Paul Lafargue and the Founding
of French Marxism, 1842–1882

Paul Lafargue
and the Founding
of French Marxism
1842–1882

Leslie Derfler

Harvard University Press
Cambridge, Massachusetts
London, England
1991

This book is printed on acid-free paper, and its binding
materials have been chosen for strength and durability.

Library of Congress Cataloging-in-Publication Data

Derfler, Leslie.
   Paul Lafargue and the founding of French Marxism, 1842–1882 /
Leslie Derfler.
      p.   cm.
   Includes bibliographical references and index.
   ISBN 0–674–65903–1
   1. Lafargue, Paul, 1842–1911.   2. Socialists—France—Biography.
   3. Socialism—France—History.   I. Title.
HX264.7.L34D47   1991
335.'.0092—dc20   90–36659
[B]   CIP

For Ingrid and Linnea, Astrid, and Elin

Contents

Illustrations

Acknowledgments

I want to express my gratitude to the many generous people who helped make this book a reality: to Olga Meier, who sent me copies of Marx family letters not included in her compilation *Les Filles de Karl Marx,* and to Michelle Perrot for suggesting that I ask for them; to Yvonne Kapp, the biographer of Eleanor Marx, for sharing insights; to Jean Cavignac, the archivist of the Gironde Department, who made available much relevant material; to Mme S. Benoist-Guesde, the granddaughter of Lafargue's longtime associate; to Mme F. Winoek, of the Centre d'Histoire des Mouvements Sociaux et du Syndicalistes; to David Webb, of the Bishopsgate Institute in London; to Diana Cooper-Richet and to Denise Fauvel-Rouif, who manages the Institut Français d'Histoire Sociale; and to Götz Langkau and the staff of the Internationaal Instituut voor Sociale Geschiedenis in Amsterdam.

I am also grateful to the staffs of a number of other institutions, including the Bibliothèque Marxiste de Paris (formerly the Institut Maurice Thorez), especially Dominique Candille; the Archives de la Préfecture de Police, especially M. Coutarel; the Archives Nationales; and the Bibliothèque Nationale. In addition I thank, for information sent to me, M. L. Marchand of the Archives Municipales de Toulouse, Pierre Gerard of the Direction des Services d'Archives of the Haute-Garonne Department, Elio Selino of the Fondazione Giangiacomo Feltrinelli in Milan, D. Antonyuk of the Institute of Marxism-Leninism in Moscow, the Biblioteca Nacional José Marti in Havana, and David Heron of the Hoover Institution. For making me feel that Florida Atlantic University's library could handle almost any request I had, very special thanks to Dahrl Moore, who directed its interlibrary loan department in the period when I was researching this book. My appreciation also goes to my colleagues in and outside of

Florida: Marilyn Boxer, the late Louis Greenberg, Joy Hall, Jan Hokenson, Arthur Mitzman, Ray Mohl, Sandra Norton, Vincente Rangel, John Schwaller, Jack Suberman, and Yvette Thomas. Several visits to foreign libraries and archives were made possible by grants from the National Endowment for the Humanities, the American Philosophical Society, and Florida Atlantic University's Division of Sponsored Research. Oscar Arnal, Joel Colton, and Patrick Hutton provided helpful criticism of early papers drawn from this research. Patrick Hutton and Steven Vincent read assorted chapters; they and the anonymous readers of the completed draft deserve my very real gratitude for their comments. It need hardly be said that the mistakes that remain are mine and not theirs. Thelma Spangler found many typographical errors. I also very much appreciate the help given me by my editor, Elizabeth Gretz.

I am pleased to acknowledge the permission granted by *Nineteenth-Century French Studies* to reprint part of my article "Paul Lafargue: The First Marxist Literary Critic" (17, nos. 3–4, spring-summer 1989, 369–384), and by *Biography: An Interdisciplinary Quarterly* to reprint portions of my article "Paul Lafargue and the Beginnings of Marxism in France." An early draft of parts of the first chapter appeared as "Paul Lafargue, le milieu cubain," in the *Bulletin de l'Institut acquitain d'études sociales* 45 (1985), 13–26. Unless otherwise stated, the translations throughout the book are mine.

Finally, very special recognition to William Cohn, author of a doctoral dissertation on Lafargue, who welcomed me in his home and with rare generosity made available all the information at his disposal.

Paul Lafargue and the Founding
of French Marxism, 1842–1882

Groups, organizations, or nations have no independent status apart from the conduct of individuals who are related by behaving towards each other in certain ways ... These collectivities exist and behave the way they do only insofar as the people composing them act in certain ways.

—Heinz Eulau, *The Behavioral Persuasion in Politics*

Socialism must not be considered in the abstract, detached from every condition of time and place.

—Emile Durkheim, *Le Socialisme*

Introduction

George Lichtheim has suggested two possible meanings for the term "French Marxism": either the "adaptation of Marxist theory to French conditions or the growth and development in France of a socialist (later also a Communist) movement which after a century still relates itself to Marx."[1] Whether one puts emphasis on the importation and assimilation of foreign theories and strategies or on the progress of a national revolutionary movement that chose to accept those theories and strategies, the role played by Paul Lafargue in bringing Marxism to France looms as all important. The disciple and son-in-law of Karl Marx, Lafargue, together with Jules Guesde, founded both the first French collectivist party, the Federated Socialist Workers Party (Fédération du Parti des Travailleurs Socialistes de France), in 1880, and the first French Marxist party, the Workers Party (Parti Ouvrier Français, or POF), in 1882. He served as the chief theoretician and propagandist for Marxism in France during the three decades that followed, and he was the first Marxist to sit in the French legislature. In addition, he pioneered in the application of Marxist methods of analysis to questions of anthropology, aesthetics, and literary criticism.

Lafargue was born in 1842 in Cuba of mixed racial descent. As a medical student in Paris in the mid-1860s, where his studies had turned him to positivism, Proudhonism, and republicanism, he joined in demonstrations against the Second Empire and was subsequently forced into exile. He resumed his studies in London in 1866, became something of a fixture in the Marx household, and in 1868 married Marx's middle daughter, Laura. The newlyweds moved to Paris, where they worked to expand the influence of the International Workingmen's Association and to turn it from its well-entrenched Proudhonism to Marxism. They fled the general repression that followed the fall of the Paris Commune; police began to work actively to apprehend them after Paul's attempts to reestablish a branch of the

International in Bordeaux and rouse the Bordelais against the Thiers government. They next went to Spain. There Paul sought, unsuccessfully, to instill Marxism against widespread anarchist opposition. Later, after a ten-year stay in London, the couple returned to France, where Paul worked to introduce Marx's thought and helped to found a new, wholly Marxist party, the Parti Ouvrier, in 1882. It developed from a schism in the short-lived Federated Socialist Workers Party, whose anti-Marxist majority, under the leadership of Paul Brousse, maintained a separate existence, following a strategy based entirely on gradual reforms and constitutional procedures.

This book surveys Paul Lafargue's career to 1882 and, through the lens of his life and experiences, examines the development of Marxist socialism in France to that point, culminating in the foundation of the Parti Ouvrier. After 1882 Lafargue, an impassioned polemicist, continued to work to influence the development of his party. The POF remained a modest messianic sect until about 1890, but then became increasingly integrated into national political life. The party reached its apogee in the 1890s, when its revolutionary ideology softened and its internationalism gave way to parliamentarianism and patriotism—only to return in the first decade of the new century to a militant posture and a reductionist, simplistic schema. Lafargue played a role in the founding of the Second Workingmen's International and was elected to the French national legislature, but he repudiated any appointment of socialists to positions in a nonsocialist government. He supported a newly unified French socialist party, founded on a Marxist program, and until his and his wife's dramatic suicide in 1911, attempted to keep it on a revolutionary course.

Lafargue is usually linked with or subordinated to Jules Guesde, and is certainly less well known than Guesde, whose name became synonymous with the Workers Party (often referred to as the Guesdists). But Lafargue was in fact Guesde's mentor, was regarded as the more able thinker, and doubtless because of his close ties to Marx and Engels, initially had greater political prestige within the party leadership. Lafargue's role as theoretician deserves emphasis. He introduced and applied Marxist thought, translating (here Laura Lafargue's role was predominant) and popularizing the *Communist Manifesto,* the *Eighteenth Brumaire,* sections of *Anti-Dühring* (which became *Socialism: Scientific and Utopian*), and other works. Lafargue formulated the first political strategy followed by the French Marxists, which in calling for ideological purity demanded total hostility to anarchists and reformists. He showed himself Marx's disciple in insisting on economic determinism, on the primacy of the concept of class struggle, and on the theory of surplus value. More original contributions issued from his insistence on breaking the domination of bourgeois values, in much the same way that eighteenth-century *philosophes*, whom he admired and whose materialism he ceaselessly evoked, had eroded the intellectual and cultural foundations of the aristocracy. Here he anticipated the notion, later formulated by Antonio Gramsci, that a ruling class maintains its power by exercising an intellectual and cultural hegemony. In his most famous pamphlet, *The Right to Be Lazy,* Lafargue showed the advantages that labor could derive by rejecting the bourgeois work ethic. And he made one of the first attempts, certainly the first in France, to apply methods of Marxist analysis to literary and aesthetic subjects, especially to reveal elements of "social control" discovered through analyses of the bourgeois novel.

Despite the crucial part they played in the social and political changes of the past century, early French Marxists, active from the late 1870s on, are not widely known and are even less widely appreciated, particularly in the English-speaking world. This is especially true of their theoretical contributions.[2] However, although there has been no adequate biography of Lafargue,[3] there is an enormous literature on the origins of French socialism, which are not Marxist, and an ongoing debate about the nature and reception of Marxism in France during the early Third Republic. The introduction of Marxism into France by those associated with Jules Guesde, who is generally credited with its dissemination and with the founding of the party created to promote the socialist cause, thus provides the larger context within which Lafargue's life and writings take on their meaning.

Early interpreters of the founding of French Marxism describe the "Guesdists" (though they were not yet known as such, even by themselves) as bringing Marxism to France and so provide what might be called the group's "romantic" image.[4] Both the American Samuel Bernstein and the longtime associate of Guesde and Lafargue, Alexandre Zévaès, in books on the beginnings of Marxism in France published in 1933 and 1947 respectively, view Lafargue and Guesde—the two are seldom distinguished, but the bulk of the authors' attention is given to Guesde—as working to bring Marxism to French labor. For

Bernstein, even the first series of *L'Egalité*, the newspaper founded by Guesde in 1877, began to promote revolutionary collectivist doctrine and so is seen as a precursor to the minimum program for the new collectivist party drafted by Marx with Engels, Lafargue, and Guesde in 1880. Zévaès' history of Marxist penetration, in contrast to his recollections (which vary, according to his fortunes in the party hierarchy), insists that it was "pure Marxism" that was presented to the French working class at both the Marseilles and Roubaix workers' congresses in 1879 and 1883.[5] Milorad Drachkovitch also sees Guesde as a Marxist upon his return to France from Switzerland in the mid-1870s, as never deviating from that stand, and Guesdist propaganda as enabling Marxism to make headway, demonstrated by Lafargue's eventual electoral victory in 1891.[6]

Shifts by the Guesdists between reformist and revolutionary strategies have preoccupied students of French Marxist history. Between 1880 and 1882 Guesdists followed Lafargue's admonitions to work for reforms, particularly at the municipal level, in order to widen their basis for recruitment, but they spared no effort to apply the teachings of revolutionary collectivism during the rest of the decade. Although beyond the purview of this volume, their emphasis was to shift again, in the 1890s, toward a parliamentary and hence reformist approach. Reformists, while not disclaiming revolutionary options, saw the vote as the chief means to implant socialism: by establishing public services at the municipal level, for the followers of Paul Brousse; by transforming society, not only economically but morally and philosophically, for the disciples of Benoît Malon. The anarchist antecedents and the trade union origins of the skilled workers who were most politically active made for loose, almost nonexistent, structures and permitted overtures to interested parties. Guesdism, in contrast, before it subscribed to a "gradualist" approach, was materialist in doctrine and small and increasingly disciplined in membership. It made light of universal suffrage and the revolutionary potential of organized labor, and expressed neutrality with regard to the defense of republican institutions.

Several explanations, relevant to the period covered in this book as well as later years, have been offered for these gyrations. For Georges Weill, the party leadership came to realize that the likelihood of victory through an act of force had been overestimated. Aaron Noland describes the efforts of Guesdist legislators to enact measures of social reform to win recruits and secure additional votes, a policy that in-

creasingly committed the party to work within a capitalist framework. The specific need to present French voters, most of whom in
1880 still worked on the land, with an attractive agrarian program is
stressed by Carl Landauer. Claude Willard's comprehensive history
of the Guesdists before 1905 cites their superficial assimilation of
Marxist doctrine that led them first to underestimate the usefulness of
the vote, then to overestimate it, and consequently to open themselves
to charges of dogmatism and sectarianism. Elsewhere I have attempted to show that Guesde was concerned not only with the defense of party interests but with the strengthening and perpetuation of
his position as its leader, and hence was unable to separate personal
needs from party considerations.[7]

Though he did not always agree with its strategies, Lafargue devoted his energies to promoting the interests of his party. An early
chronicler denied that a biography of Lafargue was possible "outside
of the history of the French workers' movement, chiefly of the Parti
Ouvrier Français, the name of the Guesdist party." Willard recognizes
Lafargue as the party's "only theoretician," whose "curious and quick
intelligence," whose ability to analyze and synthesize (which was
based on "a vast and detailed documentation and on a far-reaching
cultural framework, especially in philosophical subjects") and whose
long intimacy with Marx and Engels enabled him to assimilate, "much
better than Guesde, though still imperfectly, the method of historical
and dialectical materialism." These advantages shielded Lafargue
from the intellectual "sclerosis" that progressively afflicted Guesde.
Moreover, "Lafargue did not work in an ivory tower. His works were
tied closely to his militant activism," and he assiduously defended
attempts to repudiate, revise, or otherwise relate Marxism to rival
approaches. "More so than Guesde," Willard concludes, "Lafargue
can be considered the vigilant guardian of the doctrine (as well as its)
popularizer."[8]

Other writers, including some on the left, are less appreciative.
Lafargue has been caricatured above all by the disciples and admirers
of Georges Sorel, who see the Guesdists as bringing to France not
Marxism but merely distortions of it, and only the work of Labriola,
Sorel, and Croce as able to repair the damage. They condemn
Lafargue as the *fantaisiste* of French Marxism, as possessed of an
"incorrigible lightness" and "great pretension." Lichtheim agrees that
"what passed for Marxism in the 1880s" was at best "an approxi-
mation and at worst a caricature, whose only value, from a later

Communist viewpoint, lay in keeping alive a tradition upon which Leninism could be grafted with ease." Leszek Kolakowski calls Lafargue a "hedonist Marxist," and such critics as Neil McInnes see him as a pamphleteer, a simplistic popularizer who "scarcely introduced more than the name of Marx into France—the least that a son-in-law could do," who was more interested in polemics than rigor and guilty of major errors: overestimating the revolutionary potential of the Paris Commune, incorrectly analyzing the agricultural situation, and (later) willing to ally socialism with the nationalist and authoritarian movement associated with the popular General Boulanger (though also willing to ally socialists with Dreyfusards) and underestimating the likelihood of a European war. The Paris street directory may reflect this impression of Lafargue. It lists no street with his name, although Guesde, Jean Jaurès, Marcel Sembat, and Edouard Vaillant are represented. (Lafargue is mentioned but underrepresented in the street directories of the "red belt" of Paris' industrial suburbs.)[9]

The Parti Ouvrier never won the allegiance of more than a minority of French workers, and precisely because Lafargue was its only theorist Willard equates the failings of Guesdism with those of Lafargue. He places special emphasis on Lafargue's inability to apply Marxist methods to the study of specific realities. Lafargue's—and consequently, his party's—inability to use dialectical reasoning and statistical analysis derived from their larger failure to properly assimilate Marxist thought. While claiming scientific accuracy, they instead produced dogma "which nourished revisions" and allowed questions to be posed in contradictory terms, as, for example, "revolution and reform," or "patriotism and internationalism." Rather than a progressive assimilation of Marxism, the doctrinal evolution of the Parti Ouvrier appeared as "a succession of sectarian and opportunist motives." Willard believes that the theoretical inadequacy of Marxism in France, certainly before the turn of the century, strategically and doctrinally weakened French labor. Michelle Perrot, too, has commented on Lafargue's superficial grasp of Marxism, and cites Engels in support of her criticism. The Guesdists, she contends, never really brought Marxism to France, and the "messianism" they did bring, whether it placed faith in revolutionary victory or in parliamentary victory, provided an obstacle to it. Although his thesis focuses on the Guesdists after 1905, Jacques Girault agrees that with regard to the challenges they confronted—reformism, revolutionary syndicalism, and the threat of war—their inadequate grasp of Marxist methodology and their consequent dogmatism accounted for their failure to meet them successfully.[10]

Similarly, Daniel Lindenberg, though denying that Guesdism was Blanquist or Bakuninist (its only similarity with Blanquism was a common acceptance of armed insurrection, which the Parti Ouvrier, never systematically extolled) or that its usefulness was limited by its bureaucratic tendencies (it was entirely too amateurish), concluded that the Guesdists diffused Marxism badly and poorly, and anyway were not the only ones doing so. He admits that Lafargue was "certainly the sole French theorist to have understood something of Marx's policy" but argues that Lafargue's pamphlets and best-known speeches "owe less to Marx than to his Proudhonist and Bakuninist formation." In a work marked by its sensitivity to nuances of expression and its ability to appreciate diverse points of view, Maurice Dommanget applauds Lafargue's ability as pamphleteer to make Marxism, hitherto scarcely known in France, more widely accessible. Lafargue may have been excessively materialistic and prone to exaggeration, but he was less dogmatic than Guesde. In any event, for Dommanget this demonstrates the difficulties experienced by Marxism in making headway against an intellectual tradition owing much to its humanistic and Rousseauist origins.[11]

In his history of French socialism during the Third Republic, Georges Lefranc, speaking from a reformist standpoint, also condemns the Guesdist legacy. Although Jaurès enjoyed sufficient prestige to prevent the total disappearance of reformist alternatives following the unification of the diverse socialist groups in 1905, after World War I what Lefranc terms "neo-Guesdist" leadership prevailed, and both Paul Faure and Léon Blum are included in this category. Recourse to nineteenth-century revolutionary intransigence, both in tactics and in doctrine, produced a sterile and rigid socialism, unable to accommodate such twentieth-century experiences as the Russian Revolution, fascism, the Depression, and the New Deal. Those within the unified Socialist Party who sought accommodation with a changing capitalism by shifting tactics and adjusting doctrine received little encouragement.[12]

What, then, was the legacy of Paul Lafargue? That the legacy was real is insisted on by Marxist writers. If the party of Guesde and Lafargue never managed to become the political avant-garde of the French workers' movement because of its sectarianism, its opportunism, its bureaucratic direction of the trade unions initially affiliated with it, or a combination of these factors, it succeeded in putting French labor on a new track. Georges Cogniot points out that "to a working class that had made a cult of spontaneity," it taught that "workers could not hope to free themselves without the compass provided by scientific revolutionary theory." Willard agrees that long after its disappearance as an independent force in the French workers' movement, Guesdism left a heritage claimed by both Socialists and Communists. Thus it is impossible to dissociate Lafargue from the context of Marxist ideological penetration.[13]

Recent studies of French socialism in the late nineteenth century place emphasis on sociological, rather than on ideological, explanations. Annie Kriegel and Michelle Perrot argue that participation in local government transformed revolutionaries and accounted for their "integration" into political society. Robert Baker's study of Guesdism in the Nord Department during the thirty years before 1914 dismisses doctrinal or personal approaches in favor of a structurally based analysis. In the 1880s ideology shaped organization, but by the turn of the century the need to preserve the party's organizational framework influenced doctrine. Donald Baker insists that it makes more sense to describe Guesdists before 1914 not as revolutionaries or reformists but as protesters, who "provided a middle ground between the two options but effectively limited the likelihood that either of them would succeed."[14]

In his study of the origins of the French labor movement, Bernard Moss identifies the trade organization of skilled workers and not Marxist theorists as providing the roots of French socialism and as responsible for its federalist structure. These artisans left a legacy that, if revolutionary, aimed at a "federalist trade socialism where the means of production would be owned collectively in a framework of federation of skilled trades." And this, Moss says, rather than Marxism, is what the Guesdists reintroduced to France in the late 1870s. When in the following decade they took a new direction, the creation of a unitary and centralist Marxist party, the Guesdists were repudiated by a labor movement that remained faithful to its trade origins. Lafargue is intimately associated with this change in direction, because it was under the direct influence of Marx and Lafargue that Guesde was instructed to create a centralist party, with "a single national program representing its unitary class interests."[15]

Unlike other observers, Tony Judt believes that a discussion of "success" or "failure" is misleading. In an essay on the French Left in the nineteenth century, he rejects several alternative hypotheses concerned with the impact of Marxism on the French labor movement: that in its narrow Guesdist form it restricted the appeal of socialism to a wider audience; that its theoretical inadequacies weakened labor and deprived it of "cogent doctrine and workable strategy"; and that whether doctrinally sound or not Marxism was a force that promoted division in the French labor movement. He argues that although Marxists were few in number, so were other groups, and that Marxists did achieve a respectable minority in certain industrial areas. Consequently their impact was not as limited as their critics maintain. The Marxism voiced by Lafargue, however "superficial," was familiar to French ears, used to the "moral optimism and social positivism which was the characteristic tone of the older French socialism." In any case, Judt asks, did the German socialist party achieve a trade union membership of four and a half million because Kautsky was a "better" Marxist? "Far from dividing the French labor movement, Marxism after 1880 offered it the nearest thing to a common if ideologically flaccid dogma." The French party, moreover, was "no more different" from the German than the German was from the Italian or than both were from the British Labour Party. Responsible for its lack of greater success were not the inadequacies of French Marxism but the "complexities of the revolutionary tradition" and its appeal in a country where power was centralized and hence provoked antiparliamentary sentiment. Judt concludes that we cannot compare French socialism with other varieties before World War I and call it a failure; we must allow it its own identify and treat it on its own terms.[16]

Certainly within the Second International, Lafargue was appreciated as the best, even as the only French Marxist theoretician. Karl Kautsky telegraphed at the time of his death that "scientific socialism lost with Lafargue one of its most distinguished scholars and fighters," and at Lafargue's tomb Lenin paid homage to "one of the most gifted and most profound propagators of Marxism."[17] For his defenders, Lafargue played a predominant role in diffusing Marxism in France. He doubtless committed errors and inclined toward dogmatism. Like the eighteenth-century intellectuals he admired, he let himself be led by a "taste for paradox," for the "easy quip" and by "the wish to dazzle"; yet they insist that at the time his audacity stamped him as the one French theorist who "continuously and in a creative way" tried to apply Marxist analysis to hitherto untouched areas, to the most difficult and diverse ideological and economic problems.[18]

1 Cuba

... the blood of three oppressed races runs in my veins.

—Paul Lafargue

Santiago de Cuba, that nation's second largest city, lies in the extreme easternmost part of the island, in Oriente Province, and was one of the first towns founded by the Spanish in the sixteenth century. It extends like an open fan facing marshy shores fringed by coral reefs and cays. Behind, the city is hemmed in by the wild and rugged Sierra Maestra mountains.[1]

The development of the town and surrounding area was strongly affected by revolutionary events in the late eighteenth century. Colonists on the nearby French possession of Haiti, the western half of the island of Hispaniola, which could be seen across the windward channel from Cuba's eastern shore, fled the slave uprisings of the time and took refuge in Cuba. Spain had ceded Saint-Domingue, as Haiti was then called, to France in 1697; it had become France's most prosperous and populous colony in the Americas and one of the world's chief coffee and sugar producers. Known as the "jewel in France's colonial crown," Haiti had made France the envy of every colonial power.[2]

Yet the façade of riches and beauty concealed problems that became all too apparent with the outbreak of revolution. Disease and ill treatment by the Spaniards had all but annihilated the native Arawak Indians, and the French colonists who were living there even before the cession used imported African slaves to develop sugar plantations on the north coast. During the course of the eighteenth century the colonists expanded southward, and as was the case throughout the lesser Antilles, society became stratified into French, Creoles (in the Spanish sense of the term, native-born white descendants of the European settlers), freed blacks, and black slaves. Between the blacks and the whites were mulattoes, who aspired to the privileges of the whites and who feared the blacks. The rugged mountainous areas concealed runaway slaves, army deserters, and impoverished free men and women of all colors who eked out a miserable existence. By 1789 there were over 450,000 slaves and only 40,000 whites and 27,500 "free men of color" (mulattoes and blacks).[3] Whites controlled all aspects of economic and social life, and the resulting racial and social tensions made Haiti a tinderbox. The spark that ignited it was the French Revolution.

The revolutionary slogan of liberty, equality, and fraternity, without reference to color, raised the hopes of the underprivileged. Even planters (who owed money to merchants in France) took advantage of the Revolution to press demands for autonomy. When the National Assembly in 1791 ordered that all free men and women of color (born to two free parents) enjoy the same political rights as whites, however, the furious whites refused to obey.[4] And when the French-descended Creole planters tried to prevent mulatto representation in the French National Assembly and in local assemblies on the island, both mulattoes and slaves rebelled. Their revolution started a race war: whites murdered blacks, blacks murdered whites, and mulattoes were the victims of both. To supplement the depleted ranks of French troops on the island, white civilians in the cities and towns invited in British soldiers for protection. Inspired by the egalitarianism of the French Revolution and under the leadership of Toussaint l'Ouverture, a former slave who had been made an officer of the French forces on Hispaniola, the blacks formed guerrilla bands. In 1793, together with the generals Jean-Jacques Dessalines and Henri Christophe, also former slaves, Toussaint began to drive the British off the island and eventually forced them to withdraw. Slaves were freed while many whites were killed or forced to flee. News of the rebels' phenomenal success filtered into the slave states of the United States, and fear of slave insurrections spread through the American South.

Toussaint completed his conquest of the island by 1801, Spain having ceded eastern Hispaniola to France in 1795. He abolished slavery, and proclaimed himself governor general. Intent on recapturing the island from "the Bonaparte of the Antilles," Napoleon in 1802 sent 10,000 troops under General Leclerc to "restore order," but his troops, ravaged by disease, could not secure the interior. Even though Toussaint, betrayed and captured, died in a French prison, French troops were forced to withdraw. Haiti became independent in 1804, and all remaining whites were expelled.

During this period of upheaval, perhaps as many as 20,000 French colonists, panic-stricken and afraid, set sail for the beaches of eastern Cuba, little more than forty miles away. At the outset, the Spanish authorities worried about the settlement of so many refugees (the total Cuban population then numbered about 200,000), fearing they were carriers of revolutionary contagion.[5]

A more enlightened view was taken by the new governor of Santiago, Sebastian Kindelan. He assumed his post in 1799 and appreciated the skills that the French emigrés could bring to his underdeveloped area. By permitting the refugees, some of whom arrived with only the clothes on their backs, to settle as grateful guests in a town too small to lodge them, he provided them with the opportunity to remake their lives.[6] They were able to rebuild their fortunes and at the same time contribute to the rapid development of coffee plantations in the nearby mountains.

Accustomed to European comforts and traditions, the French developed technology and the arts: they introduced scientific farming, opened roads, built small villas with gardens, and established theaters.[7] Schools of music and dancing were opened by well-bred Frenchwomen. Most of the French community in Santiago lived on or near Galo Street, literally, Street of the Gauls. During the period of the Terror of 1793–94, the worried Spanish had increased their surveillance. Even so, in 1802, the year that witnessed the greatest number of new arrivals, the government distributed land to French families, and the more enterprising among them leased or sold large tracts to others. Thus it was that French immigrants settled in Cuba, receiving protection from the Spanish government and, in the process, enriching themselves.[8]

Among the immigrants was a mulatto from Haiti, Catalina Pirón. Her son Francisco (François) Lafargue, the father of Paul Lafargue, was born in Santiago.[9] In 1891, when the question of nationality came up during Paul Lafargue's candidacy for the Chamber of Deputies, his mother offered proof of her husband's French citizenship. On November 24 of that year, the newspaper *Le Matin* published the notice sent by the French consul in Santiago certifying that François was a Frenchman and that his name was to be found in the French Registry. His mother Catalina had arrived in Santiago sometime between 1796 and 1805. His father, Jean Lafargue, a Frenchman born in Bordeaux, had disappeared and was probably killed in one of the uprisings. The widow found shelter in Santiago along with other emigrants from Haiti.[10]

The suffering of the French emigrés was renewed when Spain and France went to war in 1808. In the spring of that year Spain rose up against Bonapartist rule, and the colonies similarly refused to recognize the king imposed by France, Napoleon's brother, Joseph. A decree calling for the expulsion of the French in all territories belonging to Spain forced most of the Santiago refugees into renewed exile. Perhaps as many as 16,000 chose to go to New Orleans.[11]

However, the authorities did not confiscate the property of those who departed. The edict signed by Governor Kindelan granted the French forty days to sell their property or to entrust it to others for future sale.[12] Catalina Pirón and her son were among those who went to Louisiana. They had little in the way of savings, and led a precarious existence in New Orleans. Unable to find work, despite the economic activity of the great port, the boy and his mother peddled fruit on the city's streets.[13] While living in London in the 1870s, Paul Lafargue was to refer to ownership of property in New Orleans, but apparently this was procured by François at a later time. The exiles returned to Cuba after 1814, when Ferdinand VII returned to Madrid and Cuba once more offered refuge to the French. Included were Catalina Pirón and her son. In the years that followed, François prospered as a cooper and a landowner. In 1834 he married Ana Virginia Armaignac.[14]

François' wife had come to Cuba in a similar manner. Her Father, Abraham Armaignac, whom Paul Lafargue said came from a Jewish-French family, had also lived in Haiti. (In October 1888, on a visit to his aging mother, Paul was told by an aunt that his maternal grandfather was a "blue-eyed, fair-haired Jew" named Abraham Armaignac.)[15] Armaignac had returned to the island from France, where he had been sent by his family to complete his studies, to find a revolution raging, which forced him and his family to flee to Jamaica. There Armaignac lived in an illegal union with a Caribe Indian, Margarita Fripié, with whom he had a daughter, Ana Virginia, born in Kingston. This daughter became Paul Lafargue's mother.[16]

Lafargue later boasted, and the claim was often repeated, that "the blood of three oppressed races ran in [his] veins" and that he was, in fact, an "international[ist] of blood before [he] was one of ideology."[17] In 1882 Lafargue took exception to a Clemenceau speech that divided the races into two categories, those capable of discipline and those condemned to disappear, and he remained sensitive to issues of color.[18] When at an international congress the American Marxist Daniel DeLeon asked Lafargue about his origins, he promptly replied, "I am proudest of my negro extraction."[19] Paul (Pablo), born in Santiago on January 15, 1842, was his parents' only child, as far as we know.[20] He was baptized September 19, 1842; in the documents his mother's name was spelled Armainac and his maternal grandmother's name, Frijié.[21]

Lafargue wrote little about his childhood in Cuba. However, he told his brother-in-law Charles Longuet in 1891: "I lived my first years in the midst of lumber and shavings. My father was a cooper in Cuba. Through long years of work he amassed a small fortune that allowed him to facilitate my studies in the Bordeaux lycée."[22]

Lafargue began his primary education in a small private school registered as the Cuban Institute. It was owned by Juan Foch, a Cuban educator and author, according to a statistical record of the primary schools of Santiago and their students.[23] That Paul did not attend a French school, but rather one where classes were taught in Spanish, may be explained by the reforms in the Santiago schools prompted by the University of Havana. The school enjoyed an excellent reputation; its new methodologies appealed to wealthier elements who found more traditional schools lacking. It was said to have provided the equivalent of the best European preparatory education, offering courses in the arts, sciences, and modern languages.[24]

Cuban writers today point to the Cuban nationalism and the anticolonialistic sentiments directed against Spain of at least two of Lafargue's teachers, Domingo del Monte and Pedro Santacilia. Both men wrote poetry, and it was in their poetry that their political views were revealed. During the time he taught at the Cuban Institute, Santacilia's poems, seditious and unsigned, were circulated. (He later supported the Narenso López conspiracy against Spain, and in exile in Mexico married the daughter of President Benito Juárez.)[25] It is likely that his teachers introduced the first notions of civil and political rights to the young Lafargue, and they may have encouraged his appreciation of these values in a class- and color-conscious society.

The account of Lafargue's early schooling offered by Raul Roa, a historian and former foreign minister under Fidel Castro, differs only in details. According to Roa, the family's comfortable economic situation permitted Lafargue to attend the reputed Colegio de Santiago, whose owner and head, Juan Bautista Sagarra, "was one of the most prominent figures of the educational reform movement." Roa agrees that one of Paul's teachers was the poet and conspirator del Monte, subsequently "persecuted by the hired assassins of the colonial regime," and we can only speculate about his influence on the boy. (Del Monte, a romantic poet and essayist, was charged with participation in the Escalera conspiracy and eventually fled Cuba.) Roa places stress on the Cuban and Creole origins of Lafargue's "obsession with sunshine," his "Dionysian feeling for life," his "impetuosity . . . [and] abundant wit," and even "a preference for roast suckling pig."[26] At the very least, this description reinforces the notion that Lafargue, during his early school years, not only received a good education but was exposed to some social restlessness on the part of his teachers. Still, he left Cuba at the age of nine, and we need not place excessive emphasis on these early childhood experiences.

Perhaps yielding to the pleas of relatives in the Bordeaux region, and certainly anxious to open wider horizons to the intelligence of his son, François leased his coffee plantation and left Cuba with his family toward the end of 1851. Perhaps, too, he was influenced by the general apprehension Cuba experienced in May 1850 over the stirrings of revolution. (It was this anxiety that caused the political repression Santacilia was reported to have fled.) Slave revolts, both real and threatened, in 1843–44 had led to 4,000 arrests made by the Spanish government, and a conspiracy to establish an independent republic or to work for annexation by the United States was crushed by the authorities in 1851.[27] More to the point, and reinforcing the father's desire to satisfy ambitions for his son, is the fact that *mestizos,* those of mixed racial origin, had little opportunity for economic or social advancement. Those of African descent were denied access to advanced education.[28] Repression directed against the black *mestizo* middle class in 1844 strengthened official discriminatory policy, and may well have influenced the Lafargues' decision to relocate to France. François Lafargue thereafter lived as a *rentier,* an investor of private means, in Bordeaux, according to Gironde Department notarial records, and a new chapter opened in the life of his son.[29]

The family settled in the Saint-Seurin Fondaudège section in Bordeaux, and in 1858, for 3,000 francs, François bought a lot at 56 rue Naujac from a Frenchman who lived in New Orleans and whom François may have met in America. The house must have been built quickly, because by November 1859 the family was living in it. On his arrival, Paul was called "the Creole," and because there was considerable anti-Semitism in the Bordeaux region, those who knew his grandfather Armaignac called him "the Jew Lafargue Armaignac."[30]

François was financially comfortable. Not only did he own property, but on his arrival in France was able to lend 50,000 francs (at 5 percent interest) to the owner of a Bordeaux hotel, receiving a mortgage in return. In July 1856 he bought an estate outside the city (Salleboeuf, Entre-deux-Mers) for 30,000 francs, but did not farm it and sold it two years later at a 3,000-franc profit.[31] He appears in the notary acts as an investor in search of sound returns, lending at prevailing rates and usually taking mortgages in return. Having relatives in Cuba, he kept a small house in Santiago, valued at 4,000 francs. Not until 1866 did François order the release of "a female negro slave named Geneviève, about forty years old." That he had not previously done so doubtless angered his son, who came to reject the bourgeois and colonialist attitude of his parents and hence his entire early life.[32]

In 1852, when Paul was ten years old, François took him to the lecture of an agricultural expert speaking on drainage. Paul later recalled that when the lecture was over and the gentlemen farmers were chatting, one of them described how a republican could be identified: "Hang him by his feet and if forty sous fall out of his pockets, you can let him down. He is not a republican."[33] It was then fashionable for comfortable bourgeois elements who supported the Empire to ridicule republicans. Lafargue later commented that for these Bordeaux farmers, the Empire of Louis Napoleon meant social order and the safeguarding of property. Lafargue's father would not have resented the anecdote, for he possessed his own *petite propriété* of seventy acres in the winegrowing area around the city.[34]

In Bordeaux the young Lafargue began his studies with a private tutor, one Roger-Micé. He then entered the lycée in Bordeaux, but apparently changed to the lycée in Toulouse, with the intention of ultimately studying medicine, and received his Baccalauréat from there in 1861.[35] His studies corresponded to the curricula for secondary education established in 1858. Students preparing for medicine studied both science and literature, and so Lafargue was solidly grounded in the classics. His contemporary, Georges Clemenceau, born in 1841 and also to be diverted from medical practice by politics, was similarly examined in classical languages, literature, and philosophy. This was the curriculum that opened the way to any university, including faculties of medicine.[36]

Lafargue did not perform military service, an omission for which he was criticized in 1891, at the time of his candidacy for the Chamber of Deputies. Some supporters said that his parents had bought him a replacement, then a perfectly legal and widespread practice. His colleague Jules Guesde argued, mistakenly, in retrospect, that Lafargue was exempt by reason of his foreign birth.[37] Lafargue himself insisted that he had drawn a lucky number in 1863, and he reminded his critics of "the state of mind" of young republicans at the time: far from condemning those who "escaped their servitude . . . in the party one envied their lot."[38] But in another article he described his father as a republican at heart and as having paid for a replacement so as not to have his son serve the Empire.[39]

According to the testimony a family acquaintance gave to the Commission of Inquiry investigating the origins of the Paris Commune, Lafargue went to Paris to begin studies in pharmacy and may even have worked in one. If so, he apparently changed his mind and enrolled in the Faculty of Medicine. He soon found that university teaching under the Empire was disorganized and inadequate. Students were plentiful in the schools of Law and Medicine. Between 1866 and 1870, the three medical faculties in France awarded an average of 474 doctoral degrees a year and these numbers raised fears of overcrowding the profession.[40]

In addition to their large enrollments, these schools were located in crowded neighborhoods. According to a nineteenth-century historian of education, *"L'Ecole pratique,* with its dissection halls, shadowed on all sides by high neighboring buildings and attached to the maternity hospital, was congested, lacked air and hallways, and was a center for infection." In the 1870s, and presumably a decade earlier as well, four years of course work and one or two years of work on a thesis (written in Latin) were required. Yet the clinical method predominated, and it was by being close to the sick that the physician learned his profession.[41] Costs were modest, at least for parents with only one son and even for those less comfortable than the Lafargues: tuition, fees, examinations, certification expenses, and all materials amounted to less than 2,000 francs a year, 12,000 for all six.[42] And after the first year opportunities for tutoring and other work, in addition to salaried internships available at the beginning of the fourth year, eased the financial burden. Even so, a high attrition rate was cited in a contemporary handbook: of the 800 students who registered each year at the Paris Faculty of Medicine, over half failed to complete a degree.[43]

The minister of education, Victor Drury, had made some minor reforms, but complaints persisted that the curriculum failed "to keep up with developments in science" and that too much teaching was based "on dogmatic lectures before large audiences." Doctors in the wards had received the right to teach, but unlike their counterparts in London who dominated medical education, French physicians enjoyed considerably less academic authority.[44]

With the development of science under the positivist currents of Claude Bernard's Société de Biologie, laboratory research and experimentation supplemented clinical observation. Lafargue, like others of his generation exposed to these winds of renovation, became a positivist, a practitioner of the system of thought that insisted on empirical and scientific methods and that denied any validity to metaphysical speculation. Yet he was fascinated by the theories of the eighteenth-century Austrian physician, F. A. Mesmer, who proposed that all matter was composed of a universal fluid. Mesmer believed that material objects, living and nonliving, exerted physical tidelike influences on living beings and that medicine could make use of this "animal magnetism" to cure and prevent human illness.

Numerous radicals and socialists received medical training: in addition to Clemenceau and Lafargue were Paul Brousse, Albert Regnard, Edouard Vaillant, and others. Conceivably their training as scientific observers of reality contributed to their knowledge of working-class misery and encouraged them to place reliance on environmental improvement. No doubt Lafargue's attempts to apply renovation to social issues and his move to the political left, ultimately leading to his preference for an activist's life, brought about a break with his parents. Certainly his parents were distressed by their son's absorption with politics and with radical politics in particular.[45] During his years at the Faculty of Medicine in the Latin Quarter, Lafargue was caught up in the swirling political currents of the Second Empire, currents themselves inspired by changes in economic conditions.

2   The Student Radical

Blanqui transformed us, corrupted us all.
—Paul Lafargue

Industrial development in France increased significantly during the Second Empire—and so did the size of the working classes. The volume of industrial production doubled between 1852 and 1870; foreign trade tripled, outstripping the growth of any other European nation; and other indices, ranging from railway track to steam power, jumped by more than that. The rate of growth was particularly acute in Paris. In 1870 the city contained 450,000 industrial workers, 100,000 more than in 1848. In the population at large, in contrast, not only was a majority still engaged in agriculture, but industry was still decentralized and small scale, with 94 of every 100 firms employing fewer than ten workers. The typical worker was still an artisan, working for himself or for the employer who more often than not worked alongside of him, but in either case, in a workshop rather than in a factory.[1]

Economic prosperity suffered a check in the early 1860s. Although wages held steady during the decade ending in 1867, averaging a little under five francs a day, purchasing power fell. A metalworker's daily wage in the 1850s could buy almost seven dozen eggs or their equivalent; in the 1860s, it bought only five dozen. Workers in the food industry, chiefly women, could buy two and a half dozen eggs, or the equivalent thereof, with their daily wages; in the previous decade they had earned the equivalent of almost three dozen. Held responsible were the Empire's economic policies, particularly its low tariffs, and both industrial unrest and opposition to the government mounted proportionately.

Louis Napoleon took steps to liberalize his Empire, to give the legislature more of a voice and to establish a dialogue between it and his government. At the same time, he decided to tolerate, if not legally acknowledge, the existence of trade unions and bring to an end the long-standing prohibition against strikes. The political struggle between those who defended and those who condemned the Empire, largely a republican opposition, nevertheless intensified, for while the progress toward "liberalized authoritarianism" cost the emperor much of his conservative support it failed to win converts on the left. In 1857 opposition candidates had received only three quarters of a million votes; in 1863 they won two million; and in 1869 they received three and a third million, 45 percent of the total vote cast.[2]

In Paris republican opposition to the Second Empire also appeared in the press and in popular demonstrations, particularly in the Latin Quarter, and it was in this climate of opposition to Napoleon III that Lafargue got caught up in the flow of French politics. Short-lived journals took an increasingly critical political stance and, if repressed, soon reappeared under different names. Already inclined to materialism and scientism, students embraced the positivist ideology that served as philosophical support for their materialistic and agnostic leanings. And students of medicine were among the most outspoken critics of the regime. Educated as much in natural science as in medicine, they drank in the philosophy of positivism and materialism. They devoured Claude Bernard, Comte, Darwin, Feuerbach, Fourier, Emile Littré, Saint-Simon, Hippolyte Taine, and Kant and Hegel as well. Lafargue acknowledged this when he wrote of his classmates as constituting a "new generation."[3] They were influenced, too, by the teachings of the social critic Pierre-Joseph Proudhon and the revolutionary Auguste Blanqui.

Blanqui was heir to the tradition of direct revolutionary action, calling for the seizure of the state and for then using it to sweep away all obstacles to reason, to education, to true enlightenment. However, his repeated attempts at a *coup d'état* against monarchy, empire, and later, republic all failed for lack of adequate planning or support and half his life was spent behind bars. For almost half a century Blanqui's name dominated reports of illegal and insurrectionary activity in Paris. Even during periods of imprisonment or exile, instructions somehow reached a dedicated and disciplined corps of disciples. Blanqui was the pupil of the aged conspirator Filippo Buonarotti, himself the last survivor of the Babeuf conspiracy against the Directory in 1793. Obsessed with the seizure of power, Blanqui first appeared on revolutionary barricades in 1830, and he now dedicated himself to the overthrow of Napoleon III.

Out of the nucleus of student admirers who became acquainted with the old conspirator, a Blanquist youth movement emerged in the 1860s. They were attracted both by the man and by the legend. As Blanqui, first in his cell and then as a fugitive from justice, expounded on the revolutionary tradition to which he had been exposed and to which his own career had contributed so much, these young men were moved by his rejection of a comfortable career and saw the life they wanted to imitate. They would become disciples; the old man, *le vieux,* would be their mentor, and like him they would be revolutionaries.[4]

Accordingly, a network of friends and acquaintances took shape in the Latin Quarter. It began in 1864 with about fifteen students, nearly all middle class, some wealthy, graduates of provincial lycées, and preparing for careers mainly in law and medicine at the University of Paris. The medical students among Blanqui's first disciples included Paul Dubois and Charles-Victor Jaclard; Edouard Losson, Eugène Protot, and Gustave Tridon studied law. Most had distinguished academic records, but had found their studies stultifying; they drifted from their classes to the intellectual ferment of Left Bank bohemianism. Attracted to the positivism of Comte, to liberalism, to revolutionary ideas, they saw religious dogmas as imposed; and because they associated religion with the despised Empire, they had become republicans. Now they were revolutionaries inspired by Blanqui.

They moved from talk to demonstrations. They heckled the imperial family. They chose to follow Blanqui's example and identify themselves with the "damned of history"—his phrase for those who preferred to be pariahs for the sake of justice. They saw themselves as the elite of a revolutionary avant-garde, a view reinforced when they successfully arranged Blanqui's escape from the prison wing of Necker Hospital in 1865. Thereafter Blanqui lived in seclusion at the home of an old friend, a medical doctor and fellow radical, Louis Watteau, in Brussels; he rarely visited Paris, and then only in disguise.[5] Not all who idolized Blanqui, however, joined his organization: Charles Longuet, editor of *La Rive gauche,* the best-known student newspaper, Clemenceau, Jules Vallès, and Lafargue were "second-degree" Blanquists, only loosely affiliated.

Proudhon, in contrast to Blanqui, rejected any revolutionary seizure of the centralized state and indeed rejected the centralized state. He created no organized movement, and his chief attempt at practical reform, a free credit system in 1848, failed completely. Yet Proudhon's impact was to exceed that of almost any other French social theorist and French labor was to draw as much of its inspiration from Proudhon as from Marx. The French workers' movement had declined after 1848, and its revival in the 1860s was in part the result of the popularity and influence of Proudhon, its chief exponent. After their disillusionment with politics, workers had turned away from the state, and their chief demand now centered on greater freedom for their professional organizations, the approach advocated by Proudhon.[6]

In his writings, Proudhon reflected the fragmentation of French industry; that is, he shared the outlook of the artisans among whom he spent his life. These people were threatened by finance capital, and Proudhon found the origins of poverty not in the maldistribution of the means of production but in the maladministration of exchange. Society was to be based on cooperative associations, ideally small federations of self-governing groups of producers.

Rejecting an arbitrary and all-powerful state, Proudhon rejected as well Marx's idea of a political revolution to bring about social reconstruction. He held that workers must depend on themselves and rely on economic rather than on political methods. Suspicious of centralized power, whether held by the old ruling elite or by workers, he offered a "federalist" solution, a scattering of power and property so that no one group could dominate others. Republicanism, for which he once held "comprehensible enthusiasm," was found inadequate; time had "opened his eyes" and he now renounced such "phantoms of a juvenile imagination." He placed confidence in the workers, who raised the question not of changing government, but of changing society.[7] His vision of a decentralized structure of workers' associations that would instill public regard for republican virtue and foster social solidarity has led some observers to see Proudhon chiefly as a moralist.[8] And Proudhon was noted for his passionate honesty and for his image as a man of the people. He was loved by Courbet, who painted him; respected by Baudelaire, Tolstoy, and William Morris; indeed, an entire generation of socialists and humanitarians was influenced by his thought.[9] However, his program, if the word is appropriate, was more individualist than socialist: for Marx his ideas were typical of a preindustrial stage of industrial development, and Marx had devoted an entire book to refute him.

Proudhon, then, was not a militant revolutionary, but he managed to restore workers' confidence in themselves; aware of their position, they could assert their own destiny. And Lafargue, too, who as a student revered Proudhon, was at that time less concerned with Proudhon's economic analyses than with his moral imperatives, among which he included Proudhon's atheism, not surprising in view of Pius IX's recently published encyclical in which the pontiff denounced progress, liberalism, and modern civilization and denied that the Church must ever come to terms with them. Proudhon believed that God was the personification of evil. If there were no God, he argued, there would be no property owners. In boldly attacking the three pillars of the existing order, God, the state, and private property, numerous would-be anarchists and revolutionaries saw Proudhon as their teacher.

What is clear is that Lafargue was influenced by Blanqui's politics and by Proudhon's moralism, but it was probably the atheism preached by both men and their disciples that most attracted Lafargue. He attributed to Proudhon "the honor and initiative of having freed morality and economic science of all supernatural elements," of having gone further than his generation, which was still concerned with the struggle of theology with science. He attributed to Blanqui "the honor of having provided the revolutionary education of a part of the youth of our generation."[10] A student radical movement was the most prominent feature of this revolutionary ferment, and whether Blanquist, Proudhonist, or, more likely, a mixture of both, it comprised the source of Lafargue's own radicalism.

It was also during his years at the Faculty of Medicine that Lafargue, like many republican opponents of the Empire, became a freemason. Yet the record is not clear. One account describes him as a member of the lodge *L'Avenir* and as having later been dropped for failure to pay dues. *L'Avenir* was a free-thinking lodge that attracted law and medical students.[11] The lodge's archives in the Bibliothèque Nationale, however, which include membership lists from 1865 to 1874, contain the names of other medical students but not those of Lafargue and Jaclard. Lafargue must have belonged before 1865, belonged to another lodge, or belonged to none. The point is not vital: as Jacques Girault argues, republicans and socialists often joined without any real commitment to masonic principles. Whether in or out of *L'Avenir,* Lafargue rubbed shoulders with Blanquists and Proudhonists, and it was the importance of "free thought" to all three of these movements that attracted him to them.[12]

In spite of Proudhonian doctrines, which appealed to the independent craftsmen who comprised a majority of the French labor force, workers, during the economically depressed years following the crash of 1857, began going on strike and began intervening in political disputes. There was a reawakening of the workers' movement, dormant since the June Days of 1848. By 1863 this rising activity took such concrete forms as producers cooperatives and credit societies, which acted as savings banks.[13] Nor were politics ignored. In the 1864 legislative elections, Paris workers ran their own candidates. And in September of that year a French delegation in London helped to establish the International Workingmen's Association (IWMA, or the International, later designated the First International).

The selection of the IWMA organized in France was influenced by Proudhon and Blanqui. A mentor of Lafargue at the Faculty of Medicine, Jules-Antoine (Tony) Moilin, became a member, and although it is not clear when Lafargue joined, it was probably Moilin who helped persuade him to do so. Moilin had published several works on socialist economics as well as on physiology. He was a left-wing radical who was later condemned to five years' imprisonment by the Empire. He was freed by the Commune, for which he worked in Paris' sixth arrondissement, and ultimately was executed by the Versailles troops.

The event that brought an end to Lafargue's student life at the University of Paris—and ultimately to his medical career—was the International Students' Congress at Liège. The congress took place from October 29 to November 1, 1865, and constituted what the French socialist Benoît Malcon called "a veritable awakening of Latin youth."[14]

In 1860, when a French invasion was feared at the hands of Napoleon III and a wave of patriotic sentiment swept across Belgium, students in Liège came together to welcome their king; they established a General Students' Association to perpetuate their union. The next year the group sponsored a festival, which included students from other Belgian universities. The authorities noted with dismay that the students declared themselves atheist and anticlerical. In 1863 the association honored the insurgents in Poland, but internal strife broke out when Catholic members charged that its executive committee was dominated by radicals and extremists.

To preserve the association, its leaders decided to repeat the festival first held in 1861; students from the four Belgian universities would be invited to discuss "all questions of vital interest to the future of the young generation and to the future of the country." Although the agenda focused on educational reform, few doubted that political issues would invariably be raised. Both former students and foreign students were invited to attend.[15]

Some radical students in Paris made plans to attend the forthcoming congress. Lafargue, who by now may have had acquired something of a reputation as a radical, was elected to an organizing committee and agreed whole-heartedly with its plan to have the French delegation seize the opportunity to stage an anti-Bonapartist demonstration.

He at once set out to secure the participation of the Blanquists in the congress. In a letter to an unnamed Blanquist student leader, Lafargue predicted that no less than 4,000 students, including 750 from France, would participate.[16] He described the opportunity offered by the congress "to make our ideas known," specifically the elimination of all restraints limiting the individual conscience. Education was held as the basis of all social change. "Revolutions are serious and profitable only when they come from below; revolutions from above only bring about a change in personnel. Revolutions must be social and not political. And education is the most powerful revolutionary lever that I know." It was necessary to extend it to all social categories and, "given your strength in Paris, your help is necessary."

The passion of the twenty-three-year-old Lafargue then burst through: "In the name of justice and humanity we beg you to stir yourselves and agitate others. Is it not better to move in one direction or another than to remain indifferent? Indifference is worse than death." In a more practical vein he held out the possibility of railroad discounts for the students who planned to attend. He included assurances that congress promoters had been advised of the questions the students were going to raise, "and we know that you will not leave us isolated."

The arrival of the French students in Liège on October 28 caused astonishment, thanks to their eccentric appearance. Largely Blanquists and Blanquist sympathizers, they came bearded, wearing broad-brimmed hats, carrying knapsacks, and shouting slogans while parading to the center of town. Included were Pierre Delboy, the budding Blanquist journalist Germain Casse, Blanqui's lieutenant Ernest Granger, Jaclard, Protot, Albert Regnard, Aristide Rey, Tridon, Henri Villeneuve, and Lafargue.[17]

Perhaps a thousand or more students attended the congress; the majority came from the University of Liège.[18] The university refused the use of its premises, but the relevant minister made a casino available to the delegates. The French contingent constituted the largest foreign group. These young French socialists, atheists, and positivists, according to the police informants present, dominated the debates and turned them to subjects of interest to themselves, which led to much commotion.[19] Indeed, so pervasive was their domination, it was claimed that all was orchestrated by Blanqui.[20] That this was not the case, however, was revealed by the extensive participation of Catholic students and other moderate elements.[21]

On the arrival of the French at the meeting hall, the Belgian students burst into the *Marseillaise*. They were thanked by the Blanquist medical student Aristide Rey, who spoke of "the tyranny that oppresses France." Lafargue asked that red ribbons be worn in the buttonholes of the French students. Some preferred green, the color of the Belgian flag, but Lafargue urged the red, "which will triumph here and elsewhere."

Students marched around the hall, behind their respective national flags, in the opening day ceremonies. But the flag of the Paris delegation, carried by the Blanquists Casse, Villeneuve, Tridon, and Lafargue, was replaced by black crepe, to represent a nation "in mourning for liberty" and French "grief" under Napoleonic rule. More moderate elements, who opposed the gesture, found a French flag, and about half the French students followed it. Lafargue later admitted that he and his friends "were not the least ardent in the anti-Bonapartist protests."[22]

On the first day, before turning to the agenda and a discussion of educational questions, the congress allowed the airing of personal philosophies. Atheism was proclaimed and religion denounced as a threat even to morality. When it came to Lafargue's turn to speak, he defended materialism as a doctrine. By his own admission he was "very young, not only in years but in enthusiasm." He argued: "Science does not deny God; it does better; it renders Him useless."[23] "There is no divine will," he went on, "that can govern our human acts . . . The religious idea is a product of human intelligence," and he insisted on the sustained effort required to reject that belief. Mankind, interdependent by nature, must unite in the great principle of mutuality "and reject any extraterrestrial idea that has no foundation in reality. War on God! That is progress!"[24] He contrasted the Catholicism of the spiritualist with the materialism of the positivist, but acknowledged the force and durability of the Catholic faith. "Four hundred years ago we undermined it and it is still solid, unfortunately. But its hour is sounding, and necessarily so, because Catholicism is contrary to science and above all to morality." He acclaimed "our great teacher in everything, Proudhon," and won sustained applause when he recited Proudhon's formulas: "God is evil," and "property is theft."[25]

The press ignored the discussions of educational themes and the majority that supported deist—not atheist—speakers. They preferred to focus on the French radicals, and at times it appeared that the dais was occupied exclusively by French students and their Belgian counterparts who cited Comte and Proudhon and articulated their revolutionary ideas, sometimes eloquently, but were often rejected by many of their listeners.[26] All the speeches were described by the Paris students' own newspaper, *La Rive gauche,* especially in the issue of November 5, 1865. The influential conservative dailies *Le Temps* and *Le Journal des débats,* however, placed emphasis on the few who spoke of the next revolution and of the need to break bourgeois resistance by "fusillade and guillotine." The important Paris cleric, Monsignor Dupanloup, in a pastoral letter censured the congress; he saw it as proof of divine furor, and the Catholic press condemned the "horrors of Liège." At separate gatherings following the conclusion of the congress Blanquist students, before returning to France, paid homage to their chief,[27] and Belgian members of the recently formed International Workingmen's Association, Desiré Brismée and César de Paepe, spoke of a coalition of workers and intellectuals as a prerequisite for the establishment of the good society.[28] It may well be here that Lafargue learned of the IWMA for the first time in some detail.

It was also here that Lafargue met Blanqui. The old revolutionary had followed the French delegation's activities at Liège, and wanted to meet some of them.[29] In his account of the meeting, Lafargue recalled that when Blanqui was young secret societies had recruited chiefly in the Latin Quarter, and that Blanqui had continued to seek recruits from among students. (He had been expelled from the Sorbonne in 1831 for inciting student unrest.) From his prison cells Blanqui had instructed a generation of youth in opposing established governments and had shaped the Jaclards, Protots, Regnards, and Tridons. Now the young student anxiously awaited the veteran, haloed by martyrdom and hated by the bourgoisie, "seeing face to face the man of whom the bourgoisie had made a monster, as it had of Marat."[30]

The "bourgeois image" of Blanqui, of which Lafargue was well aware, had been best expressed by Tocqueville, for whom Blanqui's appearance before the Constituent Assembly in 1848 had aroused "disgust and horror." Tocqueville said "he had sunken, withered cheeks, white lips, and a sickly malign, dirty look like a pallid, mouldy corpse; he was wearing no visible linen; an old black frock coat tightly clad his lean and emaciated limbs. He looked as if he had lived in a sewer and had only just emerged."[31]

Now Lafargue was "astonished" to see a small man quietly enter the room. He was "simply dressed, with white beard and hair, finely textured skin, a long tapering nose (all revolutionaries had such a nose, Blanqui later said, laughing), two small eyes, deeply sunken and bubbling with life, a gentle and sympathetic voice, nervous and well-shaped hands." Lafargue had heard that he always wore black gloves to hide nailless fingers tinged with blood.

Twenty students gathered around him, and Blanqui seemed to take pleasure in their presence. He spoke of their role as revolutionaries and of their need to work according to their capacities. He sounded as if the Empire would crumble the following day, and he clearly sought to inspire ardor for the struggle within his listeners. Blanqui told them he hoped they would never experience what he went through. He also told them not to listen to the old, even himself, when they spoke of things contrary to the students' aspirations. Blanqui was then sixty-two, and in spite of years spent in prison seemed young and alert. He was able to climb stairs effortlessly and had kept up with scientific discoveries; the impression given was that of a vital and virile man. Recounting the meeting, Lafargue credited Blanqui with having turned him to revolution. "Blanqui transformed us, corrupted us all." He was overcome and never tired of appreciating the lessons and advice "given without pretention" by *le vieux*. It was difficult for an ebullient young man not to be overwhelmed. "To Blanqui falls the honor of having made the revolutionary education of a part of the youth of our generation."[32]

The French government was clearly embarrassed by the students' behavior, and Louis Napoleon's advisers feared that the radical rhetoric would be taken as a sign of diminished support for the Empire. The Church was upset by the atheism shown and, in what came to be called the "affair of the schools," demanded that the government act. The widespread indignation prompted calls by the clerical and Bonapartist press to punish the students involved. The public prosecutor in his report commented on "the angry response produced by the regrettable attitude of some French students at the Liège Congress and Brussels meeting . . . who did not fear disowning their country's flag," and he promised that the government would reply to the "legitimate demands of public opinion."[33]

When the Academic Council of Paris met December 12, 1865, only one student heeded the summons to appear. Others, including Lafargue, paid no attention. These well-to-do young revolutionaries could ignore the threat of an expulsion or loss of a scholarship, and their refusal to testify intensified hostility against them.[34] The council, genuinely offended yet also yielding to pressure, voted to expel seven students from the University of Paris for "desecrat[ing] the flag and "attack[ing] the principles of social order."

The expulsion order gave rise to an outburst of unrest and defiance. Lectures were disrupted, professors booed, courses stopped, and clashes between students and police led to arrests. In the Senate Monsignor Dupanloup denounced the materialist doctrine and revolutionary theories voiced at Liège. There was repeated disorder in the Law School, and more than eight hundred medical students signed a protest stating that the expulsions were irregular, unprecedented, and arbitrary, violating individual liberty. No law forbade the French "the expression of their philosophical views outside the borders of the Empire."[35] Violence broke out in the Faculty of Medicine on December 18, a demonstration took place in the Faculty of Law and more arrests were made. To enter university facilities identification now had to be shown. Finally, all courses were suspended pending the outcome of an investigation. Academic administrators were divided: some found that the excessively harsh penalties only provided wider publicity for radical views and preferred to let public opinion decide the matter; others were pleased with the expulsions. Calm was restored by the time of the Christmas break; rumors of a ministerial crisis and the impending departure of the education minister Drury also helped to dampen protest.

The students appealed the expulsion decision on December 19, and the Imperial Council on Public Education, presided over by Drury, met December 26. The students now appeared, but only to submit a formal statement that denied the authority of the council to judge events that had occurred in another country. Aside from minor modifications, the expulsions were allowed to stand. Together with four medical students, including Albert Regnard and Charles-Victor Jaclard, and two law students, Germain Casse and Edouard Losson, Lafargue was expelled forever from the University of Paris and for two years from all other universities in France. Others received shorter penalties.

Lafargue's parents were clearly upset over the interruption of his medical studies. But they were determined that he should complete them and practice, nevertheless, and they made it possible for him to pursue them in London—although he did not yet speak a word of English. Whether the initiative was theirs or his we do not know.[36] Why London? Lafargue could have gone elsewhere. Was it because by now he was very much caught up in politics? Was he attracted to London because it was the seat of the International Workingmen's Association, founded the year before and influenced by the founder of a new and supposedly scientific school of socialism, Karl Marx?

3 Arrival in London

It was as though a veil had been torn from my eyes.

—Paul Lafargue

Lafargue sailed for England in mid-February 1866. On his arrival in London, he made his way to a hotel owned by a Frenchman outlawed for opposing the coming of Louis Napoleon to power in 1851, and was there for the February 24 celebration of the 1848 Revolution.[1] Eventually he found a room at 35 Kentish Town Road. The greater metropolitan area, soon to reach a population of over four million, was pushing out in all directions, adding fifty miles of new streets and more than 17,000 houses each year. By 1880 it resembled an oval patch with a horizontal axis ten miles long, a vertical axis a little less. The city advanced into the surrounding countryside by "thrusting out tentacles from the metropolitan heart," but one still found countryside between the tentacles.[2]

Lafargue studied physics and chemistry under a Dr. Carrière, himself a refugee, at Saint Bartholomew's Hospital. Apparently Lafargue hoped to take an English medical degree and then his qualifying exams in Strasbourg on his return.[3] One of the oldest hospitals in the world, with twelfth-century foundations resting on Roman foundations, Saint Bartholomew's, or "Bart's," as it was more commonly called, was in central London, almost in the shadow of Saint Paul's Cathedral. The hospital had been added to over the centuries, with the result that piles of masonry covered at least an acre or two: there was medieval architecture on top of Norman, Georgian on top of Tudor, and Victorian encrustations on top of everything.[4] Lafargue had to pass through gateways connecting the inner courtyards that lay among those grey stone structures. The rambling buildings contained mazes of long white-washed corridors and tunnels, permeated with the fumes of carbolic acid and alcohol and interrupted by enormous stone stairways leading to numerous high-tiered amphitheaters.

Not long after settling in London, Lafargue paid a visit to Marx, whose ability to mediate between English trade unionists and Continental socialists had enabled him to dominate the International's General Council.[5] Lafargue presented his letter of introduction from Henri Tolain, a labor organizer and leader of the Paris section of the International. The visit was intended as a simple courtesy, but Lafargue's impetuosity led to a fervent discussion, lasting, according to Lafargue, much of the night. It proved decisive; Lafargue was "seduced and conquered," because the impression made on the "Creole," as Marx described him to Engels, was such that he returned again and again.[6] Writing a quarter of a century later, Lafargue placed the date of his meeting with Marx a year earlier, in February 1865, a few months after the founding of the International. "I had come from Paris to bring him news of the progress made there by the young organization," he wrote in his memoirs of Marx. "I was then 24 years of age; all my life I shall not forget the impression made upon me by that first visit."[7]

This earlier date, however, is not corroborated by any other source, and is contradicted by the testimony of Charles Longuet, Lafargue's future brother-in-law. Longuet, already active in radical politics, was in England in early 1865, yet reports that he first met Lafargue at the Liège Students' Congress in October of that year and that the expelled Lafargue went to London in February 1866. Moreover, the first mention of Lafargue by Marx comes in letters Marx wrote in March 1866.[8]

Lafargue's version is also contradicted by the IWMA's membership list for the period. Lafargue is listed as having paid dues in 1866 and after, but not earlier. And according to the archives of the Institute of Marxism-Leninism, as examined by the Russian historian, G. P. Novikova, Lafargue met Marx at about the time of Lafargue's admission to the General Council of the International, in early March 1866.[9] Lafargue's memory, then, was very likely at fault. The 1866 date also appears more legitimate because in 1865, before the Liège Congress, Lafargue was relatively unknown, even in student republican circles, and there is little reason to think he would have been sent as an emissary to Marx from the International in France.[10]

Yet if misdated, there is no reason not to accept the rest of Lafargue's account; he adopted Marxist doctrine in stages through long conversations held during evening strolls on Hampstead Heath. Lafargue described these talks in glowing terms. Here he "acquired [his] education in economics," although "unfortunately" the notes he kept were among the papers seized during the time of the Paris Commune and burned by the police. Marx, he said, expounded his materialistically based theory of the development of human society "with that fullness of proof and reflection that was all his own. It was as though a veil had been torn from my eyes; for the first time I sensed clearly the logic of history and could trace back to their original causes the seemingly contradictory manifestations in the evolution of society and of ideas. I was as though dazzled and for years the impression remained [vivid]."[11] This and subsequent encounters would prove a turning point in Lafargue's life, greatly influencing his decision to choose politics over medicine, and Marxism over Blanquism or Proudhonism.

At a meeting of the International's General Council held February 27, 1866, Lafargue was proposed for membership by Eugène Dupont, a council member and the IWMA's corresponding secretary for France. A watchmaker, Dupont had fought in the June Days of 1848. He had then emigrated to London, and was ultimately to settle in the United States. On March 6, at the following week's meeting, Lafargue was elected unanimously.[12] A fellow council member was Charles Longuet, until Longuet's return to Paris in July. Doubtless because of his fluency in Spanish, Lafargue soon showed an interest in Spain's labor movement and specifically in attempts to organize a section of the International there. Almost immediately after his election to the council, he published an article in *El Obrero*, the newspaper of the federation created at the first Spanish workers' congress, which had been held in Barcelona the previous December. The article, which appeared March 18, described the IWMA's steps to operate mutual credit associations on an international scale. Nine days later Lafargue was made secretary of the International for Spain, and he was to hold the post until 1870.[13]

His work on the council, however, was largely administrative, concerned as its members were with such questions as the collection of dues, preparations for forthcoming congresses of the International, dissemination of council decisions, and the recruitment of British trade unions.[14] Lafargue seconded Marx's suggestion that the International's 1867 Congress, scheduled for Lausanne, discuss the "practical means enabling the IWMA to fulfill the function of a common center of action for the working classes," and he received the council's request to translate into French its "address" to the general membership laying stress on the necessity of concerted political action.[15]

In spite of his growing fascination with Marxist thought, Lafargue had by no means discarded his earlier Proudhonism, and his occasional "lapses" at council meetings aroused Marx's ire. Marx was well aware that his chief ideological competition in these early years of the International was Proudhonist mutualism and that it was the latter which accurately expressed the outlook of a Latin European proletariat still retaining a strong artisanal consciousness.[16] Proudhonists, who opposed strikes and political parties and stood for mutualism, in fact dominated these first congresses. (The best Marx could get at Lausanne was a vague resolution favoring the political emancipation of workers as a requisite for their social emancipation.)

In the spring of 1866, French students published an appeal to their German and Italian counterparts calling for international solidarity and for an end to all national differences. The appeal was defended by Lafargue at the International's General Council meeting of June 5, 1866, when the council was debating the line to take in the war, then imminent, between Prussia and Austria. Lafargue's defense was entirely in keeping with his Proudhonism, particularly with the Proudhonists' rejection of nationality as meaningless and as opposed to the liberation of peoples. Two days earlier, a Lafargue article in *La Rive gauche* had lumped Italian nationalists Mazzini and Garibaldi together with Bismarck and had denounced all three as equally reactionary.[17] These views evoked criticism of Lafargue at the council meeting of June 19, many of its members rejecting the comparison. A chastened Lafargue replied that he had written in his individual capacity and not as a council member, upon which his colleagues passed a resolution declaring themselves "not responsible for Citizen Lafargue's views."[18] Lafargue continued, however, to take an independent line in the columns of *La Rive gauche*. In the July 1 issue he dismissed the concept of nationality as "null and void," as one with which workers had nothing in common, and he insisted that nationalism only concealed imperialist aspirations and that class divisions would replace divisions between nations.[19]

For Marx and for most of the council, Lafargue and his fellow students rightly condemned predatory wars but missed the "historic" character of the wars of unification of the 1850s and 1860s in Italy and Germany, which were seen as progressive steps. Writing from Margate, where he was resting, Marx had already complained to his daughter Laura: "That damned boy Lafargue pesters me with his Proudhonism, and will not rest it seems, until I have administered to him a sound cudgeling of his Creole pate."[20]

Marx also vented his frustration to Engels. "The Proudhonist clique among the students in Paris . . . preaches peace, declares war to be obsolete and nationalities to be an absurdity . . . As polemics against chauvinism their doings are useful and explicable. But as believers in Proudhon (Lafargue and Longuet, two very good friends of mine here, also belong to them), who think Europe must and will sit quietly on their hindquarters until the gentlemen in France abolish 'poverty and ignorance,' under the latter of which they themselves labour in direct proportion to their vociferations about 'social science,' they are grotesque."[21]

Three weeks later, Marx told Engels how during the council debate on the war between Prussia and Austria, he had ridiculed Lafargue and the other French delegates to the IWMA, specifically their repudiation of nationalities and proposed replacement of nation states with small groups that would form cooperative associations. "Proudhonized Stirnerism," snorted Marx, and he compared it with Fourierist phalansteries. "The English laughed very much when I began my speech to the General Council by saying that our friend Lafargue and others, who had done with nationalities, had spoken French to us, i.e., a language which nine-tenths of the audience did not understand. I also suggested that by negating nationalities he appeared, quite unconsciously, to understand their absorption by the model French nation."[22] Yet Marx found much to like in the energetic young student who could make himself useful as a member able to translate council directives into French, who prepared a French version of Marx's report on behalf of the General Council, and who polished the French text of Wilhelm Liebknecht's pacifist remarks in the Reichstag.[23]

Neither Marx nor Lafargue attended these congresses of the International. Marx was busy reading proofs of *Capital,* which was published in 1867, while Lafargue was trying to keep up with his studies. On September 6, 1867, delegates at Lausanne, reviewing the work of the General Council, praised Lafargue for his assiduous attendance at council meetings, and the delegates at Brussels (September 1868) reelected him to council membership.[24] According to council minutes, Lafargue regularly attended meetings until his return to France in the fall of 1868.[25]

There is also evidence that Marx tried to use Lafargue as an intermediary with French revolutionaries and particularly with the Blanquists, whom Marx badly wanted to regroup under the banner of the

International. As early as November 1861, Marx had written to Watteau at the time of Blanqui's imprisonment to express his concern "over the fate of the man I have always considered as the head of the people's party in France."[26] At the same time he wrote Engels of the necessity to raise money for Blanqui's forthcoming trial. Lafargue, still mightily impressed by his meeting with the old revolutionary, needed little urging to try to get in touch with him. On April 22, 1866, Lafargue, ignorant of Blanqui's address, wrote to him in care of Watteau. Watteau forwarded the letter, acknowledging the writer's sincerity but commenting on the carelessness with which it was written and the likelihood of Marx's influence in Lafargue's decision to write.

Lafargue modestly wondered whether Blanqui remembered his "name or face," but assured him that "never in my life will I forget the lunch that, together with several of our friends, we shared in Brussels." It was in the name of the revolution to which he was so committed that Lafargue asked *le vieux* to support the International and its forthcoming congress in Geneva. With Blanqui's presence, it would be "complete," and Blanqui was asked, in view of his acquaintance with, and influence on, revolutionaries in "all of Europe," to do everything possible to help it succeed.[27] Blanqui was not impressed: though pleased by the greater emphasis placed by the IWMA's Brussels Congress on political action, political action still trailed economic. "For me," Blanqui wrote (in a letter that came to Marx's attention), "socialism is inseparable from politics. To abstract itself from the state, to act without it, in spite of it, to claim that things are set in motion outside of it, almost unknown to it, to me always seemed an immense farce."[28]

Some Blanquists, however, their chief's advice to the contrary notwithstanding, did participate at Geneva. Because of doctrinal and tactical disagreements, as we shall see, they eventually quit the International after the Commune. Still, Marx continued to view Blanqui and his followers as an important ingredient in French socialism, and on two subsequent occasions Lafargue again tried to act as an intermediary. In 1869, before the IWMA's Basel Congress, he wrote to Blanqui through Tridon, who shared Blanqui's sentiments regarding the International and had condemned Lafargue's assignment as secretary for Spain because he knew Spanish as "pitiful."[29] A decade later, Lafargue once more sought the old revolutionary's support in reviving the French labor movement. On neither occasion was there a reply from the ailing and irritable Blanqui.

4 Laura

The young man first attached himself to me, but soon transferred his attention from the Old Man to the daughter.

—Karl Marx

Laura Marx was born on September 26, 1845, into a family beset by childhood tragedies. Of Karl and Jenny Marx's seven children, one died at birth, two others survived slightly more than a year, and a fourth died at the age of nine. The oldest, Jenny, was born in Paris; Laura and her brother Edgar were born in Brussels. Soon after their arrival in London, the Marxes had another son, Edmund, called Guido, who a year later experienced convulsions and died. A third daughter, Franziska, born in 1851, died of bronchitis the next year, and in April 1855 Edgar died, probably of tuberculosis. The youngest daughter to survive childhood, Eleanor, was born in 1855; another daughter was still-born in 1857.

Most of what we know about the Marx family comes from the letters of the three surviving girls and their mother, as well as from Karl Marx's own correspondence, particularly with Engels, who lived in Manchester until he moved to London in 1869.[1] By all accounts the daughters were talented, energetic, and charming. An atmosphere of freedom and love prevailed, in contrast to the behavior shown by Marx toward those with whom he disagreed politically. The girls admired their father, whom they called Mohr (the Moor) because of his jet-black hair. Each girl performed well in school, winning prizes and showing a special talent for language and literature. But it was largely at home that they received their education: Marx read to his children such classics as Homer, the *Nibelungenlied, Don Quixote,* and *A Thousand and One Nights.* Shakespeare was the "house Bible." Other novelists included James Fenimore Cooper and Sir Walter Scott, and these works were not only read but discussed.

The girls were devoted to their parents, especially to their father, regardless of the poverty, both real and genteel, in which they lived for so long. Unable to provide them with a better life, free of debt, Marx experienced deep and prolonged feelings of frustration.[2] Yet both parents insisted on keeping up appearances and hiding their poverty. Servants were employed, music and drawing lessons were made available, though there was no money for a piano and at times family members went hungry to pay the fees. The Marxes were determined that their daughters would have a respectable upbringing, and indeed they grew up multilingual and very much aware of the world.

The poverty of these first years in London was softened by several inheritances, by the assistance sent regularly by Engels, and finally by the annuity that he settled on Marx. In 1863 Marx had told his friend that without support his family would doubtless disintegrate; the two older girls would have to live away as governesses; and "Lenchen," Helen Demuth, the devoted servant who had accompanied them from Germany, would have to go elsewhere.[3]

Legacies from an old comrade and fellow refugee who had settled in London, Wilhelm Wolff, and from Marx's mother, valued at about 1,500 pounds, enabled the family in March 1864 to move from Grafton Terrace, "a mean little house in Kentish Town" (itself a vast improvement over their first squalid quarters in Soho), to Modena Villas, in Maitland Park, where they lived until their move in 1875 to a smaller house in the same area.[4] The Modena Villas, larger than any house they had known, was located in a newer suburb, south of Hampstead Heath. Marx had a large, airy study on the first floor overlooking a park (now built over), and each girl had a room of her own. However, the costs of the move and the almost 100 percent increase in rent tormented him.[5]

Even so, the rent, about forty pounds a year, was not excessive and contrasted favorably with housing costs in other European capitals. For middle-class families who could afford them, these houses, designed as villas of four or five stories, were readily available. A basement or half-basement held the kitchen and a sitting room; a ground floor contained a hall and two sitting rooms, back and front parlors as they were called; the first floor held the largest room in the house, usually used as a drawing room (although Engels used his as a library and work room); the upper floors had two or three bedrooms and storage areas. Marx's home was somewhat smaller than this.[6] Because these houses were built in groups of eight, ten, or twelve by the same contractor and were identical, construction costs were reduced considerably, making an eight- or ten-room house in London far cheaper than its counterpart in Paris or Vienna.

As one of Marx's biographers points out, Laura may well have been the "most elegant and versatile" of Marx's daughters.[7] Describing her to a friend, her mother said of Laura that she was "at home in everything, be it in the wide sea or at the stove or the reading room of the British Museum or in the ballroom," and, moreover, "sweet in nature and brilliant in intellect."[8]

"Laura is some degrees lighter, blonder, and more clear-complexioned," continued her proud mother, "actually more attractive than her older sister because she has irridescent green eyes under dark brows and long eyelashes [that] shine with the fires of joy." Having grown up in London, Laura of course spoke English; in addition, she knew a fair amount of French, could understand Dante in Italian, and had been exposed to enough German to read Hegel.[9] Like her sisters, she was bright, cultivated, and politically aware. Her temperament, however, according to reminiscences of family and other observers, was "less ardent, less sensitive; her activity, more limited."[10] Paying more attention to her clothes than did her sisters, and sportive, developing a taste for horseback riding, she was more attracted than they to the material aspects of life.[11]

Like other visitors, Paul was impressed by the family's inclination to give nicknames to each member of the household, even to friends. Laura was called the Hottentot, or more often, Cacadou (the word for cockatoo, in German), after a fashionable tailor in an old novel, because of her exacting taste and the smartness of her dress. Less vivacious than her sisters, she was more cautious, perhaps colder. Certainly her letters show her as more indolent. Laura was known to have fits of brooding, and she may have suffered from the presence of her even more brilliant older sister and from the favoritism shown Jenny by her father. As perhaps was to be expected, there was no shortage of suitors, and Laura was much courted. One assiduous caller was Charles Manning, of partially Spanish descent, who according to father Marx was "rich" and "decent." But Laura, he told Engels, "cool and reserved, doesn't care a pin for him" and could "damp his southern passion." In May 1865 she indeed turned down Manning's proposal of marriage.[12]

Lafargue, the more fortunate suitor, had soon fallen in love with Laura, and was to remain so throughout his life. Consequently, the model of an austere professional revolutionary such as Blanqui would never be a viable alternative. Twenty years later Paul would describe Laura as "taking after her mother, having a fair skin, rosy cheeks, and a wealth of curly hair, with a golden sheen, as if it concealed the setting sun."[13] The smitten lover became something of a fixture at the Marx household—and a burden as well, as his presence forced the Marxes, who relished the prospects of the twenty-five-year-old medical student (who exaggerated his family's wealth), to keep up appearances.

Moreover, the Marxes were upset by Lafargue's passionate courtship of their daughter. Laura herself initially found Lafargue far too impulsive. According to her mother, "it took a long time before Laura, with her quiet, cool, critical sense, could decide in his favor, the more so since to her reserved, truly English character, the passionate nature and the demonstrative manners of the young man were directly antagonistic; still, as in love opposites often attract, so it also happened here."[14] Like her suitor, Laura was sportive and liked her comforts; less combative than her sisters, she was not insensitive to Lafargue's charm and vitality.[15]

On August 6, 1866, an understanding was reached and, as Marx put it, she "became half engaged to Monsieur Lafargue, my medical Creole." Marx had long thought that Lafargue's interest in the household was political or philosophical, and he told Engels, not without irony: "The young man first attached himself to me, but soon transferred his attraction from the Old Man to the daughter." Marx explained that "she had treated him like the others, but the emotional excesses of such Creoles, some fears that the *jeune homme* . . . would do away with himself, etc., some affection for him, cool as is always the case with Laura . . . have led to more or less a half compromise."[16]

Some aspects of the couple's respective personalities are illustrated by their "confessions," a popular pastime of the period in which likes and dislikes were stated and compared.[17] Laura identified her favorite character trait as truth; Paul, as attentiveness and patience. Laura preferred men to show justice and women to show mercy; Paul wanted men to be silent and women coquettish. Laura criticized her irresolution; Paul, his impetuosity. Laura's idea of unhappiness was self-contempt; Paul's coldness; the vice she most detested was cant; he, virtue (already displaying the taste for irony and paradox that was to mark his writings). The vice she was most ready to excuse was day-dreaming; he, laziness. Her favorite poet was Shakespeare; his, Alfred de Musset; her favorite prose writers, Cervantes and Shelley; his, Rabelais, Pascal, and Balzac. He revered Marat and despised Napoleon I. Under "favorite maxim" she wrote, "know thyself"; he, "consider well before speaking" and "only an imbecile doesn't change."

Before the engagement became formal, Marx began to check his future son-in-law's references. He wrote to Moilin, Lafargue's former professor in Paris, who thereupon informed Lafargue. Paradoxically, Moilin urged Lafargue not to reveal his political views publicly: "If you want to be taken for a serious doctor, renounce for now your political writings."[18] Marx also showed concern over the articles his prospective son-in-law was sending to *La Rive gauche:* a letter to Lafargue's father November 12, 1866, thanking him for the gift of some wine and asking for some transcripts required by the College of Surgeons, closed with a request: "Will you tell your son he will very much oblige me by not making propaganda in Paris. The times are dangerous . . . He will lose nothing in economizing his polemical force. The more he constrains himself, the more he will be a good fighter at an opportune time."[19]

Most upsetting was the misunderstanding over what Paul and the family—particularly Marx but Laura as well—each defined as a semi-engagement. Lafargue made no distinction between being engaged and semi-engaged; he now wanted to become intimate with Laura. But Marx, perhaps prodded by his wife, in any case worried by Lafargue's unsettled future plans and his own precarious financial state, decided to put his cards on the table. He now spent so much time either with or worrying about Lafargue and about keeping up appearances before the "wealthy suitor" that he was distracted from his work.[20]

Laura's riding lessons had added to Marx's mounting expenses. Apparently Laura and "the Secretary for Spain," both on horseback, were "creating a sensation on Haverstock Hill."[21] Disturbed during the day, Marx had begun working nights; he was increasingly afflicted by boils, and so upset that he momentarily considered emigrating to the United States.[22] He was more convinced than ever that he had to have "positive information" about Lafargue's plans and prospects.[23] In a letter that must be considered a classic, the stern Victorian father, writing in French, asked his prospective son-in-law about his intentions.[24] It reveals that he in no way considered Lafargue a committed revolutionary; on the contrary, Marx continued to show concern with preventing Lafargue from becoming politically active.[25]

Cold and formal in tone, Marx asked for permission to make some "observations." What followed, in numbered paragraphs, were rules that might have discouraged many a young lover. First there was an ultimatum: "If you wish to continue your relations with my daughter, you will have to discard your manner of paying court to her. You are well aware that no engagement has yet been entered into, that as yet everything is provisional." He continued,

> And even if she were formally your betrothed, you should not forget that this concerns a long-term affair. An all too intimate deportment is the more unbecoming insofar as the two lovers will be living in the same place for a necessarily prolonged period of purgatory and of severe tests. I have observed with dismay your change of conduct from day to day over the geological epoch of a single week. To my mind, true love expresses itself in the lover's restraint, bearing, and even diffidence regarding the adored one, and certainly not in unrestrained passion and manifestations of premature intimacy. Should you plead in defense your Creole temperament, it becomes my duty to interpose my sound sense between your temperament and my daughter. If in her presence you are unable to love her in a manner that conforms with the latitude of London, you will have to resign yourself to loving her from a distance. I am sure you take my meaning.

Marx then raised the matter of finances: "Before definitely settling your relations with Laura I require a clear explanation of your economic position." He admitted he had a deep personal reason for asking; he had practically wrecked his own wife's life. "You know that I have sacrificed my entire fortune to the revolutionary struggle. I do not regret it. On the contrary. If I had to start my career again I would do the same. But I would not marry."

What information Marx had regarding Lafargue's prospects was not reassuring.

> I know that you are still a student, that your career in France has been more or less ruined by the Liège incident, that you still lack the language, the indispensable implement for your acclimatization in England, and that your prospects are at best entirely problematic. Observation has convinced me that you are not by nature diligent, despite bouts of feverish activity and good intentions.

Marx then got to the point.

In these circumstances you will need help from others to set out in life with my daughter. As regards your family I know nothing. Assuming that they enjoy a certain competence, that does not necessarily give proof that they are willing to make sacrifices for you. I do not even know how they view your plans for marriage. I repeat, I must have definite elucidation on all these matters.

Marx added that an "avowed realist" like Lafargue could not expect him to behave like an idealist where "my daughter's future is concerned." And to prevent any misunderstanding of his letter, Marx warned him that should Lafargue feel tempted "to enter into the marriage today, it would not happen. My daughter would refuse. I myself should object. You must be a real man before thinking of marriage, and this will require a long testing time for you and her."

On the same day, Marx wrote a long letter to François Lafargue asking for *renseignements positifs* about his economic condition before matters could proceed. The reply came soon, apparently a wholly satisfactory one: the elder Lafargue, formally asking for the designation of fiancé for his son, agreed with Marx that Paul must take his medical exams, first in London and then in France, before marrying.[26] He informed Marx that the Lafargues were well-to-do, with "plantations" in Cuba and property in both New Orleans and Bordeaux. Lafargue *père,* then a wholesale wine merchant, considered himself prosperous enough to promise that his only son and heir could count on a handsome wedding gift of 100,000 francs. (There is no sign, however, that it was ever delivered.)

Marx was understandably pleased: "So far," he informed Engels, "the thing is settled." Yet Marx did not conceal his reservations: Although a decent fellow, Lafargue was an *enfant gâté,* too much "a child of nature," and Laura would want Engels' consent. Yet Marx admitted that even though he could not help but feel jealous watching his pursuit of Laura, he "liked the fellow."[27]

The entire family saw Paul as a future physician and thought him gifted. Marx believed that he had "an extraordinary talent for medicine," and appreciated his skepticism regarding the limits to which the art could aspire. Still, he reproached Lafargue for giving credence to such fads as belief in the therapeutic powers of electricity. Marx also regretted Lafargue's two-year expulsion, but was grateful that he had a good adviser in Professor Carrière, who had gotten him access to hospitals in London.[28]

Laura's mother appeared especially pleased with the suitor's qualities, and to a German friend described him in glowing terms, particularly "his dark olive complexion and extraordinary eyes." He was "a brilliant student," and besides being devoted to Laura, was "good-hearted and generous." Recalling the religious issues raised by her own engagement, she was pleased that in this regard, at least, her daughter would not be hurt: Laura and Paul shared a common atheism. "What I consider a quite remarkable piece of luck is that he has the same principles, in particular where religion is concerned; thus Laura will be spared the inevitable conflicts and sufferings to which any girl with her opinions is exposed in society." It was "truly exceptional to find men in his cultural and social position" who shared his point of view. She added, in English, "I always thought Laura would be a lucky girl." She also anticipated a generous wedding present inasmuch as Lafargue's parents were prosperous "estate owners" and he an only child.[29]

Although, of course, aware of Lafargue's racial origins, the Marxes showed no signs of real prejudice. They did share certain beliefs, common to bourgeois and others of their era, about national traits (for example, of the French) and the supposedly emotional temperament of those from warmer climates. But their references to Lafargue's one-eighth black background were couched in affectionate and joking terms and seen as a source of amusement, not concern. To family and friends, Marx referred to Lafargue as the "gorilla," the "negrillo," and the "nigger."[30] Later, after the now-married Lafargues had returned to France, Marx asked his youngest daughter to extend his compliments to the "African."[31]

Even though an understanding had been reached, it was not easy for Marx, with his bourgeois habits, to be too close to Lafargue—now in the house more than ever—and observe his passionate behavior and general exuberance. Father Marx described the young man as a *verliebter Kauz* (literally, a screech owl in love), and often repeated that nothing would come of the whole thing unless Lafargue "calmed down to the level of English manners."[32]

Marx was both amused and exasperated by his prospective son-in-law. When Laura briefly served as apprentice teacher in a boarding school outside London, the lovelorn Lafargue posed such a sad figure that Marx was prompted to write to his daughter: "Il hidalgo della figura trista [the knight of the rueful countenance] left me at the corner of his house. After his heart was heavily shaken, he seems to part from *me* with heroic coolness." Much of the exasperation came from having Lafargue around the house (until he visited his parents in Bordeaux in early November) when money was short; the family was still desperate to hide its poverty from Laura's well-to-do suitor.[33]

But it was impossible to remain angry with Lafargue for long: his southern glibness, his taste for pomp, his enthusiasm, and his exuberance, even his bragging, overrode all complaints. Marx and his wife were both fond of him, and on December 7 Marx apologized to Lafargue for his August ultimatum.[34] And Laura, to judge by a letter to her sister Jenny, was deeply in love and feeling very romantic.[35]

That Lafargue was generous to a fault—and unmindful of money— was illustrated in a letter to Moilin. Apparently Lafargue had asked him to buy flowers, available in Paris, for Laura, only to be told how "foolish" it was "to spend so much money on a bouquet which in a few hours will wither."[36] Lafargue also showered gifts on Laura's sisters: Eleanor reports Paul's gift to her of a collection of Cooper novels.[37] Finally, on her twenty-first birthday, September 26, 1866, seven months after Lafargue arrived in London, Laura received an engagement ring and plans were made for the forthcoming marriage.

At the end of the year Paul's parents invited the three sisters to spend the summer of 1867 with them, first in Bordeaux and then at the seashore. They would travel with Paul, and he offered to pay expenses. Marx could not allow this, but to make the trip possible for his daughters used the money set aside for rent, and in order to redeem their clothes and jewelry from pawnshops exhausted what little savings remained.[38] They were gone from July 21 to September 10, forcing their mother to abandon plans for a trip of her own.[39]

When Lafargue returned with them to London, he learned that Marx—and Laura—wanted him to visit their longtime family friend and benefactor, Engels. Lafargue insisted that Marx, in turn, accompany him during the three days he planned to spend in Manchester. He really could not afford the fare, Marx told Engels, but Lafargue was not to be informed of the family's financial plight.[40] Engels thereupon sent five pounds to cover his friend's travel costs. The meeting was to prove momentous for Lafargue. Even though he had continued to write for left-wing student journals, his political interests understandably had been dampened by romantic and academic involvements. His introduction to Engels rekindled them.

5 Marriage and Politics

[Lafargue and Longuet] are ridiculous disciples of Proudhon.
—Karl Marx

What is little short of astonishing is that in addition to pursuing Laura, studying medicine, and working on behalf of the International, Lafargue found time to submit articles to the left-wing press, particularly to the revolutionary student newspaper once again housed in Paris after its year-long sojourn in Belgium. In the spring and early summer of 1866 he sent some dozen articles to *La Rive gauche*, revived by Charles Longuet in November 1864. Lafargue, we have seen, had met Longuet, three years his senior, at the Liège Congress and had renewed his acquaintance in London, where the two sat on the International's General Council. Both men shared an admiration for Proudhon, for Blanqui, and then for Marx. It was in the columns of *La Rive gauche* that the first accounts of Marx's doctrine, written by Lafargue, appeared in France.

Longuet fitted his name; he was a tall, thin, alert-looking man with a wispy beard and bright black eyes. He was always ready to debate, although when debating frequently lost in a digression. He was born in Caen on February 14, 1839, into an old bourgeois landowning family of clerical and monarchist persuasions. His great-grandfather, a lawyer, in 1789 had drafted the demands of the Third Estate for the district of Caen.[1] He was raised in hatred of the Empire, and while completing a classics-laden curriculum, moved toward republicanism and atheism.

Hardly had he started law studies at Rouen in 1863, when he founded a little journal, *La Jeunesse normande,* short-lived even by student standards, lasting as it did for all of one issue before it was seized by the authorities. In Paris, Longuet began preparing for a doctorate in law, and also studied history and the English language. He was at once caught up in the republican youth movements of the Latin Quarter and influenced by Proudhon's teachings in particular and by social questions in general. He became friendly with the non-resident medical student, Georges Clemenceau; with Anatole France; with Louis Rogeard, a left-wing professor who published vitriolic pamphlets; with yet another medical student turned to political activism, the eighteen-year-old Henry Bauer; and later with Charles Beaudelaire. They frequented the Brasserie Glaser, discussing literature, philosophy, and politics. Jules Clère, who was to publish portraits of leading Communards, described Longuet in looks and manners as "the most perfect example of a Bohemian one could meet."[2]

Together with Clemenceau, Longuet established, or helped to establish, *Les Ecoles de France*, another short-lived radical student newspaper. On June 10, 1864, for having published "unauthorized writings," he was sentenced to four months in prison and a 300-franc fine. The first issue of *La Rive gauche*, founded by Rogeard, appeared on October 20, 1864, soon after Longuet's release. Published as a *journal littéraire et philosophique*, it proclaimed its intention to give students "the opportunity to assert themselves before their detractors." Its staff, by anyone's estimate, was brilliant, including as it did Clemenceau, France, and the poet Sully-Prudhomme, and even getting contributions from Victor Hugo. Hugo's bust was given to all new subscribers, but it was Proudhon who was venerated above all. The issue announcing Proudhon's death, that of January 22, 1865, appeared with a black border on its front page.

Because of a satirical article published on May 31, 1865, ridiculing Napoleon III and defaming the imperial family, the twenty-five-year-old Longuet was again condemned to prison, this time for eight months, and required to pay a 500-franc fine. He chose instead to move the newspaper, which he now helped to edit, to Brussels, where he soon published a version of the International's provisional statutes. For this and other articles considered incendiary, the Belgian authorities expelled Longuet from the country in September 1865. After a short stay in Germany he arrived in England in late November or early December. The newspaper continued to appear, although intermittently and in different places. By December 10 Longuet was the sole editor. As a member of the International, he was received at Modena Villas and by January 9, 1866, named the International's corresponding secretary for Belgium. Both he and Lafargue were assiduous visitors to the Marx house, served together on the General Council, and eventually became brothers-in-law.

Regardless of their similar political views, the two differed in temperament and style. Longuet was more cautious but lacked both the diligence and the originality of Lafargue.[3] If he was then attracted to Jenny Marx, Longuet was too reserved or too politically involved to show it. He returned to France, subsequently served another prison term, and attended the IWMA's Lausanne and Basel Congresses in 1868 and 1869.[4]

Lafargue and *La Rive gauche* rejected religion and capitalism, but saw themselves as possessed of moral idealism and as *très sérieux*. An insight into the former's state of mind may be found in the "extensive and anguished" obituary of Aimé Cournet written by Lafargue that appeared in the issue of June 26, 1866.[5] Cournet, whom Lafargue had known and befriended in Paris, had died the previous month at the age of twenty-six, and Lafargue lavished praise on him as "a fighter in the name of atheism, socialism, and revolution." He saw Cournet as one of the "misunderstood and despised representatives of youth and intelligence whom the nineteenth century had rejected and driven to death," as it had Lafargue's literary hero Musset. Lafargue's romanticism burst through when he concluded that men had "a right to live and develop themselves," and he resented society's refusal to meet the physical needs of its members.

In addition to its literary ambitions, *La Rive gauche* fulminated against the Empire of Louis Napoleon. Its first page satirically carried quotations from his speeches given as candidate for president of the Second Republic, which strongly defended the republican idea. As a contributor, Lafargue was writing for a staff whose orientation was Proudhonist and Blanquist. The Belgian socialist César de Paepe, who also contributed articles, antagonized Proudhonists by favoring cooperative ownership of the land. Still, on most questions de Paepe was closer to mutualist than to Marxist solutions. Longuet later acknowledged that Lafargue, too, was then a Proudhonist; "not as profoundly as I, no doubt, but much more urgently."[6]

Reflecting the views of Proudhon, but also those of Blanqui and now of Marx, Lafargue portrayed himself as "representative of the youth of France, . . . [of] the future battling gallantly against the tyranny of the Second Empire," a tyranny that he saw as a concerted but futile effort to prevent the young from voicing their opposition. He asked the younger generation to part company with bourgeois republicans: "Time has opened our eyes. Now we understand these defenders of the Empire; they are a safety valve . . . we have brusquely broken with them." The government's repression of journals hostile to the regime, particularly those in the Latin Quarter, meant little: "All the young men who write for these journals affirm Atheism, Revolution, Socialism. Their number is large [and] each closure produces new combatants."[7]

As it had for Proudhon, education was relied on as a weapon by the opponents of the regime. When everything "fell still" after the June Days, Proudhon was the first to break the silence; his book *La Justice dans l'Eglise et la Révolution* was a major event. "The Empire has silenced us up to now," Lafargue continued, "but we are ready for battle! We have studied and we have read our Kant, Hegel, Feuerbach, Proudhon, Darwin, Fourier, Comte, Buchner, Saint-Simon, Taine, . . . and we have our leaders." He quoted "old Blanqui," who had told young revolutionaries "not to listen to the old, to those who lived in different times and who have forgotten."

Lafargue praised the "positivist method" as "the only one that can lead man to truth,"and urged its adoption in the social as well as in the natural sciences.[8] He hailed "our beloved Proudhon," for having "begun to clear away all supernatural elements—mystic or sentimental—from ethics and economic science." Idealism posed a priori principles insisted on as irrefutable; from them it drew deductions, such as religious teachings, "with whose reality it was not concerned." Positivism, on the other hand, related only to objects capable of subjection to experience and observation; it abandoned primary and final causes to the fruitless research of the idealists. Hence idealism was condemned as an "enemy to be overcome at any price and against which all our efforts must be directed," a theme to which Lafargue was to return time and again.

He had referred to the International, but was almost alone on the staff in doing so. On June 17 the newspaper published an IWMA manifesto. On July 8 Lafargue published a short review of a book, *Leçons de médecine physiologique*, which he interpreted in a materialistic sense, and, finally, his article of July 15, "La Lutte sociale" (The Social Struggle), the first in a proposed series, referred to Marx at length. However limited its circulation, *La Rive gauche* was becoming the organ disseminating the views of the International in intellectual circles, and a reading of Lafargue's articles shows that he was moving toward Marxism. Still, as his insistence on internationalism within the IWMA revealed, and much to Marx's annoyance, he retained Proudhonist perspectives. In the summer of 1866, "to cure

[his] very good friends, Lafargue and Longuet," who are "ridiculous disciples of Proudhon," Marx planned to have them read the refutation of Proudhon he had written twenty years earlier, *The Poverty of Philosophy.*[9]

In "The Social Struggle," Lafargue's first sustained writing effort, the materialism and positivism that later permeated his thought, reinforced by economic determinism and the concept of the class struggle, were already apparent. "The Social Struggle" was intended to introduce French readers to Marx's ideas.[10] His homage to Marx, whom he described as "an eminent German socialist," was supported by a three-page quotation from *The Poverty of Philosophy.* The articles provided the first prolonged exposure to Marxist thought (aside from Marx's 1847 book on Proudhon) in any French periodical since at least 1843, and may have been the first time Marx's name appeared in a French publication before 1870.[11] None of the French delegates to a conference of the International held in London in September 1865 had read Marx. James Guillaume, one of the heads of the Swiss section at the 1866 Geneva Congress, admitted that he was "until then ignorant of the existence of Karl Marx."[12] The Frenchman usually thought of as bringing Marxism to France, Jules Guesde, admitted that it was only after the Paris Commune that he became aware of Marx's existence.[13]

Lafargue offered a general analysis of the historic role of the bourgeoisie from its origins to the Second Empire. Like the nobility in the age of Louis XIV, the bourgeoisie was intellectually and artistically moribund; it had rejected the antireligious audacity embraced in the eighteenth century. Previously Lafargue had agreed with Enlightenment thinkers who argued that idealists had created God and original sin in order to explain the universe and human misery.[14] He had agreed, too, with positivists who rejected metaphysical explanations for observed phenomena and who insisted on the play of material forces.[15] Lafargue saw Marxism as completing the work of eighteenth-century materialists and nineteenth-century positivists: the bourgeoisie now recognized the "usefulness of religion . . . [the] necessity to provide consolation [for the poor], by placing the Bible into their hands."

The bourgeoisie maintained itself in power by relying on such social categories as judges, clergy, soldiers, and civil servants, and Lafargue attributed the existence of these "nonproductive parasites" to a system allowing for private ownership. Subsequent articles planned to trace the rise of the middle class to economic and political power and attempt a class analysis of the Second Empire (in essence arguing that the bourgeoisie and the proletariat, tired of killing and of being killed, had thrown themselves into the arms of Bonaparte). The writer would then discuss the hated Empire's moral degeneracy, which accounted for its readiness to go to war (explained as attempts to divert attention from domestic inadequacies and predicted as the cause of its ultimate downfall). For Lafargue, campaigns in Italy had twice saved Napoleon III.[16] More original was Lafargue's insistence that the bourgeoisie reinforced its hold on power by creating a cultural context that promoted its own interests. Lafargue condemned Renan and Hugo, particularly Renan's *Etudes religieuses* and Hugo's *Claire de Gueux*, arguing that such art and literature were representative of a bourgeois outlook. This early effort to apply a materialist analysis to art and literature and to relate cultural and political domination would later be expanded on considerably.

Also given expression in these first articles was Lafargue's pamphleteering talent, rich in irony and paradox. In June Lafargue parodied the Catholic catechism to condemn the iconoclasm of the "irreverent" younger generation. His simulated document aimed at showing the anxiety of an older generation of republicans fearful of the atheistic revolutionism and socialism of the young. (Lafargue had no patience with the democrats and revolutionaries of 1848, who despite their flaming rhetoric were now servile to the Second Empire.) Heavy-handed, it nevertheless made the point that it was precisely the irreverent younger generation, however much it placed stress on reason and science, that embodied the ideals of Christianity.[17]

Lafargue contributed to other journals as well, and an article in one of them showed the pride he took in his racial origins. Published by a Brussels newspaper supporting the IWMA, it took as its subject racial tensions in the United States and was signed "Paul Lafargue, mulatto."[18] He closed on a note of defiance: "They throw in our faces, as an insult, the term *homme de couleur*. It is up to us revolutionary mulattoes to pick up the term and make ourselves worthy of it. Radicals of America, let 'mulatto' be your rallying cry! . . . It means misery, oppression, hatred. Do you know anything more beautiful?" Lafargue remained fascinated by his origins. At the time of a racial disturbance in New Orleans he urged that the revolutionary example of Haiti be followed. Still, he was not obsessed by race; he had equated mulatto with proletariat and based his plea for racial harmony on

international revolution and universal brotherhood. He never identified himself exclusively with blacks, Jews, or the colonial oppressed.

Lafargue became friendly with the English positivist and reformer
Edward Beesly, who had presided over the inaugural session of the
International and served as one of the editors of the *Fortnightly Review*, and this friendship provided a tie to trade unionists. Together
with another leading British positivist, Frederic Harrison, Beesly was
highly regarded by trade union leaders, and he helped them to formulate strategies for organized labor. The movement's "aggressive"
program of propaganda and pressure on Parliament and employers
alike revealed before everything else how conscious British labor was
of the extent of its power. This obviously impressed Lafargue, as it
had Marx and Engels.[19]

As early as May 1866 Lafargue was telling the readers of *La Rive
gauche* how British agricultural workers were resorting to the strike,
which he described as "the sole means of strength for the proletariat"
and as useful in "preparing the social revolution we all await."[20] Yet
while recognizing the workers' precarious existence and miserable
living conditions, on the one hand, and acknowledging, on the other,
that the strike constituted their only means of struggle, Lafargue rejected total reliance on it because it cost workers higher prices and
lost wages. Yet, contrary to Proudhon, he admired both the virility
demonstrated by the struggle and the revolutionary component in
strikes, particularly acute when the striking worker was forced to
consider his role in economic society. Lafargue found much to admire
in the "interesting and instructive" British trade union movement,
and suggested it might well serve as a model for revolutionary socialists "who could profit from examining the organizational skills developed by workers."[21]

However much preoccupied with other matters, Lafargue had thus by
no means backed away from political interests when in September
1867 he was introduced to Engels. As Lafargue recalled the event
many years later, Marx had told him that "it is necessary, now that
you are engaged to my daughter, that I introduce you to Engels."[22]
Here the father may have been prevailed upon by the daughter, for
Laura was anxious to keep close ties to Engels and insisted that no
formal engagement could be made without his approval.[23]

The ostensible purpose of the trip was to plan a publicity campaign for *Capital*, scheduled for publication that month in Hamburg.[24] The publisher, Meissner, had asked Marx to send part of the preface for reproduction in the German press. Marx asked Engels to translate it into English for the English press, while Lafargue, or rather Lafargue and Laura, in view of her fiancé's inability to read German, were working on a French translation for *Le Courier français*, a left-wing republican newspaper sympathetic to the International.[25] In Manchester, the three men agreed to mobilize friends in Europe to promote the book; they agreed, too, to consider translations, distribution, the printing of extracts, and the recruitment of radicals to assist in publicizing it. Making use of his friendship with Beesly, Lafargue was to try and place a review of *Capital*, to be written by Engels, in the *Fortnightly Review*. Lafargue was also active in searching for a French translator of Marx's great work, and it was at Lafargue's request that Eugène Dupont wrote to de Paepe in this vein.[26] For Maurice Dommanget, who chronicled Marxism's early history there, Lafargue's presentation of Marx to the readers of *La Rive gauche* and this publication of the preface to *Capital* were "uncontestably the first introduction of Marxism in France."[27]

Friedrich Engels, born in the German Rhineland in 1820, was two years younger than Marx and had worked with him on the *Communist Manifesto* and other works. He had helped turn Marx toward a greater concern with economics. As a young man Engels had rebelled against the "penny-pinching" world of commerce wished for him by a tyrannical father, as well as against a "dreary" family home. Engels became a foe of organized religion and capitalism, but after participating in the revolutionary ferment that swept much of the continent in 1848–49 he returned to the world of business, working in the Manchester branch of the textile firm his father had founded. He was successful enough to be able to support not only himself but Marx and his family.

Now in his late forties, Engels was blond, elegant, slender, and brilliant. Though he spent much time with books, he was never bookish. He showed an astonishing versatility: he was interested in all the natural sciences, read widely, and had become an expert of sorts on military affairs. The more Lafargue came to know Engels, the more he admired Engel's universality; all subjects interested him and he was competent in many. He became a model for Lafargue. When Engels reached middle age he was able to read and write almost two dozen languages, including Slavic ones, and had even taught himself Gothic,

Old Nordic, and Old Saxon. He studied Arabic, philology, and his English was impeccable.[28] He had a great grasp of detail, keeping everything methodical, "like an old woman," recalled Lafargue. He insisted on writing in the language of his correspondent: in Russian to Russians (often exiles), in French to Frenchmen, in Polish to Poles. He possessed a powerful memory, the ability to work, to learn quickly, and to understand completely. He kept up a fine appearance and was "always neat and dapper."[29]

In the mid-sixties, Engels was leading a double life in Manchester. He then lived with Mary Burns, an Irishwoman who had made him aware of the Fenian movement and who encouraged him to prepare a history of English domination in Ireland, and her niece in a small house at the end of the city. For six days a week, from ten to four, he was the businessman, especially responsible for maintaining his firm's diverse correspondence. He had for this purpose an official residence in the center of the city where he received business acquaintances. His more suburban home was reserved for political and scientific friends. In the evening and during weekends he cast aside business concerns and became "a free man." Yet he enjoyed the pleasures shared with business acquaintances: the elaborate dinners and sport, particularly fox-hunting. His other life was largely unknown to these companions; for them he was only a "joyful companion," "able to appreciate a good glass of wine," and for some, frivolous.

These same traits were revealed to the many socialist visitors, a large number of them refugees, who enjoyed his hospitality, particularly after he was to retire from business in 1869, at the age of fifty, and move to within walking distance of Marx in London. "Until the end of his days," said Lafargue, "he remained the gay companion, the agreeable comrade," enjoying the company of the young. Marx and Engels always held each other in high esteem, and during their long separation, the one in London, the other in Manchester, they corresponded extensively. Engels was close to the family, continually providing financial and other help, as we have seen. He treated Marx's daughters as his own; they, in turn, thought of him as a second father, calling him "General" because of his competence in military matters. Hence Laura's insistence on securing his approval of Lafargue before announcing her engagement.

Approval was quickly granted; Engels and Lafargue got on well together, and by year's end a wedding was planned for the following April.[30] In February 1868, Lafargue *père* in Bordeaux sent some necessary papers. Marx was both relieved and desperate; relieved that the business was settled at last because Lafargue, although supposedly lodged in Kentish Town Road, "practically lives in our house" and accordingly drove up his expenses.[31] Marx had no money for utilities, much less a wedding, and his pleas to relatives in Holland for help went unanswered. An appeal to a close family friend, Ludwig Kugelman, who had participated in the 1848 Revolution, was now a leading gynecologist in Hanover, and who, as an unabashed admirer of Marx, was active in the International, yielded him fifteen pounds. Marx's gratitude was immediate and painfully excessive: "In the last four months I have spent so much money on Blue Books, Commission Reports, Yankee reports on banks, etc., that I had nothing left for my daughter."[32]

Once more Engels came to the rescue. On March 19 he sent forty pounds "for the wedding expenses of Lörchen and Doctor Amorosus."[33] Both Paul and Laura pleaded with him to attend the wedding, and Lafargue's bantering tone reveals how easy relations with Engels had become. Addressed to the "great decapitator of champagne bottles, to the bottomless swallower of ale and other adulterated trash," Lafargue's letter read: "You must have heard with all the world that Mr. Lafargue, medical student, bachelor, is about to marry Miss J. Laura Marx (the given first name of all Marx's daughters was Jenny), spinster . . . To give this act all its social value, it seems indispensable, I don't know why, that two witnesses be present . . . Now although you are far from having all the moral qualities requisite to the fulfilling of this respectable bourgeois function in a respectable way, there is no man whom I should like better than yourself to stand by me during so formidable a ceremony."[34]

He thanked "my ever-laughing Engels" warmly for agreeing to attend and for having praised his progress in learning English: "If you find my English good, I find your French astonishing, and you have not near you such a pretty master to correct your mistakes as I have. The French *grisettes* who have taught you have so well earnt their money that you would need them no longer for that purpose."[35]

Neither partner holding religious beliefs, there was no religious ceremony. As Marx had learned—he had asked Engels the previous December—no church wedding was legally required in England. His wife, who feared the gossip of neighbors, had not wanted a civil marriage publicized.[36] Engels provided Marx with information on the necessary legal formalities, and added, "Your wife can tell her Philistine neighbors it's because Laura is a Protestant and Paul a Catholic."[37]

On Thursday, April 2, Marx, boils swathed in bandages, and Engels went to the Registry Office of Pancras County, Middlesex, to appear as witnesses before Messrs. Matthews and Ivimey. The certificate of marriage mentioned "Paul Lafargue, twenty-six, medical student, son of Francis Lafargue, Gentleman, [and] Jenny Laura Marx, twenty-two, spinster, daughter of Charles Marx, Gentleman."[38] Marx was in pain, but Engels was cheerful, and his teasing during the wedding lunch that followed at Modena Villas made the bride burst into tears. A quarter century later, Laura recalled the experience to Engels: "By the bye, my dear General, do you remember a certain day in April, 1868, when you lunched with us after our 'laughable' journey to the registry office and how you cracked silly jokes at a very silly girl's expense and set her a-crying? Well, I'm considerably older at this hour of the day and a bit better armored."[39]

Paul and Laura left for Paris on their honeymoon that same night, taking the boat to Dieppe and stopping overnight in that "exceedingly pretty town."[40] The couple then toured Rouen, and arrived in Paris Saturday evening, where they stayed at the Grand Hôtel de l'Europe. The weather was magnificent, permitting them to stroll on the Champs-Elysées "until late in the evening." Paul's parents journeyed to Paris and remained with them for a week.[41]

Engels had returned to Manchester after spending four days with Marx, and with Paul and Laura gone the house seemed empty. By April 11 Marx was writing Laura (in English): "We feel here rather somewhat lonely." Marx was "baffled" to learn that Paul was doing some research in Paris for an article on the French economy, and he wrote to Engels about Lafargue's strange conception of a honeymoon.[42] On the same day he sent a letter to the newlyweds asking his son-in-law whether he didn't prefer a honeymoon with Laura to politics.

Even so, he had asked Paul to send some books he wanted, had asked Laura to pick up several periodicals and catalogs, and had admitted that though it was a peculiar time to ask for the needed book or article, so long as Lafargue was willing to seek them out there were others he could use.[43] In his note to Laura, excusing himself for the intrusion (he wanted her to ask about copies of *Capital* sent to friends in Paris), Marx said that he wasn't just fond of books: "I am a machine condemned to devour them and then to throw them, in a changed form, on the dungheap of history." Paul obliged, and Marx greatly appreciated his son-in-law's sending him books "at such a critical juncture; [it] speaks volumes for the innate kindness of the young man. This simple fact would go far to prove that he must belong to a better than the European race."[44]

The Lafargues returned to London about April 23, in plenty of time to celebrate Marx's birthday on May 5. They settled into an apartment in Primrose Hill, where Paul plunged himself into preparation for his final medical exams in surgery.[45] He passed them on July 2, and with his degree was admitted to membership in the Royal College of Surgeons. Qualified as an assistant surgeon, he began to practice medicine at Saint Bartholomew's, causing Marx to comment sardonically that his son-in-law was now "licensed to kill men and beasts" but that at least Marx was now in a position to "borrow" money from his daughter.[46]

In August Laura and Paul spent a holiday in Margate with Paul's parents, accompanied by Laura's mother and sisters. The vacation was necessary: Jenny and Eleanor were recovering from an attack of scarlet fever, Laura was now four months pregnant, and her mother did not want to be separated from her daughter in the last weeks before the couple left permanently for France. Marx himself paid a brief visit at the end of the month, and when he fell ill Lafargue regarded him as his "first and most important patient." The holiday was cut short, however, because Paul had to finish his internship at the hospital, and twenty pounds had to be found for Laura's household linen.[47]

Lafargue seemed to have wanted to set up a medical practice in Paris after taking his equivalency exams there.[48] In May he received a letter from Moilin approving the idea of practicing in the well-to-do Passy district, where he might attract English-speaking patients.[49] He also toyed with but rejected the idea of relocating in America and making use of the family property in New Orleans.[50] With plans for the future still unsettled, on October 15, 1868, the Lafargues left for Paris to set up housekeeping.

6 Becoming a Revolutionary

I went to London to complete my medical studies, but on my return to Paris I regularly associated with Blanqui and his friends.

—Paul Lafargue

In later years Lafargue described himself as a thoroughgoing Marxist by the time he returned to France in 1868. His recollections of his strolls with Marx on Hampstead Heath and of his work on the General Council convey the image of his father-in-law's confidant, a disciple handpicked to carry on Marx's work. If this is taken at face value, then indeed the 1866–1868 period was "a turning point" and his course of action was clear: a life of political activism.[1]

Yet once back in Paris, Lafargue was uncertain about his future; things were less decided than he liked to think when he looked back on these times. He still intended to practice medicine. Not only Marx but Engels too wanted him to take his equivalency exams.[2] Laura was expecting their child at the end of the year. But Paul was becoming involved in politics, having joined the active Vaugirard section—one of the neighborhood branches of the Paris section—of the IWMA. He was also meeting with his former Blanquist friends, and there was talk of launching a newspaper that the old revolutionary had in mind as well as of working on a French translation of the *Communist Manifesto*. Paul wrote to his sister-in-law Jenny of his doubts: "I do not know yet on what foot to dance. Should I remain in Paris or not . . . I have been to see the Minister [about having his medical degree recognized in France]. He was very pleasant, but what will be the result?"[3] Lafargue again considered moving to America.

The police showed fewer doubts about the intentions of the son-in-law of the man who was seen as heading the dreaded International. Lafargue was placed under police surveillance almost as soon as he arrived in France, and the dossier that was to recount much of his political career was opened. An agent then described him as looking four or five years older than his age, as a little over average height, with a dark complexion and light brownish hair, a mustache and chin tuft, heavyset yet possessing "an air of elegance."[4]

The Lafargues found a furnished apartment at 25 rue des Saint-Pères, on the Left Bank, where they remained until the end of December. They then moved to an upstairs flat at 47 rue du Cherche-Midi, also on the Left Bank but closer to Montparnasse than in the Latin Quarter proper. The streets in this district retained a medieval flavor, although much of central Paris had by now been transformed by Louis Napoleon's prefect, Haussmann, who had driven new boulevards through the city, replaced old buildings, and built additional parks.

Jenny was to stay with the Lafargues to help after the baby came, and Laura warned her sister that the furnishings were not luxurious and that theirs was a "Bohemian style"—one that she did not "ever intend to give up entirely."[5] Paul sketched the floor plan of the apartment and indicated Jenny's room, which he described as charming and overlooking the street. "There is only one little problem; it is too expensive—1,000 francs. Ah bah! Maybe I shall earn it—sleeping. You see, I sleep very well." Their furniture finally arrived and was described by Laura as secondhand and with "the most impossible coverings in existence, in all sorts of colors."[6]

On January 1, 1869, nine months to the day after their wedding, Laura gave birth to a son, Charles-Etienne, nicknamed at first Fouchtra, later Schnaps or Schnappy. Laura experienced difficulties before and after the birth; at the end of February, she wrote that she had spent most of nearly every day in bed for the past three months.[7] Concerned yet filled with pride, Marx told his friend Ludwig Kugelmann that he had been a grandfather since January 1, "my New Year's gift."[8] On March 26 Laura's two sisters, later joined by their mother, came to France to help, and although Jenny had to return to her job on April 14, Eleanor stayed on for seven weeks. Grandmother and aunt doted on the new arrival: Eleanor had "never seen such a lovely child." Many photos were exchanged, and accompanying letters described the baby as "most affectionate" and "a great mimic."

"I have not read much since many weeks," Laura complained to her sister Jenny, who had wanted to know how she was getting on with her copy of Fourier. "Little Schnaps" did not "feed on philosophy in his cradle . . . [and] is not at all fond of reading nor of seeing others read. He is so amusing too that it is rather difficult to do anything else than play with him."[9] Her complaints became more strident after the arrival of their second child (in early January 1870). She was, she said then, always occupied with the babies, who caught cold and had sore throats, so that she was "shut up anew in prison." Jenny, who was later to experience similar feelings with her own children, proved a sympathetic listener. It was all the more difficult for Marx's daughters to bear their isolation because they were politically aware and had even been active on behalf of political causes. Their letters as girls had contained references to Irish Fenians, English politics, and factional fighting within the International, and the gulf between upbringing and adult reality steadily widened.[10]

Feeling confined and frustrated, Laura became critical of her husband. Lafargue was closer to his children than many Victorian fathers were, but he was doubtless not fully aware of his wife's isolation. He was conscious of the "women's question" in the socialist movement, and his party was to be the first to champion the union of women and the working class: the 1879 congress founding a workers' party called for complete equality of the sexes in private and public life, and the party's rhetoric, if not practice, always included women's rights.[11] Yet Laura's letters contain references to a cigar-smoking emancipated woman whom she, as wife and mother, found threatening. "Formerly," she told Jenny, her husband "would hear nothing of women outside of the kitchen and the ballroom; now he prefers seeing them in the reading room."[12]

She became irritated by Paul's friendship with Paule Mink, a feminist and fiery socialist speaker, writer, and newspaper editor, founder of a cooperative society for women workers and a relentless critic of Napoleon III's bourgeois Empire. In the last years of the Empire Mink spoke to large crowds throughout the country on freedom of the press, union solidarity, women's emancipation, and the abolition of property. Born of dissident members of the Polish and French nobility, she was reared in the revolutionary tradition of 1830 and now won support for socialism by describing the low wages and the suffering endured by women working for importuning employers and capitalist profits.

An unsympathetic police agent found her "ugly, slightly deformed, and sloppy, with a strong mouth, big nose, and missing teeth," but he admitted that "when she spoke she was completely metamorphosed, for her face lights up with sparkles in her eyes." An unmarried mother who bore eight children and raised four, she got into trouble with municipal authorities over the choice of her children's names: her first-born, for instance, was called Lucifer-Blanqui-Vercingétorix.[13] Mink lived a hand-to-mouth existence on lecture receipts and occasional socialist party subsidies, tutoring, proofreading, and was finally driven to advertising in socialist newspapers for "any kind of work." She tried to explain socialism to poorly educated workers and assure them they had nothing to fear from women's equality with men. The solution to the women's question, she tirelessly repeated, lay in socialist revolution: "The emancipation of labor will liberate humanity without distinction of sex." Equality under capitalism was dismissed as useless because female members of parliament would do no better than their male counterparts and because female employers would prove no less despotic.

It was the emphasis placed by Mink and other feminists on "the duties [*devoirs*] of women" that riled Laura, presumably because she then had too many *devoirs* of her own. Laura scathingly referred to another friend of her husband who was "probably . . . busy as usual in making all sorts of propaganda, from atheism and woman's emancipation down to gymnastics." As noted by Sheila Rowbotham, "Laura, clinging desperately to a fragile sense of herself as an independent person, [found] emancipated women disturbing, and even talking of women's rights just hot air."[14]

The Lafargues' situation became pressing when Paul learned that the French did not recognize his English degree and that consequently he could not practice without more extensive exams than he had anticipated. Marx told Engels on November 7 that "Paul . . . has the ill luck of not having his English diploma honored at all, but [they] insist upon his running the gauntlet of five new examinations, instead of the one or two as he had expected."[15] Moreover, the Academic Council refused to let him take his exams in Paris. Not knowing whether they would have to relocate near a provincial university, Paul and Laura postponed buying more furniture; they might only have to resell it. As their financial situation worsened, they borrowed even from Helen Demuth, regretting that they could not pay her back. Paul eventually was excused from three of the examinations, but was required to take the other two, and in October got permission to take them at the University of Strasbourg. He chose, however, to remain in Paris.[16]

He found various pretexts for his refusal—Laura's illness, then her second pregnancy, later the illness and death of that child, a daughter—

but both his parents and his parents-in-law were forced to accept his growing inclination toward revolutionary activism and literary and philosophical criticism, presumably the explanation for Lafargue *père*'s refusal to provide the funds once promised and for a growing estrangement between Lafargue and his parents. Paul had polished Laura's translation into French of Marx's *Communist Manifesto* in time for Jenny to take it back to London,[17] and was now asking Marx for permission to use his name in attempts to promote the proposed Blanquist newspaper. Marx reluctantly agreed but noted that "your father will think I pushed you to more or less premature political action and prevented you from taking the steps necessary (and which I am continually urging you to take) to pass your medical exams and establish [yourself] professionally."[18] Marx disapproved of Lafargue's growing commitment to politics in general and to his Blanquist friends in particular; he did not want him to run any risks in Louis Napoleon's police state and urged him to go to Strasbourg and take his exams.[19] Marx had reason to fear that François would hold him responsible for bringing an end to his son's medical career. "As it is," Marx wrote his daughter Jenny, "he has not much reason to delight in his connection with the Marx family."[20]

For a number of reasons, including concern over his daughter's poor health, complaints from François that Paul was abandoning his career, and the wish to explore the possibility of a French translation of *Capital,* Marx decided to visit the young couple in Paris.[21] Paul had found a French translator, Charles Keller, whom he described as "young and poor [but] enthusiastic and intelligent," and as already having started work.[22] Keller was a Swiss who sat on the IWMA's Paris Federal Council (a sectional or branch council, in contrast to the International's executive body, the London-based General Council) and had previously translated medical literature into French. In an undated letter, Lafargue added that difficulties in the translation had arisen but that he hoped to show Marx the progress made.[23]

Marx had written to the Lafargues of his intended visit. After the receipt of his letter, a stranger called, asking whether Marx had arrived. The couple suspected the police, who since 1858—when the conspirator Orsini attempted to assassinate Napoleon III—held almost unlimited power to expel or imprison anyone suspected of hostility toward the Empire. Warned, Marx decided to postpone his trip until the summer, and it was not until July that he left for Paris.[24] Traveling under the name of Williams, he stayed unbothered in a hotel in the rue Saint Placide from the sixth to the twelfth. On the basis of promises made to him by Paul, he wrote François on July 10 to assure the elder Lafargue that his son had not abandoned his studies, but that because of Laura's illness he had postponed his examinations. So as not to worry Marx's wife, this had been kept a secret: Paul would take the examinations after a seaside rest prescribed for Laura.[25]

A more realistic appraisal was sent to Engels: "[Lafargue] is too absorbed by politics and this can end badly; already all his friends are Blanquists." By the following spring Marx realized that his son-in-law preferred a political to a medical career, and in April 1870 he finally admitted defeat: he only asked Paul to tell his father that "I have as little influence on [you] as he has," and to "go to Bordeaux and pacify him."[26]

It would have been difficult for Lafargue to have acted otherwise. With the dissolution of the Legislative Assembly, election fever was sweeping France in the spring of 1869. Attempts to liberalize the Empire and so stave off opposition had failed: a freer press and the right of political assembly were restored in 1867 and the right of the legislature to question the government, the following year. Even so, there was every indication that Louis Napoleon's dictatorship was meeting increased resistance. His move toward "liberalized authoritarianism," on the one hand, was costing him conservative support. The opposition, on the other hand, was growing and in 1869 secured three and a third million votes, 45 percent of the total cast, and could believe in the imminent downfall of the Empire.[27] Working-class discontent had expressed itself in the one weapon available to it, the strike. The average number of annual strikes (and more important the number of participants in them) was increasing, reaching its peak, 116, in 1870, compared with an annual average of 81 in the 1855–1859 period and only 43 in 1859–1864. And the political liberalization that had made this activity possible was itself a response to industrial discontent.[28] Lafargue was but twenty-seven years old, had a record of participation in student revolt, and had married into the Marx family. Almost coincident with his arrival, he had renewed ties with old friends and had made new ones, particularly in the Vaugirard section of the IWMA. In the midst of this ferment he could not stand aside, and doubtless recalling Marx's earlier attempts to woo Blanqui, he joined the militant socialist wing of the Blanquist movement. During the year that followed, he focused his energies on Blanquism and later admitted as much: "I went to London to complete my medical studies, but on my return to Paris I regularly associated with Blanqui and his friends."[29]

Between February and June of 1869, Blanqui resided illegally in Paris with various associates at different locations. While taking care to avoid arrest, the old revolutionary witnessed the demonstrations to which his followers attached so much importance: commemorations of the French revolutionary past, of 1792, of 1848 (and later, of 1871), complete with the symbolic rites and festivals that permitted their organizers to view themselves as guardians of revolutionary tradition. The erection of monuments, the holding of pilgrimages, and the publication of newspaper reminiscences also numbered among Blanquist strategies. When Lafargue pointed to the danger he exposed himself to, Blanqui replied with a smile, "I always carry my safe conduct with me," and took from his pocket copies of *Pays* and *Constitutionnel.* "If taken and searched, I will soon be freed when these Bonapartist and reactionary journals are found on me."[30]

Blanqui was more of a propagandist than a theoretician. (What theory he had was based on the mechanistic materialism of the Enlightenment.) He placed his revolutionary hopes in young people and wanted them to serve as the general staff of a secret society organized to upset the Empire and seize power. Detailed plans were formulated, for example that calling for the occupation of the Ministry of War and the Prefecture of Police to frustrate repression. Groups of ten, knowing only their leader and hence limiting the risk of police infiltration, were established. When Blanqui wished to inspect his cohorts, he arranged with leaders to assemble their groups on a certain corner at a certain time, and *le vieux,* unperceived, reviewed them. A lieutenant of Blanqui maintained that these followers numbered about three hundred in 1868, strongest in working-class districts in and around Paris.[31] Lafargue met with others every week at the house then frequented by Blanqui, that of a man named Casavan, "who lived on the isle of Saint-Louis, on a street with the macabre medieval name of la Femme sans Tête."[32]

To what extent was Lafargue's involvement with the Blanquists sanctioned by Marx, and to what extent was Marx's interest in Blanqui used by Lafargue to justify that involvement? If, as Lafargue told Blanqui, Marx still considered Blanqui "the head and heart of the proletarian party in France" and still wanted to win his support, then Marx could not help but approve of Lafargue's efforts both to keep

Blanqui informed of developments within the international socialist movement, particularly with regard to the German parties, and to try to recruit Blanquists to the Marxist cause.[33]

Admittedly the differences between Blanqui and Marx had widened as any sympathy Marx may have held for the concept of a revolutionary elite gave way to a conviction of the need for a broadly based class movement. Blanqui had given orders to boycott the International's first congresses, although in 1868 a Blanquist group headed by Edouard Vaillant had disobeyed, creating a schism between insurrectionists rejecting a mass base and those seeking wider support for a revolutionary movement.

In May 1869, Lafargue wrote Marx that Blanqui lacked faith in the German social democratic movement, and accounted for this view in terms of the old revolutionary's patriotism and anti-German hostility.[34] Although holding no illusions about converting Blanqui and his disciples to Marx's teachings, Lafargue hoped to turn them away from Proudhonism, and took pleasure in telling his father-in-law that Blanqui not only had read the copy of Marx's attack on Proudhon's thought, *The Poverty of Philosophy,* which Lafargue had given him, but was circulating it among his friends.[35] He added that "Blanqui has the greatest esteem for you." Similarly Laura informed her father that Jaclard, an important Blanquist disciple, was seeking authorization from the International's General Council to form a new Paris section.[36] Envisioning himself as an intermediary, Lafargue helped to keep Blanqui and Blanquists, on the one hand, and Marx and the International, on the other, on speaking terms.

In the spring of 1869, pressed by his admirers, Blanqui thought of launching a newspaper, intended to mark a renovation of Blanquist thought and practice.[37] It was to be called *La Renaissance,* and Blanqui planned to keep costs down by taking advantage of new printing technology and by relying on advertising, especially from the new department stores. The subscription list showed that Lafargue, in spite of his financial problems, contributed two hundred francs, twice the average donation.[38]

Blanqui wanted to have enough copy on hand for several issues, and Lafargue gave him a lengthy piece entitled "Mutualism, Collectivism, and Communism." He was astonished to see Blanqui put it in a drawer unread, commenting only that "all these discussions on the possible forms of future society is revolutionary scholasticism. It is more urgent to criticize primary education." Noting the younger man's discomfiture, Blanqui added, "we must not formulate doctrine but fight the Empire. Like you, like Marx, I am a communist, but I don't say so. I only want to seize the state through revolution to ameliorate the proletarian's working conditions and existence, [not] for the sake of confrontation. Violent and interminable quarrels among the socialist sects before 1848 over the nature of future society prevented us from taking action."[39]

The newspaper never materialized. The 30,000-franc deposit required by the Empire could not easily be raised because the name of Blanqui frightened away potential backers, and when the sum was finally raised, war intervened.[40] Apparently Moilin, who had promised a sizable contribution, backed out at the last minute, but by the end of May money, in the form of a legacy left to Tridon, had been found. It was then that Paul asked whether he could list Marx's name among the contributors.[41]

Although there was no shortage of copy, both Lafargue and Blanqui wanted to publish an article from Marx. Wanting to oblige, the latter nevertheless pleaded pressure of work. We have already seen that his real reason, as confided to his daughter Jenny, was his fear that "old Lafargue should suspect [me] of pushing his son to premature political action and make him neglect his professional duties."[42]

Lafargue often saw Blanqui, but it was with the young Blanquists that he was especially friendly: with the Levrauld brothers, Léonce and Edmond, one in business, the other a medical student; with Jaclard, yet another medical student who had found medicine tame; with Tridon, Blanqui's devoted disciple, wealthy, consumptive, a Proudhonist before being converted by Blanqui, and who wrote a pamphlet on the Hébertists, whom Blanquists saw as forerunners of their own movement; with the rising left-wing lawyer, Protot; and with Regnard, still another physician who had turned to Blanquist militancy.

Even so, Lafargue's London exposure and conversion to Marxism had cooled his admiration for *le vieux*. Years later Lafargue recalled that when Blanquists left the International in September 1866 (at the time of the Geneva Congress), he had not joined them: he had been won over to Marx. Blanqui was the conspirator of 1830, the man of the secret societies who had not adjusted to the economic and social events that made conspiratorial strategies less and less useful; such groups might overthrow a government and even set up a republic, but could not prepare a class for social revolution. The eighteenth-century

Encyclopedists and bourgeoisie had laid the foundations for the 1789 Revolution not by plots but by public propaganda that had sapped the social bases of the Ancien Régime. This was why Marx had dissolved the secret Communist societies and had organized the International.[43]

Also recollected by Lafargue were Blanqui's "sentimental idealism" and "Italian superstition," the cult of *la patrie* that shut out internationalism, however much Blanqui remained "a scientific spirit nourished by modern knowledge and eighteenth-century materialism." The likelihood of war had lessened considerably thanks to the emergence of a revolutionary German party that "would make every effort to oppose any war with republican France." Blanqui, however, doubted that the party wielded much influence (and in retrospect was of course correct). Lafargue believed that Blanqui's ignorance of domestic developments in Germany accounted for his conviction that if revolution broke out in France, the king of Prussia would invade the country. Engels reinforced Lafargue's views: while Blanqui was a political revolutionary, he was a socialist only by sentiment; while aware of proletarian misery, he was lacking in theory.[44] More difficult for Lafargue to shed than his Blanquism, however, was his Proudhonism.

7 The International

Each new working class movement, each new strike, is attributed
to a greater or lesser degree to the International.

—Laura Lafargue

It was not Blanquists but Proudhonists who dominated the French
labor movement and consequently the French sections of the International. They had helped to found the association, and they provided the chief opposition to the collectivists in its early congresses. At
Geneva in 1866 they rejected strike action as "barbarous" and preferred to place emphasis on cooperative associations for workers;
they denounced a legal eight-hour day as violating "freedom of contract"; and they refused any discussion of women's place in the labor
force, basing their objections on "physical, moral, and social"
grounds. These attitudes proved unacceptable to the more pragmatic
English and non-French-speaking Swiss sections.

At the Lausanne Congress in 1867 French Proudhonists denied any
right of the state to intervene in matters of education: these were best
left to parents. In the debate over nationalization, they opposed the
increase in state powers that would follow a widening of its economic
base. Collectivism won a victory at the Brussels Congress of 1868,
when the International went on record as favoring the nationalization
of the means of production, but did so only by overcoming the objections of the French and French-speaking Swiss delegates. The ideological clash between collectivists and Proudhonists peaked the next
year at the Basel Congress, in September 1869, when the French
delegates' opposition to the common ownership of land was overcome.[1] The Proudhonists among them included Henri-Louis Tolain,
who spoke for the trade unions (and who in 1867 went to London to
ask the General Council's help for striking Paris bronze workers);
Eugène Varlin, who was more willing than most Proudhonists to rely
on political action; and the revolutionary anarchist, Mikhail Bakunin,
who represented the French section at Lyons as well as an Italian
section.

Engels acknowledged the domination of Proudhon's ideas—and by implication the absence of Marx's—in France and generally in southern Europe when in 1872 he regretted that "for twenty-five years workers who speak Latin languages possess[ed] no other socialist intellectual nourishment than the writings of this socialist of the Second Empire."[2] The 1873 *Dictionnaire général de biographie et d'histoire* discussed Proudhon but failed to mention Marx. The *Grand Dictionnaire Larousse* of the same year confused Marx with Lassalle, and gave only four lines to *Capital*. The article on Proudhon in the 1878 edition required almost twenty-five columns; that for Marx, the same two and a quarter columns previously published in the 1873 edition. It was not so much a question of national bias as of ignorance.[3] Still, the preference of French workers in the 1860s for trade union, rather than for political, activity strengthened Proudhon's appeal to a labor force still artisanal and only beginning to industrialize. Labor leaders like Tolain rejected politics; those like Jean-Joseph Barberet rejected socialism.[4]

Although Lafargue was impressed by Blanqui, he had long admired Proudhon and had credited him with having freed morality and economics from the supernatural. His future colleague Gabriel Deville once reproached him for his anarchist leanings: "You have had the fortune to meet Marx; if you had not you would have been one of our most brilliant anarchists"—and Lafargue acknowledged the legitimacy of the observation. (Almost forty years later Lafargue, alone in his party, was willing to accommodate syndicalism, and Gustave Hervé called him "a misled anarchist among the Guesdists.")[5]

Certainly Lafargue felt obliged to reassure Marx that he had abandoned his Proudhonism. At the end of May 1869 he told his father-in-law of an article he had written criticizing Proudhon and of another defending communism. He let Marx know that he regarded political and not economic strategies as the most useful. On the eve of the legislative elections, he described the attitude of Paris workers, who, he believed, rejected both the government and its liberal republican opposition. Still, he anticipated good results from "serious candidates" like Gambetta, Raspail, and Rochefort.[6]

In a letter written in late October, he stressed the need to organize and unify workers along ideologically correct lines, that is, Marxist and not Proudhonist.[7] In view of growing proletarian strength, Lafargue thought the time ripe for the founding of a socialist party, "if only to make liberal deputies deal with a new political force." Even without a newspaper and thus limited to reliance on public meetings and demonstrations, a party could have an impact.[8] By April 1870 he told Marx that most members of the Paris section of the IWMA agreed with him on the need for a more centralized structure and on "the clear and precise understanding that the working class has its own individuality as a class antagonistic toward the bourgeois opposition." And a newspaper was now "available": *La Marseillaise,* the journal run by the arch-critic of the Empire, Henri Rochefort, was "fully under the control" of the IWMA. Marx may have thought these accounts exaggerated the International's influence, but he admitted that he was being kept abreast of developments in France by his son-in-law.[9]

Laura Lafargue was equally optimistic about the IWMA's growth in Paris and in France, and was sending progress reports on Keller's translation of *Capital.* Keller's only regret was that without a publisher to provide advance royalties, he had to turn to other work. In three months he had apparently translated the first three chapters, although not without criticism from Marx over the use of some French terms.[10]

Thus Lafargue worked to spread Marx's teachings, then virtually unknown in France. As already mentioned, he had prepared a final draft of Laura's translation of part of the preface of *Capital* and of the *Communist Manifesto.*[11] He helped prepare a new translation of the IWMA statutes, which restored passages referring to workers' political action eliminated by earlier Proudhonist translators, particularly Tolain, at the time of the founding of the IWMA in 1864. Despite reservations shared by Marx and Engels about Lafargue's linguistic skills, Marx had relied on his son-in-law to translate them faithfully from the English. But it is clear that at least with regard to his own and Engels' writings, Marx had his daughter in mind.[12]

Lafargue, too, relied on his wife to translate from the German, a language he could not read, and after she perfected her French his role seems to have been a limited one. Engels had great faith in Laura's command of languages. (Fifteen years later he found Edward Aveling not competent enough to help Samuel Moore prepare an English translation of *Capital;* he wanted Laura to take a hand, much to Moore's relief.)[13] Engels praised her translation of one of his publications as reading "like the original." He again revealed his faith in her ability when years later he told Louise Kautsksy that "there is only one person in Paris or its suburbs who knows French and that person is not French . . . but Laura."[14] Even though fluent in German, however, she did not dare translate into that language a weekly column her husband was later to write for the German socialist press, though she was much pressed by the party leader, August Bebel.[15]

In contrast to England, where the International had increased its influence by supporting strikes and preventing the use of foreign scabs—and may have reached an affiliated trade unionist membership of over 50,000—slower growth took place on the Continent (the Lafargues' optimism notwithstanding).[16] The Paris headquarters of the International consisted of a nine by twelve foot rented office at 44 rue des Gravilliers, in a shabby district, and still the rent could not be paid. The French Marxist Charles Rappoport was to refer to the First International in France as "a great soul in a small body."[17] The Paris Prefecture of Police had nevertheless placed the IWMA under close surveillance, identifying Lafargue and other members of the Vaugirard section to which he belonged.[18]

More rapid headway was made by the French branch beginning in 1867, due to both an upsurge in strike activity and the intervention of the IWMA in such successful strikes as those of the Paris metalworkers and the Roubaix textile workers. In Roubaix strikers received an average wage increase of 25 percent. Laura credited a growing International for the surge of labor unrest.[19] Whether a cause or a consequence of more labor militancy, expansion of the French branch meant more neighborhood sections and regional federations as well as a diminution in the appeal of Proudhonism. Yet as Marx complained, there were still fewer than six hundred members; local groupings drifted in and out of the parent organization; and income from dues of ten centimes a week failed to keep up with even meager outlays. The treasurer reported that between 1865 and 1868 he never held more than fifty francs at any one time. Even so, the government saw the International as a powerful subversive organization: in 1867 it prosecuted the IWMA in the Paris Court for illegal political activity but managed to have it condemned only as an unauthorized association. The branch in Paris was reduced to a hundred members. Its reorganized executive was then prosecuted for supporting a construction workers' strike in May 1868, and the members of the executive were sentenced to three months' imprisonment and fined. The rue des Gravilliers office closed and a central structure disappeared, although individual groups continued to exist. The Brussels Congress of the IWMA, meeting later that year, declared the Paris section moribund.[20]

Relentless government persecution, however, brought with it seeds of renewal. Shocked by the damage inflicted on the Paris branch and by the trial and imprisonment of its leaders, left-wing Proudhonists began to show more sympathy for political action. They were led by the bookbinder Varlin, who represented France at the International's Basel Congress in 1869 when he succeeded the more intransigent Tolain as spokesman for French labor. Though Tolain had claimed the right to strike and to unionize (the demand for which marks the point of departure for French syndicalism), Varlin and his colleagues between 1866 and 1870 created a syndicalist organization extending throughout almost all of France. Varlin worked at night at his trade and during the day at creating links among unions, so that workers in one city, for example, could provide strikers in another with cash reserves.[21] Supported by other younger, more ardent men such as Zéphrin Camélinat, a metalworker who had helped to found the International in France; Antoine Bourdon, an engraver and one of the first members of the French section; and especially Benoît Malon, a self-educated dyer who had attended the International's Geneva Congress in 1866, Varlin led efforts to revive the IWMA in France. (Although he abandoned his earlier Proudhonism, Varlin never became a Marxist, however.) It was no coincidence that each of these men, members of the Paris section's executive and accordingly sentenced to prison, began to turn to political action. Unlike their predecessors, moreover, they saw advantages in an internationalist approach and in workers' reliance on the strike.

Internationalists in Paris had been influenced by the defense and explanation of Marxism made at the 1867 Lausanne Congress. Proudhonists, in turn, were hurt by the collapse in 1869 of the Proudhonist labor-credit bank, which showed the inadequacies of credit-based theories. The collectivist victory at the Basel Congress and the endorsement of political in contrast to economic action was the result. A majority of the French delegates to the Basel meeting believed revolution in France was so close that the next congress was set for September 1870 in Paris. This explains in part why the French government stepped up its persecution. No reliable figures exist, but the number of individual French members could never have exceeded a few thousand, and only thirty-six local sections were reported in 1870 by the French branch's (reorganized) Paris Central Committee.[22] The need for reorganization called attention to the need for ideological clarity, and hence provided an opportunity for disseminating Marxist thought.

The year 1869 was marked by revolutionary agitation in France, prompted by the government's attempts to liberalize the Empire and by the legislative elections scheduled in May. The poverty of workers was becoming more and more evident. Though wages increased by 17 to 30 percent during the Second Empire, living costs rose by nearly 50 percent and food by more than that. Rents had more than doubled because of the rebuilding of the city: demolition of old working-class districts had forced the former inhabitants to move to the outlying areas and to the suburbs, raising transportation costs. (Previously workers had lived in the same buildings as wealthier tenants, but on the upper floors.) The typical working day was twelve hours; the typical working week, six days.[23] In the capital, working-class hostility to the Empire was such that the government did not dare name official candidates for the election. The republican opposition was victorious in Paris—where it amassed an enormous majority—and Lyons, and was strong in other big cities. In the country at large, the opposition made huge gains, winning three and a half million votes to the four and a half million won by government candidates (in 1863 the difference had been three and a half million), and sending about thirty republicans to the legislature. The same year the first strikes in large industry took place. Government troops sent to the Saint-Etienne coal basin fired on a crowd, killing thirteen and wounding nine in the "massacre" of June 16. In the Aveyron Department, in south central France, striking miners on October 20 attacked soldiers guarding the forges, provoking fire and leaving fourteen dead and twenty wounded.[24]

Hence Lafargue's difficulty in turning his back on politics, in relocating to a provincial university town to complete work on a French medical degree. The Empire was in crisis. There was an explosion of republican activity, and revolution appeared imminent. Although Lafargue overestimated the political impact of the IWMA and the role it could play in the May elections and in the forthcoming 1870 plebiscite, he went to meetings and worked to unite the IWMA's different Paris neighborhood sections.[25]

Paul and Laura planned to spend August and September in London; they would bring some of the Keller translation to Marx and help to celebrate Marx's birthday. On the way they stopped at the seashore at Dieppe, as recommended by Laura's physician, a stay made possible by funds sent by François Lafargue at Marx's urging.[26] Laura was pregnant again, and not feeling well, and their son was also ill and had been for some time—one letter described the boy's gastrointestinal trouble and special dietary needs. They had to prolong their stay in London, not leaving until October.[27] Writing from Hanover, where he was visiting Ludwig Kugelmann, Marx pleaded with Laura not to leave London too soon and to consult with a physician Marx recommended highly.[28]

On their return to Paris, the Lafargues found the city agitated. The opposition was still reveling in its success in the May election. Clerical workers were on strike, and the opening of the new legislature, scheduled for October 26, had been postponed until the end of November. The populace was especially upset by the news of the acquittal of the Bonapartist prince Pierre Bonaparte, who in fit of rage had murdered a staff member of *La Marseillaise,* Victor Noire. For exasperated opponents of the regime, the *affaire* shriveled the already-waning prestige of the Second Empire. In the weeks that followed, Lafargue pushed French efforts in the International to establish a tighter organization and ultimately a socialist party. He must have been active in other organizations, too; one evening he attended a meeting of a freethinkers' society, the Libres Penseurs de Paris, with six hundred other men and women.[29]

On January 1, 1870, a year after the birth of their first child, a baby girl, Jenny (nicknamed Schnapine and Maigrotte), was born. "Too soon," Laura commented to Engels, adding sardonically, "[we will] soon sing one, two, three, four, five, six, ten nigger-boys."[30] Laura's confinement was not as difficult as before, Paul reported to Jenny, but she was "still in her room," and he complained of having "an invalid and two helpless creatures to care for." Very likely, Laura was unable to nurse her child: a long and difficult confinement and the childbirth itself, unrelieved by analgesics or anesthetics, was sufficiently exhausting to account for her reluctance to breastfeed, at least immediately. Much to the displeasure of the midwife, Paul insisted on cow's milk, rather than permit a wet nurse for the infant. It was doubtless a poor decision: the child survived less than two months. In one respect, his advice corresponded with nineteenth-century medical practice, which was now linking the still largely unregulated but widespread practice of commercial wet-nursing with high infant mortality. In another, it did not, because physicians, until the sterilization of cows' milk became common practice in the 1890s, preferred breastfeeding, even if it had to be outside the home, to bottle feeding. Yet as a medical student in both Paris and London and as a political radical, Lafargue was surely aware of the evils associated with commercial wet-nursing and with the criticisms levied against the practice. He was doubtless aware, too, of the newly invented feeding bottle widely advertised and discussed in the British medical press in 1869, which according to *A Practical Treatise on the Diseases of Infancy and Childhood* (1870), explained why physicians now encouraged bottle feeding as a viable alternative to breastmilk more than "at any time in the past."[31] Hence the advice and training received by physicians of the period was contradictory. The effect of the tragedy—and of the subsequent deaths of his two other children, Schnaps and another son in 1871—is only hinted at by the Lafargues in their letters, but might well have caused Paul to question the beliefs of his once-intended profession, or his own abilities, or both, and so reinforce his decision not to practice.

In his letter acknowledging receipt of the news, Marx said simply: "I have suffered myself too much from such losses not to profoundly sympathize with you. Still, from the same personal experience I know that all wise commonplaces and consolatory speech uttered on such occasion increase real grief instead of soothing it." He asked for news of "little Schnappy," his "greatest favorite," whom he thought must suffer from the cold, "so adverse to *la nature mélanienne* [dark-skinned nature]," and on which he blamed the newborn's death.[32] He then commented on the ten-year-old publication of "a certain M. de Gobineau," who sought to prove the superiority of the white race, himself probably having descended "not from an ancient Frankish warrior but from a modern French *hussier* [doorman] . . . For such people it is always a source of satisfaction to have somebody they think themselves entitled to despise."[33]

The Lafargues found themselves in even worse financial straits: bills had to be paid, Paul was unable to earn a living by writing, and their chief source of income, an allowance provided by François Lafargue, was inadequate. The couple borrowed from relatives and friends alike. Even after Laura's recovery their style of life remained modest. After one caller, smartly dressed, appeared, Laura admitted: "Paul and I were as usual considerably more shabby than genteel."[34]

*   *   *

In early 1870 Paul became associated with the republicans involved with *La Marseillaise*. To his consternation, he did not publish many articles, nor did his Blanquist friends. One article shows the view he held of the state. Another, "La Viande," discussing the raising and selling of meat, described the gulf between retail prices and those actually received by small producers. Although for fifteen years the market price for cattle had fallen, consumer prices for meat were at their highest. The absence of constraints on retail butchers was held to be responsible, and Lafargue called on the state, even though bourgois, to stop its collusion and begin controlling consumer prices.[35] It was at about this time that Lafargue, possibly at Blanqui's suggestion, began reading the works of Victor Hugo and collecting material about him for a series of articles and ultimately a political biography.[36]

He wrote more frequently for the free-thought weekly, *La Libre Pensée,* edited by Henri Verlet, whom he had recommended for membership in the International the previous April. Verlet, whose real name was Henri Place, was a militant Blanquist who had written to Marx asking permission to establish a new Paris section of the IWMA. Through Lafargue and with the approval of the General Council, Marx replied in the affirmative and sent Verlet's credentials to his son-in-law on April 18, 1870. The accompanying letter warned French socialists about the dangers of "sectarianism," urging they avoid all labels (*etiquettes sectaires*), either "communist or any other," in the International.

Marx explained his warning.[37] "The general aspirations and tendencies of the working class emanate from the real conditions in which it finds itself placed. They are therefore common to the whole class although the movement reflects itself in their heads in the most diversified forms, more or less phantastical, more or less adequate. Those to interpret best the hidden sense of the class struggle going on before our eyes—the Communists, are the last to commit the blunder of affecting or fostering sectarianism."[38] It was a curiously prophetic admonition for the strife-ridden French movement in which Lafargue was to spend his political life.

In a letter the next day Marx advised Lafargue of the presence in the International in Paris of a schoolteacher named Paul Robin, who was the agent of the revolutionary anarchist Mikhail Bakunin.[39] Robin would do his best to "discredit the General Council" in Paris as he had done at Geneva and to prepare for "the dictatorship of Bakunin in the International Association." Marx reviewed a Bakuninist "conspiracy" to set up an organization within the International aimed at converting the larger organization "into an instrument of the Russian Bakunin." Bakunin's "Alliance" had a three-point program: (1) to at once abolish inheritance, which would only frighten the middle classes and the peasantry, and which was an example of the "superannuated idealism that considers the actual jurisprudence as the basis of our economic state, instead of seeing the economic state as the basis and source of our jurisprudence"; (2) to establish equality among classes; and (3) to have the working class abstain from politics, which revealed Bakunin's failure to see that "every class movement . . . is necessary and was always a political movement."

Marx concluded his biographical account of Bakunin and his "intrigues" with a warning that "this damned Muscovite has managed to create a great scandal in our ranks, to make his personality a watchword, to infect our Workingmen's Association with the poison of sectarianism, and to paralyze our action by secret intrigue." The Lafargues, in turn, kept Marx informed about Bukuninist attempts to spread propaganda in the Paris sections and particularly about the efforts of Robin, who "had his foot in every door and was now distributing Bakunin's newspaper right and left." Lafargue promised to work against Bakunin's influence, which he saw as waning in the aftermath of the proposed abolition of inheritances, and specifically to "prevent the tightening of lines tying Bakuninists and Varlin," who remained outside of the Bakuninist and Maxist camps.[40]

La Libre Pensée, founded by Verlet in January 1870, reflected a radically atheistic and anticlerical standpoint (a foundation of Blanquist thought), and Blanquists, including Tridon and Regnard, were instrumental in running the journal. Blanqui himself contributed occasional articles, and Lafargue anticipated its conversion into a political newspaper that would appear three times a week.[41] Atheism was held as necessary, both because faith was seen as irreconcilable with science and because atheism forced one to come to terms with the real world and so increased the sense of human responsibility, "without God or master," as the Blanquists liked to say.

The newspaper was committed to the "uncompromising pursuit of the triumph of reason and truth," and Lafargue embraced an anti-idealistic and antireligious line in articles that criticized biblical texts by pointing to the contradictions contained in them.[42] He cited Darwin extensively, considering him, with Michael Faraday, the discoverer of the theory of electromagnetism, one of the greatest Englishmen of the century.[43] He condemned papal infallibility by applying natural selection metaphorically to Christianity, depicting it as an aged man and the church as senile and "decrepit."

It was in *La Libre Pensée* that Lafargue also published his first attempt at literary criticism. For some time he had believed that he possessed literary talent. Longuet recalled that Lafargue in 1868–69 submitted proposals for comedies that he had in mind to Alexandre Dumas, "who did not refuse to help him with his own experience and with advice."[44] No play or novel of Lafargue's—if any were written—has survived, but references to them are found in the family correspondence. Eleanor, who thought his writing had value, in 1888 asked her sister about a play Laura and Paul had written and urged them to produce it, and Engels referred in several letters to a novel Paul was supposed to be writing.[45]

In early March 1870 Lafargue went to the Odéon Theater to see George Sand's *L'Autre*. He had deliberately waited until the third night, reasoning that all who went to see the play for social rather than artistic reasons would have already gone and he would be surrounded by what he called the "true public." Suitably impressed, he predicted a successful run for the play and applauded the performance of its leading lady, Sarah Bernhardt. In a review written for *La Libre Pensée*,[46] Lafargue nevertheless called for greater reality and less imagination in character development: he regretted that the modern theater still "awaits its Balzac." Other critics had complimented Sand and were only sorry that she had introduced such social questions as the subordination of women into the theater.[47] Lafargue only regretted that she appeared content with moralizing.

The plot concerned the daughter of an adulterous union, a theme then popular in the French theater, which provided Lafargue with the opportunity to comment on upper- and middle-class women who alleviated their boredom by resorting to adultery. Other playwrights had the wife repent (and Lafargue deplored the double standard implied). Sand, however, asked that more pity be shown for the "the lonely and cast-off wife of a brutal husband." Lafargue rejected such pity as "humiliating." When his critique began to shift to economic analysis, condemning a system in which women must marry to assure themselves financial security and criticizing Sand for neglecting these realities, the article was cut off, doubtless because of editorial disagreement over his polemicizing.[48] Lafargue's interest in literature and aesthetics grew in the years to follow and became a distinguishing feature of his role as a Marxist theoretician, anticipating the criticism that was to characterize the work of such twentieth-century Marxist thinkers as Georg Lukács, Henry Lefebvre, and Raymond Williams.

Lafargue published occasional articles on the status of women.[49] In them he attacked the legacy of Proudhon, who had insisted on female inferiority. On the contrary, Lafargue retorted, "the woman of our century will become free and take possession of her *personne*," and in a historical analysis he tried to show that in all stages of societal development—hunting, agricultural, city-state, modern—women were enslaved because they were condemned to bear and raise children. Persuaded by his reading of Darwin that men were in no way superior, Lafargue anticipated that the forthcoming emancipation of women would render the debate over Proudhon's view useless. Here he differed from other radicals of his day, such as Verlet, whose articles on women reveal a deep-seated male chauvinism. (Later, after reading the American anthropologist Lewis Morgan and Engels' own contribution, Lafargue was to reject simplistic explanations and see the issue as part of a larger societal problem.) He signed these articles Laurent-Paul Lafargue and sometimes Paul-Laurent, an amalgam of his and his wife's names, to distinguish himself from another, more conservative, writer.

Lafargue spent much of his time working to establish a federation of the International's Paris sections that would be based on a firm Marxism rather than the mutualism on which the French section had been founded in 1865. His fellow French Internationalists, as we have seen, had gradually become aware of the need for political action, and at a March 5, 1870, meeting their delegates decided to create a federation of the eleven Paris sections. A committee, of which Lafargue was a member, was elected to draft by-laws. On March 18 this committee adopted draft statutes and voted to convoke a general assembly of the sections the following month to ratify them.[50]

These meetings, too, were highlighted by the struggle between Proudhonists, who unsuccessfully opposed any central organization, and collectivists. Orthodox Proudhonists refused on principle to attend the assembly or to join the new federation. Lafargue complained that they did "everything possible to oppose a federation and preferred to keep completely apart." "In the last days of the Empire," he wrote, "the Proudhonist group was considered outside the International."[51] The General Assembly opened at 1 P.M. April 18, and was presided over by Varlin. Lafargue, who attended and actively worked to ensure that the Paris sections did not support Bakunin, wrote that there were 1,200–1,300 IWMA members present as well as delegates of diverse workers' groups. Overcoming Proudhonist opposition, they approved the proposed by-laws, and so created the Paris Federation. The decision is significant in the history of the First International, particularly in view of the emergence of Bakuninism and its struggle with the General Council, for it was the only ruling of all the IWMA sections that clearly voted to put into practice the organizing principles of the International. A proud Lafargue wrote Marx on April 20 that the majority sensed the need of centralization and for a "clear and precise awareness by the working class of its individuality as a class and of its hostility to the bourgeoisie," and that Marx would have been happy to have attended such a demonstration.[52]

The aim of the Federation was "to facilitate relations of all kinds among the diverse groups of workers." Its administrative organ was the Federal Council, composed of delegates from the sections, with one delegate for each fifty members of the IWMA. The Federal Council was to report regularly to the London General Council on the situation of the International in France, and the General Council was to keep the Federal Council informed of IWMA circumstances outside of France. At its April 26, 1870, meeting, the General Council acknowledged Lafargue's role in bringing about the collectivist victory and praised Varlin for his initiative.[53]

The gulf widened between "orthodox" Proudhonists led by Tolain and collectivist Proudhonists under Varlin and Malon, tied to the International.[54] By mid-April there were four French regional federations of the IWMA: in Paris, Lyons, Marseilles, and Rouen. The task now was to unite them in a national federation, a step urged by Varlin. In a letter to her father commenting on the growth of the IWMA in France, Laura, taking a few hopeful signs as a national trend, said that "sections are formed each day and that each new working class movement, each new strike, is attributed in a greater or lesser degree to the International." Lafargue echoed his wife: he credited the IWMA with bringing out a larger working-class vote and with generating a sense of self-awareness and a willingness to take action. As was so often to be the case, Lafargue's analysis was overly optimistic and, at the least, premature. The decline of Proudhonism in the IWMA did not mean the decline of Proudhon's influence in the French labor movement: the Paris Commune was to call for a federalist solution; the defense of municipal liberties was undertaken by French socialists like Malon, Brousse, and Jean Allemane; and revolutionary syndicalism was to echo Proudhon's federalism and moralism.[55]

The new Paris Federation took shape during the government's plebiscitary campaign of 1870. Napoleon III's proclamation of April 23 told voters they would be asked whether they supported the tentative steps taken to liberalize the regime. An affirmative vote would indicate approval of the Empire; a negative one, condemnation of the measures taken. Delegates to the first meeting of the Paris section debated the tactics to follow with regard to the forthcoming plebiscite. Lafargue and Marxist speakers sought abstention, and wanted to publicize their reasons in a manifesto. Blanquists too urged abstention. A twelve-member committee was set up, including Lafargue, to draft a socialist manifesto calling for workers, both rural and urban, not to vote but to reassert the demand for a democratic and socialist republic. The statement was published in *La Marseillaise* on April 24, signed by Germain Casse, the newspaper's editor; Alphonse Humbert, a militant Blanquist who had been an early member of the International; Emile Duval, a metalworker who similarly had become a Blanquist member of the IWMA; and Lafargue.[56] It was the first time that Lafargue's signature appeared on a document drafted by the French branch of the International, and his name was followed by the simple description, "member of the Vaugirard section." The government seemed unable to stop the International's propaganda campaign against the plebiscite. Even so, although bourgeois republicans too denounced the plebiscite, they refused to join forces with the IWMA; they urged a negative vote in contrast to the socialists' demand for abstention.

The overwhelmingly affirmative vote, seven and a half million against a little more than one and a half million, was even more positive than expected and was understandably seen by the government as a victory for Napoleon III. The opposition had come mainly from Paris and other large cities, and the government stepped up its repression of the International with renewed confidence. A pleased Marx nevertheless wrote to Engels that such official frenzy revealed the difference between an ineffectual secret political organization and "a real workers' association." The government, he said, saw the IWMA as a serious political threat because of its growing membership and its success in encouraging strikes.[57]

On April 30 the minister of the interior, Emile Olivier, aiming to strike at all republican opponents but especially at the socialists, ordered the arrest of a number of IWMA members who had protested against the plebiscite, on the grounds that they were conspiring to overthrow the Empire. It appeared that the government, upset by the syndicalist surge, was returning to a more authoritarian Empire. In London, the General Council, in a protest drafted by Marx, condemned the vagueness of the charge. The Lafargues, in their letters to Marx, were euphoric over what they saw as the International's importance; "today, the working class, thanks to the International, which has made immense progress since the last elections, takes cognizance, is aware of its strength and wishes to act at all costs."[58]

The size of the International should not be overestimated. Although in June 1870 the public prosecutor claimed its total membership to be over 800,000, of which almost 434,000 were in France, he not only exaggerated wildly but failed to distinguish between individual members (perhaps only 2,000 in France) and trade unions and parties that had joined collectively. Still, in England, trade unions with memberships totaling about 50,000 (of over 800,000 union members) were affiliated with the International. And though it is impossible to secure accurate estimates for France, strikes by French workers during 1868 and 1869 swelled the IWMA membership there by over 50,000. In the spring and early summer of 1870, the French sections of the IWMA were growing rapidly, demanding a ten-hour day and an increase in salaries.[59] Lafargue asked Marx to have the General Council accredit him as the council's representative to the Paris Federation, and the council, meeting on May 17 and reacting to the arrests in Paris, voted unanimously to name Lafargue its special correspondent.[60]

The trial of thirty-eight accused IWMA members opened June 22. The government, in its attempt to break the growing workers' movement, had indicted the organization as a threat to the regime and as a "formidable threat to society" at large. The collective defense amounted to an indictment of capitalism. Several of the accused were sentenced to prison terms and/or required to pay fines, and the Paris branch was declared dissolved.[61] A similar trial, with similar results, took place in Lyons. The IWMA in France lost experienced leaders and its most active militants, including Varlin. Yet the setback proved temporary; as foreign policy crises multiplied, the International regained its strength. The Paris Federation protested the likelihood of war in *Le Reveil* on July 12: under the guise of defending national honor and preserving European equilibrium, political ambition threatened European peace with destruction and loss of life. The Federation called on its "German brothers" to join it in a show of solidarity. Other sections made similar appeals, and Lafargue wrote Marx in July that "the campaign opens for the French government under very bad auspices with regard to domestic tranquillity."[62] The French government nevertheless declared war on Prussia on July 19.

Faced with mounting criticism at home, having failed in his foreign policy, Napoleon III saw war with Prussia as inevitable. Even though Austria and Italy were unwilling to become involved, the French government hoped that in the event of war one or both of the Catholic powers would side with France. The immediate cause derived from the successful French protest against a German prince taking the vacant Spanish throne and, when Prussia withdrew his candidacy, the French determination to force the issue and win a promise that the candidacy would not be renewed. The demand was made at a meeting between the French ambassador and the Prussian king. An account of this meeting, edited by Bismarck, made it seem France had suffered a diplomatic setback that contributed to its willingness to declare war.

Goaded by public opinion, looking forward to the prestige that military victory would bring, but without allies, without adequately prepared armies, and hence with little chance for victory, the Empire went to war. Even though aware that the government was doing its best to whip up enthusiasm, Parisians, Lafargue observed, supported the war. People in the provinces, however, appeared hostile. He reasoned that the failing Empire had resorted to war this time, as it had in 1866, to cover its domestic inadequacies.[63]

At the time his daughter was born, Paul had written Laura's sister Jenny that they expected to leave rue du Cherche-Midi sometime in April and that soon he would start looking for "a little house with a garden." Laura added that it might be in the suburb of Neuilly, where there was a better chance of finding a garden and economizing, although she admitted that she was not "delighted" at the idea of living outside of Paris.[64] Six months later Laura wrote Jenny they were looking in Levallois, a suburb northwest of Paris, and after having rejected half a dozen apartments and cottages had finally found a little house, "very pretty but unfortunately very nearly gardenless" at 7 place de la Reine Hortense (Levallois-Perret).[65] The house was well situated, with trees and some open space. Other houses, even though surrounded by "trees covered with apricots and cherries that made one's mouth water," were so isolated that she feared thieves and burglars, who were doing "a terrible trade just now" in the Paris suburbs, "and as Paul very frequently comes home late at night we might have had to pay very dearly for our fruits and flowers. We have therefore given up the idea of having a large garden—not without regret, as you may suppose."[66]

Paul was more enthusiastic. Unpacking in July, he wrote Marx that they had fled Paris because the city was full of smallpox. "Now we have got out" on a little road near the fortifications, "with a beautiful garden 110 meters square." They could leave Schnaps, now tubby and active, there all day. His parents had drawn closer because of him. "If this admiration for their offspring continues," Paul wrote, speaking of himself in the third person, "I believe that Paul and Laurent's . . . partnership will become stronger every day, for the silliness which acts as the connecting link in their union will become so great that all corrosives, social or otherwise, will be powerless to dissolve it."[67]

In the war Prussia took the offensive, and because it was superior in numbers, leadership, and morale, the French suffered repeated defeats. At the news of the first few losses in early August, street demonstrations broke out in Paris. Napoleon III, though ill, had taken personal command, but surrendered a large army on September 2. Two days later a republic was proclaimed in Paris, and a provisional government set up by Paris deputies. Laura's parents, worried about the Lafargues' safety, had tried to persuade them to leave the capital and stay with Paul's parents; on the day the battle of Sedan was fought, Marx wrote in fury: "Those idiot Lafargues' delay in beating a retreat to Bordeaux is inexcusable."[68] They finally did so only weeks before the Prussians surrounded Paris in mid-September; in fact they were forced to leave their home because the government ordered the houses surrounding the fortifications to be pulled down. But even before their decision was precipitated by events, the Lafargues had decided to store their furniture and relocate in Bordeaux:

for their son's sake, who was still in poor health; because Laura was once more pregnant; and no doubt because they could not stay even had they wanted to, inasmuch as all *bouches inutiles* (wives and children) would be forced to leave.

It was natural for them to think of Bordeaux after deciding to flee Paris; Paul's parents were there and his father was a friend of the republican mayor, Emile Fourcand, a wealthy merchant who had amassed a fortune trading in colonial foodstuffs. A liberal, he proclaimed the existence of a republic on September 4.[69] Paul, of course, had lived there as a child and as an adolescent and knew the city well.

Moreover, both Lafargues were dismayed by the apathy of most Paris workers and by the enthusiasm of others, who, optimistic of victory, relished the excitement.[70] The delayed departure was explained by Laura: Paul was furious at the idea of having to give up his house and garden, "where he has done wonders, pruning, planting, and spoiling trees and vegetables and flowers."[71] To Marx's relief the Lafargues arrived in Bordeaux September 2 and moved in with Paul's parents.[72] He might have anticipated that within weeks his son-in-law would again immerse himself in revolutionary activism.

8 Bordeaux

The drowsy Bordelais ... interested in money-making, eating, and drinking, only fear the red specter.

—Paul Lafargue

Bordeaux sits at the mouth of the Garonne, about sixty miles from the sea and fifteen miles upstream from where the Garonne and Dordogne rivers meet. Already a commercial, political, and cultural center in Roman times, and the economic hub and political capital of medieval Aquitaine, the port enjoyed renewed prosperity from the sixteenth through the eighteenth centuries with the development of the wine trade and new West Indian commerce. Between 1700 and 1791 the previously stable population more than doubled, going from 45,000 to 110,000, the greatest such increase of any major French city.[1]

By the middle of the nineteenth century, because of its coastal trade with other French ports on the Atlantic, the city had overcome the loss of Haiti and its cane sugar. Bordeaux shippers sent 60 percent of their cargoes to Norman ports (chiefly wine to service the Paris area). Although by the beginning of the nineteenth century railway construction had cut this coastal trade by two thirds, the loss was overcome by an extension of overseas navigation. Bordeaux could not compete with Le Havre for the North Atlantic trade, but its exporters moved into the South Atlantic, trading with New Orleans and Mexico. Under the Second Empire, despite the competition of Marseilles, firms operating out of Bordeaux got the concession for passenger liners to South America, which was also becoming an important market for French wine. Ships sailing from Bordeaux could also be found off Indochina, New Caledonia, and later, Senegal and Africa's west coast.[2]

Because of its trade, and regardless of its rank as France's fourth largest city (with a population of about 200,000 in 1870), Bordeaux did not experience industrial growth (aside from ship building) until the end of the Second Empire. It was never a "working-class" city, as

Lafargue regretfully reminded himself. As early as 1848 the writer Théophile Gautier noted that its workers "suffer with resignation," and municipal authorities attested to their *bon esprit*. The city was conservative, sending *ultras* to the Chamber of Deputies in 1815, giving Louis Napoleon 60 percent of its votes in the 1849 presidential election, and overwhelmingly supporting the Second Empire in 1852. The Bordelais held a reputation as "reserved," and experienced few of the "great moments of enthusiasm" known by Paris and the south.[3]

Still, the potential was there. After the Prussian victory over Austria in 1866 a conscription bill, intended to enlarge the French army by requiring "good numbers" to serve actively in the reserve, generated disturbances in Bordeaux and Toulouse. Although not implemented, the proposal contributed to republican gains in the elections of 1869, and republican strength was such that the city voted no in the 1870 plebiscite.[4] News of the French army's surrender to Prussia led to street agitation: crowds gathered in the Place de la Grand-Théâtre, from which they marched on the Prefecture to cries of "Gambetta." On September 4 the Bordelais welcomed the news that a republic had been proclaimed.[5]

Lafargue nevertheless resented the Bordelais' generally compliant attitude toward the war and, after September 4, their reluctance to pursue it with vigor. Shortly after his arrival he wrote Marx that "the situation in Bordeaux is reactionary. The wine merchants and shopkeepers would welcome the Prussians. They care little for what is going on in Paris. Bordeaux eats, sleeps, drinks, and plays."[6] Quiet, stately Bordeaux with its wide streets, monumental gates, and spires and steeples was transformed by the war as refugees from the north flocked to the city. There were crowds of people everywhere. Parades were held daily with bands playing patriotic songs, adding to the commotion. Restaurants and hotels were jammed, and National Guardsmen were seen on horse and on foot. The theaters were filled with people enjoying operettas, comedies, varieties, and cabaret.[7]

Lafargue described his frustrations in detail to his sister-in-law Jenny, particularly his attempts to find a newspaper offering a more radical alternative. He held forth on "the drowsy Bordelais . . . more interested in money-making, eating, and drinking, whose only dread is *le spectre rouge* [while] the great ruling classes [are] more concerned with exterminating Reds than Prussians." Lafargue showed enthusiasm over Gambetta's *levée en masse* and shared his dream that armed workers would dictate the next constitution; Jenny, more realistic, refused to underestimate the conservatism of the French peasantry.[8]

Paul's frustration was matched, and doubtless in part caused, by his and Laura's unhappiness with their personal situation. Schnaps remained ill and required constant attention.[9] They badly missed Paris. In the same letter to his father-in-law he admitted, "we are bored as beaten dogs in this horrible Bordeaux; praying God to deliver us from here." Laura complained that their situation was "odd": Paul was abused by his father for trying "to make himself useful to the International"—he was away from the house most of the day involved with newspapers and political work—while at the same time his Paris friends reproached him with being away from the capital. The elder Lafargue was now bedridden, and Madame Lafargue's health was deteriorating, for which Laura blamed François' "temper, which must make life in common with him very nearly intolerable. Now that his son's family was out of danger, he only looked for ways to make himself and others miserable."[10]

Bad enough, their situation worsened after François' death on November 18, 1870. Laura, in an advanced state of pregnancy, was particularly distraught: she told her sister the news was so disagreeable, some of the details so "grotesque," that she had put off writing and was still suppressing a good deal of it. "Never in my life," she wrote, "have I been so abused as here by my venerable mother-in-law—since M. Lafargue's death *bien entendu*." Paul was treated "in the rudest manner possible by her," and on the one occasion Laura defended him, she was told "in not the politest manner in the world to hold [her] tongue." One incident was described in detail: the mother-in-law's refusal to have an additional fire lit in the bedroom where Laura and her son were obliged to spend much of the day, despite the fact that both of them were suffering from bad colds: "I cannot go into details: suffice it to say that she got to grudging us the food we ate, the wine we drank, the oil we burnt and the wood consumed by our fires. *I am really* ashamed for the sake of Paul's mother to give you further examples of the mean and petty warfare she waged against us—the Lord knows why."[11]

When the couple "resolved to bear it no longer" and decided to move to a furnished apartment, the mother moved out instead, taking most of the furniture. Given their precarious finances, the Lafargues were in no position to argue. They preferred having the house to themselves, however "denuded" of furniture, linen, and kitchen utensils.[12] Hence it was at 56 rue Naujac that the twenty-five-year-old Laura gave birth to another son, Marc-Laurent, on January 31, 1871.[13] Marx sent ironic congratulations to Paul: "It is necessary to produce new defenders of France, and you and Laura seem seriously and successfully engaged in that patriotic business."[14]

With his father's death Lafargue found himself heir to about 100,000 francs (4,000 pounds or 20,000 dollars), but in the form of investments—some in New Orleans property, municipal bonds, and other American bonds, and the rest in French mortgages and shares in the Orléans railway. (The rue Naujac house went to Paul's mother.)[15] The amount of the estate was sizable but, when compared with other legacies that year in the Bordeaux notarial archives, not extravagant; it was an "average-sized fortune." On December 23, 1870, the estate was divided between Paul and his mother. Although François had previously tried to sell his two houses in New Orleans, he had not succeeded. One, worth 25,000 francs, went to his widow; the other, worth 28,000, went to his son.[16] The bad feelings between mother and son were not assuaged by the elder Lafargue's death; she shared her husband's views and did not approve of Paul's politics. Paul informed Marx that he had spoken with a lawyer about selling the mortgages; he would have to take a loss, yet was considering investing "elsewhere than in France." Could Engels invest the money in England if the mortgages were sold?[17] Even so, there was enough cash available to finance a summer trip to the Pyrenees for the Lafargues, their children, and Laura's two sisters in the summer of 1871.

Lafargue had thrown himself into republican and socialist activity in Bordeaux. He had welcomed the proclamation of the Paris deputies establishing a republic on September 4, 1870, and had rallied to the idea of national defense. Later he identified himself "as one of those who [on September 4] in Bordeaux, overturned the equestrian statue of Napoleon III and proclaimed the Republic."[18] He and other republicans debated means of strengthening the new regime and continuing the war, a decision not yet taken by the provisional government.

With Paris under siege, the minister of the interior, Léon Gambetta, escaped from the city by balloon to reorganize French defenses. His delegation spent two months in Tours before coming to Bordeaux in early December. Included in Gambetta's entourage and serving as his chief of federal police was Lafargue's Blanquist friend Arthur Ranc, who had been on the staff of *La Marseillaise*. He unsuccessfully tried, according to Lafargue's version of events, to persuade Lafargue to accept a prefecture (that is, to head one of the eighty-three *départements* into which France was divided).[19]

Born in 1831, Ranc had attended law school, but decided instead on a career in journalism and politics. Staunchly republican, he had been condemned to a year in prison by Napoleon III's government for conspiracy, and to avoid a later charge had fled to Switzerland. Benefiting from an 1859 amnesty, he began to write for Paris newspapers. When the Empire fell he was named mayor of Paris' ninth arrondissement, but chose to depart with Gambetta. Lafargue refused the prefecture offer, and in turn proposed a seizure of the goods of Bonapartist deputies responsible for the war, suppression of indirect taxes, and government aid for soldiers and their families.[20] Thirty years later a more conservative Ranc denied he had made such an offer; he had lacked the authority to fill prefectures and had only promised to inform Gambetta of the situation in Germany—specifically a shortage of supplies—as learned by Lafargue from a German source in the International.[21]

It was natural in this atmosphere for Lafargue to join with radicals and socialists, who were in a minority in Bordeaux, and support efforts either to use one of the city's existing newspapers or to open a new one to disseminate Internationalist propaganda. His letters to London indicate that he was managing (but may have been exaggerating his role) the short-lived *Défense nationale,* a workers' newspaper. At least three issues were published and sent off to Marx.[22] He also wrote for the revived republican newspaper, *La Tribune de la Gironde.*

This newspaper had seen suppressed by Louis Napoleon the day after his coup of December 2, 1851. It reappeared September 15, 1870, opening its columns to IWMA members and carrying on its masthead the three revolutionary dates of 1792, 1848, and 1870. It was published between September 15 and November 19, 1870, and was then forced by the government to suspend publication.[23] Lafargue knew the editors of *La Tribune* and so was able to publish occasional articles there.

Finally, together with Pierre Delboy, his comrade-in-arms at the International Students' Conference at Liège and now representing the far Left on the Bordeaux Municipal Council, Lafargue contributed to a third paper, the city's major republican daily, *Le Républican de la*

Gironde, in existence since 1792.[24] As early as September 7, a Lafargue article called for defense of the Republic. He blamed poor generalmanship and inadequate preparation for the French defeats as well as corrupt profiteers who failed to deliver the weapons paid for. In view of foreign aggression and domestic threats, particularly from Orleanists, republicans needed to organize and the IWMA could play an important part in this effort. He praised the International as a vehicle of social regeneration, which was precisely why it was so feared and so hated by the nations of Europe, and readily identified himself as a member.[25]

Lafargue's article contained the first more or less Marxist analysis of events published in the Bordeaux press. Lafargue attacked the Orleanists and their "spokesman" Adolphe Thiers as representing the commercial bourgeoisie and the forces of high finance and as controlling government jobs. Thiers had brought republicans and Bonapartists into his government to set them against each other, and it was necessary for republicans of all persuasions to join forces in order to overcome both Bonapartists and Orleanists and preserve the Republic. He urged the working class to form a party and affiliate with the International, and asked that Bordeaux republicans support it as their best means of solidifying the newly proclaimed regime. Upbraided were the Orleanists and the moderate republicans who unwittingly allied with them to protest against workers who organized themselves and so continued the previous government's prosecution of the International in Paris.

The "specter" of the International had become a reality, Paul told Jenny, and the papers were filled with it.[26] It was natural for him to work for the reestablishment of a Bordeaux section of the International, and his role may have been significant here.[27] A section had been founded in 1867. It was represented at the IWMA's Lausanne Congress, but had become moribund and under its president, a shoemaker and former disciple of Cabet named Vézinaud who had converted to mutualism, disappeared in the first few days of the war.[28] By the end of September, Paul was able to tell Marx that he had published a French translation of the IWMA's salute to the Republic in *La Tribune,* and that copies would be sent to the French sections.[29]

Yet we do not see Lafargue's name on reports of protest meetings held in the city or on lists of subscriptions undertaken to send volunteers to the army.[30] He was listed among the delegates of the federated National Guard companies as having belonged to an

IWMA-affiliated "Central Committee." And his signature, together with 140 others, appears on a poster printed by the "Central Committee members of the International and workers delegation," dated January 7, 1871, denouncing the government as then organized and asking that there be representation in it "for the people and for the Commune."[31]

During this period Lafargue fervently favored national defense (and ignored Marx's internationalism, although now that the nation was a republic fighting an apparently annexationist-minded Prussia, Marx's sympathies lay with France). Did IWMA members hope to buy U.S. surplus Civil War material and even recruit volunteers in Spain and in the United States? A unit of Spanish volunteers had fought in the French republican army late in 1871 (in the Jura mountains area). Was an attempt made to recruit these veterans in a Spanish legion by the Bordelais Central Committee, presided over by IWMA member Jean Dargance, who after being accused of deserting the army in 1854 had taken refuge in Spain? A former teacher, he was to play an active part in what has come to be known as "les troubles de Bordeaux" in April 1871. If such attempts were made or even considered, it is unthinkable that Lafargue, who was fluent in Spanish and who had represented Spain on the International's General Council, was unaware of them.[32] Lafargue had tried to persuade Ranc to continue the war. Ranc later confirmed Paul's patriotism. As long as the war lasted, Ranc wrote, "he did not yield to Internationalist intrigue. He spoke and behaved like a patriot, as a Frenchman."[33]

On October 28, in a letter intended for the IWMA's General Council, Lafargue told Marx that a reorganized Bordeaux section had been established the previous week. He took some credit for it but admitted that the group, if "'enthusiastic,'" was small, and he asked to be put in touch with its counterparts in Lyons and Marseilles.[34] A Lafargue article in the October 31 issue of *La Tribune de la Gironde* also announced the news "with pleasure," and provided a summary statement of Marxist objectives. The newspaper, in its short life, published occasional IWMA communiqués. Lafargue's focus was on national defense, however, not on the internationalism preached by Marx, who from the standpoint of the class struggle did not distinguish the French Republic from the Prussian monarchy. Lafargue even downplayed collectivization, given diversity of views within the section. He rather called for a continuation of the war, even after the anticipated surrender of Paris, in the belief that Prussian resources, as he had informed Ranc, were in short supply.

At a meeting of the General Council in London, October 25, Marx reported that "Lafargue [was] making great propaganda" at Bordeaux.[35] Together with another member of the Bordeaux branch, a former magistrate named L.-J. Perilhou, Lafargue published social-ist and communalist articles and extracts from Proudhon in *La Tribune*.[36] He may have helped to draft the address of the Interna-tional hailing the coming of the Republic, which the French press initially refused to print. Finally he managed to publish a French translation, albeit "with numerous and heartbreaking misprints," in *La Tribune*.[37]

The Versailles government, relying on a parliamentary investiga-tion of the Paris Commune, later exaggerated the influence of the International in manipulating events. The involvement of Marx's son-in-law Lafargue in the IWMA, however minimal its actual role, came as a windfall to a regime eager to find an international socialist con-spiracy behind the Commune. A lengthy police biography, prepared twenty years later, credited Lafargue with reestablishing the Bordeaux section and, in his capacity as its corresponding secretary, with sign-ing all manifestos and declarations emanating from it.[38]

It is difficult to follow the development and activities of the new section, however, because *La Tribune de la Gironde,* the one news-paper interested in reporting events related to it, suspended publica-tion November 19 when its editors were mobilized. As early as October 28 Lafargue was complaining of the difficulties he experi-enced in getting the paper printed in Bordeaux, for which he blamed reactionaries in the city.

Three months later he was more optimistic about the section, which had been "going better for some time now." Lafargue translated and made available to its members Edward Beesly's article on the Inter-national published in the November 1870 issue of the *Fortnightly Review*. Wanting to do more, he asked Marx for the addresses of sections in other towns in order to "open up communications and establish a kind of centralization, which after the siege of Paris could be taken up on a much bigger and more active scale."[39] In early February, commenting on three demonstrations carried out by the International's Bordeaux branch, Lafargue, now its corresponding secretary, regretted that there were "only four or six sections and a thousand members here."[40] He expected the war to continue: the fall of Paris seemed to produce a "new fervor," and real republicans feared that an unfavorable peace could mean the death of the Republic. Still, his concern about the countryside's lack of interest in continuing the struggle, the absence of a radical newspaper to disseminate a radical and patriotic point of view, and an exceptionally cold and snowy winter accounted for an injection of healthy realism.

Radical republicans showed themselves powerless, however, as news of the war became increasingly worse. To national consternation, word came that on October 27 Marshal Bazaine, commander of the Metz garrison, had surrendered his army of 120,000 men, huge amounts of material, and "the strongest fort in France." The surrender made victory on the Loire, where Gambetta had organized the nation's defenses, impossible. Orléans was abandoned December 3. Le Mans gave way soon after. These losses shattered hopes of freeing Paris, and by December the city was in a state of siege. The government, Gambetta aside, decided to ask for an armistice. It included the stipulation that German soldiers were not to enter Paris while the nation elected an assembly that could ratify the armistice and have the power to negotiate a peace treaty with Prussia.

According to the terms of the armistice eventually signed on January 23, 1871, the nation was to elect an assembly to decide on peace or continued war. This election campaign, and the intention of the national government to sit in Bordeaux, accounted for *La Tribune*'s reappearance on February 2. Now called *La Tribune de Bordeaux,* it carried on its masthead the revolutionary motto, "Liberté Egalité, Fraternité," and it promised to serve as the "energetic organ of the Republican party."

In the elections of February 8, carried out by means of department-wide lists of candidates rather than by single-member constituencies as under the Empire, voters elected an Assembly containing about four hundred monarchists, two hundred republicans, and thirty Bonapartists. Elected were local notables from the relatively untouched provinces committed to peace—and only incidentally to a restoration of the monarchy. The list of candidates supported by the *Tribune* was put together in large part by Delboy. The city, like many of those in France, voted for conservative republicans and supported the list headed by the seventy-year-old Adolphe Thiers, defeating the republican list headed by the one member of the provisional government who had opposed the armistice and had wanted to continue fighting, Léon Gambetta.

Upset by what he perceived as a reactionary victory in the election for a National Assembly, Lafargue wrote Marx that republicans might be better served by an Orleanist monarchy than by conservative republicans; the enemy would then be easily identified and a revolutionary-republican alliance could be established. Marx preferred a liberal republic, which would allow workers to organize and thereby develop greater class consciousness.[41]

Lafargue could only follow these and subsequent events with dismay, especially the ratification of the peace treaty giving Alsace and Lorraine to Germany together with a promise to pay a huge indemnity.[42] He managed, however, to publish a rejection of government denunciations of the IWMA as a "red specter" and a denial of charges that it was responsible for the disasters encountered.[43] After the Assembly, which he contemptuously dismissed as "our honorable *ruraux* [rustics]," left Bordeaux for Versailles, Lafargue noted how quiet the town was and how the hotel and restaurant owners "must be suffering."[44]

He never forgave what he called "bourgeois patriots" for their "betrayal" of French interests, and he contrasted them with Paris workers who had wanted to fight on. As members of the National Defense government, the former had installed themselves in the still-warm place of the emperor. But when the first shells hit Paris, their patriotism confronted the prospect of property losses, and fell far short. In his 1906 pamphlet *La Patrie en danger,* Lafargue went so far as to accuse the government of "starving and bleeding" the Paris population in order to lead it to surrender.

On February 23 the Bordeaux section sent a protest denouncing the armistice to the National Assembly, which it addressed as the "representatives of capitalist ownership." It was signed by the member of the section, a hatter named Barbier, who had presided over the meeting that drafted it, and by Lafargue, as secretary.[45] The protest rejected the peace then being prepared as "precipitating France into the abyss of shame and ruin" (doubtless Lafargue's words, on the basis of his letters), and in view of the "desire for vengeance" and the "necessity of conquest," as perpetuating the "regime of permanent armies and war."

The statement especially denounced "bourgeois rhetoricians" who did not want to defend the country, and asked "the representatives of industrial and financial capitalist property" to refuse to take responsibility for the shameful peace.[46] Marxist themes resounded amid cries of patriotic anguish in a March 17 article in *La Tribune*. Lafargue told his critics: "You can denounce us; your governments can massacre us, but so long as economic fatalities exist which divide the nation into two antagonistic classes, the flag of social demands will rise."[47]

Lafargue's spirits revived enormously when news came that Paris, sorely tried by the German siege, resentful of the conservative Assembly's determination to end hostilities and of its lifting of emergency relief measures, and fearful of the Assembly's perceived hostility to the Republic, on March 26 established an insurrectionary government, the Commune, and elected to it radical and moderate republicans, Proudhonists, Blanquists, and members of the International. He exuberantly wrote Jenny: "What an awakening in Paris! We're trying to organize something in Bordeaux. Perhaps in a few days, with the help of some friends in the National Guard, the prefect will be shown the door."[48] A historian of the provincial communes has credited Lafargue with adding a socialist voice to the "Bordeaux Commune," although, as we shall see, a Bordeaux Commune never formally existed.[49]

After the Paris Commune was proclaimed, *La Tribune de Bordeaux* published extensively the news from the capital, printing lengthy extracts of the *Journal Officiel de la Commune* as well as government communiqués from Versailles designed to isolate the capital. On April 2 Paris was besieged again, this time by the Versailles army, with the cooperation of the Prussians, to destroy its independence. *La Tribune*'s editorial staff took the side of the Communards, arguing that they had shown restraint in the face of repeated government provocations and had resorted to insurgency only when the government sought to disarm them. On April 10 the newspaper published a Communard appeal, found posted on the walls of the city, to the rest of the country. At the same time the battalions of the Bordeaux National Guard began to organize themselves, and members of the Bordeaux branch of the International began to publish a weekly newspaper. But this was not Lafargue's work, because on April 6, a little over two weeks after the establishment of the Commune, he was in Paris.

9 The Commune

The ruling classes are more interested in exterminating Reds than Prussians.

—Paul Lafargue

Lafargue went to Paris for several reasons, one of them a wish to undertake a research project. When he had written to his sister-in-law Jenny in mid-March inviting her and Eleanor to vacation with the Lafargues in the Pyrenees, he had asked her to bring documentation relating to the International, whose history, he said, he planned to write: it would be both a narrative and a collection of documents designed for all IWMA members. Having gotten *La Tribune* to publish IWMA texts had aroused his interest in compiling one.[1] Conceivably Lafargue would gather documentation in Paris as well. Jenny urged her father to join them, but he pleaded the pressure of work on the second volume of *Capital*.[2] Lafargue may also have wanted to visit friends of his student days; Jaclard, for example, was serving as regimental commander in the Commune.[3] And he may simply have wanted to see what a revolutionary government, especially in Paris, was like. He admired the spirit of the Paris workers who had crossed German lines to join provincial armies.

Was he on a mission of some sort to go to Paris and then return to Bordeaux? Marx identified Lafargue as a "delegate" from Bordeaux to the Commune so that he could obtain *pleins pouvoirs*—although for what purpose he did not say.[4] Consequently there is speculation, but little evidence, that he received orders from the Communard leadership to return to Bordeaux and promote an insurrection in southeastern France.[5] Jenny believed her brother-in-law went to Paris to secure authorization to organize a revolutionary army at Bordeaux.[6]

Whatever the reason, Laura, who after his departure had no news of her husband because the Versailles government had cut communications, grew frantic. "To make matters worse," she wrote Jenny, "my poor baby has been so ill that during eight or nine days I expected every moment to see him die." Paul had not intended to remain away so long, and might be unable to return or send word. She would go to Paris to join him, but could not leave her children even if they were healthy and certainly not if they were ill. Accordingly Laura asked that her sisters postpone the visit they had planned. "As to my feeling lonely, I am used to being alone. Paul since many months is hardly ever at home and I have hardly stirred out of the house for the last six or eight months." Jenny reassured her sister in an April 18 letter that interrupted rail and postal services accounted for his silence and prolonged absence and that regardless of what Laura had said she would come by steamer as soon as possible.[7]

On his arrival in Paris, Lafargue walked through the city, struck by the calm. He went to the Hôtel de Ville, and in euphoric terms described what he saw there at seven in the morning. "Part of the square was illuminated by a joyful ray of sun, enveloping the National Guards, some sleeping outstretched on the flagstones, others cooking, others polishing weapons, others smoking their pipes . . . However, up close the cannons and machine guns showed their murderous muzzles." Lafargue contrasted the idealism of Paris under the Commune with that under the Empire. Around the barricades and in the midst of debris, he saw children playing and traffic and pedestrians circulating freely. He heard no reports of thefts or murders. The wealthy—and the prostitutes—had departed to the suburbs, the latter to service the Prussians, whom they found "more generous but less knowledgeable than the French." Everywhere he saw "active children and chatting women."[8]

From Paris Lafargue supplied his father-in-law with his impressions of the Communards and the general population: all were enthusiastic and hopeful of taking Versailles, but as revealed to him by a Communard chief, Edouard Vaillant, seriously short of leaders. Could Engels "place his talents at the service of the revolution" and work out a plan of military operations for the defense of the city?[9] Although not happy to learn that his son-in-law was in the besieged capital, Marx at a General Council meeting April 25 acknowledged receipt of the information. Regrettably the letters had been "sifted" and consequently delayed by both the French and the Prussian governments, which dated most of Lafargue's news.[10] Still, Marx was struck by how ignorant the rest of France was of events taking place in Paris, and struck too by Lafargue's optimism. The latter was con-

fident of victory, for "Paris was becoming invincible . . . already possess[ing] a well-organized citizen army supplied with victuals and
munitions; and each passing day adds to the importance and solidity
of that army."[11]

His hopes, of course, proved wholly unrealistic. When the Versailles government believed that its army was ready, troops were sent
to enact a bloodier version of the June Days of 1848. Personally led
by the cavalry officer and war hero General Gaston Galliffet, the
Versailles forces broke into the city on May 21 and in a series of
fiercely fought street battles, advanced barricade by barricade until
the last Communards were executed in the Père Lachaise cemetery.
Hostages (including the archbishop of Paris) were shot and buildings
set afire by the retreating Communards, while government soldiers
executed mercilessly. Between 20,000 and 30,000 Parisians died in
the seventy-two days between March 18 and May 28, under the eyes
of watching Prussian troops and to the horror of Europe. Insurrections in other principal cities, Lyons, Saint-Etienne, Toulouse, and
Marseilles, met with similar, though less bloody, results.

As was true for many socialists, the Paris Commune proved a for-
mative and traumatic experience in Lafargue's life. He never forgave
the government and its chief members, Jules Favre, Jules Ferry, Jules
Simon, and especially Thiers, for whom his hatred remained undi-
minished. Thirty-five years later, in a *Humanité* article, Lafargue
could still cite Thiers' "cowardice, cupidity, and venality," his "nar-
rowness of spirit," his "overcrowding conceit," and the "betrayals of
his public life." He reminded his readers of Thiers' accountability for
the massacres of republicans under Louis Philippe and of the insurgents of 1848. He "crown[ed] his bloody life with the butchery of the
men of the Commune."[12]

The Commune strengthened Lafargue's animosity toward bourgeois capitalist society and became the subject of countless articles.
He attributed its defeat to the lack of any support from outside of
Paris and to the fact that the "necessary economic transformation"
had not been carried out. Lafargue acknowledged the reforms
achieved but denied that the Commune had restructured society or
had even attacked capitalist power. "The insurrection of March 18
was far from being a socialist movement." It was, however, patriotic
and was supported by the International.[13] A similar analysis explained the failure of radical republicans in Bordeaux: "In 1871
power fell into the hands of people not prepared to receive it." This

in turn explained why "no socialist program was carried out by the Communards."[14] Even so, he compared the resistance shown to that of workers' uprisings in earlier revolutions. In 1789 and 1848 "it took two months of struggle and eight days of massacre to overcome the jobless Paris workers."

Lafargue remained especially bitter about *la semaine sanglante,* the bloody week of government repression. It was worse than 1848; it was the "Saint Bartholomew of the working class." The Prussians had conformed to the rules of war and respected the rights of prisoners, unlike the "bourgeois patriots" after the defeat of the Commune. Never were the vanquished treated so badly; never was such a "bloody orgy" so prolonged. Lafargue said that the "Versaillaises" never could have inflicted on Prussian prisoners the "infamies and crimes" committed against the prisoners of the Commune without unleashing the indignation of the civilized world. But bourgeois capitalists of both hemispheres were in agreement: war against socialists was "more ferocious and more barbarous than any ever fought against nations." "Bourgeois patriotism," he would recall in 1906, "had shown itself more concerned with property interests than with the interests of France."[15] The fear of German shells falling on Paris had prompted the surrender; the same fear of property loss accounted for the suppression of the Communards.

In early April the republican-dominated Bordeaux Municipal Council, which had shown sympathy for the insurrections that had broken out elsewhere, decided it was not prepared to go so far. Even *La Tribune,* which initially stated its support for the uprisings in Paris and Lyons on March 29, openly rejected the pro-Commune stand of a new socialist paper, *La Fédération. La Tribune* deplored the presence of Communard agents in Bordeaux, blamed the upsurge in anti-Versailles agitation on them, and seemed pleased that the police and the National Guard were able to handle all incidents.[16]

La Fédération was a radical newspaper that had made its appearance on April 16, during Lafargue's absence, as a biweekly with hopes of becoming a daily. It never called itself an organ of the IWMA, but its staff, as well as Lafargue, who associated himself with the journal after his return to Bordeaux, were for the most part members. Articles struck both Marxist and Proudhonist chords: a sovereign commune, universal suffrage, workers to own the instruments of their labor and so eliminate capitalist exploitation, and free belief. Unlike *La Tribune* it maintained open and strong support for the Paris Commune, and its disappearance on May 21, 1871, coincided with the demise of the Commune.

There were "disturbances" in Bordeaux for several days in mid-April. Posters proclaiming sympathy with the Communards in Paris and calling for similar change in Bordeaux had covered the walls of the city center. Rumors flew about the refusal of local and regional troops to fight for Versailles. Excited crowds formed, and no longer restrained by government troops (who had departed with the Assembly) but benefiting from the presence of more sympathetic National Guard units, readily staged demonstrations in the streets. On the evening of April 16, two hundred young people went to City Hall to proclaim the existence of a commune. These events were described by city and departmental officials as the work of agents sent by Paris and of the Bordeaux section of the International—and specifically of Lafargue as a directing force—an impression reinforced by the support the Paris Commune and the IWMA received regularly in *La Fédération* and occasionally in *La Tribune*.[17] But with the arrival of government troops and the unwillingness on the part of most Bordeaux citizens to support the demonstrators, coupled with pleas for reconciliation by most of the city's newspapers and a diversion of interest to the forthcoming municipal elections, calm was restored.

Thus although the city favored republicanism and supported administrative decentralization, there was no commune in Bordeaux. The last gasp of discontent came in the form of a national congress of French cities, called for by the Bordeaux and other provincial municipal councils and designed to put pressure both on the Versailles government and Paris to find a peaceful solution. The congress was scheduled to convene in Bordeaux, but Thiers effectively prevented this from happening by invoking legislation enacted in 1855 that forbade municipal councils from debating state affairs and by ordering the arrests of municipal councillors headed for Bordeaux. He ignored republican complaints that rights of travel and association were being trampled and successfully intimidated most delegates. The Bordeaux Municipal Council, which sponsored the congress, agreed to cancel it and use less dangerous means to express discontent. For the historian of the provincial communes this repression was "as important a victory as the breaching of the Saint-Cloud gate."[18] Thiers also enjoyed the fullest authority that the National Assembly could provide: the right to declare martial law. And the public prosecutor was ordered to take action against spokesmen of conciliation who proposed treating the Paris Commune and the National Assembly on an equal footing.

With twenty-one other IWMA members, Lafargue ran in Bordeaux's municipal elections, called by Thiers in hopes of dividing his opponents and thus prolonging the success won by his supporters in the February vote for the National Assembly. Republicans had won a majority in Bordeaux in February, and at an April 28 meeting of the Bordeaux section of the IWMA its members asked republican candidates for municipal office whether their programs matched that of the Communards in Paris. When it was clear that they did not, the IWMA members then presented their own list of candidates, including Delboy and Lafargue (who ran as "Laffargue, landlord").

The slate of IWMA members received only enough votes to permit its three most highly placed candidates to be elected.[19] Lafargue was unsuccessful. Eliminated on the first ballot of April 30, he blamed his defeat on the lack of publicity at his disposal. He believed that as news of a workers' party in Bordeaux spread, the International would steadily increase its membership. Still, his chief concern seemed less one of winning political office than of working on his writing, specifically his history of the International, which he said would further its propaganda.[20]

Again, Lafargue's optimism, which at one point had led him to think that most of the National Guard would support insurrection, proved excessive. The IWMA list was put together after impassioned debate, but it was moderate republicans who were elected, and their victory coincided with the conservative reaction that culminated with the destruction of the Paris Commune. *La Tribune,* which had published Beesly's abbreviated history of the IWMA, introduced and annotated by Lafargue, and which planned to publish all the IWMA proclamations and circulars in order to publicize the International, was seized at the end of May.[21]

Lafargue had never shown admiration for the political courage of the Bordelais. When after the elections to the National Assembly Bordeaux republicans feared retribution in the form of exile or deportation and asked that their electoral committee be dissolved, Lafargue dismissed them with contempt in a letter to Marx.[22] Years later, in 1899, he recalled how discouraged he had been. Those who had cursed the leaders of the new Third Republic—the Thiers, the Favres, the Ferrys—for their centralist tendencies now drew back, wondered whether the more radical Varlins, Tridons, and Malons were capable of governing France, and refused to support them.[23]

The government had not hesitated to blame the International for the Paris Commune, for the outbreaks in other French cities, and for the "disturbances" in Bordeaux. According to the report of the parliamentary committee subsequently charged with investigating the origins of the Commune, the International had "a powerful impact on the people." In reality, in spite of all its efforts, the French branch of the IWMA was weak, its connection with the Girondin radicals who published IWMA manifestos in *La Tribune*, minimal. *La Tribune* deplored the International's pleas for support of the Paris Commune as impractical; it was better to follow the program of "progressive" radicals. Still, the newspaper maintained its support for the IWMA candidates in the municipal elections and that was why it was subsequently suppressed by the authorities. In his testimony to the investigating committee, Mayor Fourcand of Bordeaux denied the existence of any ties between the city government and the International, but admitted that as in all the major cities of France, there were representatives of the IWMA in his. He knew Paul's father, but had never met the son: he knew only that he was told by the prefect of the Gironde Department that Paul Lafargue received posters to put up in support of the Paris Commune. They were pulled down by the police and he had been forced to flee.[24]

Lafargue had been instrumental in reorganizing the Bordeaux section of the IWMA. He had gotten *La Tribune* to publish IWMA texts. Earlier he had founded *La Défense nationale*, which called for the revolutionary pursuit of the war. In his work for the International, he had shown organizational skills. The association had been nothing when he arrived, and he had helped it to reemerge, at least to the extent of running candidates for municipal elections and establishing newspapers, however short-lived. In all this Lafargue was much less a spokesman for Marxism (a majority of IWMA members were Proudhonists) than a patriotic French citizen demanding continuation of the war effort.

He had not avoided police attention. On April 23 the Bordeaux public prosecutor, in a report to Versailles, described the arrests carried out and indicated that Lafargue, referred to as a Cuban national, was under surveillance and that a dossier on him had been started. The prefect of the Gironde Department, Ferdinand Duval, held Lafargue's complicity as a matter of "grave concern." Duval went to

Toulouse to coordinate efforts with the prefect of the Haute-Garonne Department, Emile de Kératry, and both men telegraphed Versailles to tell of the steps taken and to get instructions.

The report from Bordeaux had identified Lafargue as a member of the International and as a "fanatic" subject to imminent arrest. Ignorant of this communiqué, Lafargue sensed no personal danger and may not have been aware that the judicial apparatus had been set in motion.[25] Subsequent investigation by the authorities shed more light on his activity. An anonymous witness, one only described by the First President of the courts of Bordeaux and Toulouse as a "very honorable resident of Bordeaux, well known to us," drew the attention of the authorities to Lafargue. According to his deposition, he was a close friend of Lafargue's parents. He described Paul as "an active recruiter [for the IWMA] and as an assiduous member of its nightly gatherings," as a "great disappointment" to his mother, someone who had gotten into "bad company" and who, according to his father, "infects all he touches [and] the threat of whose doctrines makes his old mother tremble . . . and who killed his father." He had begun life by seducing a young girl and fathering two illegitimate children, then abandoning his three victims. Madame Lafargue was innocent of all her son's wrongdoings, and the blame lay rather with his radical teachers in Paris.[26]

The witness, however close to the family, obviously interspersed opinions with his facts. There were even allegations of bombs. Almost all the testimony was accepted by the Bordeaux Court on August 20, 1871. Though he was identified in prefectural and juridical reports, however, a warrant for Lafargue's immediate arrest was not issued: there was simply not enough evidence. The report of the Bordeaux public prosecutor, while placing blame on Lafargue, similarly showed the impossibility of unearthing the necessary evidence.[27] He acknowledged Lafargue's relationship to Marx, "the high priest of the International organization," but concluded: "It does not seem to me that he is preoccupied with any more than recruiting members for that organization; he cannot be charged with anything indicating participation in the destruction that has taken place." The central commissioner of police, whose men had Lafargue under surveillance, agreed.[28]

What, then, accounts for all the attention paid to Lafargue? The parliamentary committee investigating the Paris Commune and other municipal insurrections, including the disturbances in Bordeaux, had gotten fragmentary responses, and the focus shifted to the role of the press, to the International, and to its "animator," Lafargue. For any-one trying to portray provincial uprisings as a result of foreign con-spiracy, Marx's son-in-law was an excellent target. The real, and more complex, explanations lay in the popular resentment of Paris (and the political centralization it stood for) by local and regional authorities who consequently distinguished France from its capital.

All this, however, lay in the future. When Jenny and Eleanor finally arrived in Bordeaux on May 1 and found Paul had returned from Paris, they looked forward to going to the Pyrenees as planned. With the fall of the Paris Commune at the end of the month, Lafargue believed that as an active organizer for the International he was not safe in France, and he had gotten his passport so that they could decamp as fast as possible. In fact no supporter of the Commune was safe from denunciation, arbitrary arrest, and worse, especially not Marx's son-in-law. Even so, in his last days in Bordeaux he helped to organize a new section of glassworkers, and he and his sisters-in-law had visited their factory. The great heat, the poor health of the work-ers, and the child labor and night work left a vivid impression on them.[29] In any event, when the Commune was destroyed there was no reason to remain in Bordeaux.

On June 2 Lafargue, his wife, their two children, and his two sisters-in-law left the city for the Pyrenees, stopping first at Saint-Gaudens and then at Bagnères-de-Luchon (both in the Haute-Garonne Department), where they had planned to stay "a few months." Jenny planned to take advantage of the mineral waters for which Luchon was noted.[30] This was a small town of about 4,000 inhabitants, close to the central Pyrenees on the Spanish border, at the juncture of the One and Pique rivers. It had been developed in the eighteenth century as a fashionable resort and contained numerous hotels, rooming houses, and small casinos. Laura described the coun-try as "marvelous," writing, it "dazzles us, and we would have liked to live there." The air was "admirable," and the area justified all the difficulties and expense of the trip. Recognizing the danger, however, she expressed a wish "to practice pistol shooting."[31]

The poor health of the children explains the delay in leaving Bor-deaux. Of special concern was the infant, Marc-Laurent: like the daughter who had died, he required constant attention. But the threat of arrest was real enough. As both an outspoken advocate of the

Commune and as an organizer of the International in Bordeaux, Paul was a marked man. In mid-June the police intercepted Lafargue's June 13 letter to Marx ("Sir Williams") from Luchon, a letter whose contents we do not know but which convinced the authorities that Paul was indeed dangerous.[32] The alias was necessary: for the French police Marx was "Bismarck's agent," the "great chief" and the "commander-in-chief" of the terrorist International. The postal authorities received orders on June 14 to look for and intercept any future Lafargue correspondence, which prompted one Ministry of the Interior official to comment on the order: "If Paul Lafargue is so dangerous as that, if it is clear he was sent to Bordeaux to foment an insurrection; why not arrest him?" The idea that Paul had been sent by Paris Communards to promote unrest and revolution in Bordeaux probably originated at this time.[33]

The efficiency shown by the police casts doubt on the accusation made by the First President of the Bordeaux Court that the Luchon police were ineffective and that "the family of Karl Marx and his son-in-law, who had an important role in the International, were able to spend two [sic] months at Luchon in absolute secrecy and that only a disinterested warning had aroused a higher authority."[34] Only the coordination between the different services proved faulty; the Bordeaux public prosecutor was not kept informed by the police or by his colleagues in Paris, on whose orders the correspondence had been seized.

In Luchon the group found a cottage on the banks of the Pique, well situated for an escape to Spain.[35] Marx's two daughters called themselves Williams, while Lafargue registered as "Mora" or "Maura," according to the police who kept an eye on them. They lived in isolation, seeing no one except their doctor. During their stay, Paul corresponded with Marx, and enthusiastically agreed with the latter's analysis of the Paris Commune. A letter dated August 1, 1871, shows that Paul was aware of Marx's *Civil War in France*. Doubtless Marx had sent him an English copy, which had already been published. The Lafargues translated it into French, and suggested a possible French publisher, Lacroix of the Librairie Internationale. Paul admired the work. Of all he read of Marx, he said, "it was the strongest; it struck all the popular chords."[36]

The net tightened at the end of July when an anonymous informer told the authorities of Lafargue's presence. Alerted, de Kératry and Baron Desazaras (the Toulouse public prosecutor) placed the cottage under surveillance and had Lafargue's papers in Bordeaux seized and sent to the Ministry of Justice. Marx had anticipated that the government would take action because of the "eminent role" Lafargue had played in Bordeaux, and almost coincident with their arrival in Luchon Marx had wanted the Lafargues to cross into Spain, readily accessible thanks to the Spanish passport secured by his Cuban birth.[37] On June 13 he had written to his children to say that he was "in possession of full information," doubtless passed on by a German businessman acquaintance of his who traveled regularly between Paris and London. Marx advised them to move to the Spanish side of the Pyrenees, where the "climate" was better. In carefully chosen words, he wrote, "Paul's health will deteriorate and may even be in great danger if he hesitates any longer to follow the advice of medical men who know everything about his constitution and have besides consulted his doctors at Bordeaux."[38]

Yet Paul remained in Luchon six weeks after he received Marx's warning. Then, on July 26, Paul and Laura's six-month-old son died. "It was a truly sad visit," Jenny later wrote, "for Laura's youngest child was ill during the whole time, like the child who had died earlier, he was not strong, and died after dreadful pains."[39] The death may have prompted Paul's decision to leave France. But as late as August 1, he felt he was in no imminent danger; he refused Marx's "invitation" (probably to come to England), and added: "We do not know yet what we are going to do."[40] Apparently he shrugged off the judicial inquiries begun in Luchon and at his mother's home in Bordeaux, including the seizure of his correspondence.[41] The seized correspondence, however, revealed nothing. These events were discussed in the press at the time of Lafargue's election to the Chamber of Deputies in 1891, when newspapers hostile to his candidacy reported that he knew he was under surveillance and had fled to avoid arrest.

Then, warned by a friend in early August, he learned that his arrest was imminent. De Kératry, together with Desazaras and Attorney-General Delpech, went to Luchon to take charge of the investigation. In the morning of August 4, only a few hours before the arrival of the police, whose search of the cottage unearthed documents and letters concerning plans for IWMA recruitment in the Midi, Paul crossed the frontier. He followed a mule path from Luchon by way of Port de Portillon to Bosost, "an ancient and rather derelict town twenty-five miles away."[42] He was soon joined by his family and would remain in Spain, working to spread Marxist ideas, until the following summer.

Paul Lafargue in his late teens, posing in dress uniform (although he never actually performed military service).

Friedrich Engels, Karl Marx, and Marx's daughters (*left to right*) Laura, Eleanor, and Jenny in 1864.

Laura Marx around the time she first met Paul Lafargue, in 1866.

Paul Lafargue near the time of his marriage to
Laura in April 1868.

Paul Lafargue (detail).

Karl Marx in 1867, the year that *Capital* was published and Paul Lafargue became engaged to Laura.

Friedrich Engels in the 1860s, probably not long before he met Paul Lafargue.

Jules Guesde, who with Paul Lafargue founded
the French Workers Party.

Charles Longuet, who married Marx's
daughter Jenny.

Laura in the early 1880s, after the Lafargues' return to France.

10 Escape

I never met such an intelligent and well-read gathering of workers.
—Paul Lafargue

On August 6, 1871, Laura, her surviving son, and her two sisters went to visit Paul in Bosost. They had planned to spend only the day, but the three-year-old Schnappy fell seriously ill with dysentery. Having lost one child only a few days before, Laura insisted on staying another day or two with her husband, while Jenny and Eleanor returned to Luchon in the evening. On reaching the frontier, the two young women were delayed by French customs officials, and then, because they were Lafargue's sisters-in-law and Marx's daughters, their English passports were disregarded and they were arrested by the police under de Kératry's command.

The two sisters, whose rooms in Luchon had already been searched, were questioned separately by the authorities, who did their best to elicit damaging testimony from them. One sister was told that the other had already "confessed," a "dirty trick," fumed Eleanor, and they were told that the Lafargues too had been placed under arrest. The young women had been up since five that morning. They were interrogated until about two the next morning, and refused permission to write their parents. It is no wonder that repeated attempts to entrap them met with some, though not much, success. Sixteen-year-old Eleanor won the admiration of the public prosecutor when he learned that at the time of her arrest she had tried to swallow a note she believed might be seen as incriminating.[1]

They spent the night at the *gendarmerie,* "for [their] own safety," de Kératry told them. The Toulouse press described Jenny and Eleanor as "emissaries of the International on the French and Spanish frontiers," but assured the inhabitants of the Haute-Garonne Department that the prefect was taking energetic measures to ensure their safety. Things might have gone worse for the young women if a letter in Jenny's possession, from the murdered Communard Gustave Flourens, had been detected. Apparently left alone for an instant, she had slipped the letter into an old ledger lying about. "Possibly it is still there," commented Engels, relating the incident ten years later.[2] Eleanor believed that it was the government in Paris and not the local officials who wished to keep them under detention: "It appears that de Kératry after the first evening did everything he could to get us free, but Thiers wished us to be imprisoned." She did not think much of police procedures. "They looked in the mattresses for bombs, and thought that the lamp in which we had warmed the milk for the poor little baby who died, was full of *pétrole!* And all that because Lafargue is Mohr's [Marx's] son-in-law."

Two days later, on August 8, the officials changed tactics. They blandly informed Jenny and Eleanor that an error had been made. They were free to leave; Lafargue was innocent and free to return to France. The young women were even given a letter intercepted from Lafargue's banker in Bordeaux containing 2,000 francs, and Jenny was asked to write her brother-in-law accordingly. The sisters rightly reasoned that a trap was being set and that although released, they in fact remained prisoners because their passports had not been returned. The police held their passports for another ten days. Rather than use the proffered *laissez-passer* to cross into Spain and warn Paul herself, Jenny asked one of Paul's friends to send him the means to get to the interior of the country.

Unable to lure Lafargue back over the frontier, the Toulouse public prosecutor and some assistants crossed into Spain themselves on August 10 and got in touch with their Spanish counterparts, who were under orders from their government to apprehend all escaped Communards. Assured that Lafargue's arrest was imminent, Desazaras returned to Luchon. To his consternation he learned the next day that Paul had fled Bosost during the night, and he charged the local authorities with incompetence. Apparently their plan to require Lafargue to present himself at the police station on the grounds that all strangers in the area must submit their passports for validation had raised his suspicions, and he was then warned by someone of his forthcoming arrest. Guided by peasants who held no admiration for the authorities of any nationality, Paul was led over mountain paths, known, according to Jenny, "only to guides, goats, and English tourists," further into Spain.[3]

The frustrated police returned to the Lafargues' room at three in the morning, breaking in but discovering nothing and only disturbing

Laura and her sick child. They threatened to arrest her, but perhaps because of the hotel keeper's intervention—he shamed the police by saying that the Spanish government would never extradite her—chose not to. Desazaras questioned Laura on August 13, but learned nothing. He was convinced, however, that Lafargue was somewhere in Spain and probably close by, because his wife was still in Bosost and his two sisters-in-law, though by now granted permission to leave France, chose to remain in Luchon. Spanish police officials placed Laura under surveillance, but when they went to question her, they found that she had gone, having been warned of their impending visit.

These well-timed warnings gave rise to a legend of a network of conspirators directed by Lafargue. In his August 17 deposition to the court, the French public prosecutor made such a charge, exaggerating the few references to members of the International found in Lafargue's papers and adding that it was a well-planned operation to develop the IWMA in Spain. He went so far as to include Jenny and her sixteen-year-old sister in the conspiracy. A letter dated August 28, 1871, from the Gironde Prefecture to Paris reinforced these claims and hinted at Lafargue's involvement in a plot to link all the European sections of the International.[4]

A more realistic explanation was given by Jenny Marx. Because a Frenchman in Luchon informed some Spanish friends of the Lafargues at Bosost of the impending arrival of the two French officials, these friends, in turn, were able to warn Laura. French and Spanish republicans in the Pyrenees, Jenny went on, "form a league . . . against their respective governments. In our case, they acted as spies . . . untiring in their attempts to bring us news." Ultimately, de Kératry had to give orders that no one be allowed to cross over to Bosost without proper authorization.[5]

On August 20, the day their passports were returned, Jenny and Eleanor learned (probably from the French officials) that Paul had been seized by Spanish authorities in Graus, between the frontier and the nearest railroad, and had been led under escort to Huesca.[6] To relieve Laura's anxiety, Jenny and Eleanor made plans to go there. When they later heard he had been released, they instead began their return journey to London. At the time Spanish officials informed the French of the arrest, they had intended to extradite Paul, a promise confirmed by the Spanish minister of the interior. But apparently they changed their minds.

Paul's own account, in a letter to Marx of August 16 and in a newspaper article published a decade later, provides some missing details. He said that he was warned in Bosost by the very officer charged with arresting him, who told him that he would return to carry out his orders, giving Paul one and a half hours to leave and cross the frontier. Paul admitted he was "astounded": he didn't know the man "from Adam and Eve," but following his advice "to the letter" he left with a guide, "hoping to reach Madrid before the Spanish gendarmerie could carry out its orders." After three days' travel in the mountains, however, he was arrested in a "small village" and brought to the provincial capital at Huesca. As he described it to Marx, "Two civil guards accompanied me on foot with loaded rifles on their shoulders, while marching me on muleback . . . along the narrow trail . . . In the villages I passed through, I was taken for an important person, pockets full of money and protected by the police. I had prestige. It amused me. The police were happy with such a prisoner . . . Everything was primitive in the Spanish Pyrenees; wine and food were abundant, and at twenty-five sous a person, I had gargantuan meals."[7]

The governor of the province, "a real *caballero,*" received him cordially with "wine, cigars, and good political conversation." The French government, for which the governor showed no sympathy, had asked for Paul's extradition, accusing him of "murder, pillage, arson, and every other offense contrary to common law"; hence the necessity of the arrest. While waiting for the Spanish government to decide how to respond, Paul promised not to leave the city, and it was in Huesca that he read of the arrest of his sisters-in-law. "Ten days later," on August 21, he was released. When he wrote of this long afterward, Lafargue contrasted the humane behavior of the Spanish authorities with that of the French. The French ambassador had been unable to secure his extradition because the republicans in the Spanish government refused to grant it. Then, for a number of reasons, the demand was dropped by the French government: because none of the charges could be substantiated, because extradition applied only to ordinary and not to political crimes, and because, as a Cuban, Paul also carried a Spanish passport, an issue that later raised questions about his French nationality.[8]

During his stay in Huesca, and with the cooperation of some die-hard republicans, Lafargue tried to organize a section of the IWMA. He was convinced that the Madrid executive of a powerful secret society, El Tiro Nacional, which was capable of mobilizing the population of Huesca to "raise the town, to paralyze the action of the gendarmes, the troops, and the police," and which had earlier made good the escape of another political prisoner, had issued similar orders for his own escape "in case of need."[9] He then went to San Sebastián to join his wife and ailing son.[10]

San Sebastián is picturesquely situated in northwest Spain on the Bay of Biscay, but after having taken up residence at the Hôtel de France, Paul had little time for sight-seeing. Although the town was already a fashionable seaside resort, his own neighborhood was "fairly industrialized," containing linen and calico mills and lead and chalk factories. Here Paul groped for ways to organize a section of the International among these workers and among rail- and metalworkers in nearby Tolosa. He hoped to start a weekly newspaper there and suggested that Engels could contribute to it. With Laura's aid he translated a biographical account of Marx for a Spanish socialist newspaper; he asked for information on the German party to transmit to the Spanish press; and, aware of discord between the followers of the anarchist Bakunin and the handful of Marxists within the Spanish branch of the International, he informed London of whatever details he had. He also tried to arrange for a Spanish edition of Marx's *Capital*.[11]

He had also not neglected attempts to publish a French edition of *Capital*, and by the end of January—at the suggestion of a fellow lodger who, like the Lafargues had left France after the Commune— had found a "first-rate" publisher. Maurice Lachâtre was a graduate of France's military academy, Saint-Cyr, who had developed a taste for travel and politics. He had opened a Saint-Simonian school in France without government approval, for which he was indicted and imprisoned in 1843. He then operated a publishing house in Paris, which among other works produced the scandalous *Histoire des papes: crimes, meurtres, emprisonnements, parricides, adultères, incestes depuis Saint-Pierre jusqu'à Grégoire XVI; Mystères du peuple,* by Eugène Sue; and *Les Crimes Célèbres* of Alexandre Dumas. After the upheavals of 1848, he published a multivolume *Dictionnaire universel* with a progressivist anticlerical twist, which won him a second jail sentence. Lachâtre preferred exile to prison; he fled to Spain, returning to Paris in 1864 to publish several revolutionary newspapers, including Félix Pyat's *Combat,* during the Prussian siege. Sought by the government for fighting in the Commune, he again fled to Spain, to San Sebastián, where he met Lafargue.[12]

In December 1871, the two men negotiated a first French edition of *Capital*. Keller, who had undertaken the task of translation two years earlier, had taken an active part in the Commune, where he had been wounded and had then fled to Basel. In Switzerland he developed a taste for anarchism, and later was to publish literary works under a pseudonym. Now he was bound by other commitments and unable to complete the work. Another translator, Joseph Roy, was arranged for by Paul. Roy was first suggested to him by Ludwig Pfau, a journalist and poet, whom Lafargue had met in Paris in 1867.[13] Pfau had tried to translate *Capital* himself, but found he lacked the necessary competence and suggested that Paul get in touch with Roy, who three years earlier had translated two volumes of Ludwig Feuerbach's works.

The contact with Roy was cemented by Longuet and former Communard Edouard Vaillant, now in exile in London.[14] According to Vaillant, Roy had begun to translate *Capital* privately. Born in 1830, the son of a Gironde baker, Roy had served a two-month prison sentence for "subversive" journalism during the Empire. It was their common opposition to Napoleon III's government that brought Roy and Vaillant, then a science student, together. Acting on Lafargue's suggestion, Marx immediately sent the German edition to Roy. But he soon expressed reservations about Roy's work; he had, he said, expected better. Even after the work was under way, at the end of 1872, Marx made a final attempt to secure a different translator, Lafargue's old comrade-in-arms at Liège, Victor Jaclard, and his wife, Anna Corvin. Jaclard, too, had fought in the Commune. Apparently, however, he was found inadequate as a translator—or it may have been his Blanquism that was suspect—and Roy continued at his task. Not until 1875 did this French edition of *Capital*, published in fascicles costing two sous each in order to permit the widest possible distribution, appear. A one-volume edition was published in 1876. The French edition was the second foreign translation to appear. (The Russian, published in 1872, was the first.)[15]

If Lachâtre was "a little maniacal" as a book publisher, he was also a demanding businessman. On his own initiative, Lafargue offered to pay an unsolicited subsidy (of 2,000 francs) in order to become "a partner" and so let Marx have legal control over the translation.[16] Marx approved, stipulating that if costs were not recovered, he would pay the sum advanced by his son-in-law "with interest," adding that he preferred a "cheap popular edition."[17] The final contract was not signed until February 1872, but Lafargue was able to defer payment until May. Even though all the parties concerned pressed forward, the need to communicate by post between London, Paris, Madrid, San Sebastián, and Bordeaux (Roy's home) delayed negotiations considerably.

Both Marx and Engels had long followed events in Spain. Marx had studied the history of popular revolts in Spain in the first half of the nineteenth century, and when in 1854 a military rebellion had led to revolution he drew on his research for articles published in the *New York Daily Tribune*. Engels had interested himself in the country's military history, had contributed articles on aspects of the peninsular war of 1811–1813 to an American encyclopedia in 1858, and later published a study of "The Spanish Army" in *Putnam's Magazine*.[18] In August 1871 Engels became the International's corresponding secretary for Spain and Italy and hence placed himself in the forefront of the General Council's struggle against Bakuninist anarchism. He was convinced that the anarchists' "abstention" from politics was ruining chances to establish a workers' party in these countries.

But he was optimistic about ultimate Marxist success. His optimism issued from his belief that in Spain everything rotated around the Madrid section of the International and that some of its members were now receptive to Marxist ideas. Perhaps Lafargue could win the Madrid—and possibly even the Barcelona—Federal Councils away from anarchism and pave the way for a Marxist victory throughout the country. Paul was qualified for such a task: he was fluent in Spanish and possessed the experience gained as the IWMA's secretary for Spain in 1868–69. Hence the excessive emphasis placed by Engels on even the smallest change in attitude shown by Spanish socialist leaders.

None of this proves that Lafargue's coming to Spain was ordered by the General Council, as was later charged by anarchists. That he decided to stay on in Spain, however, can be attributed to the insistence of Marx and Engels. They had hoped that the Franco-Prussian War might open an era of insurrection, but thus far only two uprisings had taken place: the Paris Commune and a rebellion in Spain. On learning that Lafargue had visited Madrid and made contact with two leading members, Francisco Mora and José Mesa, perhaps even quickening their conversion to a Marxist stance, Marx and Engels were encouraged. Both men wrote Lafargue (the letter was Marx's, the postscript, Engels') in November, providing a summary of recent developments in the International, particularly of what they called a "Bakuninist conspiracy," a secret "International Alliance of Socialist Democracy" within the IWMA eager to seize control of the parent organization. They admitted their great unhappiness with the anarchist-controlled Madrid Federal Council, which was no longer replying to their communications, and Marx in particular wanted Lafargue to "act." He promised to send his son-in-law English and French copies of the revised and enlarged edition of the IWMA statutes and rules.

In his postscript, Engels anticipated a schism in Spanish socialist ranks. He had sent an ultimatum to the Madrid council, asking that it work to further the interests of the International, that is, to reflect the Marxism championed by the General Council in London. If it failed to reply, or sent an inadequate reply, "we shall immediately send you full powers for the whole of Spain. Meanwhile, like any other member, you have the right . . . to form new sections. It is important that, in the event of schisms, we should retain a foothold [*pied-à-terre*] in Spain . . . even if the entire present organization deserts with bag and baggage to the Bakunist [*sic*] camp; and we could rely on you alone in such circumstances. So do what you can to resume communications everywhere with the people who would be useful to us in that situation. Those Bakunists want to transform the Int[ernational] into an *abstentionist* organization, but they will not succeed. What happens to them as a result of this abstention from politics is that *they themselves* make politics the most important point."[19]

The anarchist-oriented leaders of the International in Spain believed that labor could best further its interests by rejecting all political activity, a position that Marx and Engels reasoned only worked to strengthen existing bourgeois parties. With the experiences of 1868–70 and 1871 behind him, Lafargue, too, appreciated the consequences of Bakuninist abstention: he was very much aware that with no political party representation, French workers had been crushed by both Empire and Republic. He readily agreed to lead the campaign in the Spanish press and in person against Bakuninism. And although his first reports to Engels have apparently not survived, in view of the elation they caused they must have been optimistic.

                              *   *   *

Lafargue had traveled alone to Madrid in September and met members of the Federal Council, in particular, Francisco Mora, a self-educated shoemaker and now the council's general secretary, and José Mesa, the printer who edited *La Emancipación*, the newspaper of the Madrid section and the first Spanish socialist paper. Originally Bakuninist, the newspaper under Mesa had recently taken an anti-Bakuninist line.[20] A republican, Mesa had lived in exile in France from 1866 until the Spanish Revolution of 1868. After the Paris Commune, he joined the International. The movement of Mesa and some of his friends to Marxism—a conversion to which Lafargue added the finishing touches—was already under way.[21] In a lengthy letter to Engels, Lafargue had given his impressions of the country and of the IWMA in Spain.[22] He commended the people he had met in the most favorable terms. "The men struck me as very superior; I may say that I never met such an intelligent and well-read gathering of workers; their knowledge was in sharp contrast with the ignorance of the Spanish bourgeoisie."

He made similar comments about the farmers he had encountered, whose anticlericalism he found striking. He then offered an analysis of sociological factors, speculating,—wholly inaccurately, as events were to prove—that Marxist propaganda could be easily carried out, for "there really is no peasantry in Spain, not in the proper sense of the word." In the parts of Spain he had traveled through, he had not seen isolated houses in the fields; agricultural workers lived in towns and villages like other workers and were in touch with them. Hence the ready participation of peasants in insurrections.

The country's "great evil," he believed, lay in its affinity for secret societies. He spoke of Bakunin's influence, and of the widespread if "erroneous" belief, held even by the leader of the bourgeois republican party, Francisco Pi y Margall, whom Lafargue had met, that Bakunin had introduced communism into Spain. Bakunin was responsible, he said, for turning people away from political action, which was especially harmful since secret societies were wholly political. Engels received Lafargue's news with "great pleasure," and although he "regretted the necessity which has made you go to Madrid, it is a real piece of luck that you should be there now."[23]

Aware of Mesa's conversion and impressed both by Lafargue's optimism and by the decision of the Madrid section to publicize in *La*

Emancipación the Marxist-oriented resolutions voted at the IWMA's London Conference the preceding September, Engels enthusiastically but prematurely told Paul in December, "we have every reason to be satisfied . . . in Spain the case is won," and "the victory gained in Spain greatly reduces the field of struggle."[24] Engels informed the General Council that the International in Spain conformed to Marxism.[25] Lafargue, caught up by the very enthusiasm he had inspired, modestly played down his own role, dismissing all doubts that "the Madrid Council has the best will towards you" and providing assurances that "it is not I who have pressed them in this direction, for I thought best to let them act as they see fit . . . Barcelona itself has come out against Bakuninism."[26]

The details of Lafargue's relocation to Madrid are not clear. We know that the family left San Sebastián in late December, arriving in the capital on the twenty-fourth. The day before his departure, he said simply that he was "obliged to leave." On December 26, two days after his arrival in Madrid, he declined to give details because Laura—in a letter which has not survived—had already done so.[27] Only later did Lafargue explain his September visit to Madrid: the governor of San Sebastián "ordered me to leave the province in six hours and go to Madrid under police surveillance."[28] He hinted that the police were looking for him and that he still might be forced to leave Spain. In London a distressed Jenny told a family friend that Laura was again left alone with a sick child in a strange country. "We couldn't imagine on what pretext Paul was again expelled. The IWMA, of which he established a section, was not attacked at this time by the Spanish government."[29] In Madrid he remained half hidden, under the rather transparent alias of Pablo Farga.

Lafargue continued to supply Engels with information on the International in Spain and on his attempts to publish a Spanish edition of Marx's *Poverty of Philosophy*. (Marx, who read these letters, showed impatience at the absence of any reference to his daughter and only surviving grandchild; the letter was "a mere blank in regard to that dear little sufferer.")[30] To combat abstentionism, Lafargue was convinced, one had to combat Proudhonism. He told Engels that "Proudhon is the great obstacle here. His book is considered the most socialist," and he asked that Marx write a new preface containing an analysis of conditions in Spain, for the Spanish edition of his attack on Proudhon.[31] Lafargue completed his translation in March, and published some chapters in *La Emancipación* under the title "Theory of the Class Struggle." To keep him at his task, Marx had the General Council the next spring send excerpts of its draft circular, *Les Préten-dues Scissions dans l'International* (Alleged Splits in the International), aimed at the dissidents who threatened "to destroy our organization" by rendering the General Council "meaningless and impotent."[32]

But by the end of December, Lafargue's optimism had somewhat faded. He was distressed that even the little news sent by the General Council in London was no longer being translated by the Madrid section. (Apparently the translator had relocated to be near his *novia* [sweetheart], "who clearly took precedence over international socialism.") Although he may have thought it unlikely that he would be able to remain in Madrid, Lafargue nonetheless began making himself at home. He disliked a bullfight he had seen, and pitied the poor horses; couldn't the International's secretary for Spain do something about that? If he were to put down roots in the city, he would teach English (here he asked Engels not to laugh) to Spaniards in the IWMA.[33] More important, he was satisfying himself that there was indeed a Bakuninist plot to undermine Marxist control of the International.[34] Lafargue did, in fact, stay on in Madrid to fight anarchism and promote Marxism. However, in order to understand the nature of the struggle that was to engulf him in Spain—and later in France—we must turn first to the most powerful spokesman of revolutionary anarchism.

11 The Anarchist Alternative

I want to abolish the state . . . which up to now has meant the enslavement, suppression, exploitation, and humiliation of mankind.

—Mikhail Bakunin

Mikhail Bakunin, the son of a Russian aristocratic landowner, was a man of enormous stature and strength. He possessed great charm and personal magnetism, producing an impression of overwhelming vitality and power. While his theories were confused and his writings invariably incomplete, he always seemed to be on the scene of revolution: Paris in 1848, Dresden in 1849, and has been referred to as "the Garibaldi of socialism."[1] He had fled after the Dresden uprising was quelled, was captured by the Prussians, and turned over by them to the Austrians, who yielded him to the Russians. He was twice sentenced to death by courts-martial. Imprisoned by the tsar's police, he spent six months with hands and feet chained to the walls of his cell, and then over seven years in solitary confinement. Banished to Siberia, he escaped, and after three years in London resumed revolutionary agitation in Italy and Switzerland, having missed the post-1848 reaction. His antistatist collectivism, or anarchism, was shaped by Italian Carbonarism, Proudhonian theory, the Slavophile cult of the peasant, and by his own predilection for secret revolutionary societies.

At the International's Basel Congress in 1869 he appeared as the "incarnation and symbol of revolution." His speech demanding the abolition of inheritance rights—and the reaction to it—brought him into conflict with Marx, who prepared the General Council's response that inheritance was the consequence and not the cause of the institution of property holding. The enthusiasm the speech evoked showed the extent of Bakunin's influence in the International. For Marx it was a dangerous influence, one that would "confuse and disorganize" the working-class struggle because Bakunin rejected all authority, all restrictions on individual liberty. Like Proudhon, who influenced him strongly, Bakunin saw in the omnipotence of the central state and its institutions an essential denial of freedom. Until this power was destroyed, there could be no hope for economic emancipation of the workers. Hence Bakunin called for an end of the state, church, banking system, universities, civil service, army, and police, all seen as "fortresses erected by the privileged against the proletariat." Also like Proudhon, Bakunin arrived at "a free grouping of individuals into communities, of communities into provinces, provinces into nations, and, lastly, nations into united states—first of Europe, then of the whole world."[2]

Bakunin called the collectivism defended by Marx "state communism." "I am not a communist," he explained, "because communism, by concentrating all property in the state, necessarily leads to the concentration of all the power of society in the state. I want to abolish the state . . . which up to now has meant the enslavement, suppression, exploitation and humiliation of mankind." He rejected all political action by workers that did not aim directly at social revolution, all participation in legislative elections, all campaigns for social reform, any attempt to win influence in the state; they were all "betrayals of the revolution," because they created the illusion among workers that revolution was not necessary for emancipation. He idealized the small peasant communities he had known in Russia, and put no faith in the great proletarian hordes of industrialized northern Europe; he (rightly) predicted their tendency toward embourgeoisement. His method, like Blanqui's, was the seizure of power by an uprising (there was no vote in Russia), led by the young educated classes and taking advantage of the revolutionary force he perceived in the peasantry. Hence unlike Proudhon, who repudiated the violent overthrow of social institutions, Bakunin's anarchism relied on force. And unlike Marxism, with its founders, texts, and ideology, anarchism had no fixed credo. It was, rather, "a great libidinal movement of humanity to shake off the repressive apparatus created by hierarchical society."[3]

We have seen that the Proudhonist tendency of federalism in the IWMA was yielding to the centralized communism of Marx, and that at the same Basel Congress a resolution approving land nationalization gave the final blow to Proudhonist domination. Even so, Bakunin's influence was spreading from French Switzerland and southern France to newly formed Italian and Spanish sections. Marx held the support of English trade union leaders, Germans, and German Switzerland, and he was determined not to lose the two principles that had triumphed in the IWMA—the need for political action and the common ownership of the means of production—especially after the defeats suffered by the International in the Franco-Prussian War and in the aftermath of the Paris Commune.

Bakuninist ideas were seen by Marx and Engels—and consequently by Lafargue—as "muddled utopian fantasy." Socialism for them was based on the facts of history: on the development of capitalism, of which socialism was the outcome, and which was producing an intellectually mature and organized working class led by a socialist party, the prerequisite of social revolution. Bakunin saw the conditions for social revolution in the semifeudal economies of Italy, Spain, and Russia, and particularly in the poverty and despair of their agricultural masses. It would be relatively easy, therefore, to unleash revolution; all that was necessary was an act of violence that would lead to the destruction of the state. For Marx, no sudden act, and certainly no peasants, would produce revolution; the political power of the state was the result of the capitalist social system and was used as an instrument of the propertied classes. Marx had written in the *Communist Manifesto* that "political power, properly so called, is merely the organized power of one class for oppressing another." He argued that the state would wither away only in a classless society, because then it would no longer be an instrument of class domination: class distinctions would end only with the substitution of socialism for capitalism. The state was thus a consequence, not a cause, of exploitation.

The conflict between Marxism and Bakuninism flared up not over questions of theory, however, but over the organization of the International. Marx saw it not as a secret insurrectionary society but as an extension of the labor movement in the different countries and as a democratic federation of workers affiliated in sections headed by an executive council. Bakunin accepted this centralization of authority at first, but came to oppose it when he decided to contest Marx's leadership and use the International to implement his own strategies. In June or July of 1868, after relocating to Switzerland the previous year, Bakunin joined the IWMA's Geneva section. No simple recruit, he was eager to play a leadership role equal to that of Marx. Accordingly he founded a new organization, the International Alliance of Socialist Democracy, which he intended to affiliate with the International but only as a distinct branch. Consisting of the most "devoted" revolutionaries—that is, the followers of Bakunin—and designed to provide a general staff for the larger organization, the Alliance formally applied to the General Council for affiliation in December 1868. In his letter to Marx, Bakunin described himself as Marx's disciple.[4]

Yet by its own "Rules" and as acknowledged by Bakunin in his correspondence with his lieutenants, the Alliance was designed as an International within the International, with its own sections, officers, and congresses.[5] Bakunin had found the International lacking the necessary revolutionary fervor and incapable of organizing and leading an insurrection; the Alliance would provide a revolutionary infrastructure, and hence needed to preserve secrecy. In marked contradiction to his theoretical advocacy of absolute liberty, its members would subordinate their personal freedom to a strict discipline, like that of the Jesuits, in which "the individual is lost in the collective will, in the life and activity of the organization." In addition, Bakunin saw Marx as a German and as a Jew, as an authoritarian "from top to toe," and the General Council as "a pan-Germanic agency," a German committee guided by a brain like Bismarck's.[6]

In reality, the International was never under Marx's control; he could not prevent British trade unionists from disaffiliating in 1865 or the collapse of the IWMA itself in 1872. Marx's leadership was exerted by balancing different elements: Proudhonists, trade unionists, followers of Mazzini, and his own supporters. He asked for an increase in the General Council's powers in 1871–72, but he did this not to turn the International into a "unified and disciplined party," as anarchists would charge, but to meet such emergencies as the repression of the Commune and the growth of national (separatist) tendencies, and particularly to cut short Bakunin's influence and his aim of transforming the General Council into an office of information and statistics. The IWMA operated in the open, while the Alliance was a conspiracy. The charges leveled at Marx derived from his style and the elements of infallibility in his theory.[7]

Marx and the General Council rejected the Alliance's bid for affiliation. They believed that a separate structure would mean the establishment of two rival groups that could not remain united and that Bakunin's real objective was control of the International. Bakunin thereupon agreed to dissolve the Alliance as an independent organization and to let its branches become sections of the International. On these terms the General Council accepted affiliation. For the followers of Bakunin, the Alliance had indeed disappeared: for the supporters of Marx, it continued to exist in secret. Both sides may be right. The difficulty might be overcome, as it was for Bakunin's biographer, by keeping in mind "the vague and unreal character of the associations created by Bakunin." Apparently just as the Alliance was to form an "inner circle" of the International, a still more select—and secret—directorate would compose an inner circle of the Alliance, and it was this, rather than the Alliance itself, that maintained a shadowy existence.[8] In any case, Bakunin was always able to gather disciples; he organized new sections and won control of existing ones in Italy, in French Switzerland, and in Spain. As portrayed by Alexander Herzen, Bakunin, the man of action, understood peasants—and brigands; he had a "direction"; he possessed an immediate appeal that Marx lacked, and hence it was he who was the creator of the peasant anarchism of southern and eastern Europe.[9]

Marx had written to Lafargue, as we have seen, as early as April 1870, describing these struggles with Bakunin and complaining that "this damned Muscovite" was still using his Alliance to convert "our Association" into an instrument of his own. Hence Lafargue was adequately warned of the threat Bakunin posed to the International, and when made aware of the preponderant role of Aliancistas in Spain, he prepared to work in Madrid to secure the evidence necessary to discredit Bakunin.[10]

The Franco-Prussian War and the indictment of the IWMA after the Commune compelled the General Council to postpone congresses in 1870 and 1871. Instead, Marx persuaded its members to hold a private conference in London in September 1871. Called to prepare the next congress, the conference was dominated by Marx: a majority of those attending were General Council members, and consequently the resolutions voted were Marxist, that is, anti-Bakuninist insofar as they called for political action and prohibited branches of the International from forming "separatist bodies."[11] A resolution affirming the need for workers to establish political parties of their own as a means of emancipation was fiercely opposed by Bakuninists, who preferred to "abstain" from political strife.

Six weeks later, those sections of the French Swiss Federation controlled by Bakunin (the Jura Federation, made up of anarchist building workers and watchmakers and run by James Guillaume, a schoolteacher who edited a radical newspaper), rejected the London conference as a properly constituted authority, denounced what they termed the authoritarianism of the General Council, and called their own congress at Sonvillier, in the Jura Mountains. They drafted a circular that Guillaume sent to sections of the IWMA in France, Belgium, Spain, and Italy, accusing Marx and the General Council of dictatorship and of transforming a "free association of autonomous sections into a hierarchical organization subject to authoritarian powers."[12] Anarchist members of the IWMA in these areas were particularly receptive and some of them even proposed the breakup of the International into its component parts.

A major battleground, it was becoming clear, would be Spain, which had been in a state of chronic uprising since the end of the 1860s. Revolution had come in September 1868, in the form of a popularly supported military revolt. Like that in France in 1789, it was a middle-class revolution, joined by peasants and workers. But—at the risk of oversimplification—once the monarch was ousted, revolutionary unity came to an end: the upper middle class sought a constitutional monarchy free of clerical and feudal ties; the middle class favored a republic; workers were disorganized and without leadership. Marx saw it as a bourgeois revolt, and the General Council's "Address to Spanish Workers," drafted when the revolution broke out, called on them to organize and join with other republicans to fight for a democratic republic. Otherwise the IWMA had shown little interest in economically retarded Spain, and Spain had not shown much interest in the International.

The country possessed a semifeudal economic structure, with industry, except in Catalonia, largely undeveloped. A tradition of *pronunciamientos* (insurrections) and conspiracies contributed to the country's political instability. Millions of poverty-stricken land-hungry peasants and even the relatively few urban workers preferred regional solutions to widespread misery. There was considerable unrest in the rural south and center, where the breaking up of common lands had encouraged peasant uprisings, five since 1840.[13] In the wake of dynastic and constitutional crises, military coups, workers' uprisings, and aristocratic counter-revolutions, the country seemed ripe for social revolution.[14]

An anarchist approach seemed therefore favored by conditions in Spain: the absence of any industrial proletariat in the capital (Madrid was an administrative center, with crafts and shops rather than industry); a peasantry that worked on large landed estates (with absentee landlords in Andalusia and elsewhere); and the vast majority of the population living in the villages *(pueblos)*, "human in scale, intimate in cohesion, with a comforting solidarity and spirit of mutual aid," rendering the remote centralized state less desirable and the Spaniard more susceptible to libertarian ideas and methods.[15]

Socialists were relatively few in Spain, and beyond a benevolent radicalism, the reforms proposed by the lower middle class possessed few social implications. There were two textile unions in Barcelona, the only ones of any importance, but they were weak, and strikes in factories, scarce. Because of their hunger and poverty, Spanish workers were "disinherited, illiterate, and violent."[16] What social views they held were Proudhonist and mutualist, thanks in part to the work of a young Catalan, Francisco Pi y Margall, a Madrid clerk and founder of the Federalist Party. Although a reformist, Pi y Margall rejected centralized authority.

Such was the working class found by Lafargue. Only a small minority was organized, and organized workers competed poorly with liberal-sponsored cooperatives. The failure of republicans to establish a republic in 1869 reinforced suspicion of all political movements and strengthened ideas of intransigence and revolution. The Spanish workers' movement was thus born in conditions less advanced than in England, France, or Germany.[17]

Although the need for a united workers' movement, enrolling industrial, rural, and artisanal elements, was clear, there was no IWMA presence in Spain until 1868 when Bakunin, who was sure that social revolution was about to break out, sent an address to Spanish workers on behalf of the Geneva section, urging them to follow political upheaval with economic change (contradicting the sequence derived from Marx's analysis). He followed this in late October by sending his agent, Giuseppi Fanelli, to organize Spanish sections of the International. The first, in Madrid and Barcelona, formed the basis for the Spanish Federation of the IWMA.[18]

Fanelli was a veteran of the 1858 uprising in Lombardy. He had given up a promising career as an architect and engineer for revolution, first under Garibaldi and then Mazzini. He had fought for a Roman republic in 1848 and for a Polish republic in 1863. Forty years old when he came to Spain, he could point to twenty-five years' experience as a conspirator. After the establishment of the newly founded Italian kingdom, he became a deputy in 1861. Thereafter he made use of the national railway pass given all deputies to spend literally years riding trains, living on a pension awarded because his health had been ruined as a political prisoner of the Bourbons, preaching social revolution to the peasants in the villages, and returning to sleep on the train at night.[19]

The heavily bearded Italian arrived in Barcelona one day in December 1868, after a train trip from Geneva. His mission was to take advantage of the revolutionary ferment that had recently driven Queen Isabella from the throne and allowed workers the right to form associations openly—and hence organize the Alliance and the International in Spain. By all counts he should have failed: his funds were inadequate (even his ticket to Spain had been purchased with borrowed money) and he could scarcely speak Spanish and lacked an interpreter. Yet when he began to speak he transformed his listeners; his gestures and tone "conveyed with electric effect the richness of his libertarian visions and the bitterness of his anger toward human suffering and exploitation."[20]

Used to the moderate expressions of Spanish liberals, the workers who heard him appeared stunned. Fanelli won them over, and by January 24, 1869, they had created a Madrid section of the IWMA. On that day Fanelli met with his Madrid converts for the last time; a small group of typesetters, housepainters, shoemakers, not industrial workers but artisans, numbering less than twenty. In addition to the shoemaker Mora there were Tomás González Morago, an engineer, and Anselmo Lorenzo, a typographer and later the most prominent figure in Catalan anarchism. Within weeks Fanelli had achieved the same results in Barcelona. There he met more sophisticated and skeptical types, but they were similarly persuaded. Included was Rafael Farga-Pellicier, a printer and journalist who helped found the International in Barcelona and edited its newspaper there, *Federación*.

Fanelli acknowledged that he had blended the International and the Alliance, with the result that the most active IWMA members in Spain, the Aliancistas, confounded the two organizations almost totally.[21] The Spanish Alliance of Social Democracy was anarchist in politics, collectivist in economics, atheist in religion. It stipulated that there would be no revolutionary activity that did not have as its object "the immediate and direct triumph of the workers' cause."[22] By early 1870, with recruitment high among Masons and mutual aid societies, the Madrid section of the IWMA could claim 2,000 members. There was even greater success in Barcelona, the real economic capital of the country. A textile center and seaport, it had a poverty-stricken industrial proletariat that not only was receptive to social change but was also imbued with an intense regional loyalty and a readiness to contest the centralization imposed by Madrid.

Early in 1869 Fanelli left Spain. Once back in Switzerland he learned that Bakunin had accepted the General Council's directive that the Alliance be dissolved as a separate organization and that its sections be enrolled as branches of the International. But by then Fanelli's work in Spain was completed.[23] He died of tuberculosis eight years later, at the age of forty-eight, and the scope of his achievement in Spain is only now beginning to be recognized.[24] In less than three months, speaking no Spanish and meeting no more than an occasional Spaniard who understood his French or Italian, he had, according to Gerald Brenan, "launched a movement that was to endure with wavelike advances and recessions for the next seventy years and to affect profoundly the destinies of Spain."[25] His converts numbered in the thousands.

Even an efficient police force would have found laws against the International difficult to enforce, and police inefficiency furthered its growth in Spain. The uncertainty of the political situation and the apparent inability of the Constitutional Cortes to find a ruler for the vacant throne also contributed to the development of an anarchist-dominated IWMA.[26] The first congress of the Spanish section of the International, which took place in June 1870 in Barcelona, was dominated by the Aliancistas. And the Alliance and the International were so closely linked for Fanelli's disciples that they initially adopted the Alliance's program for the Madrid and Barcelona sections.[27] Lafargue was to note that even those on the Spanish Federation's executive like Mora and Lorenzo, who did not identify themselves as Bakuninists, believed that the Alliance professed "an even more revolutionary socialism than did the International."[28]

The congress, although taking an antistatist stand organizationally, nevertheless made an attempt to work out a compromise and leave individual workers free to act "in the political arena." The structure proposed remained the framework used by the Spanish sections for several years; it provided for "organization by trade and by locality" and was consequently the model Aliancistas wished to have the entire IWMA adopt. The five members of the executive elected by the congress, Francisco and Angel Mora, Lorenzo, Morago, and Enrique Borrel, were all Madrid anarchists who had met Fanelli. In the first six months of its existence, the Spanish Federation issued much propaganda, published new periodicals, and recruited widely among workers and the urban poor.

In December 1870, with the support of liberals and the army, Amadeo of Savoy came from Italy to try to rule as constitutional monarch. Then the example of the Paris Commune struck fear in the governments of Europe. Early in 1871 great strikes broke out in Barcelona, and the government, sensitive to agitation, insecure, and determined to restore order, jailed many IWMA members. The Federal Council, prematurely as it turned out, fled to Lisbon, only to return in three months, but not before having helped to found a Portuguese branch.

But the council lost two members, Borrel and Francisco Mora, who stayed in Lisbon nursing the personal and ideological "grievances" that would account for the former's withdrawal from active politics and bring the latter to the Marxist camp. Most of the reorganizational work of the council, largely carried out by Angel Mora and the indefatigable Lorenzo at a full congress held in Valencia in early September 1871, resulted in the establishment of a more structured, more centralized (and in the view of many anarchists, more cumbersome) organization.[29]

This impulse for greater centralization came from new men on the Federal Council, particularly José Mesa and Pablo Iglesias, and from Francisco Mora, no longer committed to anarchism. Within a few months these *autoritarios,* as the anarchists called them, had established a stronghold within the Madrid branch of the Spanish International and were exchanging blows with Bakuninists. Thus conflict had begun before Lafargue's arrival on the scene; his appearance in Madrid in December brought matters to a head.

12 Our Man in Madrid

> [Lafargue] is one of our best men in Madrid.
> —Friedrich Engels

On January 7, 1872, using his Spanish alias and without introducing himself as Marx's representative, Lafargue attended his first meeting of the IWMA's Madrid section. Upon hearing a resolution that had first been proposed by the Jura Federation, he became aware, he said, of how widespread Bakuninist influence was in the very heart of the Spanish section, an awareness subsequently strengthened when Spanish IWMA journals reproduced circulars issued by Swiss anarchists. Lafargue did not participate in the discussion of the resolution that followed, and only *La Emancipación* issued a protest—which, however, was not allowed to be read at section meetings.[1]

The *Emancipación* editors, together with a handful of others, refused to obey Bakunin's orders as transmitted by Morago, who had become a leading Alliance spokesman. Lafargue built upon the editors' doubts either to win them over, as was the case with Mesa, who became Lafargue's chief ally on the Federal Council, or to nurture their newly found interest in Marxism, as was the case with Mora and Pablo Iglesias, a Galician typesetter.[2] The three had founded *La Emancipación* the previous June, and Lafargue arrived at a time when rivalry between Mora and Morago was moving from the personal level to the ideological.[3] Anarchists like Max Nettlau later argued, in an interpretation of events used by G. D. H. Cole, that before Lafargue's arrival the Spaniards had hardly been affected by the Marxist-Bakuninist debate "that was rending the International asunder" and that Lafargue was sent to Spain with a "definite mission" from Marx and Engels to fight the Alliance.[4] The historian of the Spanish Socialist Party, Juan José Morato, stated unequivocally that Lafargue, who began to write for *La Emancipación,* won the editors over to Marxism and as evidence cited Lorenzo's admission that he learned more Marxism from Lafargue in a few months than during his many years of study.[5] The newspaper, which took an ever stronger Marxist line, published texts from London, often written by Engels. According to anarchists it tried to "dazzle its readers with Marx's talent . . . and lead them by the nose to political action." What is not in doubt is that after Lafargue's arrival, *La Emancipación* presented itself as the sole spokesman in Spain of the IWMA or, more precisely, of its London-based executive.[6]

Lafargue had left France so quickly there had been no time to arrange his affairs. Accordingly, at the French Consulate in San Sebastián on November 14, 1871, he designated Jean Theodore Lamarque, a Bordeaux businessman, to handle matters relating to his property.[7] Laura and her son had remained in San Sebastián when Paul first went to Madrid, where he stayed with Mesa. Both during his earlier visit and after his relocation to the capital, Lafargue's articles for *La Emancipación* and his letters to London reveal a total immersion in IWMA affairs and in Spanish politics. His extensive correspondence with Engels, and to a lesser degree with Marx, contain lengthy reports on the Spanish situation for publication in other countries and requests for information about the International for Spanish consumption.[8]

Lafargue was showing an interest in and developing a familiarity with the business of newspaper publishing. He urged Engels to send a weekly bulletin to all IWMA branches. A newspaper was too expensive, but a newsletter could be produced cheaply using a lithographic press to reproduce communications in English, French, and Spanish for all International newspapers published by the various regional federations.[9]

Because Lamarque, complaining of police harassment in Bordeaux, informed Lafargue that he could no longer handle his affairs, Lafargue asked Engels for financial advice and listed his assets for the latter to manage: "some railroad shares, some American bonds, and the sum of about 6 or 7,000 francs." The rest, because they consisted of mortgages, "can stay in my notary's hands." The meticulous Engels wanted precise information. Paul must send details "by registered letter" for him "to examine," and he required definite instructions about the remittance of cash.[10] To ease the financial burden, Marx recommended Lafargue to Charles Dana, editor of the *New York Sun,* as the newspaper's correspondent in Spain, but anticipating that nothing would come of it, promised also to write on his son-in-law's behalf to the *New York Herald.*[11]

In Madrid, where his status was still tenuous, he lived in semi-obscurity under his assumed name.[12] As part of his efforts to establish a workers' party, Lafargue again visited Pi y Margall, who had translated Proudhon's *Du principe fédératif* and who was speaking out against the abuses of centralized power. Understandably, Pi y Margall offered no support and told him Spanish workers did not want a party of their own.[13] Lafargue's chief concern, however, was to gather sufficient evidence to demonstrate the existence of Alliance domination of the International in Spain, and in the weeks that followed he secured copies not only of the statutes of the Alliance but of instructions sent by Bakunin to his Spanish followers. Certain that an underground anarchist society with headquarters in Switzerland existed in the Spanish Federation, he traveled through Spain (together with Mora and Lorenzo), ostensibly recruiting new members but at the same time attempting to set up pockets of opposition to Bakuninism.[14]

Secrecy was necessary because on January 16, 1872, the liberal minister Praxédés Matéo Sagasta ordered the dissolution of the International in Spain, charging that it aimed at "destroying the family, destroying society, obliterating the country, [and] forcefully eliminating all elements of known civilization."[15] Although seemingly repressive, the decree was scarcely enforced. Nevertheless, the Federal Council insisted that the three men work under cover. Because the emissaries also intended to weaken Alliance influence, Lafargue approved.

His tactics were these: the London conference had prohibited secret organizations within the IWMA, and in relating the history of the Alliance in Spain and describing its subordinate relationship with Swiss anarchists he tried to show that the Alliance had never been dissolved, and that behind closed doors it still guided the Spanish International. Lafargue was correct,[16] and when he revealed the existence of the Alliance in *La Liberté*, the organ of the Belgian section of the International, he was denounced in the newspaper Morago began to publish in February 1872, *El Condenado*. Historians sympathetic to anarchism add that Lafargue also came to Madrid precisely to win the Spanish Federation over to Marxism and orient it toward political action. Hence Lafargue's support for an alliance with republicans and for the establishment of a workers' political party. While other Federation journals, like Barcelona's *La Federación*, urged abstention from politics, *La Emancipación*, on January 27, 1872, called for the establishment of a proletarian party to win political power. On March 3 the newspaper published Lafargue's letter asking republicans to respect the International's program.

Bakuninists answered charges of the Madrid groups with charges of their own. In the early spring of 1872, before the forthcoming Saragossa Congress and anticipating Marxist attacks, Spanish Bakuninists formally dissolved the Alliance in Spain. The Madrid Marxists maintained that it continued to exist in secret.[17] In March the dispute flared up when the *Emancipación* group, admittedly representing only itself, spoke in the name of the Federal Council to ask for a rapprochement with republicans. The editors had wanted to provoke republicans to take a harder line and, to encourage them, promised socialist support for a republic. The Madrid branch of the Federation, after much debate, disavowed the act and expelled the six editors.[18] The Saragossa Congress sought to heal the schism and settle differences between the followers of Marx and those of Bakunin by both rejecting the action of the six and annulling the expulsion.

The congress, the second held by the Spanish branch of the International, as a long-term objective wanted to consider a comprehensive reorganization plan that would clarify the relationship between the General Council in London and the Spanish Federal Council. Lorenzo and Lafargue were instructed by the Federal Council to prepare a draft report.[19] "Therefore it is we who will settle the question," a worried Lafargue wrote to Engels. "As this responsibility alarms me, I beg you and Marx yourselves to draft all the statutes which ought to govern the powers of the General Council . . . I beg you not to breathe a word of this to anyone—what an outcry there would be if the Bakunists got wind of it!"[20]

On Monday, April 8, although officially prohibited as an illegal gathering, the Saragossa Congress opened its doors to the forty to forty-five delegates who attended. All the workshops in the city had closed to permit workers who wished to do so to attend the opening session, and after this show of force, the authorities permitted the congress to continue in a smaller hall.[21] Lafargue, who represented a new section, Alcalá de Henares, and his friends demanded the expulsion of the Aliancista Morago, whom they described as "the moving spirit of the Alliance in Spain" and as having come early to Saragossa "to work up an atmosphere." Lafargue's own late—and unexpected—appearance upset Morago and the Bakuninists; they accused him first of spying for the police and then of carrying out a special mission for London.[22]

Lafargue made a mark at the outset. When the delegates had earlier learned of the governor's refusal to authorize the meeting, many had proposed abandoning the congress. Paul read Engels' letter to them: what they suffered in Spain was "child's play" and it would be unworthy to leave. A Lafargue-sponsored resolution "not to vacate the hall save at bayonet point" was approved. In preliminary skirmishing, Lafargue (together with Lorenzo) drafted a report on property ownership, defended strikes as necessary for the establishment of trade unions, and repudiated cooperatives should they create interests separate from those of the International.[23]

Then, in the long-anticipated confrontation, Bakuninists, led by Morago, asked for greater sectional autonomy in contrast to Lafargue's request for greater centralization. Lafargue helped defeat a proposed reorganizational scheme based on almost total autonomy, but he failed to get the Marxist-inspired statutes adopted instead.[24] The Congress accepted neither the Alliance's plan of reorganization nor Lafargue's; it kept the rules adopted at Valencia. And although delegates rejected Bakuninist demands for the immediate convocation of a general congress to discuss reorganization, they demonstrated their resolve to move in the direction of greater autonomy. They went on record as approving the resolution voted at a Belgian (Bakuninist) congress the previous December that defined the role of the London General Council as an "information center."[25] Lafargue, however, then secured the majority that voted to delay implementation. As a final attempt at conciliation, the *Emancipación* editors were taken back, the earlier decision to expel them annulled, and a public retraction of attacks on them in the Madrid Federation formally requested.[26]

Alliance strength was such that the Saragossa Congress elected a Bakuninist Federal Council. Of the former members not committed to anarchism, only Lorenzo and Mora were reelected, and the latter refused to serve. London had lost its influence in the new council, and after Saragossa the Madrid Marxists appeared as a simple faction trying valiantly to stem an anarchist tide.[27] Again, the chief explanations were the influence of Fanelli, who had made the Alliance and the International one and the same, and conditions in Spain that lent credibility to anarchist overtures. Yet the more independent Lorenzo was designated secretary-general. The delegates also voted to move the headquarters of the Federal Council from Madrid to Valencia, which for Lafargue made sense in as much as it was done "to avoid the endless quarrels that would certainly have broken out in M[adrid]—the source of what Marxist strength there was—or in Barcelona had the Council been transferred there."[28] But this too constituted a Marxist defeat.

In spite of these setbacks, Lafargue saw the Saragossa Congress as a success because of the "favorable impression the Congress created in Spain," because the Alliance, in its push for greater decentralization, had been forced to reveal itself, and because its reorganizational plan had failed to win a majority.[29] Engels initially accepted this overly optimistic analysis. He told the General Council that Bakunin's "small but active faction . . . ended in total defeat" and wrote Theodore Cuno, a German socialist soon to emigrate to the United States, that although anarchists controlled the International in Spain, "our people won a victory" and "the Alliance loses its influence with every day that passes." The congress, he explained, realized that the interests of the anarchists and the International were not the same, and it was "one of our own best men who settled the matter."[30] Following Lafargue's lead, Engels reasoned that after the expulsion of Mesa, Mora, and Iglesias, the new Federal Council had after all renominated Mesa and Lorenzo, and he found the Spanish police "frightfully stupid" for not deporting Lafargue.

Within a month Engels had revised his estimate. "The victory," he told Wilhelm Liebknecht, "was not as complete as [Lafargue] told us."[31] The delegates had endorsed a Bakuninist view of the General Council as a clearing house for information. Still, Lafargue continued to merit Engels' praise. After only three months in Spain he played a "predominant role" and had managed to win over a majority of the Spanish Federal Council with only Lorenzo remaining neutral. The problems at Saragossa were due to the "Spanish situation."[32]

Engels was right; Lafargue had not won over the delegates. Yet under his pseudonym he had published accounts of the Saragossa Congress in the April 28 and May 5 issues of *La Liberté,* the Belgian socialist newspaper for which he was a correspondent, denouncing the Alliance but giving more space to his own reorganization plans than to those of his opponents. His accounts aroused criticism, and on May 5 the newspaper printed several letters of protest. The May 10 issue of the *Bulletin* of the Jura Federation commented on the *Liberté* articles and denounced Lafargue's "intrigues" and aim, as Lafargue told Engels, of forcing Bakuninists "into the open."[33]

Had Lafargue minimized the defeat because of an inherent tendency toward optimism? There had been some successes in the Spanish Federal Council, which had temporarily taken a Marxist line. *La Emancipación* had published extracts of *The Poverty of Philosophy* and the *Communist Manifesto.* But the council was never very influential in Spain, where the sections were autonomous, and in the years to follow Marxism suffered a near total eclipse in that country.

Engels nevertheless held out hopes for the future and continued to appreciate Lafargue's work. Referring to a recent article he told Liebknecht that "Lafargue works enormously and very aptly in Spain . . . *La Emancipación* is now the best newspaper we have" and wrote Laura that her husband's articles, on subjects ranging from Chartism to German and French socialism, flowed as "a cool spring in the desert of abstract declamations which reigns among the Spaniards." Engels anticipated that Lafargue's information would destroy Bakunin. To Cuno he again referred to Lafargue as "our best man in Madrid."[34]

Within a few weeks the battle was on again. Although formally dissolved to lull suspicion, the Alliance was very much alive. On June 2 *Emancipación* editors, influenced by Lafargue, publicly condemned the Federal Council for supporting the secret society, and as proof of the council's duplicity pointed to a letter from Bakunin to Morago.[35] The Madrid Marxists charged the Aliancistas with still meeting secretly, and in a circular sent to every section of the Spanish Alliance asked them to dissolve their organization once and for all. In turn, a week later, the *autoritarios,* including Lafargue, were again expelled from the Madrid section of the Spanish International, and this time there seemed little likelihood that a future congress would reinstall them.[36]

At a meeting of the Madrid Federation's general assembly on June 9, the Marxists, particularly Mora and Hipólito Pauly, with support from Lorenzo, all former Aliancistas, tried to expose the tactics used by the secret society. Lafargue proposed the creation of an investigating committee and insisted that its findings be circulated, in order "to crush forever their secret intrigues that agitate and tear the International apart."[37] Gossip, slander, organized maneuvering, and bitter invective obscured basic political differences. Suspicious of Lorenzo's friendship with Lafargue, the Bakuninists on the Federal Council conspired against him, even opening his mail from Madrid. Infuriated, Lorenzo resigned from the council and left Valencia, but, committed to anarchism, later returned. In the June 12 issue of the Jura Federation *Bulletin,* Bakunin labeled Lafargue "the habitual weapon of

Mr. Marx" and "a mound of refuse."[38] Marxists, in turn, impugned Bakunin's character, publicly casting doubts on the sources of his income and trying to revive the rumor that he worked for the police.

On June 27 Lafargue published his pamphlet, *A las Internacionales de la región española* (To the Spanish Internationalists), a thirty-two-page attack against the Aliancistas.[39] He had previously sent a copy to Engels, telling him he intended to resign from the Madrid Federation on the grounds that it was controlled by the Alliance and then inform its members that, now able to speak freely, he would reveal all he knew of the conspiracy.[40]

Lafargue related the history of the assault against London's "absolutism" and the Madrid Marxists, and he blamed non-Spaniards for it. Obeying orders, Spanish Bakuninists in the IWMA had refused to debate and had renewed their attacks at the Saragossa Congress. In response to Morago's charge that he was a spy using a false name, Lafargue told how he had to flee France and take a new identity. He took credit for helping Huesca republicans found a section of the IWMA. Once in San Sebastián he had gotten in touch with Internationalists and helped to organize them. He was then ordered to leave, and went to Madrid under police surveillance; hence his need for a pseudonym.

Having become convinced at Saragossa that the Alliance was responsible for these attacks on Marx and on Marxist strategies, he "believed it [his] duty to denounce that secret society in the heart of the International." He cited Bakunin's letter to Morago and circulars from the Jura Federation to show how Bakuninists aimed to transform the IWMA's General Council in London into a statistical and correspondence office. If, as the Jura anarchists wanted, the "autonomy of the sections [were] absolute," it would render the International powerless. Lafargue opposed "doctrinaires who wish to change our association from a militant body solidly organized for struggle into a platonic gathering devising an ideal for future society."

He told how the Alliance was refused recognition by the General Council, whose "authoritarianism" it had condemned. Here Lafargue elaborated on an abbreviated history of the Alliance in Spain that he had earlier sent to Engels.[41] He defended London's emphasis on industrial legislation, specifically a reduction of working hours, calling a twelve-hour day stultifying and eight hours sufficient to produce the necessities of life. It was now that he began presenting ideas on the need for leisure time and on the workers' own ignorance of this need. The Madrid Federation was right to identify the Alliance as the source of all dissension between Madrid and the Spanish Federal Council, which under Bakuninist domination on the one hand preached anarchy and on the other wanted to control all the regional councils.

Lafargue sent a copy of his pamphlet to the editors of the Jura Federation *Bulletin*. In his covering letter he sarcastically condemned the authoritarianism of the Alliance and criticized the naïveté of its supporters like the Communard Benoît Malon.[42] All this material found its way into the pamphlet published later by Lafargue and Engels, with Marx's blessing, to expose and discredit Bakunin.[43] (After revealing evidence of the "Bakuninist conspiracy" in several countries—with the section on the Alliance in Spain based on the information gathered by Lafargue—the authors justified the Russian's expulsion from the International.) Lafargue indicated his willingness to make these disclosures at the IWMA's forthcoming Hague Congress as well as to provide additional information on anarchist activity in Portugal. "The International in Spain," he confidently informed Engels, "will never go over to the Bakuninists."[44]

On July 8, a month after their expulsion from the Madrid section, the Madrid Marxists established a "New" Madrid Federation, the first all-Marxist organization in Spain and the parent of the Spanish Socialist Party. In its struggle against anarchism, it included many of the future leaders of Spanish socialism: Mesa, Iglesias, who was to found the Socialist Party, Mora, the Party's historian and secretary, and Juan José Morato, Iglesias' biographer and another party historian.[45] The decision had been foreshadowed as early as June 15, when *La Emancipación* had added to its masthead the words: "Defensor de la Internacional." The newspaper and its editors were recognized at once by London as working "to keep Marxism alive in Spain." Later in July, Marx and Engels, acting for the General Council, wrote to the Spanish branches that the General Council now possessed proof of a secret society, the Alliance of Social Democracy, which pursued its own ends—of which most of the IWMA was ignorant—and its own strategy of spontaneous revolution rather than political work; this group was guilty of "treason against our association." Engels informed the Spanish Federal Council that the next general congress, to be held at The Hague in September, would investigate. To facilitate the investigation, he asked for a list of all Alliance members and their functions in the IWMA.[46]

The Marxists' expulsion isolated them and, on the eve of the congress in The Hague, rendered them even more powerless. The great majority in the established Madrid Federation, like all the Spanish regional federations, supported the Aliancistas.[47] The New Madrid Federation, despite Lafargue's efforts, was promoted by only a few small trade unions in the Madrid area, and *La Emancipación* wielded little influence.

Given this prevailing anarchist sentiment, why had Marxism temporarily won in the interior of Spain? For a twentieth-century observer of the Spanish political scene (the socialist foreign minister in the 1936 Popular Front government), the visits of neither Fanelli nor Lafargue explain as much as do historical differences. Castilians, said Julio Alvarez del Vayo, "more sober politically," traditionally held "a greater awareness of the existence of the state." Other Spaniards were less disciplined, "in constant conflict with authority and an enemy of the state because the State had been Castile."[48] Lafargue, too, recognized regional hostilities and the deep roots of anarchism in Spain. Complying with Engels' request to collect documentation for London's forthcoming attack on Bakunin, he pointed to Fanelli as having founded the International in Spain and as having preached abstention from politics, but recommended that Fanelli be "left out" of it, "for there are many people here who have a personal liking for him and these Spanish fellows set a great store by personal relationships." Lafargue also recognized the importance of perceived insults and slander in Spanish political quarrels.[49]

While identifying the Alliance as a conspiracy and asking that energetic action be taken, Lafargue also proposed that no Aliancista be given IWMA funds for travel to any congress, and that to implement this Engels should openly denounce the Aliancistas as conspirators.[50] Lafargue would go to The Hague and, with Laura, would leave for Lisbon in a few days. Engels was already notifying IWMA members that Lafargue had "accus[ed] Bakunin of having drawn up and sent to Spain secret instructions on how the International was to be controlled there," and that Bakunin was "enraged" at having been exposed.[51] On July 28, 1872, identifying Lafargue as his source of information, Engels proposed to a subcommittee of the General Council that the Spanish Federal Council be suspended. The Spanish council did not contest the decision, and the disappointed Lorenzo resigned as its secretary. He had been close to Lafargue, and was torn between London and Geneva in his sympathies. On the same day *La*

Emancipación published the names of important Aliancistas, an act that intensified hostility between Bakuninists and Marxists.

The expelled Marxists, whether acting maliciously and in reprisal for their prior expulsion,[52] according to the Bakuninists, or whether complying with Engels' request, exposed their former comrades to the police by making their identities known. Lafargue explained that the Madrid Marxists did so after learning of the intention of the Bakuninist-dominated Federal Council to send delegates to the forthcoming congress with funds supplied by the International. To prevent this, Mesa demanded the names of all Alliance members to send on to the General Council.[53] Thirty-six years later Lafargue again defended himself against charges that he had endangered Alliance members by revealing their identities. He also recollected that the Alliance had denounced him in *El Condenado* for having attended the Saragossa Congress, forcing him to remain underground.[54]

Thus when Lafargue left Spain at the end of July, he had failed in his "mission." The International in Spain was split into hostile factions: only a small minority supported London, while the majority embraced anarchism. The New Madrid Federation he had helped to found was isolated, with few ties to the working population, with no support from any sizable organization and, on the eve of the congress in The Hague, entirely without influence. The Cordoba Congress of the Spanish IWMA, meeting that December, favored such measures of social reform as the eight-hour day and free compulsory education. Still, it revealed its Bakuninist orientation by its refusal to permit its elected executive any authority over regional and local groups: it would be little more than a correspondence bureau.

The Marxists seceded from the main Spanish Federation the next month, and shortly afterward disappeared as an organized group. A short-lived Federal Republic collapsed in Spain within two years of its founding in June 1873, unable to withstand regional insurgencies that proclaimed full independence from any central government. By the following year two military uprisings had brought an end to the Republic and had reestablished a monarchy.

Lafargue's decision to leave Spain may also have been prompted by a personal tragedy—the death of his and Laura's only surviving child. His son's health had continued to deteriorate: "Schnaps is getting worse," Paul wrote his sister-in-law Jenny October 10, 1871. "We have put him back on milk. He only eats and drinks milk with bread," he later reported.[55] Paul and Laura were mystified: in mid-April Paul admitted he did not know what to do.[56] The boy had recovered somewhat in March, then declined until his death in July. Upon hearing the news, Jenny postponed her wedding to Charles Longuet.[57] Lafargue told Engels simply: "Our poor little Schnaps, after eleven months of physical and mental suffering, is dying of exhaustion."[58] Jenny Marx ascribed it to the boy's never having recovered from the cholera he had the previous August.[59] Lafargue was greatly affected by the loss of his third child; he became increasingly pessimistic about medicine and threw himself even more deeply into the work of the International.

Although the New Madrid Federation did not survive the collapse of the Republic and the proscription of working-class organizations, its former members kept in touch, meeting in Madrid cafés. Guided by Iglesias, the former *Emancipación* editor, they were resolved to found a party. Of cautious temperament, the product of a bitterly poor childhood, and in ill health throughout his life, Iglesias was devoted to his mother, living in her dingy apartment until her death and marrying only in middle age.[60] A patient man, capable of careful preparation, and using the Madrid typesetters' union as a base, in 1879 he formed the nucleus of the future Democratic Socialist Workers Party (PSOE), which was organized officially in 1888 and came to be identified with him. Although its members saw themselves as orthodox Marxists, the party followed a reformist road. Those in the party kept in mind the realities of Spanish life: an influential oligarchy, the timidity of the lower middle class, the retarded economy, and a weak proletariat. These all indicated a long struggle, which required work, organization, education, and liberal reforms that stressed the winning of basic political rights. Socialists seemed dull indeed in contrast to the anarchosyndicalists.[61]

What precisely had been Lafargue's "mission"? Engels had told him to keep a "*pied-à-terre*" in Spain, even if the International there deserted to Bakunin, and to collect evidence showing how the Alliance dominated the Spanish Federation for use at the IWMA's forthcoming Hague Congress.[62] Measured from this objective, Lafargue succeeded. The creation of the New Madrid Federation meant that the Marxist movement could send a delegate to The Hague, and it was this group that seven years later founded the Spanish Socialist

Party. In Morato's account, Lafargue "introduced Marxism into Spain. [He] exercised a decisive influence . . . the first stage of the Spanish socialist movement. He had a great impact on Iglesias; what was obscure and incapable of clarification by Lorenzo and Mora was illuminated by Lafargue."[63] Lafargue, was "in reality the founder of the socialist party . . . because the initial effort came from him."[64] Engels too acknowledged the importance of Lafargue's role in Spain: "[His] presence in Madrid at the decisive moment was of incalculable value to us and to the whole Assoc[iation] . . . As for the articles in *La Em[ancipación]* . . . for the first time the Spaniards were treated to true science."[65]

From an opposite point of view, Lafargue's arch-critic, Max Nettlau, agreed on the importance of his role. "Perhaps never was such a flourishing movement invaded by an individual who assigned himself the task of destroying the revolutionary elements." The "authoritarians" tried to impose their system on all of the International, and this provoked surprise in Spain. The situation there was not understood in London. Mesa and Lafargue, to win control of the International in Spain, sowed discord, tried "to divide and destroy it," and turn it from its chosen task.[66] Anarchist historians rightly describe the IWMA in Spain as anarchist from the outset, as formulated by Bakunin, and with the exception of the "Lafargue episode" as remaining anarchist. Nettlau's relevant chapters, both in his biography of Bakunin and in his study of the International and the Alliance in Spain, are entitled "The Intrigues of Lafargue in the Heart of the International," and the heading anticipates the interpretation that follows. In his attempt to create a workers' party, to establish electoral processes and reverse the anarchist tide, Lafargue was determined "to break the solidarity of the [Spanish] movement with the libertarians of other countries and to pry into the secrets of this movement which had given him hospitality."[67]

Yet Nettlau contrarily provides as well the testimony of Anselmo Lorenzo, who denied having fallen for "Marxist intrigue": "with respect to Lafargue I tell you that this man worked with great discretion and no doubt developed judgment, especially on individuals, and treated them as individuals. With me he behaved correctly."[68] In any event, Marx was convinced that his suspicions of Bakunin were well grounded and that with Lafargue's evidence he could prove his case at The Hague. He was able to do so, but the price paid would be the destruction of the International.

13 The Hague

If the General Council did not presently exist, it would be necessary to invent it.

—Paul Lafargue

On July 30, 1872, Paul and Laura set out on the journey to Portugal, one he described as "a trifle long, a trifle hot, and a trifle arduous: thirty hours on the train in heat that would have hatched out lice on a pane of glass." Fortunately an "eighteen-pound watermelon" slaked their thirst while crossing the "desert of La Mancha." They revived at once in Lisbon, thanks to cooler weather and a city that was "the most picturesque we have ever visited." Lafargue at once got in touch with the local branch of the International: he found its members Aliancistas, who "however have seen through the Jura intrigue." For the forthcoming congress, Paul urged them to endorse the organizational plan published in *La Emancipación* and to demand that the Alliance be dissolved. Because they were apparently unable to send one of their own members to The Hague, he suggested that they agree to have Engels represent them but ultimately was to do so himself.[1] At the end of August the couple embarked for Holland.

In The Hague they complained of expensive lodgings and poor food, but finally found a furnished room a long way from the center, and because of this experience volunteered their services in helping to find housing for other delegates. The Dutch language was "difficult," but French was widely spoken, and if Lafargue was unable to make himself understood, Laura, "flaunting her German" and already making progress in Dutch, came to the rescue.[2]

On September 1, Marx, his wife, their daughter Eleanor, and Engels arrived. It was the first and only time Marx attended a general congress of the IWMA. Longuet, too, was there.[3] The next day, a Monday, the Sixth Congress of the International opened. Sixty-five delegates represented branches in fifteen countries, but Bakunin did not attend, having no doubt estimated that he controlled only a minority of them. The anarchists were led by Guillaume, who spoke for the Jura Federation. As early as May 17 Lafargue had proposed that the next congress be held in England, because "the Bakuninists would be done for there before they ever appeared," and his suggestion may have played a part in designating the Dutch location.[4] Thanks to the size of the French and German delegations alone, the Marxists were assured of a majority, but to strengthen it Engels had paid the fares of "five obedient delegates" from London and had also invited five sympathetic Spaniards, while rejecting five of their anarchist countrymen.[5] It was clear that the bitter controversy between Marx and Bakunin, in a state of sporadic eruption during the past three years, was somehow going to be resolved in Marx's favor.

In their spring attack on the Bakuninists, *Les Prétendues Scissions de l'International,* Marx and Engels defended the authority of the General Council and insisted that Bakunin, in recognizing the autonomy of the sections, wanted to fragment the IWMA. It was the first time they used the term "anarchist."[6] On June 15 the Jura Federation published a reply in its *Bulletin,* a series of attacks by Bakunin and several associates on Marx and Engels, and a rebuttal of Lafargue's charges, calling him "the apostle of the Marxist law" and marking the first time the term "Marxist" was used, at least in a pejorative sense.[7] These exchanges accounted for the heated atmosphere in which the congress opened.

The Dutch looked on in some bewilderment at this gathering of "foreign-looking bearded men" consuming great quantities of "coffee, beer, and sandwiches" and meeting in a building that was a cross between a summer theater and a hayloft, with the remains of scenery still hanging from the low-beamed ceiling and with tables arranged in horseshoe fashion on the floor below.[8] Theodore Cuno, who represented a German section, described the visiting dignitaries: "[Engels] was a tall bony man with sharp cut features, long sandy whiskers [and] a ruddy complexion," who looked over the crowd and said, "everything goes well; we have a big majority."[9] An Amsterdam newspaperman was also impressed by Engels: "His manner of speaking is quick, determined, and he convinces the observer the man knows exactly what he wants . . . In conversation with him one learns something new with every sentence he utters." Marx, sitting behind Engels, had a "big woolly head, dark complexion, grey hair and beard, and wore a black broadcloth suit. He put a monocle in his right eye when he wanted to look at anyone intently. Far from appearing authoritarian, he believed that no one, because of an accident of birth, should exercise authority, and he never used titles such as Herr, Mr, Monsieur or Signor."

The same newspaper described Lafargue, sitting next to Engels, as a dark Creole and as possessing "a respectable, even noble," appearance, although laughing rather more often than necessary. His was a "good-natured face tanned by the Andalusian sun," and one "would not guess he defends those pernicious predatory theories which he dares to advance." His "grinning countenance" and "jaunty careless- ness . . . makes one doubt his seriousness." Laura was found "a pleas- ing presence." Ludwig Kugelmann, whose "loan" to Marx had helped to finance Laura's wedding, was also present at the congress as a member of the German delegation. He described her to his family as "a beautiful, elegant, and amiable woman . . . slim and young-looking [who] took a passionate interest in Party life and seemed to have given herself up to it entirely."[10]

The Marxist majority nodded with approval upon hearing prelim- inary speeches focus on the need for a central authority. The Paris Commune had gone down to defeat because it was isolated, and if other European capitals had risen in support the outcome might have differed; hence the necessity of relying on political strategies. Anar- chists rejected this analysis, and Guillaume neatly summed up the two opposed viewpoints: "The majority wants to conquer political power in the State; the minority wants the opposite, the destruction of po- litical power."[11]

Lafargue represented the New Madrid Federation as well as the IWMA branch in Lisbon. Not recognized by the Bakuninist-dominated Spanish Federal Council, the Madrid Marxists had applied directly to the London General Council and had been duly recognized. In his July 12 letter to Engels, in which he had announced the formation of the new federation, Lafargue asked whether it "would be an advantage if I went to the Congress as a delegate," and the reply was no doubt positive.[12] Bakuninists, on procedural grounds, violently opposed his right to represent Madrid: those who had been expelled belonged to a miscellaneous section, itself not recognized by the parent federation.

For the English journalist, Maltman Berry, the debate over whether to accredit Lafargue was the "battle of the day."[13] The Bakuninists had wanted everyone's credentials examined by the entire congress; Lafargue said that only contested credentials should be examined, and his motion carried. After Vaillant's credentials were approved (he had been denounced by Bakuninists as "royalist" and "bourgeois"), they tried to discredit Lafargue's. Morago attacked him violently, denying that the New Madrid Federation had been legally constituted. "As Lafargue unfolded his evidence," recalled Berry, "the Bakuninists were rushing wildly about, shrieking and howling interruptions."[14] Similarly relying on violations in procedure, Lafargue said that the Madrid group had been expelled by only fifteen voting members of the Spanish Federal Council and without the required notice. Continually interrupted, he in turn denounced the Bakuninists for treachery.

Engels spoke in support, stating flatly that the new section had been accepted by the London Council in an attempt to save the International in Spain. He then posed the question: was the IWMA to be dominated or disorganized by an irresponsible secret body? This could not be allowed. More debate followed, but because of the voting procedure, which allowed one vote for each delegate present regardless of the number of mandates an individual carried, Lafargue's credentials were approved by the Marxist majority.

The question of the organization of the International, specifically a resolution to approve the London Conference's collectivist declaration, topped the agenda. Lafargue passionately defended the General Council's authority. "The full liberty of the working class," he said, "requires that the means of production—today found in the hands of individuals—become common property . . . To carry out all these goals, the working class must increase its political power and be independent of [existing] political parties . . . If the General Council did not presently exist, it would be necessary to invent it." Without it the federal councils would lack direction and the International would be composed of a "disconnected multitude . . . without any power." He dismissed critics of the General Council as authoritarians in their own right.[15]

Guillaume defended the right of "free" federations to reject an "authoritarian head," and asked the delegates to limit the role of the General Council to that of a secretariat. However, his claim that the International had not organized any strikes requiring central direction was denied by spokesmen for the Paris bronze workers and the Newcastle engineers, who acknowledged that they had indeed asked for help. Bakuninists were on more solid ground when they pointed out that Lafargue represented only 9 or 10 separatists in Spain whereas they spoke for more than 17,000 workers. However, the Marxist-dominated congress approved the London Conference's call for political action by a 39–5 vote.[16]

On the last day, September 6, the Alliance's fate was debated. In testimony reinforced by references to a detailed notebook, Lafargue related the history of the organization, beginning with the recruitment of the first members and concluding with the struggle waged against the General Council at the Saragossa Congress. He showed Bakunin as having drafted secret instructions in his own hand for his followers on the Spanish Council in order "to seize leadership."[17] The delegates ratified the vote of an investigating committee that had earlier voted unanimously to oust the Alliance from the IWMA. After hearing Marx raise charges of personal fraud committed by Bakunin (unjustifiably, as later research was to reveal), the congress voted to expel Bakunin and Guillaume and ordered the publication of a full account of the Alliance's activities.[18]

Lafargue voted to expel the two anarchist chiefs, but abstained, contrary to Marx and Engels, on the vote to expel a third associate, Adhémar Schwitzguebel, a Swiss disciple of Bakunin and one of the leaders of the Jura Federation, maintaining that Schwitzguebel had been "led astray" but perhaps had been merely eager to refute charges he was "Marx's puppet." Then, to widespread consternation, the delegates approved Marx's proposal to move the headquarters of the International to New York, conceivably preferring its disappearance to its fall into anarchist hands. Lafargue lamely defended the choice as "the only place, besides London, which offers the necessary guarantees for the safety of the archives and for the international character of the Council's composition."[19] Finally, in his capacity as representative of the Lisbon and Madrid sections, he proposed that the new General Council establish an international trade union federation and decide on conditions for membership, and his resolution to that effect was adopted unanimously.[20]

When the congress was over and before returning to London, Marx took his family to the nearby seaside resort of Scheveningen, where he invited several friends for dinner and a concert on the terrace of the Grand Hotel.[21] One guest was Theodore Cuno, the young German engineer who was soon to emigrate to America, where he was to help found the Knights of Labor. He later recalled that in making introductions Marx said jokingly: "Cuno, I am told that you are going to

America, so you may do there what one of my daughters has done toward solving the color question, by marrying a nigger, for Lafargue is of colored descent."[22] As always, Marx seemed to remain aware of, and perhaps somewhat self-conscious about, his son-in-law's heritage, but to regard it as a curiosity or conversation piece rather than as a barrier or an object of prejudice.

Two weeks later, the Bakuninists met for a congress of their own at Saint Imier in the Swiss Jura. French-speaking Switzerland, Spain, and Italy constituted the strength of the Bakuninist camp, for Belgium was divided and France was engulfed by the repression that had followed the Paris Commune. Among the French in Switzerland was a young radical journalist with anarchist connections, Jules Guesde. Guesde, too, had rejected the "authoritarianism" of the General Council and had denounced its "dictatorship." Together with Guillaume he later attended the Jura Federation's Sonvillier Congress in November, and as secretary of that congress drafted a manifesto condemning the General Council.[23] Bakunin's resolution to regroup was carried unanimously, and a purely Bakuninist International, with its center in the Jura watchmakers and most of its members in Mediterranean countries, confronted the Marxist. It was precisely this awareness of anarchist strength that had prompted Marx to move IWMA headquarters to New York.

Morago and Pellicier represented Spain at Saint Imier, and they called for the Spanish congress to be held at Cordoba in December 1872, which ratified the decisions taken at Saint Imier.[24] Following the road taken in Barcelona and confirmed at Valencia in 1871, the Cordoba decision placed Spain firmly in the Bakuninist camp for the next half century. The "great sultan from London," as one of the anarchist delegates said, was rejected; the victory of the authoritarians, organized by Lafargue—"a refugee from the Commune," according to a historian of Spanish labor—represented only "an insignificant minority."[25] The structure of Spanish socialism was thoroughly decentralized: the sections remained sovereign, and the central Federal Council became the "bureau of correspondence and statistics" they had tried to make of the London Council. And this may have suited conditions in Spain, where the first task was to make half-starved uneducated field laborers and factory workers conscious of their grievances and power. Conceivably, the orthodox (Marxist) approach, relying on political parties or, as was the case in Britain, on well-structured trade unions, would necessarily have failed.[26]

The tactic pursued in the years to come was that of gathering groups of poor workers, regardless of their opinions, for mutual protection against their employers. There were occasional strikes, and if they succeeded membership soared. During periods of reaction membership shrank to a kernel of militants. Momentarily bolstered by the decentralized Republic, anarchists survived the repression launched by the restored monarchy by operating in stealth. They retained a mass following by combining their doctrines with those of revolutionary syndicalism.[27]

Mesa had wanted Lafargue "to make the sacrifice" of returning to Spain "to help us reorganize the Spanish Federation and to put *La Emancipación,* dying, back on its feet again," and he asked Engels to persuade Lafargue to do this. If Lafargue did return, however, he did not stay long.[28] A letter from Eleanor to her sister Jenny dated November 7, 1872, reveals that Paul and Laura were then in London. Eleanor's letter complains of the Lafargues' cold treatment of the former Communard, Prosper Olivier Lissagaray, whom she was engaged to marry.[29]

Lissagaray had escaped to London, where he was helping to rehabilitate other French exiles and preparing a book on the history of the Commune. Because he was twice Eleanor's age, among other reasons, Marx was upset by the prospect of this new son-in-law and refused to recognize the engagement. His wife, too, believed that two Frenchmen in the family were enough (Jenny was by now married to Charles Longuet): however charming, "they were not without their weaknesses." Although he admired Lissagaray's history, Marx also found his daughter's suitor irresponsible, flamboyant, and untrustworthy. He feared that Eleanor would have to make the same sacrifices her mother had. There were also doctrinal differences: Lissagaray was a frequent visitor to the Marx home, and though his utopianism had cooled, he was unable to accept the need for a disciplined party.[30] Marx had shown the same concerns with Lafargue seven years earlier, but in 1866 Lafargue had prospects and the promise of financial support, whereas Lissagaray had none. Echoing his father-in-law's sentiments, but to Eleanor's confusion and distress, Lafargue refused even to shake hands with Lissagaray.[31] He came to detest him and the "individualism" he preferred. Lafargue may also have harbored a certain resentment toward authentic Communards because he was not one of them. By the next year the eighteen-year-old Eleanor was forbidden to see her suitor, and distressed by her family's disapproval, she began to suffer from nervous depression.[32] She resolved to become financially independent, and soon left the family household.

There is some speculation, based on Paris police reports, that Lafargue was back in Lisbon between January and May 1873, where he found a less than enthusiastic reception. The police lost sight of him, and certainly not much is known of his activities during this time. He could not play a useful role in Spain because he was discredited in "anti-authoritarian" socialist circles.[33] With Bakuninists firmly in control of the Spanish IWMA, there was little more he could do in that country. There is no real evidence to corroborate a return to either Portugal or Spain, however, and it is more likely that the Lafargues, who had returned to England the previous fall, remained there. Now thirty-one years old, Paul had spent seven years, under the tutelage of Marx and Engels, working for the First International. The experience gained would be used in efforts to combat anarchism and promote collectivism within the ranks of French labor, but before that happened politics would be set aside in efforts to earn a living as an exile.

14   The London Exile

> I prefer to keep my distance from the refugees. Placed in an artificial setting, they can only exhaust themselves in petty and personal quarrels.
>
> —Paul Lafargue

Outlawed in France, no longer useful in Spain, Lafargue began living as an exile in London. During the next ten years he reached near-fluency in speaking and writing English, though he was a poor linguist, and he met some of Europe's future leading socialists, people like the young Karl Kautsky, later the Second International's leading theoretician, and Eduard Bernstein, the future German Social Democratic leader, who were then making pilgrimages to Marx and Engels.[1] Even so, it was a painful and distressing life, because of material difficulties experienced in the wake of his refusal to practice medicine and because various business ventures, particularly electroplate engraving, proved unsuccessful. The couple now began to make repeated appeals to Engels for financial aid.

Though Laura's husband proved as incapable as her father of earning a living, she must have relished living in the same city as her family and friends. By the end of 1874, when the Lafargues relocated to Hampstead, 27 South Hill Park, she lived not far from her parents. Laura had recovered her health and looked so much younger than her age that after nine years of marriage she was often addressed as "Miss." Her mother commented on her "happier state of mind."[2] The Longuets, also unable to return to France, lived nearby at 58 Fleet Road.[3] For Marx and his wife, who now had all of their family with them, it was a time of great satisfaction.

Lafargue had never been strongly disposed toward practicing medicine. After his marriage, once settled in France, he admitted that he considered the profession artificial and lacking justification. Writing to his sister-in-law Jenny in 1870, he said with sarcasm: "Dr. Lafargue has been very happy to see you put all his colleagues to the door like donkeys. The happy result you got by your own medication should make you persevere along this track."[4]

Qualified to practice in England, he refused to do so, explaining that he "did not believe in medicine."[5] The deaths of his children confirmed his belief that good hygiene was more important than medical expertise and, as we have seen, doubtless made him question his own abilities as well.[6] When their last-born had taken seriously ill, her sister Jenny had begged Laura to "listen to the advice of *maman* in this matter" and take a wet nurse.[7] Laura blamed the lack of good medical care for the death of Schnaps. Urging Engels to get the best possible advice for himself in 1883, she added: "If immediate steps had been taken, and *could* have been taken in the case of my boy Etienne [Schnaps], he would be alive now and fourteen years old."[8]

In 1882, replying to a critic who accused him of having made "a fortune" in London by exploiting young workers, Lafargue emphatically denied the charge: "The truth is, that instead of working at my trade of doctor, which I did not practice because I do not believe in medicine, I earned my living in the manual craft of photolithography and from engraving by the Gillot process; and instead of selling my pen in radical journals, I did not earn a red *liard* [quarter of a sou] for my writings, although I wrote badly for the International and workers' party in England, Spain, and France."[9]

Together with Eugène Dupont, the former General Council member, he instead opened an engraving business. Neither this partnership nor a subsequent one with a different associate survived.[10] One partnership was dissolved because Lafargue apparently failed to pay his associate for his time.[11] As a commercial photoengraver, Lafargue used a new process invented by the Frenchman Firman Gillot, and that he had some artistic talent was shown in the full-page political drawings he sent to the second series of *L'Egalité* beginning in January 1880.[12] Working at one point out of his kitchen, Lafargue made plates for printing and design, even inventing an electroplating technique he believed was a real contribution to the industry.[13] He put in long hours, was always on the verge of securing a profitable order, but never seemed to get one. His mother-in-law acknowledged that he worked hard, but she found his perpetually buoyant nature irritating. He was forever citing the praise evoked by the quality of his work and pointing to promises of future orders. For him, "the sky was always full of violins," and she wished he had stuck to medicine.[14]

Lafargue was unsuccessful in the lithography business—among

other reasons, because despite Engels' urging he did not press his clients for payment: he found it easier to have Engels cover his debts.[15] Laura was obliged to give private language lessons. Other, more speculative, ventures failed as well. Lafargue had invested some funds gotten from his parents in English stocks. There was a plan to publish guidebooks, which Engels strongly opposed as financially unsound.[16] Engels was critical of Paul's business sense, and on one occasion told him, "One might think you were dying to be robbed: how can I advise you on business when you give me all the information afterwards?"[17] According to Engels, the particular agreement Paul was prepared to sign required him to give up his rights and so jeopardized his investment.

Hence Lafargue's letters to Engels begin twenty years of pleas for financial help. After supporting Marx for years, Engels supported his daughters and their husbands. Almost every appeal made by the Lafargues was answered. The editors of the Engels-Lafargue correspondence included two dozen requests for the period 1874–1880, and omitted fifteen others because they lacked biographical interest. A letter written December 28, 1874, was typical: "I have done my best to wait until January 15th without pestering you with requests for money, but I cannot succeed in getting paid a penny, everyone drives me from pillar to post; so forgive me if I ask you to send me £30, of which I have the utmost need."[18]

And the following August, when evicted from the house in which he and Laura were living, Lafargue planned to move to another he had rented, where he would combine his workshop and living quarters:

> When I asked you the other day for £20 to cover my removal, I expected to move my workshop only at the end of this week. But since then I have seen the man in charge of the repairs in my new house and he promised me to finish everything by this Saturday or next Monday; the landlord of the Hampstead house is anxious for me to leave as soon as possible and I hope he will let me off one month's rent if I leave in the course of next week; as Laura has no objections and would even prefer to move during the fine weather, I think I ought not to miss the opportunity. I shall need another £50 to pay my landlord, whom on the 24th of next month I shall owe three quarters' rent, rates, gas, water, etc., and for the removal and various alterations in my new house; for I shall use the downstairs kitchen as a workshop and shall be obliged to buy a gas stove to do the cooking upstairs.[19]

The moving expenses proved greater than figured, and an additional £30 was required.[20]

The new house was located at 225 Camden Road, in north London. In 1877 the Lafargues moved to the address they would retain until their return to France, at 37 Tremlett Grove, off Junction Road in Islington.[21] The 1881 census return shows the Lafargues as the only residents. Paul gave his age as thirty-nine, Laura's as thirty-five, and his occupation as "nonpracticing surgeon."[22]

At the end of 1874, Lafargue planned to sell the house in New Orleans left to him by his father.[23] The rest of his inheritance had long since disappeared: only the house, valued at $3,500 and which had been renting for $600 a year, remained. Earlier Paul had wanted to use it as collateral for Engels' "loans," but Engels had refused to take the mortgage.[24] The couple became more and more importuning, soon giving no reasons to Engels for their requests. Because of his generosity, the Lafargues managed to keep a maid—Laura complained about servant girls—and even to take occasional vacations at the seashore.[25]

Not even a falling out between Lafargue and Engels during the last six months of 1874 interrupted the flow of checks. The former Communard Auguste Serraillier, now a refugee in England and working on a commission basis for Lafargue, protested to Engels that he had not received his full earnings. Paul denied the accusation, and sent his version of events to Engels on June 9, voicing the hope that Marx, "too ill and too bored by the whole business," would not be bothered by it.[26]

There was no communication between Lafargue and Engels until December. When Lafargue needed more money, he turned to his father-in-law, apparently deciding he was not so ill that he could not, after all, intercede with Engels on his behalf. "I am not asking Engels directly because I believe him prejudiced against me and because he has no confidence in my business."[27] He also informed Marx of his need to find a new realtor in New Orleans and possibly to visit the city himself in order to sell his property. No reply from Marx exists, but he may have helped secure the loan, for when Engels and Lafargue were again in touch the latter asked for another £360, which added to £240 outstanding would match the £600 anticipated from the sale of the house.[28] Lafargue managed to sell his house, but these funds were exhausted in three years. Threatened by bankruptcy in the spring of 1877, Lafargue again considered emigrating to the United States, either to set up an engraving firm or to work in an established shop.

Engels, always generous, sometimes provided help before being asked. He not only sent money but extended hospitality, by having the Lafargues join him on vacations, for example.[29] And the Lafargues were at least sincere in their appreciation. Laura best expressed their gratitude a few years later: "It is too late in the day for me to feel surprise at any fresh act of kindness on your part, but it is never too late for me to be sensible of your goodness and to thank you for it. And I do so."[30]

The International, as anticipated, had effectively dissolved after its move to New York, and there is little evidence of active political involvement by Lafargue throughout much of the 1870s. On his return from The Hague he had worked with Engels on the report on the Alliance ordered by the congress, completing it by mid-1873. Containing much of the evidence gathered by Lafargue as well as less legitimate material—such as the text of the infamous "revolutionary catechism," found in the papers of Bakunin's unscrupulous protégé Nechaev and attributed to Bakunin—the 140-page tract, *The Alliance of Social Democracy and the International Association of Working Men,* concluded not only that a conspiracy had existed within the International in Spain but that the Alliance aimed at taking over the International. A tendentious, polemical indictment aimed at workers in Latin Europe, it was written in French between April and July 1873 and published in London.[31] The authorship was long attributed to Marx, but Engels confided to his and Marx's friend, Friedrich Sorge, who had led working-class and immigrant groups in the American branch of the International: "It is Lafargue and me who wrote it together; only one or two pages of the conclusion is Marx's," and he predicted, prematurely, "the thing will go off like a bomb among the autonomists, and . . . Bakunin will be stone dead."[32]

Even so, Lafargue's correspondence with Engels during the first few years of his exile shows only one reference to socialism: that he would get two of Fourier's books to Marx.[33] Sensitive on the subject, Lafargue tried to justify his political aloofness. He told a fellow socialist, Paul Brousse, then in Spain promoting anarchism, that he had earlier taken an activist role and would do the same in London if a truly English movement existed. Until then he preferred to remain apart from other refugees: struggle in an "artificial milieu" only made one exhaust oneself in "luttes de boutique ou de personne" (petty or personal quarrels).[34]

As would so often be the case, Lafargue turned to more scholarly pursuits, writing—and by the late 1870s, publishing—on a variety of socialist and labor themes. Lafargue clearly preferred writing to photoengraving, and the time he devoted to it may help explain his failure as a businessman. In 1878, with considerable help from Laura, he excerpted and translated parts of Engels' *Anti-Dühring,* which appeared in a monthly, *La Revue socialiste,* two years later. On June 3, 1879, the newspaper *La Révolution française* published his article on the strike waged by Durham miners.[35] Certainly he was working as well on *Le Droit à la paresse (The Right to Be Lazy),* published in serial form in *L'Egalité* in 1880. He was also trying to apply Marxist methods to literary criticism; he prepared a draft study on the economic antecedents of the Romantic movement. Although Lafargue hoped for publication in a major literary journal, the article did not appear in print until 1896.

Nor did the French refugees in London, received with indifference at best and hostility at worst, confronted by a language barrier, divided into quarrelsome factions living in poverty in and around Soho, and watched by the police, inspire much of an activist role for Lafargue. There were between 1,100 and 1,200 men, and almost as many women and children. The Gladstone government, to its credit, refused demands to extradite them. Marx was in touch with these refugee groups. According to Paris Prefecture reports, he addressed at least one of their meetings in late December 1878 with Charles Longuet and pleaded illness when asked to speak at others.[36] The scholars among them compiled accounts of the uprising. Several worked in the British museum, whose "most admirable library," for Jules Vallès, compensated for "the most appalling city that I know."[37]

There could be found Vallès, Lissagaray, Regnard, Vaillant, and other Communards. Edouard Vaillant, introduced to Marx by Longuet and named to the IWMA's General Council soon after his arrival, together with other Blanquists, had condemned the decision to transfer the International's headquarters to New York and abruptly resigned. Blanquists also disagreed with Marxists over the nature of the Commune; Marxists saw it as more than a re-creation of the revolutionary Commune of 1793, while Blanquists saw the IWMA as entirely too reformist.[38] Vaillant, who secured a British medical degree, lectured at London's University College. Longuet, who had commanded a Communard regiment, served on the National Guard's Central Committee, and drafted most of its declarations, on his arrival in London similarly sat on the General Council and voted at The Hague for the move to New York.

Longuet had narrowly escaped capture during the last days of *la semaine sanglante,* having been sheltered by a military doctor friend, and with the aid of a priest escaped to Belgium. Declared undesirable and expelled by that country's government, Longuet had sailed to England and made his way to Maitland Park.[39] He was a frequent visitor to the Marxes' house, and courted and became engaged in March 1872 to the twenty-seven-year-old Jenny. The two seemed compatible; neither cared to display emotion or to make themselves centers of attraction. They were married in October, and relocated to Oxford, where Longuet looked for work as a teacher of French but found only part-time tutoring posts.[40]

Although suffering from asthma, and busy keeping house and caring for her children (four by 1879), Jenny had to teach German in a parochial school to make ends meet.[41] Longuet was forced to leave Oxford because, according to his wife, "the dandified scholars who had taken lessons during this trimester were doubtless so shocked at seeing the name Longuet among the delegates to the International Congress they decided to have nothing to do with their former teacher." Nor was he appointed to a chair of French literature at London's Kings College, even though he placed first of the 150 candidates seeking to fill it. In addition to his other qualifications, he submitted recommendations from Victor Hugo and Edgar Quinet.[42]

The two brothers-in-law were compared by Eduard Bernstein. "Lafargue could pass for a Frenchman of the South, with that touch of the bizarre that Daudet ironized in *Tartarin de Tarascon,* clever, frank, exaggerated. Longuet was a live debater, with a quick intuition, but politically organized like the prudent northerner, able to form an accurate estimate of the real virtues of a proposal." Marx on occasion showed disenchantment with the ability of both sons-in-law to absorb his doctrines, but especially despaired of Longuet's Proudhonism, which he had never really shed but had only supplemented with Marxist ideas. Yet for Bernstein, Proudhon, with all his defects, understood and better reflected the spirit of French democracy than the majority of the socialists of his time. Longuet "shaped his policy independently of Proudhonist crotchets and absorbed enough Marxism to adapt his theories skillfully to his own policy ... He had neither the diligence nor the originality of Lafargue; he himself did not dig for gold, but he had the eye of the expert who can distinguish gold from the less valuable metals, and the talent of the practical coiner." Longuet's realism was to turn him toward a more gradualist approach to socialism. The political differences that began to distinguish Longuet and Lafargue even came to the attention of the Paris Prefecture of Police.[43]

Throughout the 1870s, amnesty for those who had participated in the Commune was both hoped for and feared by Marx and his wife. With most of the refugees impatient to return, he knew that he would miss his daughters and grandchildren and that the separation would likely be a permanent one. The amnesty of July 1880 finally permitted most of the exiled Communards to return to France. Lissagaray returned immediately, to open a left-wing newspaper that welcomed anti-Marxist contributions. His relationship with Eleanor was over, but we shall see that memories of the quarrel with Lafargue had political consequences in the 1880s. Longuet, asked by his friend Clemenceau to manage the foreign affairs section of Clemenceau's newspaper, *La Justice,* departed soon after. He temporarily left his family in London, but Jenny and the children soon joined him.[44] Longuet, given his landed and provincial origins and more aware than Lafargue of the deep conservatism and parochialism of the French peasantry, took an ever more moderate line. Under Clemenceau's influence, he rejected the need for an independent workers' party and adopted a socialism that was more compatible with French attitudes.

Although Lafargue was not to return to France for another two years, in 1882, his interest in politics revived as the French workers' movement showed signs of revival. The defeat of the Commune had proved disastrous for the French labor movement. Surviving Communards who were not in prison had fled to Switzerland, to Belgium, and to England, as we have seen. By the end of the decade Jules Guesde, Benoît Malon, and Paul Brousse were all in Switzerland flirting with anarchism. The Thiers government was convinced that socialism had been eradicated. The Dufaure Law of March 14, 1872, aimed against the International, forbade any propaganda calling for societal change. In campaign speeches to the voters of Paris' ninth arrondissement, Thiers said, "Socialism is no longer spoken of. We have gotten rid of socialism."[45]

Nevertheless there was a mild resurgence of the labor movement in the second half of the decade. Here and there emerged short-lived cooperatives, mutual associations, workers' circles, and trade unions, all placed under police surveillance. Like that which followed the failure of Chartism in Great Britain, this revival took the form of trade unionism, and the model was that offered by the journalist Jean Barberet. "Barberettisme," a mixture of radicalism and Proudhonism, was totally reformist, rejecting all forms of violence, even strikes, preferring class collaboration, associations, and cooperatives, together with full support for the new Third Republic.[46]

This revival was signaled by the calling of the first workers' congress since the Commune. Held in Paris in early October 1876, it was dominated by the old arts and crafts workers and their organizations, which supplied the backbone of Barberettisme. The republican bourgeois press congratulated the 350 delegates for their moderation. Still, a congress had been held and had even spoken of workers' candidates, although not so much to win political power as to voice complaints. At a second congress, convened in Lyons in 1878, a "collectivist motion," doubtless inspired by a more or less Marxist group led by Jules Guesde and gathered about the small struggling weekly newspaper, *L'Egalité*, received eight votes.[47]

Lafargue followed these stirrings of a French socialist movement closely. He was now firing off letters to French newspapers in defense of Marxist ideas. He complained, for example, that the editor of *La Revue sociale*, an anarchist paper, had published an article by Johann Most, the German anarchist who had settled in America, which was critical of German Social Democratic Party (SPD) deputies like Liebknecht.[48] Regardless of his own precarious economic state, Lafargue extended an invitation to Blanqui to visit England, to stay with him and his wife, and to meet Marx, "who has followed all your political career with great interest [and who] would be very happy to meet you." Since the Commune, he told Blanqui, none of the bourgeois radicals had worked out a program able to impress workers; hence "you are emerging as our standard-bearer."[49]

This was reminiscent of Paul's 1868 efforts, and very likely he was again inspired by Marx, who only a few years earlier had believed that because of Bakunin's and Blanqui's influence France was lost to the International. Observing the trend of events in France, Marx and Engels considered who might lead a resurgent socialist movement. Of the younger socialists, only two, Guesde and Lafargue, seemed promising, but neither appeared to possess the necessary requirements. Though an excellent speaker, the radical Guesde was only a recent convert to Marxism. Lafargue had led an anti-anarchist struggle in Spain, but was a poor speaker, seemed ideologically rigid, and was now unknown in France. Hence Marx's courtship of Blanqui—and encouragement for Lafargue's initiative.[50]

There is no evidence of any reply. And it was of course Marxism that was to secure a foothold in French political life and to return Lafargue to politics. In the spring of 1879 there began an exchange of letters between him and Guesde.

Guesde had written to Marx in March or April (replying to a letter of Marx, which has not survived). Apparently Marx had approved of Guesde's polemic against Longuet, published in *La Révolution française*. Invoking the need of a class party independent of bourgeois radicalism, Guesde assured Marx of his acceptance of collectivist theory, exaggerating his longtime support of it.[51] As he had with Blanqui, Marx no doubt designated Lafargue to reply for him. Lafargue said he was happy to be communicating with Guesde, which suggests that their thirty-year relationship began with this letter.[52]

In his reply and in subsequent letters, Lafargue acted as an "eminence grise." While keeping Marx and Engels informed, he did not hesitate to advise Guesde himself. He assumed a senior position at the outset and made numerous recommendations: on advertising in a projected new series of Guesde's newspaper, *L'Egalité;* on attaching more importance to strikes and other working-class demonstrations; and on other matters.[53] Even if demonstrations, like cooperatives, proved counterproductive, Lafargue said, they helped develop administrative skills, and at least in regard to the usefulness of strikes, there is evidence that Guesde was persuaded.[54] The coming together of Guesde and his associates in Paris and Lafargue in London was to return Lafargue to an active political role and to prove momentous for the beginnings of Marxism in France.

15 The Guesdists

We learned socialism at the same time we informed our readers, and it is incontestable that we sometimes made mistakes.

—Gabriel Deville

At the end of the 1870s Marxist ideas were scarcely known in France. Aside from *Capital* only a handful of Marx's texts were available in French, and only a handful of intellectuals, mainly young, were aware of them.[1] A recent convert was Mathieu Basile (or Bazile), or to use the pseudonym he adopted, Jules Guesde.

Guesde was four years younger than Lafargue, having been born November 11, 1845, on the isle of Saint-Louis in the heart of Paris. His father was a teacher who operated a private school in Passy, then a suburb not yet incorporated into Paris. After earning his Baccalauréat, Jules held successive posts in the Ministry of the Interior and in the Seine Prefecture. Reading Kant, he told an interviewer in 1893, turned him to atheism, Hugo, to republicanism, and Proudhon, to radicalism. It was the Commune that brought him to socialism.[2] Absent was Marx. Guesde was not a disciple like Lafargue and was always to keep some distance from Marx. He became a journalist, and because of his opposition to Napoleon III took his mother's maiden name to avoid compromising his father.

In Montpellier Guesde managed a radical newspaper, *Les Droits de l'homme,* and used it to denounce the war for which he held the Empire responsible. On the staff was a young physician equally hostile to the Empire but also active in the International, Paul Brousse. With the establishment of the Republic, Guesde called for a *levée en masse* in full support of a revolutionary struggle. For defending the Paris Commune, he was sentenced to five years' imprisonment by a republican court. Without waiting for a trial, he fled to self-imposed exile in Switzerland.

While in Geneva he affiliated with the Bakuninist Jura Federation of the IWMA, and accordingly attacked Marx and the General Council's "authoritarianism" and "intolerance." Guesde then relocated to Italy, where he ceaselessly spread Bakuninist propaganda throughout the industrial north. Hungry, homeless, often in rags, but driven by an indomitable will, he ruined his health. Three years' association with anti-Bakuninist socialists whom he met in Milan and a close reading of Lassalle in Italian translation, however, led to his break with anarchism. Guesde retained revolutionary zeal, but no longer possessed a doctrine. He found one after his return to France in 1876, while writing for the radical press and mixing with revolutionary-minded students. He said he then became a Marxist, an affiliation seen at the time as a German import. Guesde was described by his friend Gabriel Deville, however, as more of a Lassallean.[3]

A number of factors accounted for his conversion: his admiration for socialist organization in Germany, where a unified party had been created the previous year; his reading of *Capital,* published in French translation between 1872 and 1876; and, most important, his exposure to Marxist thinkers in the Latin Quarter.

Intellectuals, particularly those frequenting the Café Soufflet (not to be confused with the rue Soufflot), debated "Utopian" and Marxist socialist theories. Included was Emile Massard, born in Belgium, who had fought in the Commune and was later imprisoned with Guesde in 1878 for attempting to organize an international labor congress. Another, a moving spirit of the group, was Gabriel Deville, a law student who was soon to ask Marx for permission to publish a condensed version of *Capital.* (Lafargue may have assisted here; in an undated letter to Deville, he said he had showed Deville's request to both Marx and Engels.)[4]

Born in 1854 of a prominent republican family, Deville came from Tarbes, in the Department Hautes-Pyrénées. As a seventeen-year-old student in Toulouse he had joined a Marxist section of the International. (The repressive legislation of March 14, 1872, had not prevented the establishment of new sections, and young people affiliated precisely because the IWMA was outlawed.) The Toulouse section favored political action and so differed from those inclined toward anarchism. This preference, in turn, led members, Deville included, to tackle Marx's works, particularly the installments of the Roy translation of *Capital.*[5]

In Paris, where he was to complete his law degree, Deville moved into the circle of Latin Quarter radicals in 1872. What Marxism there was, was then a youth movement comprised of students who wanted to move beyond Jacobinism and the Commune. They rejected Blanquism as theatrical and self-defeating, and as idealizing revolution. They sought a more objective approach, and so were attracted by Marx's view of history as a vast unfolding of a socioeconomic process that transcended the concerns of political activists. A dispassionate science, it saw the logic of history as leading capitalism to its destruction in a crisis that was revolutionary but did not require street riots and coups.[6]

Deville had achieved some notoriety by directing, on behalf of a professor friend, the first more or less collectivist election campaign in France. In 1876 a by-election for the Chamber of Deputies was held in the Saint-Germain area of Paris. The area was a maze of tiny streets and alleys inhabited by wage earners receptive to radical ideas. On the initiative of Deville and a colleague, a "Radical Republican" committee (the term socialist was not used) was established and chose a left-wing educator as its candidate. Deville drafted his program, which asked for the return of property to its "legitimate source," labor. The campaign fared poorly because the workers preferred a cooperativist approach.[7]

According to a contemporary photograph, Deville had something of a dashing appearance; he was dark (Lafargue was convinced he had Moorish blood),[8] and wore a mustache and a short pointed beard. A mediocre orator but a good jurist, he pioneered Marx's theories in France and may well have been the first Frenchman to promote collectivism within the country.[9] A scrupulous economist, he was the only leader of the eventual French Marxist party to interest himself in Marxist economics and able to understand the algebraic formulas in *Capital*.[10] Moreover, of all the Guesdist chiefs, only Deville could read German (although not easily; he worked from the French translation in preparing his summary of *Capital*).

Guesde was also influenced by Karl Hirsch, a German socialist and longtime correspondent of Marx, who with Wilhelm Liebknecht had helped found the first German Marxist party in 1869. (A merger of these Marxists and Lassalleans produced the united German Social Democratic Party—the SPD—in 1875.) Because of difficulties with the German government Hirsch had emigrated to Paris in 1874, where he worked as a correspondent for the German socialist press.[11] Guesde learned most of his Marxism, however, through conversations with José Mesa. Events in Spain had forced Mesa, hounded by the Spanish government after the fall of the Republic, to take refuge in Paris. He earned a good living as correspondent for two Spanish fashion magazines and in June 1875 had visited Lafargue—and Marx and Engels—in London.[12]

In 1875 Mesa became friends with Hirsch, and while maintaining his interest in Spanish socialism also became involved with the renewal of the workers' movement in France. Impressed by Guesde's articles in *Les Droits de l'homme,* Mesa became acquainted with him as well. According to Deville, Mesa proved more decisive an influence than Hirsch in converting Guesde to Marxism. He was, Deville wrote fifty years later, "the first theoretically knowledgeable Marxist" in France, although his influence was long underestimated because Mesa "acted without noise . . . motivated by the necessities of his existence."[13] It was Mesa and Hirsch who reconciled Guesde with Lafargue when the two disagreed and when Guesde tired of Lafargue's harping tone. It was also Hirsch who, after several visits to London, hopelessly in love with Eleanor Marx, in 1872 proposed marriage to and was rejected by her.[14]

Guesde became a leader of the collectivist-oriented group: he had the prestige of a Commune-inspired exile, considerable political experience, a caustic but talented pen, and eloquence. He worked to turn workers toward a collectivist solution and refused to separate himself from them, though labor then favored cooperativist solutions and opposed even the strike. Impressed by the founding of the SPD in Germany, he saw the need for an independent French working-class party.[15]

In November 1877, with Deville, Guesde founded and edited the weekly *L'Egalité.* The newspaper was more radical than Marxist: its masthead read "Journal Républicain socialiste." Still, a prepublication notice stated that as the Republic was the final product of political development, socialism emerged from economic development. Revolution, however, was seen as necessary. Eclectic, the newspaper also reflected bits and pieces of libertarian, utopian, and Lassallean theories. It received most of its financial support from German socialists and, in terms of expenditure of labor, was also subsidized by its staff.

Collaborating as well were a few former editors of *Les Droits de l'homme,* including Massard. Guesde published contributions from foreign socialists: August Bebel and Wilhelm Liebknecht in Germany, César de Paepe in Belgium, and from exile in Lugano, the Communard Benoît Malon.[16] Until the appearance of *L'Egalité* there had been no collectivist newspaper in France. The very words "collectivism" and "workers' party" were new and the theories advanced, often confused.[17] Deville explained the errors in the scattered attempts to publicize doctrine: "In 1877 when I was one of those who began to propagate the collectivist and Marxist theory by the newspaper, I scarcely knew the rudiments . . . We learned socialism at the same time that we informed our readers, and it is incontestable that we sometimes made mistakes."[18]

The newspaper survived for thirty-three issues, from November 18, 1877, to Bastille Day in 1878, when a court-imposed fine of 1,800 francs could not be paid. However, the growth of a labor movement continued. The Second Workers' Congress, held in Lyons from January 28 to February 8, gathered 136 delegates from 24 cities. Although the final resolution continued to condemn strikes and all revolutionary means to working-class emancipation, new themes were introduced; women's rights were defended, and the motion submitted by the *Egalité* group supported the socialization of the means of production.

The Guesdists displayed skilled political techniques as early as the spring of 1879, when the group waged a campaign in Bordeaux to send the imprisoned Blanqui to the Chamber of Deputies and to make the campaign part of the larger drive for political amnesty for Communards. Local leaders like Ernest Roche, an engraver, lacked political experience yet showed organizational skill in putting together a coalition of radicals, socialists, and revolutionaries. Deville worked to give the Bordeaux campaign national attention by promoting Blanqui's candidacy elsewhere and by making the campaign serve as a national plebiscite on amnesty, a tactic Guesdists would use again in 1891 to send Lafargue to the Chamber. Blanqui received a majority of the votes, and although the election was invalidated, the victory helped secure both his pardon and the amnesty that was enacted the following year.[19]

Lafargue contributed to Blanqui's campaign by writing an account of his first meeting with *le vieux,* at the students' congress in Liège.[20] As we have seen, he debunked stories of Blanqui as a sinister and conspiratorial figure, portraying him instead as a gracious and warm personality who encouraged young revolutionaries to find their own way rather than act as disciples. Regardless of their revolutionary rhetoric, by seeking an amnesty Guesdists were implicitly arguing that the cause of the Commune was no longer an issue, that its participants and its supporters were no longer a threat, and that a stable republic was necessary for the socialist cause—thus rendering revolutionary Blanquism innocuous and revolutionary tradition obsolete, a first step to a reformist approach.[21]

The group was distinguished by its appearance as well as by its intransigence. In imitation of Guesde, members allowed their beards to grow long and wore low-slung felt hats. Aside from Deville, who dressed like a dandy, they otherwise presented a correct appearance. Although Guesde could exert charm, the others preferred to show themselves as disdainful and aloof. Guesde gravitated toward a leadership role because of his managerial skills, his speaking ability, and his "apostolic bearing." According to one biographer, he evoked the figure of a medieval monk, "with the head of a sickly Christ, his great ivory brow, his fiery eyes behind the glass of his pince-nez, his strident voice always reaching ever higher registers."[22]

Guesde was tall (almost six feet), ascetic-looking, and thin to the point of emaciation. His skin was white and sickly. He had long romantic-looking hair and a prophet-like beard, with shining eyes that caught his listeners' attention. He was a great orator, with a torrential delivery given in a grating voice, filled with resonant phrases and caustic comments. A newspaperman who heard him in 1880 said "his clear and metallic voice vibrated like a bugle, his eloquence is lively, he gesticulates while speaking and leans over the tribune to mesmerize his audience; he expresses himself in a clear language in a scientific style, yet politically and vividly."[23] The speeches were solidly constructed, with implacable logic and making obscure theories clear to the audience. Usually after a heated denunciation of the evils of capitalist society, Guesde lyrically painted a tableau of the future under socialism. This socialism was no longer conspiratorial; it was the open presentation of a doctrine whose truth was felt to be compelling.[24]

This same ability to focus on basics led to a schematic and pedagogical approach, however, and the resulting Marxism was stripped of its nuance and richness. Guesde's was scarcely a creative application of Marxist method to contemporary problems. French Marxist historians today agree on Guesde's predisposition to cut and dried formulas inspired by the *Communist Manifesto*. His reading of the first volume of *Capital* in translation instilled in him the conviction that science was on the side of socialism. But the chief source of his economic knowledge was Lassalle, whose iron law of wages—which insisted that under capitalism salaries could not significantly rise— Guesde wrongly attributed to Marx.[25]

*   *   *

In the spring of 1879, Guesde was completing a six-month jail term. As one of thirty or forty people who had tried to organize an international socialist congress in Paris, he had violated the law enacted earlier against the International. Authorization to meet had been denied, but a number of delegates nevertheless held a preliminary gathering and were rounded up by the police. Guesde's courtroom defense consisted of an exposé of socialism, the closest description of Marxism yet spoken by a Frenchman.[26] However, the conservative republican government ignored his claim to the court that he represented a rising proletariat destined to come to power, and in the midst of the post-Commune repression in a society wholly unfamiliar with Marxist ideology, his remarks struck many of his listeners as absurd.[27] Still, Guesde's audacity, both in breaking the law and at his trial, marked him and his associates as leaders; more converts were won over, and several important unions came out for socialism.[28]

From Sainte-Pélagie prison, Guesde contributed articles to a new daily, *La Révolution française,* which was published from January 1877 until mid-June 1878. It took a stronger republican than socialist line, avoiding references to revolution but continuing to call for a congress. When Guesde became ill, he was put in the Necker Hospital, and it was from here that he wrote his letter to Marx, professing his esteem and agreeing on the need to establish a separate workers' party to win labor away from bourgeois radicalism.

Lafargue's reply (on Marx's behalf) and subsequent letters offered advice on a variety of subjects, as already noted, and his tone was both authoritative and critical. While the two men respected each other, they were never close. Perhaps Guesde's later remark, that he had conceived of Marxism without knowing the texts, was directed at Lafargue.[29] Guesde's unqualified acceptance of the iron law of wages explains in part why he denigrated trade unions and saw economic victories as less than essential. Lafargue, now contributing to the second series of *L'Egalité* and soon to the new *Revue socialiste,* edited by Benoît Malon, tried to lead him to less Lassallean views.

Malon differed from other socialist chiefs in that he was an authentic worker. Born in 1841 in the Loire Department to a family of poor day laborers, he was forced as a child to work as a shepherd. He largely taught himself to read and write. As a worker in a Paris dye-works, he organized a strike in 1866 and was one of the first to join the French branch of the International—although as an advocate of cooperatives. Like Guesde, he came to socialism without a knowledge of Marx; unlike Guesde, he never wholly accepted Marx. He was sentenced and imprisoned on several occasions for promoting labor unrest. Revealing, though perhaps apocryphal, was the anecdote told by Guillaume. One day in March 1870, Lafargue invited Malon to lunch and proudly introduced him to Laura: "This is the daughter of Karl Marx." "Karl Marx," said Malon, a bit confused, "I think I've heard the name. Isn't he a professor of German?" "No, he's the author of *Capital*. You don't know that?" Malon admitted he did not. "Is it possible? You don't know it's Karl Marx who heads the General Council?"[30]

A Communard, Malon had gone into exile in Switzerland, where he published a history of the insurrection. Now familiar with Marx's writings, he hesitated between Marxism and anarchism, and sought to reconcile the two. Malon joined the Jura Federation, although the republican victory in France and his reading of *Capital* convinced him that "without socialization of the means of productive forces there could be no emancipation for the worker" and that for socialization a labor party was necessary. He conveyed these ideas to labor leaders in France, thus moving closer to the Marxists, and later wrote for *Egalité*. Malon's *History of Socialism* (1878) reproduced part of the *Communist Manifesto*. He began publishing *La Revue socialiste* from Zurich in 1880, and continued it in France after the amnesty allowed his return. His approach to socialism remained eclectic and conciliatory, that is, reformist: "Let us be revolutionaries," he said, "when circumstances warrant it and reformists always." Throughout his life he was to keep his distance from Marx, a hostility perhaps generated, certainly sanctioned, by a certain resentment of both Germans and Jews, as shown by his articles in *La Revue socialiste*. Marx, who was well aware of this, commented to Sorge that Malon could not wait until the International had freed itself of this German Jew and of German Jews in general.[31]

Mesa had written to Lafargue about the new review. It was to be a serious, almost scholarly journal, complete with documentation and statistics. Contributions from Lafargue would be welcome. In the first issue, dated January 20, 1880, Lafargue complained of monopolists who cornered the market on wheat, driving up the cost of bread. To complete his article he had asked Guesde to supply some of the needed data.[32] Many of the suggestions made in his letters to Guesde reappeared in his articles, but the letters discussed everything: newspaper publishing, cooperatives, the usefulness of worker demonstrations and proposed reforms, foreign labor, economic theory, and the role of workers' organizations following the revolution.[33]

In the early summer of 1879, anticipating an amnesty, Guesde asked Lafargue to return to France and help run a daily newspaper (whether the forthcoming series of *L'Egalité* or *La Révolution française* is not clear) and also to contribute funds. Lafargue refused both appeals. He wanted Guesde "to have no illusions about our economic situation. I am forced to earn my living by manual labor . . . I cannot return to Paris because I have no resources, no job, and know very few people. I have no one to count on in Paris." Nor should Guesde rely on Marx and Engels, "whose resources are devoted to the German movement," then suffering under Bismarckian repression.[34]

He was negative about starting up a new daily, and doubtful of Guesde's ability to serve as editor, "a dog's life," because it was a twenty-four-hour job. He cited the need for a competent staff and adequate funds, and above all the problem of Guesde's poor health. Perpetually ill, Guesde's poverty undermined his health, and his associates time and again had to come to his aid. On one occasion, according to a police informer, they discussed "the sad situation in which Guesde and his family [found] themselves." The landlord had evicted them, and his wife and children were literally starving. Those present raised fifteen francs among themselves.[35] "A socialist newspaper," Lafargue nonetheless insisted, "should not count on advertising." Moreover, repeated condemnation of the French establishment in the paper would produce arrests and prison terms for members of its staff. (The restrictive censorship and press laws were not changed until 1881.) Consequently Lafargue preferred a weekly that took a more theoretical approach. More secure from prosecution, it would allow the time necessary to build up subscriptions.[36]

The "great depression" of the late 1870s and early 1880s was an especially difficult time for working people in France. Lower wages and higher rent and food costs, coupled with an average working day of twelve hours, generated greater working-class consciousness. Bread cost nearly two francs for five kilograms, even though an experienced miner earned only four to four and a half francs a day and a textile worker in Roubaix, three francs a day.[37] The republican victory after the May 16 constitutional crisis (when the president of the Republic forced the premier to resign) may have unleashed working-class strength to the extent that many were persuaded that the time seemed ripe for an independent political movement.

The opportunity came in the Third Workers' Congress, known as *l'immortel Congrès,* held October 1879 in Marseilles. It was a major event in the history of French socialism and the first occasion during which French workers called themselves "revolutionary."[38] In part because of preparatory work by the *Egalité* group, a cooperativist approach was rejected and a collectivist resolution was narrowly approved by the 130 delegates. They also voted to form a class-based socialist party, adding to the triumph of the tiny Guesdist contingent. The party was to be called the Federated Socialist Workers Party of France (Fédération du Parti des Travailleurs Socialistes de France) and, as implied in the name, was to have a decentralized structure consisting of six regional organizations. Each would hold its own congress; the six groups would be linked by an executive committee to carry out the decisions of an annual national congress. The exiles Lafargue, Malon, and Brousse doubtless gloated over the news.

Choice of the term "collectivist," Lafargue wrote later, was prompted by the wish not to frighten away moderate delegates: the word could encompass legal nationalization initiated by a labor party and so win support from reformists like Malon as well as from moderate anarchists.[39] Because the Marxist victory was won at a congress, the role of congresses seemed vital. In later years, Guesde reminisced about the "immortal Congress" of 1879. Congresses eventually took on great symbolic value; instead of defining theory, in reality delegates became content to ratify prepared drafts.[40]

The following month Lafargue offered the theoretical line that the forthcoming series of *L'Egalité*—and by extension, the new party—was to take.[41] It reflected Engels' simplification of Marxist thought in the parts of the *Anti-Dühring* that the Lafargues were translating as *Socialism: Scientific and Utopian*—collectivization not as the realization of such ideals as justice and equality but rather as the necessary and inevitable outgrowth of capitalism. Seen as crucial was the need to raise the class consciousness of workers in order for them to take action.

"Our program," Lafargue informed Guesde, "issues from the entrails of economic reality . . . our theories, our principles, our aspirations are the immediate products of economic facts." Proof lay in the more or less simultaneous emergence of socialist strength in all industrial societies. "We are only the spokesmen of reality, we materialists, and we are revolutionaries only because the economy is in a revolutionary state ... common ownership under another name already exists in the reality around us and everywhere can be found competing with private property, crushing it, absorbing it, and creating unceasingly a mass of expropriated human beings who feel pangs of hunger in their stomachs and hatred in their hearts and who require only a crude organization to make them conscious of their power in order to break the economic and political bonds of society."[42]

Propaganda, then, was a major focus for party activity. The new *Egalité* was to show the impossibility of private ownership not in the name of justice or equality but because economic development admitted only one conclusion: collective ownership. This view of the party as "instructor" rather than as a "general staff" reinforced the spontaneous and catastrophic outlook held by Lafargue.[43] His popularization of Engels' summation of Marxist principles provides an excellent example.

Engels wrote *Anti-Dühring* to refute the theories of Eugen Dühring, an anti-Semitic economist who had won some notoriety advocating a reformed capitalism through a strong labor movement. Three general chapters of Engels' work provided a clear and simple exposition of Marxist thought. More detailed than the *Communist Manifesto* yet more approachable for the general reader than Marx's other writings, *Anti-Dühring* had led future theorists like Kautsky and Bernstein to Marxism.[44] Engels' closing words calling for propaganda stated the mission Lafargue dedicated himself to fulfill: to impart to the "now oppressed proletarian class a full knowledge of the conditions of the meaning of the momentous act it is called upon to accomplish."[45]

The following spring, in the third, fourth, and fifth issues of *La Revue socialiste* (those of March 20, April 20, and May 5, 1880), Lafargue published excerpts from his and Laura's translation of these chapters, along with an introduction, as *Socialisme utopique et socialisme scientifique*. In June the excerpts appeared as a brochure, which became immensely popular. By 1885 Lafargue was able to tell Engels that "it strongly influenced the development of French socialism."[46] In numerous translations and editions it proved one of the most widely read socialist pamphlets published at the end of the nineteenth century.

Lafargue found no need to spell out tactics. "If with *L'Egalité* we succeed in penetrating the masses and activating them with our communist ideas, no matter how or towards what, we shall have accomplished a major revolutionary task; and we should for the moment set aside the question of tactics. Economic and political forces will impose themselves on us to the extent that our strength will increase and at that point we shall see what line to take."[47]

His optimism was boundless and no doubt contagious. He was convinced that worldwide revolution was imminent. In its bourgeois form it could occur at any moment in Russia, "because in Russia the proletariat and big industry do not yet exist"; under these conditions parliamentary government would then be created. That, in turn, would "shake the European financial system and fracture the dorsal spine of European reaction while unleashing revolutionary storms; the Russians on the one side and the Americans on the other are preparing the terrain for us; in five or six years Europe will be on fire."[48] All that was necessary was to explain Marxism to the masses and they would be won over.

Force, however, was a weapon "not to be rejected." The capitalist state was "not an abstraction, [but] represented power that had to be assaulted and taken," and he reminded Guesde of the importance of food riots during the French Revolution.[49] Still, any activity bringing workers together, including support for reform, would be useful. Here he cited Engels, who while rejecting a program based on reform, nevertheless believed that "we must promote unrest as ardently as possible and take in hand the question of hours of work as of the first importance, in order to give breath to the working masses."[50]

Indeed, in his lectures to Guesde and in articles published during the 1879–1881 period Lafargue appeared to place near total emphasis on reform. Capitalism survived because of the surplus value of labor it accumulated, which explained capitalists' efforts to lower wages and increase hours. Hence the need for socialists to work for higher wages and lower hours. Not only would this weaken capitalism, but—hinting at themes he developed in *The Right to Be Lazy*—it would allow the worker to "develop his individuality, to increase his physical and intellectual needs."[51] Moreover, labor would then resent all the more keenly any lowering of the conditions of life during periods of crisis and struggle all the more fiercely against the prevailing economic system.

Thus it was in the capitalists' own interest to have the state regulate "wild competition" and so ensure the steady flow of surplus capital. A series of articles on French railroads called attention to their owners' willingness to accept government regulation in order to avoid the disastrous economic consequences of cutthroat competition. For the sake of economic growth, Lafargue quipped, they might even "appreciate the need for nationalization."[52]

Similar arguments were made for the municipal regulation of grain speculation. The government that already provided subsidies, tariffs, and credit to entrepreneurs should also purchase and make grain available to consumers. This would drive down the price kept artificially high by speculators.[53] Again, reforms were possible—and necessary—in capitalist society. Not only would working-class lives be improved (supporting Engels' belief that agitation for a shorter work day was essential), but reform would permit the economic system to develop to the point of making socialist revolution possible.[54] Lafargue continued to believe in the need for a political party to offer immediate gains, and that recruitment for such a party would be furthered if it took up a popular cause.

Nor was other municipal action to be neglected. Even though successive socialist conquests of municipal councils offered no substitute for the long-sought revolution, an alliance of socialist-governed cities could create a "powerful opposition" to an ever more reactionary Chamber of Deputies. From that conflict would emerge a revolutionary situation in which socialists could seize power.[55] The Commune of Paris would act as a provisional government, but, keeping in mind the lesson of 1871, Lafargue acknowledged that Paris needed the support of other cities. That, in turn, was possible only if the municipalities fell into the hands of the working-class party.[56] "The first step of the workers' party in its struggle for the conquest of public power will be its conquest of the municipalities." What might a workers' party do after power was won in the cities? In addition to securing control of the food trade and putting it into the hands of the "débourgeoisées municipalités," a party could create a network of municipal banks to made credit more widely available. The initial conquest of the cities, however, could be carried out within a capitalist framework.[57]

Returning from his workshop one day at the end of January 1880, Lafargue was "overjoyed" to find forty copies of the new *Egalité.*

More collectivist than its predecessor, its masthead read, "Organe collectiviste révolutionnaire." "At last we have an arm of combat," he wrote Guesde, "and if they let us survive a year, we will see if a workers' party won't be well-established."[58] Marx, too, was pleased: "For the first time in France," he wrote to Sorge later in the year, "we have a workers' newspaper in the full sense of the word."[59] Lafargue regularly sent articles to *L'Egalité*. In its initial issue of January 21 was published the first of his two articles on "agrarian agitation in Ireland and its economic causes." A draft had been sent to Deville, and Lafargue entered into correspondence with him.[60] Then he followed it with a series of articles criticizing Proudhon.

Writers on the staff included former Communards and those who had supported the Commune from outside of Paris: Malon; Jean-Baptiste Clément, the militant poet; and Leo Frankel, earlier the IWMA General Council's corresponding secretary for Hungary, who had fought in the Commune. Emile Massard had fought alongside his father. Eugène Dupont had followed the events of the Commune from Manchester; Brousse and Guesde were then in Montpellier; and Lafargue, of course, had been in Bordeaux. Participants and nonparticipants alike repeatedly invoked and commemorated the experience of the Commune, seeing it as a workers' revolution and as "almost exclusively proletarian." On the anniversary of the Commune the newspaper was printed in red ink. The June 2, 1880, issue offered a fully "Marxist" analysis of the Commune based on Marx's *Civil War in France*. Unsigned, but entitled "The Class Struggle," it was probably Lafargue's work. The article identified the Commune as a "brilliant demonstration of class conflict," but unlike previous insurrections, one in which the proletariat seized state power, which demonstrated the necessity of political action. "Possession of state power by representatives of the proletariat," however, was bound to bring repression; hence the Commune had not been a full-fledged socialist experience but "a necessary transition" toward it. On August 11 he repeated that insurrection in one city was no longer adequate: due to technological change, troops could be brought to the scene of any conflict. Hence the need for nationwide action and international support.[61]

Ideologically, Proudhon had given way to Marx. Lafargue criticized Tolain and the mutualists on strategic grounds: though useful in a transition to collectivism, cooperatives could never replace capitalism. The industrially decentralized world of Proudhon was gone, never to return.[62] As if to demonstrate the weight it attached to these views, *L'Egalité* in April and May began to serialize Marx's *Poverty of Philosophy* and in May also defended a newly drafted collectivist party program.

In addition to contributing articles, Lafargue sent engravings for the newspaper's illustrated back page. One compared workers' living conditions with those of animals; another displayed caricatures of an idle priest, an aristocrat, and a member of the bourgeoisie.[63] Lafargue's articles appeared irregularly and, following the newspaper's style, often anonymously. He published more regularly in the third series (December 11, 1881, to December 5, 1882). Not until August 18, 1880, did his first signed article appear. Entitled "Liberté, Egalité, Fraternité," it offered a Marxist analysis of religion as an instrument of bourgeois domination and a description of nineteenth-century revolutionary materialists as continuing the work begun by eighteenth-century Encyclopedists.

The disagreements with Guesde showed no signs of abating. Lafargue questioned articles approved by Guesde for publication, and above all he challenged cuts made in his own articles. Guesde had criticized Lafargue's draft article on the price of bread as "a call for insurrection . . . which in the present circumstances would compromise us—or worse, make us look ridiculous." He told Lafargue about his plans to find financial support, and mentioned that he had an investor or two in mind.[64] Lafargue dismissed the strategy as outdated: Guesde was "naïve in money matters . . . a man of a communist society and not a capitalist society." Better to sell shares and advertise (a course of action he now found entirely appropriate). How fitting for capitalists to underwrite the cost of their own destruction![65] Guesde was asked to send itemized costs of publishing the newspaper for Lafargue's scrutiny. Scheduling and technical changes to permit the printing of illustrations were proposed. The slogan of the International should be substituted for that currently used as a masthead. The censor could be outmaneuvered by submitting fragmented material or material pulled out of context.[66]

Mesa regretted the quarrels between the two men and dismissed most of them as procedural. Others he attributed to Guesde's "state of nervous excitement."[67] But disagreements over substantive and procedural matters were set aside when Lafargue set about polishing his draft of *The Right to Be Lazy* for serialized publication in *L'Egalité*.

16 A Pamphlet and a Program

> For the proletariat to realize its own strength it must . . . discover
> its natural instincts and proclaim that the right to leisure is a
> thousand times more sacred and noble than the Rights of Man
> advocated by the metaphysical lawyers of the middle-class revo-
> lution.
>
> —Paul Lafargue

In the spring of 1880 Lafargue rushed to complete his essay on the
working population's need for leisure time. Thanks to *L'Egalité* he
now had an outlet for publication. On June 16, 1880, the newspaper
announced the forthcoming serialization of what proved to be Lafargue's most popular and enduring piece of writing: *Le Droit à la
paresse* (The Right to Be Lazy).[1] It was Lafargue's first sustained
effort at paradox. Marked by irony and caustic humor, the work
became a masterpiece of the genre and strongly recalled similar efforts
by the eighteenth-century *philosophes*.

Lafargue's early immersion in the writings of Proudhon may have
aroused his initial interest. In a pamphlet concerned with "Sunday,"
Proudhon discussed the workingman's single day of rest from the
standpoint of "public health, morals, the family, and civilization." He
commented that on Sundays, "servants regained the dignity of human
beings and stood once more on the same level as masters." In his
introduction he subordinated "discussions of work and wages, organization and industry" to the necessity of starting with "the study of
a law which would have as its basis a theory of rest."[2] Moreover,
Marx's *Economic and Philosophical Manuscripts of 1844* introduced
the concept of the worker alienated from his labor and speculated on
the result of this alienation. Though that work was not published
until the twentieth century, the subject doubtless came up in Lafargue's conversations with Marx.

Lafargue was struck by the irony of a society where workers spent
most of their lives working and living in abstinence and where the
bourgeoisie did not produce but were arch-consumers. He placed the

blame on capitalism. His title, although often mistranslated as the "right to leisure," was deliberately chosen to attract attention. The wording apparently derived from a book by Louis Moreau–Christophe, which Lafargue found in Marx's library, whose title began with the words "Du droit à l'oisiveté" (the right to idleness). But the "right to leisure," *loisir,* and even the "right to pleasure," *plaisir,* were considered and rejected; "laziness," *paresse,* seemed best because it shocked, because it came as a cry of war.[3]

The opening paragraph dripped with sarcasm: "A strange madness has taken possession of the working classes of those nations in which capitalistic civilization dominates. This madness is the primary cause of the individual and collective sufferings which for the past two centuries have been endured by an unhappy humanity. This madness is the love of work, the furious desire for labor, carried even to the extent of exhausting the vital forces of the individual and his offspring. Instead of protesting against this mental aberration, priests, economists and moralists have doubly sanctified labour. Blind and narrow-minded men, they have thought themselves wiser than their God; feeble and despicable creatures, they have sought to rehabilitate that which their God has cursed. I appeal from their judgment to their God's, from the teachings of their religious morality and political economy to the frightful consequences of work under capitalism."

Lafargue then turned to the many church-related holidays in the Middle Ages, the abbreviated work week of the ancien régime, and writers like Virgil, Rabelais, and Cervantes who sang of leisure. He gave full reign to his epicurianism in evoking fables and old stories, and contrasted the condition of labor in earlier times with what it was in the 1880s. The working day in the thirteenth and fourteenth centuries was shorter than that of the nineteenth. Exasperated, he emphasized the "virtues of idleness," when workers are "not exhausted in body and spirit" and able at last to profit from their existence: "O idleness, take pity on our long misery! O idleness, mother of the arts and the noble virtues, be the salve of our human anguish!"

More specifically, he held work in capitalist society to be "the cause of all intellectual degeneration and organic deformation." As evidence Lafargue cited the "physical beauty and proud bearing" of people in more primitive societies, from "aborigines in Oceania . . . gazed at in astonishment by European explorers" to the "German communist tribes" so admired by the Romans. Lafargue offered examples of the moral and intellectual attainments reached by those who like the Greeks taught "a contempt for work." And he cited authorities who similarly advocated leisure, including Christ and the ultimate example of Jehovah, "who after six days' work rested for eternity."

In contrast, the races for whom work "is an organic necessity"—"... the Scotch; the Auvergnats, the Scotch of France; the Pomeranians, the Scotch of Germany; the Galicians, the Scotch of Spain; the Chinese, the Scotch of Asia"—remain "bent over their ground" or "captivated with their shops," while the proletariat, "false to its instincts, unmindful of its historic mission, has allowed itself to be corrupted by the dogma of work." Its punishment is no less than "all individual and social misery."

The church was attacked as sanctifying the status quo. Christianity had justified slavery in antiquity and glorified serfdom in the medieval world, and it now justified alienated labor. Hence Lafargue condemned the social function of religious belief and once more regretted the suppression of the many holidays of precapitalist society. He denounced those like Napoleon, who advocated longer hours as a means to curtail vice, and like Thiers, who in 1849 had said that man was destined to suffer in this life.

This was the age of steam and iron, of early industrialization in France, before industrial legislation prevailed. The maximum length of the working day had been fixed at twelve hours by the Constituent Assembly in 1848 but was often exceeded. Writing as a physician, Lafargue bemoaned the prolonged labor of women and children as detrimental to health and physique, and he bristled at the voluntary acceptance of the "religion of work" by the victorious republicans who after 1848 proclaimed the "right to work" as a revolutionary principle. The right to labor, said Lafargue, was the right to misery. Convicts worked only a ten-hour day; West Indian slaves averaged nine; while "the country that proclaimed the Rights of Man tolerated establishments requiring a sixteen-hour day with only an hour and a half allowed for meals."

Because so many hours of labor yielded more than the capitalists cared to sell at home (at going prices), they sought new markets, some in the form of colonies, and sometimes destroyed surpluses. In these ideas, of course, Lafargue foreshadowed the later analyses of Luxemburg and Lenin. Lafargue heavily criticized the proletariat, for "allowing itself to be [so] perverted by the dogma of labor" that the exhausted worker was no longer human but "debris." Yet this was not entirely the worker's fault; capitalist sentiment prevailed in capitalist society, even in the area of popular literature. Victor Hugo and Paul de Kock (an immensely popular mid-nineteenth-century writer), as well as other purveyors of current political and religious beliefs, were all censured. Here too, Lafargue's critique was an early expression of certain ideas later developed by Marxist theorists such as Gramsci and Lukács, who argued that a ruling class could exercise its hegemony by supplying the system of belief accepted by ordinary people and thus ensuring that they would not question the actions of their rulers.

One remedy, said Lafargue, lay in more labor-saving machinery, already forced on capitalists by the refusal of some workers, such as the spinners of Manchester, to toil excessive hours. An even better example was that of the United States, where a shortage of labor had led to the introduction of such devices as the mechanical reaper. Another remedy lay in a scientific restructuring of the productive process, resulting in more efficient work, which would in turn make possible a reduction in the length of the work day for each worker. Rather than exporting "surplus" commodities to underdeveloped areas, Lafargue preferred a more equitable distribution of the burden of labor: although an internationalist, he wanted greater consumption at home.

Most fundamental, however, was the need for a change in attitude. Workers must "trample underfoot" the prejudices of capitalistic religion and economics, return to "their natural instincts, proclaim the "Right to Leisure a thousand times more noble and sacred than the Rights of Man advocated by the metaphysical lawyers of the middle-class revolution," and restrain themselves from working more than three hours per day, "resting and feasting during the remainder of the day and night." Only then would the proletariat become fully class conscious and able to achieve its emancipation and that of the rest of human society. Lafargue, then, with some tongue in cheek, saw his task as one of demonstrating the labor-saving potential of modern technology, "curb[ing] the extravagant passion for work and requiring [workers] to consume the goods they produced."

Rather than a denial of work or an affirmation of leisure as an end in itself, *The Right to Be Lazy* was a celebration of life, or rather of what life could be: not merely recuperation from labor, but the essence of life itself. Far from advocating a hedonistic philosophy, it condemned only excessive and abusive labor. Leszek Kolakowski, in his history of Marxist thought, entitled his chapter on Lafargue "A Hedonist Marxism," in which he described Lafargue's communism chiefly as "an opportunity for carefree consumption" and Lafargue himself as closer to Rabelais than to Marx.[4] For Lafargue, however, more leisure meant the opportunity for more physical and intellectual development; leisure opened the prospect of "paradise on earth" rather than in the heaven of the "good Christian capitalists."[5] Here Lafargue anticipated Kropotkin, who in his *Conquest of Bread* said that "after bread, leisure is the chief aim," and by leisure meant facilities for each to follow, in time free from essential work, those individual inclinations that produce art, literature, and science.[6] One critic maintained that Lafargue's concept of the nobility of leisure was based on Marx's concept of *homo aestheticus* and had points in common with Fouerierism.[7]

Lafargue recognized the difficulties faced in changing a fixed, deeply embedded mind-set. It was easier to describe "bad truths" than to convince the worker "that the ideas with which he has been innoculated are utterly false, that the unlimited work of which he has been the victim from the beginning of the century was the most terrible scourge ever to afflict humanity, that work should become an appetiser to the pleasures of leisure, a beneficent exercise to the human organism, a [useful] passion . . . when . . . well regulated and limited."

After appearing in *L'Egalité, The Right to Be Lazy* was published as a brochure in June 1881. In 1883 Lafargue revised it and added a new preface. A new edition appeared in 1898, another in 1900 in a collection of Lafargue's writings,[8] and there were numerous subsequent editions. The work became immensely popular. According to Alexandre Bracke, the longtime socialist deputy, it was the socialist pamphlet most extensively translated after the *Communist Manifesto* and was translated into Russian before the *Manifesto*. In between and at both ends of the political spectrum it enjoyed the reputation of a small masterpiece of socialist revolutionary literature. The nationalist and anti-semitic writer Edouard Drumont regretted some "useless blasphemies," but called it "a most striking work . . . almost a masterpiece of irony." Gustave Hervé, then a militant socialist, hailed it simply as "the masterpiece of criticism of the capitalist regime," the "most acute and happiest critique of capitalism since the *Communist Manifesto*."[9]

The essay's immediate impact lay in the inclusion in the 1880 program adopted by the Federated Socialist Workers Party of an eight-hour day and a weekly day of rest. The work also had an impact on subsequent socialist thought. Karl Kautsky, who read the pamphlet and most certainly discussed its contents with Lafargue, later deemed socialism as the only means of "rendering access to the proletariat all the sources of culture . . . only [it] can make possible the reduction of hours of work to such a point that the working man can enjoy leisure enough to acquire adequate knowledge." And Kautsky made it clear he meant "not the freedom of labor but the freedom *from* labor . . . that will bring to mankind freedom of life, freedom for artistic and intellectual activity, freedom for the noblest enjoyment."[10] The "right to work and leisure" was called for in the Charter of the National Council of Resistance in 1944, the program embodying the hopes of most World War II *résistants* for greater social and economic democracy. The same attitude underlay the demand for *autogestion,* self-management, in May 1968; it was formulated not simply to increase productivity but to suppress the status of proletarian by suppressing repetitive work itself and replacing it with more fulfilling activity. Still, before the strife-ridden 1960s sales of the pamphlet were weak, and its only outlets for publication were provided by minor libertarian presses. The 1964 edition, however, brought out by Maspéro, was very successful.[11]

Subsequent French editions were published in 1974 and 1976 by Maspéro and in 1980 by Editions de la Liberté; the introduction to each made a case for the relevance of Lafargue's work to the contemporary scene. For example, Amédée Dunois, introducing the 1976 edition, placed emphasis on the demand for self-management made that year by striking workers. More intellectuals, *lycéens,* activists, *gauchistes,* and anarchists purchased the pamphlet than did workers, however, according to the preface of the 1974 edition. The work is still in print. Its message, favoring more leisure time as a right, has been taken as a precursor of more recent interest in the history and sociology of leisure and as a relevant criticism of today's consumer-based society.[12] It has also been cited as a precursor to sociological analyses of the phenomenon of leisure time in post-industrial societies. The journalist Raymond Cartier, referring to the right to work as a socialist battle cry in 1848 and to Lafargue as deliberately taking the opposite view, said: "It sufficed to replace 'laziness' with 'leisure' to find in Lafargue all the theory of modern life."[13]

* * *

Questions regarding the originality of *The Right to Be Lazy* have been raised. Lafargue did not cite an 1861 book by Maurice Cristal, who argued that relaxation for workers was a right they possessed.[14] Nor did Lafargue cite the work of Henri Brissac, in which similar statements appear. Whether he read them remains unclear. There appears less doubt that he got his title from the book he found in Marx's library, Louis Moreau-Christophe's *Du droit à l'oisiveté et de l'organisation du travail servile dans les républiques grecques et romaines* (The Right to Idleness and the Organization of Servile Labor in the Greek and Roman Republics, 1849).[15]

Lafargue may have gotten more than his title from Moreau-Christophe: *The Right to Be Lazy* is filled with exact citations taken from labor histories, geography, and economic tracts and with specific references to writers of antiquity who commented on the subject.[16] Among the ancients quoted or referred to are Herodotus, Livy, Xenophon, Aristotle, Virgil, and Juvenal, men who scorned labor and praised leisure. Many of these citations appear in the book by Moreau-Christophe. The sixteenth-century writers whom Lafargue appreciated, especially picaresque novelists who hailed carousing and *fêtes pantagruéliques,* fell outside the scope of Moreau-Christophe's work, as did the British statistics and social comment Lafargue made considerable use of. But the fact that he failed to give credit to Moreau-Christophe, and thus left the impression that he got those citations directly from the works quoted, raises the question whether he borrowed extensively from other sources as well.

Lafargue can also be criticized for the same overstatement and excessive generalization that marked Moreau-Christophe's work. Neither classical antiquity nor the Middle Ages can be treated as a whole; not all labor was servile (some artisans were free and some Romans voluntarily engaged in commercial activity); and in spite of a widespread disrespect for labor, leisure was never proclaimed as a right. But it should be noted that Lafargue never said that citizens of ancient Greece and Rome shunned all commercial or industrial activity, only that the preference of most not to be active in these areas became a reality by reason of slavery. Because citizens were not forced to labor, their right to leisure was real.

Moreover, Lafargue published his study in pamphlet form in June 1881, two months after the death of Moreau-Christophe, which raises the possibility that he deliberately waited until the one person in the best position to raise questions was no longer on the scene. Lafargue also relied on the Roy translation of *Capital* for several citations without, apart from two instances, crediting Marx.[17] Yet Engels, not reluctant to criticize Lafargue on other matters, never referred to the omissions in his correspondence. Was the absence of sources deliberate, sloppy form, or a combination of both? Certainly, Lafargue was widely if superficially read in these sources; he was capable of providing references other than those in Moreau or in Marx. His objective, of course, was to spread Marxist propaganda in popular form, which is one explanation for the absence of annotation.[18]

While Lafargue wrote and worked in London, developments continued in France. Events there as the old decade ended and a new one began could be observed with considerable satisfaction. A workers' congress had called for collectivization and had established an independent workers' party, bringing an end to the domination—though not to the durability—of Proudhonian ideas in the labor movement. An emerging collectivist press was beginning to disseminate Marxist ideas. Eight years after the defeat of the Commune, the French workers' movement had set foot on the road to Marxism.[19]

Even so, the opposition to and the discord within the fledgling party was only too apparent. Anarchists, soon reinforced by Communards returning after the July 1880 amnesty, rejected political solutions, and radical republicans who rejected socialism showed alarm at the prospect of a socialist party. A coalition of socialists and Radicals (a group of liberal republicans) set up a short-lived Socialist Republican Alliance. Longuet, now closely associated with Clemenceau, was a member. Also participating was Lafargue's old comrade-in-arms, Victor Jaclard. Rather than write for *L'Egalité,* as Lafargue had wanted, Jaclard preferred to help this coalition "introduce a new force on the doorstep of the bourgeoisie."[20]

Following Communalist tradition, the new Federated Socialist Workers Party was decentralized and composed of diverse elements. In addition to Marxists, there were mutualists (Proudhonists), who recognized the necessity of independent political action but repudiated the emphasis placed by the Marxists on revolution, Blanquists, reformists, and a handful of Radicals.[21] Personality clashes reinforced and contributed to doctrinal differences. Some resented Guesde's leadership; others could not stomach the discipline insisted on, a recurrence of the anarchist rejection of Marxist authoritarianism in the days of the First International. And the circulation of the party press was embarrassingly small: *L'Egalité,* appearing every Wednesday, had a print run of about 5,000 copies; *Le Prolétaire,* the newspaper managed by Brousse, perhaps 6,000; and the limited readership elicited references to a *presse confidentielle.*

A national legislative election was scheduled for 1881, which meant that the new party's need for a platform, or program, was pressing. Drafts emerged from various quarters: Guesde's revealed his doctrinal eclecticism; anarchists and reformists offered their own.[22] To enable Guesde and the new party to compile a statistical portrait of living and working conditions of the French proletariat, Marx drafted his detailed and comprehensive "enquête ouvrier," a 101-item questionnaire for the working-class readers of *La Revue socialiste.* It was hoped that the data gained, if incorporated into the party program, might induce "a republican government to follow the example of the monarchical government of England" in bringing about social legislation.[23]

While touring the country trying to organize local and regional groups, Guesde had found that most of the programs proposed were reformist in nature, asking only for greater civil and social rights. In Zurich, Malon saw himself as able to reconcile differences between labor groups seeking reform and more revolutionary Marxists. Once associated with anarchists, Malon had broken with them by 1876 over the question of what form of government to propose (he preferred a republic; they opposed any form of state organization), and during the next four years had moved further in the direction of reformism.

Malon favored a program that included a philosophical-historical section by Lafargue and a section on commerce and industry by Guesde. The program would be broadly based, with emphasis placed on practical reforms. He rightly believed that he spoke for most French workers, and he feared the creation of a revolutionary avant-garde out of touch with them. A reform-laden program would also enable socialists to make a good showing in the forthcoming election. He did not want workers to vote for progressive bourgeois candidates. Marxists, in contrast, favored a small and doctrinally correct party. At the end of April, Malon learned from Lafargue of Marx's willingness to help draft a program. Believing that his own influence was dominant, Malon informed Guesde that he would accept the results.[24]

Guesde, too, wanted Marx's active participation in drafting a program for the new French party. Lafargue, who had persuaded Marx to help, encouraged Guesde to visit London, assuring him that Marx and Engels would be happy to meet with him. In early May 1880 Guesde arrived and the several days he spent together with Lafargue strengthened ties between the two men.[25]

Toward the end of the month, Marx, Lafargue, and Guesde went to Engels' house to draft a program. Marx dictated the theoretical preamble, the *considérants,* and Lafargue wrote them down. Engels recalled that it was "a masterpiece of cogent argumentation rarely encountered, clearly and succinctly written for the masses: I myself was astonished by this concise formulation."[26]

The draft program called for collective appropriation, which "can emerge only from the revolutionary action of the productive class [or proletariat] organized as a distinct political party" and that such an organization must be sought "by all the means at the disposal of the proletariat including universal suffrage ... transformed into an instrument of emancipation."

Demands for specific civil liberties and social legislation included the rights of free speech and assembly, communal autonomy, and abolition of the *livret* (worker's passport), religious budget, public debt, and standing army; in the economic and social sectors, an eight-hour day, six-day week, minimum wage, equal salary for women, old-age pensions, abolition of child labor and of the importation of cheap foreign labor, employees' accident compensation, a voice for workers in factory administration, a progressive income tax and abolition of indirect taxes, and the "annulment of all contracts alienating public ownership," seen as meaning the nationalization of banks, mines, and railroads. The model was that of the SPD's program in Germany, distinguishing between a revolutionary-sounding theoretical statement and a "minimum" electoral program of immediately realizable demands capable of fruition under capitalism.

Guesde and Lafargue added references to the need of the proletariat, first, not only to win power but to retain it (having in mind Paris revolutionaries of the nineteenth century, ultimately defeated by a coalition of middle-class and farming elements in the rest of the country), and second, to understand their class interests, specifically the need to combat anarchism (a requirement whose fulfillment necessarily meant the simplification of Marxist doctrine, which may explain much of the mechanistic nature of Guesdism). Guesde also insisted, for electoral purposes, on the inclusion of a minimum wage, which Marx found "immature" but to which he reluctantly agreed.[27]

The drafters erred in not insisting on the participation of Paul Brousse, then completing his exile in London. Lafargue, as Brousse was to admit, had initially asked his help in drafting a program but had been refused. Brousse later said that he did not accept Lafargue's invitation because "having left France eight years ago, I did not know the movement well enough, [and] because I smelled a Marxist intrigue." Remembering the anarchist-Marxist struggles in the International, Brousse could not bring himself to trust the *côterie marxiste;* and he saw conspiracy in every political act of Guesde or Lafargue. Eduard Bernstein regretted Brousse's absence; he was, after all, in London and was a "trusted person of a considerable wing of the party."[28]

Guesde proposed that no further efforts be made to get Brousse to attend: he would "get involved in long-winded discussions about misunderstood phrases." Engels, who found Brousse "the greatest muddlehead I have ever encountered," agreed with Marx that this was not their business.[29] In a subsequent letter to Lafargue, Brousse voiced concern: his fears about the program had been realized. He predicted that the draft would be approved only "with difficulty," and if approved, "accepted without enthusiasm."[30]

Like Lafargue, Brousse had been a medical student drawn to positivism and scientism, but unlike Lafargue he had been attracted to Bakuninist activism. Brousse, too, went to Spain (in December 1872), where he began an anarchist newspaper intended for distribution in southern France. In the years 1876–1878 he did not shrink from advocating violence and praised, without using the term, "propaganda by the deed." In Switzerland, where he was active in the Jura Federation in the late seventies, he incurred the wrath of Guillaume, who found him excessively radical.[31] Arguing that socialism must adapt to "new circumstances" and admitting the possibility of a transition period to anarchy, Brousse came to favor participation in municipal elections and a program of immediately realizable reforms based on communal autonomy. He ultimately was won over to a wholly reformist strategy.

Anarchism provided Brousse with his ideas on public services, and he believed anarchism's federative principle should be the basis for socialist strategy and party structure. The commune—as an admin-

istrative entity—he saw as the political framework within which the
working class could secure political power and establish socialism.
Within a short time of his return to Paris in July 1880, Brousse broke
definitively with anarchism and developed a theory of municipal socialism in which the tradition of the Commune was put in the context
of a realistic and a "possible" approach. At the root of the evolution
in his thinking lay the failure of the International, for which he blamed
the centralized structure imposed on the organization by Marx and
the General Council. This anti-Marxist attitude was to characterize
the remainder of his political life: he would work to prevent Marxist
control of any French workers' party and of a new International.[32]

With the draft program completed in late May, Lafargue and
Guesde got in touch with Malon to win his backing. His stamp of
approval, they reasoned, would further the draft's chances of party
adoption.[33] Though Malon found the program too short and not
sufficiently reformist, he believed it could be revised and agreed to
support it. A month later this Marxist program was published in the
socialist press; it appeared in *L'Egalité*, for example, on June 30.
Later Malon claimed that Guesde's visit to London to put the program together had taken him by surprise, a complaint that implied he
had been kept uninformed. His correspondence showed, however, that
he had been aware of the impending visit and that he had approved the
resulting draft.[34] Lafargue, in turn, was already criticizing Malon's
eclecticism, specifically his former anarchism, which rendered him incapable of understanding the nature of the class struggle.[35] These conflicts presaged the difficulties and schisms to come.

The program was interpreted in different ways. Marxists found that
it contained reforms that were theoretically capable of realization in
a bourgeois economy, but believed that the middle class would probably reject such changes and in the process demonstrate the need for
a revolutionary strategy. Reformists hailed the reforms and the decentralization called for as a significant first step in winning political
power and as a force making for working-class unity: they simply
wanted more. Brousse was very critical. He cited what he described as
the excessive centralization of the International, and he believed that
Marx and Engels would not stop at giving French socialists advice but
would seek a controlling voice.[36] Anarchists condemned the program
as recognizing the right of the state to exist and as insufficiently

revolutionary, and an anarchist spokesman, Jean Grave, called for a negative vote. French workers influenced by Proudhonist anarchism were more critical than French socialists; various regional labor congresses meeting in the second half of 1880 rejected the program's emphasis on elections.[37]

To refute them, Lafargue wrote a searing article in the August 11, 1880 issue of *L'Egalité*. His language was especially intemperate, denouncing anarchists as "bourgeois" and "reactionary" and accusing them of creating discord in the party. Doubtless hardline anarchists would have fought the program in any event, but the article offended even more moderate elements. Those in the south of France counterattacked. Malon urged Guesde not to speak there, and noted that Lafargue's *sarcasmes sanglants* made even collectivist groups come out for anarchism. A Midi regional congress had already rejected the program.[38]

Even Bernstein, generally admiring of Lafargue, was critical: he called him a "cutting polemicist," who as the recognized "spokesman" of Marx discredited Marxism. De Paepe agreed that Lafargue's style was deplorable. In a letter to Malon he referred to "that contemptuous tone, that conceited air, that pretension to scientific and historical infallibility, that disdain of the intellectual works of an intelligent and studious proletariat [which] always annoys me, no matter from where it comes."[39]

In a letter to Brousse, Lafargue regretted the excesses in his antianarchist attacks, admitting that he and not Guesde was to blame. Still, he justified them as responses to the anarchist condemnation of Marxists as bourgeois on the basis of the reforms that the program espoused. "For a long time anarchist attacks and calumnies against German socialists wore on my nerves and I'm eager to relieve myself."[40] In August he wrote Guesde: "I am disgusted with the accusations hurled against the Germans by these anarchist empty talkers [who sound] as if nothing would have been easier for Marx and Engels to make disturbances which would have sounded the tocsin of reaction in Europe."[41] Revealing, in this context, is a police report dated August 14, 1880, which reported allegations that Lafargue was not even a real name but a pseudonym for a German socialist.

As noted earlier, an amnesty for most Communards finally became law that summer, in July, the result of a nine-year struggle. When the news reached England, the Lafargues, the Longuets, and Jenny Marx—but not her husband, who remained in London—were on a seaside holiday in Ramsgate. That fall Charles Longuet, as we have seen, left his family in London and departed to work on Clemenceau's newspaper, *La Justice,* and to look for living quarters.[42] Lafargue had initially approved of his brother-in-laws's association with Clemenceau, but became increasingly disenchanted with *La Justice*'s hard line against collectivism. Longuet, complained Lafargue, wanted to form a left-wing radical party with the "debris of the Commune, to take from and emasculate the Workers Party Program." One of the best of the moderates by virtue of intelligence and moral character, he concluded, was "moving toward bourgeois fiefs."[43] The rift between the two, occasioned by ideological differences, widened over family matters in the years to come.

With the return of the Communards (aside from Lafargue, who remained in London until 1882), ideological conflict within the socialist movement intensified, making its lack of unity apparent. The Fourth French Socialist Workers' Congress ("socialist" had been added), meeting at Le Havre in November 1880, underwent a schism. Cooperativists and trade unionists both had second thoughts about following a collectivist path; they had regained their strength in the year since their defeat at Marseilles. Having reconstituted their majority, they voted to reverse that decision. Only by organizing a subsequent congress of their own did collectivists secure approval of their program. Even this, however, required concessions to the libertarians and reformists among them. Friends of Brousse and Malon managed to inject two clauses relating to municipal socialism. Anarchists who supported a collectivist framework secured an amendment stating that collective ownership was to be viewed as "a transition stage to libertarian communism." They also won a promise that if results in the 1881 election proved unsatisfactory, it would be the last such "electoral experience": emphasis would then be placed on revolutionary action.[44]

Even so, Marx seemed pleased by developments in France. He told Sorge that "things are going splendidly in Europe . . . thanks primarily to Guesde's coming over to us and to the work of my son-in-law Lafargue . . . Even Malon, in the *Revue socialiste* . . . has had to espouse *socialisme scientifique,* that is, a *German* socialism . . . this is *the first real labor movement in France.* Until now only sects existed there . . . Because the economic section of the program consists solely of demands that had arisen spontaneously from labor and [because of] an introduction defining the common goal, [the program] is an energetic step towards pulling the French workers down to earth from their fog of phraseology."[45]

Yet this noisy audacious party, with all its hopes, consisted only of a few small groups that agreed on a few basic principles. Lafargue tried to make Marx aware of the difficulties. "You believed, because we spoke at the top of our voices of our party, of the Workers Party, that it materialized, that the party was a reality with all of its organs intact; feet and arms, stomach and head; in reality the Party is still only a mouth [*gueule*] . . . The Workers Party does not exist."[46]

And even the "mouth" was soon stilled. Because of financial problems, *L'Egalité*, after the issue of August 15, 1880, and after only seven months, again suspended publication. In announcing the decision to its surprised readers, the newspaper carried an ad for a new daily that Malon began to publish in Lyons, *L'Emancipation*. The names of Guesde, Lafargue, and Brousse were listed as staff writers. Lafargue, who as always contributed through the mail from London, published a handful of articles, but this newspaper survived for only twenty-four issues.[47]

First Guesde and then Lafargue, beginning in June 1881, also wrote for *Le Citoyen,* the newspaper run by Achille Secondigné, a Radical who under Guesde's influence became a socialist. Both Guesde and Lafargue submitted copy because they needed the money.[48] Brousse opposed their collaboration, complaining that socialist participation in bourgeois newspapers would "drain our ranks" and encourage readers to believe that the newspaper was in fact a "party organ."[49] The Marxist participants agreed that they lacked full freedom to write as they pleased.[50] From the outset, Lafargue urged Guesde to reestablish an independent newspaper or to revive *L'Egalité*, so they could again have their own organ. He suggested that it could be funded by an anonymous group, each member contributing a small amount.[51]

Meanwhile, anarchists charged that the new party was run by the "German," Marx. Marx was aware of the charge, and attributed it to an excess of "national feeling" on the part of the French Left.[52] Neither Marx nor Engels wanted to act as a "pope" of international socialism; they were not about to repeat the errors of the International. As with the German Social Democratic Party after its emergence in the Gotha unification congress, Marx—although he anticipated a schism—continued to advise the French party through

Lafargue. Even so, his connection with it, according to Engels, was "a very slender one" and the advice was "scarcely ever followed." Like Marx and Engels themselves, Marxist historians later insisted that the "Guesdist" assimilation of Marxism was imperfect and superficial.[53] But at the time Broussists as well as anarchists criticized Guesde and his associates for "submitting to the will of a man who lived in London outside any party control."[54]

17 The Road to Schism

> What revolutionary times we live in! The least revolutionary are
> the revolutionaries.
>
> —Paul Lafargue

Relations between Lafargue and Brousse continued to deteriorate, at
least on the theoretical plane. From April through June 1881, a remarkable exchange of letters between the two widened the gulf between them and revealed their differing conceptions of socialism.
Lafargue was highly critical of Brousse's "heavy involvement" in Paris
politics in Montmartre, where anarchist sentiment ran strong. Montmartre, he complained, was not France, and Brousse always tended to
be absorbed by his "narrow milieu": in Switzerland, Belgium, London, and now Paris. Lafargue also hinted that Brousse was motivated
by envy of Guesde's leadership role.[1]

Brousse denied any jealousy. He admired Guesde's polemical talent
but admitted that he and some others worried about his managerial
skills. Malon, who enjoyed a wider basis of support, was found more
suitable to head the party. It was Lafargue's perceptions of reality that
were limited: he saw only the industrial North, Reims and Roubaix,
where large-scale industry provided disciplined workers prepared to
accept Marxism. But this was by no means true of the South and the
East, where collectivist sentiment was more moderate and where the
imposition of "simplistic sectarian beliefs" sowed division. "You and
Guesde seek to bend facts to your manner of seeing . . . Where circumstances do not coincide with your doctrine, you stand with arms
crossed . . . You are authoritarians. I am not. That is the single serious
difference between us."

Lafargue rejected the charge. The 1880 program recognized the
usefulness of both revolutionary and reformist strategies and was
deliberately left incomplete in order to let circumstances define tactics. Only three goals were specified: nationalization of the instruments of production; the necessity of struggle in all areas; and

"because the appetite grows in the eating," the need to accept reforms. Yet, Lafargue pointed out, Brousse had refused to support and
had even protested against such a program. With regard to a party
chief it was he and not Lafargue who had raised the issue and proposed Malon. The party "must not incarnate itself in anyone, neither
in Guesde nor in Malon." What was needed was "the dictatorship of
the working class, not a personal dictatorship." Lafargue also opposed Brousse's view of a party newspaper as one open to all shades
of socialist thought. A "simple administrative sheet" need not defend
any particular theoretical standpoint, because a workers' party must
accommodate all points of view. But a newspaper, which seeks to
influence the movement and the party, is something else; "it must be
straightforward, know where it wants to go, and must not be a catch-
all where anyone can freely submit his prose."

Still, in its essentials, Lafargue believed that Brousse shared his
collectivist view of socialism: that property in capitalist civilization
was ready to evolve, to take a national or communal form according
to circumstances. Because revolution was imminent, however, organization, propaganda, and alliances with other progressive groups
were all required. He wrote:

> I believe that in a few years, five or six, the movement will take a
> revolutionary character. Events to take place in Russia will have a
> terrible aftereffect in Europe. Economic unrest generated by Ameri-
> can competition will grow . . . We must be ready . . . must make noise
> . . . This blatant propaganda which somewhat shocks you is indis-
> pensable to stir the masses. Along with making it we must prepare
> organized cadres to receive the new arrivals whose interest we will
> have aroused. Your view is shaped by the thought of old anarchist
> elements . . . who deny the need for rules and organization.

Brousse responded that he believed that what separated him from
Lafargue was more than a clash of personalities. Lafargue was sectarian and consequently authoritarian. Brousse saw himself, on the
contrary, as empirical, and if shown wrong capable of change and of
responding to "the force of opinion." Lafargue favored alliances with
nonsocialists and hoped to dominate them. Brousse opposed alliances, fearing that at the present state of party development they
would "mutilate, divide and pulverize the party."

Lafargue's reply revealed that he was losing patience. Brousse had
slid into a rut from which he could not emerge, a tendency developed

in the milieu of petty rivalries characteristic of refugee circles. By writing for *Le Citoyen*, Lafargue explained, Guesde and he hoped "to tame Secondigné and stamp the newspaper with our imprint." The party was to rouse the workers and excite hatred of the bourgeoisie by describing public suffering in detail and by instilling in workers' minds the conclusions drawn from economic development. In principle Lafargue favored electoral alliances with advanced bourgeois groups, "because a party is not an old virgin who must always show a prudish fear of letting herself be violated. One enters an alliance to get something: an industrial reform, a step forward for the party." To forestall any charge of opportunism, party members should not accept any post while society remained in the "bourgeois stage" of development. To Guesde, Lafargue complained that Brousse was sincere but strategically limited. "He still believes he is in the Swiss Jura . . . he cannot be counted on."[2]

Able to express himself freely to Guesde, Lafargue revealed his optimism not only for socialism but for the future of mankind. He admired the state of technology reached by the Americans, who had recently invented a compressed air machine to mine coal, and he speculated about the "disastrous" impact this would have on English mining. Had Guesde heard of the new battery, which by storing electricity "might enable us to change the movement of the wind, rivers, and tides into electricity which could be carried anywhere one wished to be turned back into light, warmth, and movement? What revolutionary times we live in! The least revolutionary are the revolutionaries."

In September 1880, about a month after *L'Egalité*, *La Revue socialiste* too was forced to suspend publication. but the major socialist setback was the national legislative election held the next summer. The reforms showed most voters as simply indifferent to socialism.

The voters had already sealed the defeat of the monarchist Right. The Senate majority that had approved the decision of the royalist president, MacMahon, to dissolve the Chamber of Deputies had been defeated in 1879 when republicans won a fifty-seat majority. MacMahon's resignation followed in the same month, and he had been replaced by the conservative republican lawyer Jules Grévy. Republicans had won regional and local elections during the next two years, and in 1881 they sent 440 of 551 deputies to the Chamber. By that time Parliament had left Versailles to return to Paris. July 14 had been declared the national holiday, and the *Marseillaise* the national anthem.

The new socialist party secured a nationwide return of only 60,000 votes. Guesde ran for the Chamber of Deputies in Roubaix, the textile manufacturing town in the Nord Department, and received a mere 494 votes. Only one socialist was elected: the poet Clovis Hugues, from Marseilles. The party's poor performance reinforced the reformist reaction to and the resentment of Marx and German theory by Brousse, Malon, and others—and also, conversely, strengthened the emphasis they placed on French traditions and needs.[3]

Socialist forces were divided going into the 1881 election. In May, anarchists accused the Federated Socialist Workers Party of electoralism and parliamentarianism. Some former Communards, including Charles Longuet, now allied with Radicals in the Republican Socialist Alliance, criticized it from the right. Broussists saw the party program as unrealizable and incomprehensible to workers. And, admittedly, given the reality of the long working day and the paucity of educational opportunity for the poor, there was little opportunity for theoretical reflection on the workers' part. The critics also condemned the party's internationalism. It was only a decade after the war with Prussia, which had revived the Jacobin tradition, and Marxist socialism and the 1880 program were seen as "German imports." Brousse's newspaper, *Le Prolétaire,* described Guesde as a German agent and called all the more loudly for reform. Followers of Guesde and Lafargue, convinced that major reform was impossible in capitalist society, wanted to use the election for propaganda purposes. In return, *L'Egalité* denounced Brousse and his lieutenant, Jules Joffrin, soon a candidate in a Paris by-election, for working to alter the party program. Thus personal and structural differences were reinforced by differences over theory and strategy.

These debates were nourished by the electoral defeat, and the incessant squabbling led the socialists further down the road to schism. Their loose coalition fell apart. Furious at what he regarded as accusations hurled against him, especially the charge that he favored a party dictator, Lafargue invested a not inconsiderable percentage of his limited income in postage in order to reply. He sent statements to the staffs of both *L'Egalité* and *Le Prolétaire* denying Brousse's charge that he had proposed Guesde as "dictator of the party."[4]

These charges and countercharges embittered relations between Lafargue and Brousse. Reporting Brousse's accusations to Malon, Lafargue wrote—but crossed out in his draft—that "Brousse left London with a plan to destroy what we did with *L'Egalité*." Malon reminded Lafargue that he, Malon, had expressly wanted Guesde to "lead" the party. Lafargue appreciated the nuance, but denied any need for a chief and in a letter to *L'Egalité* repeated his denial.[5]

Brousse refused to hear of a centralized party. While content with the structure proposed at the 1879 Marseilles Congress, which provided autonomy to local groups and to regional federations, he feared that a program coming from London would be imposed on the party. A program formulated by groups and federations, while keeping the national context in mind, could better recognize local needs and concerns, and Brousse blamed the 1880 program for the socialists' dismal electoral performance.[6]

Lafargue insisted that Guesde had to take a stand on the question of organization, and he was pleased that Guesde had apparently approved his plan to delay the formation of a national committee until a common understanding among socialist groups was reached. Without such an understanding, "we are armed only with the program that Brousse rejects." To create an executive prematurely would "hand power over to schemers." Lafargue proposed as a first step that the forthcoming Reims Congress name a five-member committee to sound out all groups on redefining the party structure.[7]

Marx and Engels, as well as German socialists, began to show concern over the party quarrel in France. An "exasperated" Malon had met Eduard Bernstein in Switzerland and had given him a detailed account. Lafargue had asked the German socialist party, in the person of Bernstein, to help fund *L'Egalité,* and presumably gave him the Marxist version of events. The confused Bernstein wrote to Engels to ask for clarification and for advice about whether to grant the money.[8]

Engels urged him not to support a new series of *L'Egalité,* and regretted Lafargue's impromptu appeal, which lacked his and Marx's approval. "Lafargue's letter," wrote Engels, "was one of those *coups de tête* that the French (I mean those born south of the Bordeaux-Lyons line) cannot stop themselves from making from time to time ... Even [Lafargue's] wife, usually able to prevent those sorts of things, did not know of it in advance. With the exception of Lafargue—who is always favorable to something happening, even anything, no matter what, we all have doubts about *L'Egalité* No. 3."

Engels believed that even with the hoped-for funding it could not survive a year and that "if Guesde and Laf[argue] wish absolutely to give themselves a reputation in Paris as destroyers of newspapers, we cannot stop them, but we do not have to help them ... These gentlemen must finally learn to count on their own resources."[9]

Engels found that the French Marxists had made "blunder after blunder": preventing Malon from accepting a post on *L'Intransigent;* Guesde's candidacy at Roubaix; their involvement with *Le Citoyen.* But even more loudly he condemned Brousse and his associates for their hostility to Marx and for having described Guesde and Lafargue as spokesmen of Marx who "wished to sell out French workers to the Prussians," a charge that Engels vigorously denied. "Workers of different lands," said Engels, "because of the theoretical and strategic contribution made by Marx and because of the reputation he enjoys place their confidence in him. When asked for advice he gives it, and it is recognized as the best. It is not that he imposes his will on others."[10]

Guesde and Lafargue exchanged ideas about running the French party, Engels went on, but left Marx and himself wholly uninformed. "Marx's advice to Guesde, sent through Lafargue, is never followed." Engels especially deplored the "impatience" of French socialists and their tendency to use the term "revolution" to excess. In a letter to Laura December 14, Marx similarly regretted her husband's "ultra-revolutionary phraseology" and the French socialists' imperfect and superficial grasp of doctrine. Engels agreed and wondered, with regard to Guesde, whether his "obsession" with revolution issued from a belief that "he will not live long and so wants desperately to see something important happen." Still, he told Bernstein, they had to struggle against Brousse's and Malon's reformism.[11]

Marx and Engels also complained to each other about their French disciples. Lafargue and Guesde "have reaped what they have sown," Engels wrote in early January, "and what we have predicted has come to pass. With their impatience they have bungled a magnificent opportunity." Instead of replying discreetly to slanderous attacks, "they fell into the trap like students, Lafargue leading the way, and replied by openly attacking in such a way as to be considered the instigators ... their polemic is infantile." Equally annoyed, Marx said that his son-in-law's polemics led him into useless debates with Malon from which he always emerged second best. Lafargue was continually put on the defensive by the Broussists for various "theoretical indiscretions."[12]

At the Fifth Workers' and Socialist Congress, held in Reims from October 30 to November 6, 1881, Brousse, Malon, and their followers, who were in the majority and were beginning to be referred to as "Broussists," denounced the 1880 program and proposed that separate local programs, drafted within the framework of a new general text, should be prepared. Their opponents, referred to as "Guesdists" or "Marxists," rejected this counterproposal, but Guesde's resolution, which provided for a single program, was shelved. (For Lafargue, the Broussist majority had been secured by fraudulent tactics, including fictitious mandates, a charge he repeated in person at the following year's Saint-Etienne Congress.)[13] In addition, *Le Prolétaire* became the official party organ and a national executive committee was elected to run the party. Apparently Guesde had not followed Lafargue's organizing strategy to the letter and had agreed that such a committee should be elected by the regional federations, thus ensuring a reformist majority. Lafargue, upset on hearing this, momentarily doubted Guesde's sincerity and threatened to quit, until reassured by a dismayed Mesa that Guesde had had no choice.[14]

In the interests of preserving party unity, Brousse and Malon did not asked for a formal vote; it was decided for the time being both to keep the minimum program and to let socialists in each constituency draft their own electoral program. Yet schism was reached in all but name. In a December by-election, the Broussists in Montmartre ignored the official 1880 program, jettisoning Marx's theoretical preamble and replacing it with a municipally based reformist socialism. They designated the Broussist Jules Joffrin as their candidate, and though he lost he made a respectable showing.

The polemical debate between Brousse and the Marxists was waged in *Le Prolétaire* and in the new (third series) *Egalité*, which started up again in December. Brousse stated his position in the issue of November 19, 1881: "We prefer to abandon the 'all at once' method practiced until now and which largely succeeded in being 'nothing at all': to divide the ideal objective into several realistic stages, to make some of our demands . . . at last possible . . . This policy . . . may be called the policy of possibilities." In the December 11 issue of *Egalité*, Guesde dismissed this "possibilism" as nothing more than opportunism. Brousse's followers at first took offense at the label "Possibilist" hurled at them by the Marxists, but then accepted it as a flag to rally around. The war of words was intensified: attacks by Brousse were responded to by attacks from Guesde and Lafargue.

According to Eduard Bernstein, the two Marxists' sharp criticism of reformist tactics amounted to a program of the "impossible."[15]

While acknowledging the great talent of Marx and Engels, Brousse condemned them for "trying to hold the entire socialist movement in the limits of their mind." He said that Marxists wanted not to expand Marxist doctrine but to "impose it, in all its details." *Le Prolétaire* added that French socialists "have had enough of the program that Guesde had set out to find in the Thames fog."[16] Engels again denied that Marx wanted to impose his views on the French movement and attributed the French party's problems to the anarchist past of Malon and Brousse, which prevented them from grasping Marxist essentials.[17]

"I am awaiting your articles," Guesde wrote to Lafargue in early December 1881. The resurrected *Egalité* was the intended medium, and Lafargue had promised to respond to the criticisms of socialism made by the conservative economist Paul Leroy-Beaulieu and to write on communal autonomy and "bourgeois sentimentality," among other subjects.[18] *L'Egalité* had resumed publication December 11, 1881, able to do so because it had abandoned its earlier refusal to sell shares and had now raised the necessary funds. In the months that followed, much of the Marxist campaign against the Possibilists was waged in its pages and much of it by Lafargue. He also, by mail, participated with Guesde, Deville, and Massard in editorial decision–making. The paper now appeared every Sunday, and unlike its first two incarnations was committed to Marxism. In a gesture of conciliation, *Le Prolétaire* welcomed its return, but within a short time relations between the two newspapers once more reflected the political hostility between Marxists and Broussists.

There was at least one article by Lafargue in each issue, and often more than one. He discussed the party platform, which he wanted to enlarge, and such themes as historical materialism and anticlericalism. He wrote on the mentality of the middle class, on the "class struggle" in fourteenth-century Flanders (which permitted him to launch an anti-anarchist attack); on Possibilism; on the length of the working day; on Catholicism; and beginning March 12, 1882, a series based on a Spanish folk legend previously embellished by Lafargue in April 1872 (in *La Emancipación*) entitled "Pius IX in Paradise."

In it Lafargue waxed ironic at the expense of the pope who had called himself infallible. He sought to show how the bourgeoisie, frightened by the progress of the proletariat, sought shelter behind religion. Throughout his career Lafargue delighted in denouncing "bourgeois palinodes [contradictions]" demonstrating how that class disguised its prejudices under the guise of eternal verities, and in confronting the "hypocritical moralizing" of popular writers who catered to the triumphant bourgeoisie of the nineteenth century.[19] He also wrote on surplus value; on capitalist exchange; and (to use twentieth-century language) on workers' participation in management.[20] On March 19, 1882, he published an article on the evolution of property, a theme to which he would return many times. Sometimes, as in the December 25 issue, Lafargue's articles filled half the newspaper (though they were not always signed, and it was usually Guesde who had the lead editorial).

"Bourgeois Politics," in the December 18 issue, offered a Marxist analysis of the need of the middle class, which he divided into industrial, landed, commercial, financial, and petty components, to win political power. On the occasion of the French acquisition of Tunis, Lafargue wrote that the act was motivated not only by nationalism but by the economic requirements of the bourgeoisie. He wrote, too, on British trade unions and communal autonomy. In addition to writing articles, Lafargue again sent sketches. He played an active role in the administration of the newspaper, requesting financial accounts and sending instructions—for the opening of a political desk to make *L'Egalité* more complete, to take but one example.[21]

When an article came as a reply to one in *Le Prolétaire,* Lafargue relied more than ever on invective and on what Marx called "ultra-revolutionary phraseology."[22] Explicitly renouncing any likelihood of reconciliation, Lafargue denounced Possibilism as an "abandonment of collectivism" and an "espousal of petit-bourgeois idealism" as well as a reversion to the federalism that in 1871 had permitted the destruction of the Paris Commune.[23] Nor were the Radicals grouped under Clemenceau spared: their "opportunism" was condemned in a discussion of German socialist electoral successes. Lafargue was chiefly responsible for the belligerent tone of the Guesdist attack, and he acknowledged that though the first series of *L'Egalité* had criticized mutualists and the second, anarchists, the third aimed at Possibilists. He insisted, however, the attack was not personally motivated but rather was launched in hopes of persuasion.

Laura's translation of the *Communist Manifesto*, published in installments in *L'Egalité* in 1882, popularized the work in France. (There had been an earlier translation in 1848, before the June Days of 1848, but there is no sign that Guesde, Lafargue, or any French Marxist was aware of it or of other translations published in 1849 and 1851.) Engels again praised her work: of the translations he had seen, hers was the best.[24]

The Marxist view of Possibilism as state capitalism and opportunism has endured in socialist historiography.[25] Yet in 1882 the Possibilist position was more popular than the Marxist among workers committed to socialism, and it was not until after 1890, when the followers of Guesde turned to reformist strategies, that Marxism was to attract mass working-class support.[26] In substituting Marx's conciliatory 1864 "Inaugural Address" to the International for the preamble to the 1880 program, it has been argued, Broussists did not practice opportunism but sought a program able to inspire workers to immediate action. In this view the Broussists shifted emphasis from a socialist to a labor party, and their failure was in part due to the Marxist attack and to the Marxists' own turn to reformism.[27] Unlike the criticism of Eduard Bernstein, who at the turn of the century questioned the basic tenets of Marxism, Broussists accepted Marx but embraced the original Bakuninist belief in the dynamics of working-class action. They held that no action unable to win the support of a majority of them should be taken. In this context, municipal socialism was seen not as a final answer but as a means by which workers could taste the realities of power and gain valuable administrative experience.[28]

Lafargue's reliance on the mail to participate in party and newspaper business was cumbersome at best, and his associates on the staff were pressing him to return to France. Mesa promised an interest-free loan for the move, but had to scale back the amount to five hundred francs.[29] Brousse offered advice on movers, urging Lafargue not to transport furniture that could be more cheaply replaced in Paris.[30] Lafargue, however, insisted that because his financial situation was still cloudy he had to be assured of a regular income. Mesa thereupon looked into the possibility of additional newspaper work; he made inquiries, but nothing materialized.[31]

In March 1882, a militant republican from Lyons who had joined the party in Paris, Léon Camescasse, became an adjustor for a Paris life and fire insurance company, Union Nationale. He had managed to secure a position for a friend and similarly was able to offer Lafargue a job.[32] Deville supplied additional information: the post paid 150 francs the first month, but raises would ensure a yearly salary of 4,000 francs after six months. It was an excellent opportunity, Deville assured him, but a prompt reply was necessary.[33] When Lafargue wanted the salary guaranteed in writing, Deville told him this was impossible and urged him to accept at once.[34] Lafargue agreed, and on April 5, 1882, returned to Paris.

Laura remained behind to look after her father, now alone and aging. Her mother had died in early December. Anticipating Paul and Laura's return to France the previous year, Jenny Longuet had written to Laura to say how sad it was that their mother was losing her children when she most needed them and how lonely she would feel after Laura's departure.[35] The old couple had spent most of July 1881 in the resort of Eastbourne. Later that summer Marx and his wife, though she was ill, visited Jenny and their grandchildren, whom they badly missed, in the Paris suburb of Argenteuil. Within a few weeks of their arrival, a telegram came from London stating that Eleanor was seriously ill, suffering from nervous depression and anorexia. Marx left for England at once, leaving his wife and Helen Demuth to return later. In October Marx himself fell ill with a serious attack of pleurisy, and had to be nursed by Laura and Eleanor.[36] After his wife's final illness and death and on the advice of his doctor, he went to the Isle of Wight with Eleanor, who was herself worn out with the strain of caring for two sick patients, her mother's death, and her impatience to "do something" with her life.[37] Bad weather was to plague Marx's last year, following him and Eleanor from France to Algiers, where he unsuccessfully sought a warmer climate. Laura, meanwhile, made plans to join Paul in France.

A period was over for the forty-two-year-old Lafargue. With his return to France his life would henceforth be even more closely bound up with the revolutionary socialist party and its struggles. His long stay in London had permitted a fuller—if still incomplete—understanding of Marxist socialism. Indeed, his reputation as the only Frenchman thus far to be saturated with Marxism, as well as his close ties with Marx and Engels, gave him the prestige that enabled him to introduce it to his countrymen.

18 The Marxists Found a Party

> This is the task of scientific socialism ... to impart to the now
> oppressed proletariat class a full knowledge of the conditions and
> of the meaning of the momentous act it is called upon to accom-
> plish.
>
> —Friedrich Engels

While awaiting Laura, who would join him in July, Lafargue moved into a third-floor apartment at 36 rue du Bac. His sister-in-law Jenny was happy to have him in Paris, and looked forward to her sister's arrival.[1] Aware that he was under police surveillance, he tried to conceal his address by receiving his mail at *L'Egalité*'s office. Within a few days, he attended an *Egalité* meeting as a member of the strike committee of the Nouvelle Fédération du Centre, the Guesdists' Paris organization established in January 1882 to counter the Broussists' Union Fédérative du Centre. When not at his job at the insurance company or at the newspaper he attended meetings of the Nouvelle Fédération executive, where he got assignments such as investigating congresses held by cooperative societies as possible sources of recruitment.[2]

He soon began an arduous speaking schedule. According to Paris police reports, he spoke at least every other day, largely to working-class audiences, providing a Marxist analysis of both ongoing events and other subjects. He spoke, for example, at Fédération du Centre meetings on socialist-governed municipalities and on reorganizing the workers' party; at the Revolutionary Socialist Circle of the Four-teenth Arrondissement on a strike of Paris carpenters then in progress; at the Young Socialists' Circle on a shoemakers' strike; and at gath-erings of similar groups.[3] Often he appeared with Guesde or other speakers; on one occasion he joined Guesde and Louise Michel to condemn a proposed French military expedition to Egypt. Michel, who had led a women's brigade in the Commune fighting, had met Lafargue in London on her return from exile in New Caledonia, and socialists did not want to lose her charisma to the anarchists.[4] He identified himself so closely with his party that his life and that of his party blended into one.

The Paris police, who had followed Lafargue's activities in London, were not only aware of his arrival but had anticipated it. In January an agent had reported that he was receiving monthly payments from *L'Egalité*. His indirect participation in the staff meetings, and even the subject of the discussion, had been duly noted. On May 19 the police, undecided about Lafargue's legal status, asked the Ministry of the Interior for instructions. No reply has survived, but apparently he qualified for amnesty.[5] The police carried out instructions to keep Lafargue, "a well-known socialist who until now lived in London," under close surveillance, and informers infiltrated party meetings and editorial sessions. At times three or more agents covered a meeting that was attended by only twelve to fifteen party members. Lafargue went about openly, but police informants reported that his apartment was carefully concealed.[6] The file on Lafargue at the Paris Prefecture, begun in 1868 and added to during his years in London, thickened as reports were filed almost daily beginning in 1882 and extending— although eventually less frequently—to 1895. The chief investigator, certainly the author of most of the reports in the early 1880s, signed himself "Ludovic," and he and his colleagues dutifully noted Lafargue's presence at every party function, even when he did not speak, and every arrival and departure from Paris. He was then described as of average height, wearing a beard, and having gray hair and a "tanned complexion."[7]

According to these reports Lafargue was not always well received, particularly when he spoke to nonworkers. He made frequent speaking trips to other towns, either alone or with Guesde. In early September the two men, with the Federation paying expenses, lectured in Lyons, Saint-Etienne, Boulogne, and the Allier Department, where Lafargue supported the Montluçon miners' strike.[8] The Paris prefect of police repeatedly asked the government for authority to arrest and expel Lafargue, basing the request on the decree that had outlawed him in 1872, but was always refused on the grounds that the recently enacted amnesty would be compromised.[9]

Laura arrived in July, and she and Paul moved to a small Left Bank hotel at 38 rue de Lille to await their furniture. In early August they moved to an apartment at 66 boulevard de Port-Royal, an eight-story building located in the southern end of the fifth arrondissement, not far from the intersection with the boulevard Saint Michel.[10]

Lafargue had wanted to live in the Latin Quarter because Guesde and Vaillant lived there and because he hoped for propaganda gains among the students. But he soon grew disillusioned with intellectuals, a disappointment he was to experience—and articulate—throughout his life. As he told a collectivist student group in 1900, "believing that it would be easy to draw intellectuals into the movement, we took up our dwelling in their cultural Latin Quarter . . . We became acquainted with hundreds of young men, students of law, medicine, the sciences, but you can count on your fingers those whom we brought into the socialist camp. Our ideas attracted them one day, but the next day the wind blew from another quarter and turned their heads."[11]

They did not expect to stay in the apartment for more than a short time. Their rooms were hardly private, divided from a neighboring apartment only by a screen. The neighborhood, Laura said, was deteriorating and no longer respectable; no family would take rooms in the building. The concierge had wanted to convert the apartments into furnished rooms, and "unsavory specimens" had already taken up "flying quarters below, overhead, and alongside us! . . . In this way we get not only all that is most 'advanced' in the way of French *jeunesse* but much of what is least desirable in the way of 'Belges,' 'Catalans,' and nondescript 'youth' generally." The worst news was that another room, screened off from their bedroom, which the Lafargues had understood would be theirs when available, proved too expensive. As it turned out however, the couple continued to live at this address for five years, until 1887.[12]

Marx traveled to Paris in August to visit his two daughters and their families. (Informed of his arrival, the police were also told that Liebknecht was coming to meet him in order "to reorganize the International to provoke trouble in France.")[13] On one occasion Marx, the Lafargues, Guesde, and Deville lunched at Mesa's home, the first such occasion for Marx. The talk was lively but so filled with "gossip and chatter," Marx told Engels, that it "fatigued" him. When, speaking of dueling, both Guesde and Deville insisted they would challenge anyone calling them cowards, he gave them "a piece of [his] mind," having found the "idiocy" and "immaturity" of their comments offensive.[14]

Other "idiocies" of Lafargue further incensed his father-in-law. Writing from Argenteuil, he told Engels that "Lafargue poses here as an important oracle" and that he found such behavior contemptuous.[15] Lafargue was especially criticized for his "infantile boasting about the revolutionary horrors of the future." He carried "the stigma of his Negro heritage," Marx fulminated. His son-in-law had "no sense of shame, I mean, thereby, no modesty about making himself ridiculous . . . It is time Lafargue end his childish boasting about his future revolutionary atrocities . . . Thus it goes with oracles sometimes; what they believe to be their own inspiration is, on the contrary, very often a reminiscence that remained stuck in memory. What Lafargue has written . . . is in reality a reminiscence from advice by Bakunin. Lafargue is, in fact, the last student of Bakunin, believing in him earnestly."

Marx's outburst was sparked by Paul's apparent support of an anarchist journal; hence the references to his son-in-law's anarchist origins. When the police published statements from an anarchist newspaper, *L'Etendard* of Lyons, Lafargue, who despised police methods, said that the anarchists wanted the same things he did and only relied on different means.[16] Lafargue's boasting seems to have issued from the prestige he now enjoyed, which intoxicated him. Returning to France after years of association with Marx and as Marx's son-in-law, he found that popularizers like Deville sought his advice.[17]

"Lafargue," Marx went on, "should reread the pamphlet on the 'Alliance' on which he and you collaborated, and he will clearly see where he has gotten his most recent ammunition . . . *and into the bargain* [Lafargue] *has misunderstood* [Bakunin]." And, in French, Marx ended: "Longuet, dernier Proudhonist, et Lafargue, dernier Bakuniste! Que le diable les comporte! [Longuet, the last Proudhonist, and Lafargue, the last Bakuninist! The devil take them!]"[18]

Nor was Marx impressed by French socialist congresses. He voiced his dismay with both "Marxists" and "anti-Marxists." "Both types," he said, for reasons that will become clear below, have "done their best to spoil my stay in France." Writing to Eduard Bernstein, who complained that Marxism was becoming discredited in France, Engels agreed that what one referred to as Marxism in France was a very special product, and that Lafargue and the other "self-styled" Marxists there had often provoked Marx to say: 'One thing is certain, that I am no Marxist.' "[19]

Marx's criticism abated, however; within a month he told Laura that he approved of her husband's most recent articles as "his best," written with "solidity and sprightliness." Apparently Lafargue had toned down his annoying "ultrarevolutionary phraseology . . . which should have been left to the anarchists [Broussists], who in reality support the present system and want to upset nothing . . . who only talk but accomplish nothing."[20] Engels at the same time was telling Bernstein that he found Lafargue's articles "delicious." That both Marx and Engels were closely following the fledgling party in France is revealed by their momentary annoyance at not receiving *L'Egalité;* Marx offered to pay the cost of a subscription.[21]

Scarcely had Laura settled in Paris when she departed to accompany her father to Switzerland for reasons of his health.[22] Marx had asked her to; he would not travel alone any longer, and told her bluntly that it was "more or less [her] duty." They were gone from August 23 to September 25, while Lafargue awaited the rest of their furniture and regretted that his wife was not there "to arrange things."[23]

Yet he was already busy speaking on the night of August 29 and on both days of the weekend that followed about the turmoil in the mining area of Montceau-les-Mines.[24] In the Haute-Saône Department, disgruntled workers had struck out at the harsh rule of the great mining companies. The miners and their supporters committed acts of sabotage, dynamited churches thought to be siding with the companies, and threatened potential witnesses. Wholesale arrests had been made, and anarchist and socialist doctrine—the two being totally confused and seen as one—was considered the source of the trouble.

Lafargue also continued to publish popularizations of Marxist thought in *L'Egalité* and in the newspaper that many of the staff were also working on, *Le Citoyen.* He now wrote under his own name and his writings appeared more regularly. His first front-page article in *L'Egalité,* "Proudhon and Strikes," appeared in the issue of June 4, 1882. It was prompted by Brousse's attack on the centralizing tendencies of the Marxists. He must also have remained involved in administrative work, for on one occasion he implored Deville to "take up his pen and contribute."[25] Still, the newspaper never exceeded a circulation of 5,000 and on November 5, 1882, *L'Egalité* once more suspended publication because of financial problems.

On his arrival in France Lafargue had found that Guesde, in addition to managing *L'Egalité,* sat on the editorial board of *Le Citoyen.* He planned to follow his colleague's example, and on April 30, 1882, the names of Lafargue and Deville were added to others on the newspaper's masthead. Since January 1881, with the addition of Marxists to its staff, *Le Citoyen* had moved to the left of its Radical beginnings and openly identified itself as socialist. Lafargue's hope that it would become an important weapon in the socialist arsenal seemed well founded: its circulation, reading 25,000, was about five times that of *L'Egalité*. By September 1882 it was dominated by Guesdists, including Henri Brissac, who had fought both in the June Days and in the Commune, and former Communards Emile Massard and Léon Picard. An arrangement was made with Union Nationale, Lafargue's employer, to make low-cost insurance available for *Le Citoyen* subscribers. The newspaper paid Lafargue a hundred francs a month, though irregularly, which let him "rub along and look for other work," and by May 2 he was on the editorial board.[26]

He submitted articles to *Le Citoyen* almost daily. The subjects varied, but most developed aspects of the workers' party program: electoral reform, rent control, bourgeois patriotism, capitalist expropriation, attacks on economic liberals like Jean-Baptiste Say and Yves Guyot, commentary on contemporary events, the venality of the press, and proposed government railroad purchases. He noted how often patriotism served as a pretext for mounting exploitation at home and abroad: when private interests were hurt, the national interest was defended. In seeking the highest rate of return, capital was not limited to one's own country. In this, as in almost every article, Lafargue's hatred of the bourgeoisie was clear. He wrote too about foreign news, on developments in England, Egypt, and Prussia; and on general themes such as religion, morality, divorce, and women's issues. He criticized his brother-in-law's evolution to Clemencist radicalism. Most important, he tried to show how much Marxism owed to and reflected the current state of scientific progress. His description of surplus value, capitalist exchange, and other Marxist themes were attempts to make theory understandable to the newspaper's working-class readers.

Le Citoyen disappeared in a power struggle at the end of October 1882. The newspaper published by Lissagaray, *La Bataille*, was in poor financial shape, and he proposed a merger with *Le Citoyen*. Though founded as an independent socialist paper a few months earlier, a majority of *La Bataille*'s staff were Broussists. When Lissagaray had charged Brousse with influencing editorial policy in order to accommodate advertisers, Lafargue had seized on the accusation to discredit Possibilism, but overstated his case. The consequence was a hardening of anti-Marxist sentiment in the workers' party.[27] As a condition of the merger, Lissagaray insisted that Lafargue resign his post. The offer was rejected by the staff of *Le Citoyen,* who refused to sacrifice Lafargue or to accept Lissagaray as their editor-in-chief. Nevertheless, on October 17, with the approval of *Le Citoyen*'s owner, who appreciated the additional circulation *La Bataille* would bring, Lissagaray succeeded in bringing the two newspapers together. The former editors tried to found a new *Citoyen,* but were stopped by the courts. The episode is only one example of the intense factionalism and personal rivalry rampant in French socialism. As one observer noted, whenever two revolutionary dailies confronted each other, one soon vanished.[28]

With the disappearance of *Le Citoyen,* the Marxist writers revived *L'Egalité.* Its fourth series began as a daily, on October 24. It survived only until December 8 and proved to be the last series of the paper, save a short-lived fifth series in February 1883 (with Guesde, Lafargue, and Deville as editors, when Guesde was running for office in a working-class district of Paris), and a single issue in April 1886. The format in the fourth series was considerably enlarged: it included sports news and stock market listings, a serial, and coverage of courtroom trials at the Palais de Justice. Lafargue continued to write extensively, contributing thirty-two signed articles in forty-five issues. He seemed to be the linchpin of these newspapers; not only did he write, but he helped to manage them as well. Yet another outlet became available to the Marxists when, beginning November 28, 1883, they began to write for the newspaper run by Jules Vallès, *Le Cri du Peuple.* Lafargue contributed occasional articles on foreign problems. Primarily because of the shortness of funds, there was constant financial juggling and never-ending rotation of the same writers as one short-lived journal gave way to another. In November 1882 Lafargue told Engels, "We spend our lives hoping and despairing."[29]

Lafargue stepped up his attacks on the Broussists' municipal socialism. The fact that only two years earlier, in 1880, he had called for these same municipal programs was ignored. Municipal socialism had been appropriated by Brousse, and to maintain a distinct identity, the Marxists, with Lafargue in the lead, modified their program in a more revolutionary way. In 1879 he had pleaded with Guesde to adopt municipal socialism; now he left this to the Possibilists.[30]

Accordingly, his articles in *L'Egalité* beginning in January 1882 and in *Le Citoyen* in May of that year, show Lafargue—and the Marxists—reversing that earlier position. Even though useful actions—like that of the city of Commentry voting funds for strike relief—could be undertaken by socialist-controlled city councils under capitalism, socialist participation in municipal politics was intended not to secure reforms as ends in themselves but rather to provide a means of enabling workers to contest other centers of power. Socialist control of city councils furnished "a school of combat" and not a panacea. Similarly, minimum programs furthered recruitment and served electoral purposes but were not to be taken as final goals.[31]

Too much municipal reform could prove counterproductive. If a worker-controlled municipality voted for reforms, immigration to that town would increase—encouraged by employers who wanted to enlarge the labor pool available. And employers could always move their firms to areas where labor costs were low, nullifying the reforms.[32] Lafargue, whether driven in reaction to the Broussists or following natural inclinations, was becoming more radical and bringing the Marxist wing of the party along with him. His 1882 articles were criticized by Broussists who pointed out how they contradicted those he had previously published.

There was also a hardening in Lafargue's personal ideology. He now broke with positivist philosophy, because it contradicted economic materialism. "Economic materialism, as taught by Marx, banishes any idealist conception from the history of human development." Comte, he went on, was theological; Comtism, a religion. "Positivism is the most elevated philosophy produced by the French bourgeoisie, a wretched philosophy, a wretched bourgeoisie."[33]

Was his earlier acceptance of municipal socialism a ploy by French Marxists to counter anarchist influence and win workers over to Marxism?[34] Certainly, Lafargue had always insisted that municipal socialism in and of itself would never achieve working-class emancipation. But he had championed its use before the Broussists had, and he rejected it when they embraced it. Under attack by *Le Prolétaire,* which pointed to his inconsistencies, Lafargue sought to explain himself. Socialist ideas, he said, change "as do the economic phenomena which produce them ... it should not be astonishing that I have modified my ideas of 1880."[35] Yet he denied any reversal of course. In 1880, with a new and virtually nonfunctioning party, the idea had been to interest workers in politics, and municipal control was seen as more enticing than such abstractions as the temporary dictatorship of the proletairat. As long as Marxists maintained a separate and distinct political identity, Lafargue throughout his career defended popular strategies aimed at the widest political audience, however opportunistic these strategies appeared to purists.

What had brought matters to a head was the Broussist-Marxist schism and the subsequent need for Marxists to focus on revolution and to deemphasize reform. Lafargue acknowledged the schism and insisted on distinguishing Marxists from Possibilists. The latter opened their ranks to all, bourgeois and worker alike, and followed the path of reform; the former rejected bourgeois members and theories, and chose revolution as the route to working-class emancipation.[36]

One position of Lafargue's was to remain constant: his concern for the interest of the small farmer. Treatment different from that accorded urban workers was seen as necessary. In peasant proprietors, he wrote, lay "the supreme hope of reaction," and threats of expropriation would scarcely strengthen their support for socialism. Instead, their taxes should be cut, their mortgages reduced, and credit reorganized in order to win and keep the allegiance of the small landholding peasant. "The counter-revolution would then lose its support and the revolution would be assured a faithful and courageous ally."[37]

Public services were another reform issue Lafargue had once encouraged but now questioned. By mid-1882 he could find few advantages: state-owned railroads and other services constituted "a reactionary and oppressive solution" and would not even "simplify the work of revolutionary expropriation."[38] What sparked this change of heart? The Possibilists were defending—and, in Lafargue's view, exaggerating—the virtues of public utilities, seeing them as ends rather than means, and here, too, his—and the Guesdists'—position increasingly hardened. However, in order to show his party's concern with improving the lives of workers—to demonstrate that their immediate needs were not being ignored by Marxists—Lafargue recommended consumer and credit-granting cooperatives.[39] Financial manipulations at home and abroad, particularly in North Africa, were relentlessly condemned, but the subject was found to be too remote to appeal to workers striving to make ends meet in the face of wage cuts and rising prices.[40]

More relevant was the question of rents. In June 1882 *Le Citoyen* launched a campaign to have the state both control and tax the rents received by landlords. Lafargue believed the campaign would benefit the newspaper and the party because "the high rate of rents is the general complaint of the Parisians."[41] Rents had been rising since the Second Empire's rebuilding in central Paris.

The issue had become acute because in the years 1876–1881, the century's largest wave of immigration into Paris had added 280,000 people to the city's population. Following on the heels of this immigration was the recession of 1883–84, already beginning in 1882, and the high unemployment especially affected the building trades. Real estate speculators kept apartments vacant rather than lower rents, and returned Communards found housing a goad with which to embarrass the government. In 1879 spokesmen for the working-class inhabitants of the thirteenth and twentieth arrondissements had asked the Municipal Council to supplement the inadequate and overly priced housing available.[42] Socialists of all views devised strategies aimed at alleviating the housing shortage: rent strikes, massive petitions, even sabotage. A progressive tax on rents to limit the profits of speculators, the construction of public housing, a tax on vacant lodgings, the expulsion of foreign workers from Paris, the condemnation of unhealthy buildings, even the confiscation of all property in the city for public use numbered among the remedies proposed. As early as March 1881, the prefect of police reported on a tenants' strike organized by "revolutionary committees."[43]

Lafargue's interest may have been stimulated by Engels. Ten years earlier, in the *Leipzig Volkstaat*, Engels had published three articles on the housing shortage in Germany, a shortage caused, he said, by the economic spurt following the payment of the French indemnity after the Franco Prussian War. Engels also blamed rapid urbanization for driving up rents. He rejected Proudhonist solutions calling for the abolition of rents and for providing workers funds to enable them to purchase their apartments as impractical. The most durable solution lay in the ultimate abolition of capitalism itself.[44]

In both *Le Citoyen* and *L'Egalité,* Lafargue published extensively on this issue. He saw it as of interest in part because it could attract both the worker and the petit bourgeois to socialism. He told the Revolutionary Socialist Circle of the Fourteenth Arrondissement that while awaiting a revolutionary solution it should demand an immediate 50 percent reduction in rent. At a debate sponsored by the Socialist Study Circle of the First and Ninth Arrondissements, citing an Irish precedent, he pointed to a renters' strike as the only way to lower rents. At a meeting of the Fédération du Centre July 5 he called on workers to organize and form neighborhood self-defense groups to contest the eviction of any one of them who might fall behind in payments.[45]

Especially relished was the prospect of a nationwide tax on rents and on unoccupied property, shops as well as apartments, because reduced profits constituted an attack on private property. Equally appealing was the way in which these tactics contrasted with those of the Broussists, who spoke of building low-rental "worker cities" with municipal funds. Lafargue rejected municipally sponsored "workers' barracks," and he saw the removal of the proletariat from the central city as a "muting of revolutionary fervor."[46] He opposed a proposed underground rail system for the same reason: it would remove workers from the "revolutionary center," enhance the value of bourgeois property, and add to the popularity of the municipal councilors who were responsible for the plan.[47]

If landlords tried to compensate for their loss of income by raising rents after the enactment of a tax, their tenants should demand significant rent reductions and, if refused, withhold payment.[48] To critics who claimed reduced rent would pacify workers, Lafargue replied that the benefit would be short-lived: if rents were reduced, employers would lower wages—and so provoke greater discontent. In any case, the need to win over shopkeepers to the party—away from the Radicals—was paramount.[49]

In the summer of 1882, Lafargue urged the formation of neighborhood-based tenants' leagues to coordinate rent strikes. Should a landlord try to confiscate his tenant's possessions in order to cover his losses, league members would assemble to intimidate the landlord or detain the concierge until the furniture was removed to a safe place.[50] Meanwhile Guesde was promoting a massive petition to the Chamber of Deputies that was designed to dramatize discontent and focus resistance, a course of action modeled on the tactics of the Irish Land League. And the press reported examples of tenants and their friends carrying off their furniture—to cries of "vive le Commune"—without paying the rent owed.[51]

But the police observed that there was little coordination among socialists, which made them less of a real threat. The socialists fought among themselves, their meetings were poorly attended, and there was a marked decline in activity when Guesde and Lafargue were eventually imprisoned in 1883.[52] Lafargue, however, was not displeased: he saw rent strikes as having created "wonderful opportunities" for working-class and petit-bourgeois agitation and as preparation for future revolutionary battles.[53]

The Sixth Socialist Congress, which opened Monday, September 25, 1882, at the Salle du Cirque in Saint-Etienne—a Possibilist stronghold—came as an anticlimax. The Marxist-Broussist split was too far advanced to be resolved. Schism, we have seen, had already occurred the previous December in Paris, where Broussists ran their own candidate on their own platform. National schism was to follow regional schism. Prior to the opening of the congress, Brousse had published a pamphlet denouncing Marxist intrigue: Marxists had tried to dominate the International, and they now were interpreting in their own way the resolutions of the workers' party. Just as Lafargue, Marx's agent in Madrid, had disrupted the Spanish movement, so was he now disrupting the one in France.[54] The implication was clear: expulsion was appropriate. Each side wanted to rid itself of the other, and the long-anticipated schism became a reality. The *Egalité* group, in the minority and threatened by a formal vote of expulsion or censure, staged a walkout and was officially expelled.

Traveling with Guesde, Lafargue had left Paris the week before, his railroad ticket and 115 francs in expenses provided by the party, to make a *"tournée de propagande,"* or propaganda tour. The two men delivered speeches at various stops on the way, anticipating the countercongress that would be called in the event an expulsion took place. Together with a former ironworker, Jean Dormoy—who, after having been blacklisted by employers in the Cher and Allier departments for his success in organizing workers, had turned to Marxism—they gave especially inflammatory addresses in the Montluçon area. The funds raised by their talks more than covered their expenses, and the surplus was used to send additional delegates to the congress.[55]

The twenty-four Marxist delegates took rooms at the same hotel. Guesde and Lafargue arrived on Sunday, before the congress opened, and in a "council of war" held that evening the delegates drafted the resolutions—on credentials, voting procedures, and other matters—that they proposed to submit. Expecting defeat, they planned a walkout, and when on Monday evening Broussists refused a Marxist proposal on voting procedures, the pretext was found.

Engels, too, anticipated a parting of the ways. He believed it un-
avoidable. When the party had been founded, he told Bebel, "Marx
and I never had any illusions it would last. It was an issue of principle:
the conflict was one of class struggle, proletariat versus bourgeoisie,
or opportunism. [The Possibilists] dropped the [1880] Program and
made it inevitable. France is doing what the Germans did—
eliminating the Lassalleans."[56] He and Marx, Engels told other socialist friends in Germany, never believed that the association of
Malon and Brousse with Guesde and Lafargue would work. Malon
and Brousse gave up the class character of the movement to win votes
and gain supporters; Guesde and Lafargue remained faithful to the
proletarian struggle against the bourgeois; hence the inevitability of
separation.[57] Or was Engels now putting the best face on a series of
blunders that had resulted in the current impasse?

For a moment compromise had appeared possible. During the debate over the verification of mandates, an accommodation was
reached. Lafargue, who believed that the Broussists had forged credentials in order to achieve a majority and who was seeking a ratio-
nale to walk out, appeared disappointed. "Having won on the
question of voting," he told Engels, "we were afraid we could not find
a suitable opportunity for the break." Groups from outside of Paris
sided with one or the other of the two factions or pleaded for an end
to the fratricidal strife. But that evening the Marxists rejected their
opponents' stand on a procedural matter, and "in a spontaneous
movement, we rose and left the hall."[58]

During the debate, Brousse and his colleagues—as Marx had anticipated and as Brousse had foreshadowed in his pamphlet—denounced
what they called Marxist conspiracy. They again compared Marx with
the pope and Marxists with the Catholic clergy: just as the clergy could
not obey the laws of their own country because their chief was in
Rome, Marxists could not obey party decisions because their chief resided in London. The letters from Lafargue to Malon, allegedly wanting to make Guesde "party dictator" and proposing that an alliance
with Radicals would benefit socialism more than would an alliance
with those Lafargue called "pseudo-socialists," Brousse's allies, were
cited and put to good use for Brousse's side.[59]

The Broussists exonerated themselves of any blame and condemned
the Marxists, whom they called "ultramontanes"—Brousse had said
it was "impossible to reconcile fire and water." Brousse's faction in
1883 took the name Federation of Socialist Workers (Fédération

des Travailleurs Socialistes; Brousse had preferred simply the Labor Party), which it retained for the remainder of its existence.[60] At the same time it dropped much of its revolutionary rhetoric. It voted to abandon the minimum program and allow each constituency to draft its own, requiring only a common preamble (a revised version of Marx's 1864 preamble to the statutes of the International), which envisaged a communist society secured by the conquest of municipal, departmental, and state power.

Lafargue denied that this was a program. The Possibilists, he said, had "formulated some basic principles which serve only to mislead fools."[61] Following their expulsion, the Guesdists opened their own congress at Roanne, 75 kilometers to the northwest. The rival Marxists took the name French Workers Party (Parti Ouvrier Français, or POF) and retained the revolutionary 1880 program. Until the early 1890s they were to remain a small minority within French socialism. In his report to the Roanne Congress, Lafargue showed his continuing concern for the plight of the small agricultural landowner. He noted they were forced out by estate holders and that the government added to their misery by increasing their taxes. The Marxists' Paris organization, the Fédération du Centre, was renamed the Agglomération Parisienne du Parti Ouvrier. It was joined, however, by only 6 Paris groups; the rival Broussist organization, though largely limited to the Paris area, contained 102. Paris, a city of artisans, went to Brousse.

Brousse's biographer has said that the split took place when it did, only two years after the party's founding, because of "the clumsiness of Guesde and Lafargue and . . . the traditional commitments of the French socialist movement." If a "conspiracy thesis" is admissible, it was a conspiracy more likely organized by the Marxists than by Brousse; and certainly that was the version of events widely believed at the time.[62] The small, wholly Marxist Parti Ouvrier, isolated from its birth until past the end of the decade, was in those years little more than a messianic sect. It lacked resources and was never to win much support in the capital and in eastern France. It fared better in the Nord Department, in Nantes, Epernay, Bordeaux, and in the mining districts of the Allier Department, where industrially disciplined workers predominated.

The expelled Marxists recommitted themselves to the conquest of political power, "not to conserve but to destroy the bourgeois state."

The Marxist and Broussist party structures remained similar: local groups combining to form regional federations, which were governed by a national congress. The Marxists, however, were initially even more decentralized. Fearing that the executive committee might fall under the control of a dissident Paris faction, they decided against situating it permanently in the capital and instead made it itinerant. It resided in each of the six regions in turn, and its members were named by the groups in that region.[63]

This did not endure. In part because Guesde and Lafargue lived in Paris, the party executive was ultimately based there and things became increasingly centralized. Yet because Paris was not a great industrial center and because not all revolutionaries joined the Parti Ouvrier, the Marxists remained a minority among socialists in the city.[64] Even so, both in the French workers' movement and in French political life, the POF emerged as the first modern political party, with local and regional organizations, a national direction, and a national program.[65] Despite attempts to erect a democratic structure, strong leaders continued to play a dominant role. As in all socialist parties, they enjoyed great personal power and prestige; some were authoritarian and little disposed to dilute their personal power.[66] And in spite of efforts to ensure democratic control through collective executives, congresses, and disciplinary committees, only a small number of militants attended party functions faithfully and furnished the leaders. Congresses were not held annually (only one, in Roubaix in 1883, was called between 1882 and 1890), and although in theory the POF executive was subject to the delegates of the entire membership, there was often no check at all; many members were too poor or too inactive to send delegates.

Lafargue's analysis of the schism ended on a positive note: like the German Social Democratic Party, the French Workers Party would emerge stronger for having experienced schism. Possibilists sought peaceful municipal reform, supported revolution only when undertaken by the international proletariat, and preferred a party open to all; Lafargue, in contrast, anticipating Lenin, argued that revolutionaries opposed the inclusion of middle-class elements. The bourgeoisie also favored reforms, provided it benefited from them, and he denounced this kind of socialism as Bonapartist, Bismarckian, and opportunist.[67]

The danger of "reformism," he had told his readers the previous June, should be clear: public housing would mean lower salaries and public transportation would mean the migration of workers to suburbs, leaving a less revolutionary Paris. The aim of their party was the "political and economic expropriation of the capitalist class and the collective or national appropriation of the means of production," and the means lay in revolutionary force. A week later he had condemned the transformation in capitalist society of some industries into public services as "the last form of capitalist exploitation" because of the many advantages the bourgeoisie would derive.[68]

After Roanne, Lafargue appeared not resigned but relieved and optimistic. "I think all that was done was excellent," he told Engels, "and if we stand firm we shall beat the Possibilists, who are nothing but Lassalleans," interested only in creating state industries like the postal service. Committed to a militant course of action, he predicted the strengthening of Marxism and the decline of Possibilism.[69] In the years to follow, Lafargue and his party in fact veered between revolutionary and moderate strategies, but Marxism itself had found political expression in France, a phenomenon that has endured to the present time.

Conclusion

As a student, Lafargue absorbed the atheism and anticapitalism that prevailed in radical circles. His acceptance of Marxism only gradually displaced his earlier commitments to Blanquism and Proudhonism, but before the Franco-Prussian War he was working to have the French branch of the First International abandon Proudhon and adopt the political action envisaged by Marx. During the war, he was determined that Bordeaux follow the example set by the Paris Commune. Similarly, in Spain, where he was forced to take refuge, Lafargue did his utmost to persuade Spanish radicals to abandon their anarchism and adopt Marxism. He failed—though the seeds of a future Spanish socialist party were laid—but was able to provide the London-directed General Council of the International with the evidence necessary to expel Bakunin and his followers. During the last years of his "London exile," he worked to introduce Marxist thought in France and promote the creation of a collectivist party, efforts that he redoubled after his return to France early in 1882 and that culminated in the establishment of the all-Marxist Parti Ouvrier later that year.

Whether it was really Marxism that he and his party were teaching has been intensely debated. Certainly it was a barebones version, relying on a few basic themes, drawn largely from the *Communist Manifesto,* that lent themselves to slogan-making: the imminence of revolution and the transfer of the means of production from private to collective ownership; the coming "expropriation of the expropriators," that is, economic materialism and the contradictions within capitalism; the belief that the bourgeoisie was "producing its own gravediggers"; and others. Initially, because of the strength perceived in the working population, organizers believed that lawful strategies could be relied on (except in the case of armed resistance by the bourgeoisie, when it would be necessary to meet force with force). It was chiefly the wish to distinguish the

Marxists from their more reformist Broussist opposition that led Lafargue—and through him Guesde and the Parti Ouvrier—to take a more uncompromising line, become more disciplined, and adopt a centralist structure. The defense of ideological purity and a party committed to it was a determinant for Lafargue in the 1880s—as it was to be for Lenin. A difference between the two men lay in Lafargue's insistence on maintaining a broad base of working-class recruitment for his party, which implied a reluctance to move too far in advance of prevailing opinion.

Was this Marxism? Lafargue and Guesde believed that it was. Blanquism, with its stress on insurrection and street demonstrations, was considered dated. France was undergoing industrial growth, and the economic centralization described by Marx as a feature of capitalism was beginning to make its appearance. In the last decades of the nineteenth century, a poorly organized proletariat was confronting a bourgeoisie wielding enormous social and political power, and the Marxist insistence on class conflict seemed entirely accurate. France, George Lichtheim acknowledges, was "catching up" with the Marxist prospectus. The issue, from a philosophical standpoint, emerged as one of moral idealism versus scientific determinism. Lafargue's understanding of Marxism, more and more shaped by Engels, was the kind passed on to French audiences: it was seen as "a further refinement of the positivist scientism they knew so well."[1] In any event, the need to combat anarchism and reach audiences wholly ignorant of Marxist thought produced superficiality and oversimplification, even had Marx's theories been thoroughly understood by Lafargue and the Guesdists. Hence the disrepute into which he fell as a simple *vulgarisateur de la doctrine marxiste* in the wake of Jaurès' moral fervor, mounting reliance by labor on the democratic process, and the teachings of scholars like Lucien Herr and Charles Andler, who, acquainted with Marx's original German texts and repelled by what they considered the exaggeration and shallowness of the POF and its leading theoretician, contended that it was not necessary to be a Guesdist in order to be a Marxist. Sorel and Croce added their voices to the growing criticism.

Lafargue was especially condemned for his readiness to provide a materialist-based analysis in any number of areas, and his expertise in some of them was limited at best. Lack of depth and rigor opened him to charges that his articles and pamphlets were more works of imagination and polemic than of scholarship. In this sense, what he produced was indeed a *marxisme vulgaire*. Yet he traveled on unexplored roads, with no guidelines or guarantees, something forgotten by critics both before the turn of the century and in the French Communist Party during its "Bolshevization" phase in the 1920s, which prompted it to retain only the most dogmatic of the Guesdist texts. (*The Right to Be Lazy,* alone of Lafargue's texts, survived because of its popularity.) Hence the durability of the distinction drawn in the 1890s between a *marxisme savante* and a *marxisme vulgaire.*[2] Lafargue, moreover, echoing Engels, persuaded his party to focus on its pedagogical role, and to introduce and popularize a concept usually means to oversimplify it—particularly, as Gabriel Deville observed, when at the same time they were passing Marxism on to their readers and listeners, the Guesdists were learning it themselves.

Lafargue insisted on the need to familiarize French workers with Marxist thought. It was a labor force that had not yet rejected Blanquism and still embraced Proudhonism, even utopian socialism, and was receptive to the radicalism then defended by Clemenceau. As late as 1885 Engels could write that even "the French edition of *Capital* remains a closed book to workers and not only to them but also to the best educated."[3] Twenty years later this was no longer true, and it may be said that much of the explanation lay in Lafargue's propaganda, which was furthered immensely by Laura Lafargue's translations of Marxist texts. Not since 1843 had the name of Marx appeared in a French publication (in a Fourierist journal) and not since his 1847 attack on Proudhon had one of Marx's writings appeared in France.[4] It was Lafargue who in 1866 brought Marx to the attention of French readers, in his *Rive gauche* description of the new "scientific socialism." After this came a stream of articles in the second *Egalité,* pamphlets, brochures, and translations (and after he again took up residence in France, lectures). It was to further propaganda as well as to accustom labor to political action that Lafargue helped to create first a collectivist, then a Marxist, party. The Parti Ouvrier, with the structure it soon adopted, a large national base, an annual national congress, an executive committee, a program, and an insistence on discipline, became the first modern political party in France. Lafargue's aim was to make Marx accessible, and if his party reduced much of his father-in-law's thoughts to fundamental schema and almost completely ignored Marx's dialectical view of the world, so complex and foreign to the tradition of French thought, Lafargue nevertheless succeeded.

This pedagogical emphasis on the uniqueness of Marxist thought is the constant underlying Lafargue's activity, to which all else was subordinated. Tactics might shift, as they did after 1882. The party became centralized and disciplined—and consequently even more isolated. But Lafargue's strategy, even at the cost of appearing contradictory, lay in distinguishing Marxism from its competitors, first anarchism, then Broussism, later Jaurèssist, or "integral," socialism.

In this regard, what is the relative importance of the man compared with the movement of which he is part? How much difference can an individual make in proselytizing a doctrine? The question can never be satisfactorily answered, and any answer will reflect the philosophy of the individual giving it. Clearly, the account here, whether describing Lafargue in France or Fanelli in Spain, attaches considerable importance to personal contacts and conversations. The role of texts and institutions in spreading a doctrine is more important, though more difficult to measure. Still, the discussion of Lafargue's role as editor of Marx's and Engels' texts and as activist in both the International and the effort to further the French workers' movement and party conveys some sense of how Marxist attitudes became part of working programs. Claude Willard, whose familiarity with the Guesdists is unsurpassed and whose Marxism places emphasis on the role of "vast impersonal forces" in history, nevertheless concludes:

> The study of economic and historical conditions is insufficient to account for the Guesdist implantation. Some structures of labor made it more receptive to Guesdism. Some historical and geographical *conjunctures* would set it more easily on the road. Even so, their influence did not make itself felt mechanically, in some inevitable manner. The importance of men and of the organizations they animated weighed heavily. The personality of the *militants*—their self-sacrifice, their oratorical gifts, their human warmth—constituted an essential factor of persuasion.[5]

Finally, the two Marxist leaders must be distinguished from each other. If Guesde gave his name to the movement, Lafargue was the greater theoretician, seeking to apply Marxist methods of analysis in areas previously untouched by it. At least initially, Lafargue's was the superior position, given his theoretical inclinations and his long intimacy with Marx and Engels. Guesde acknowledged that he did not owe his socialist and atheist formation to Marx; it had rather issued from his reading of Hugo and Kant, his hostility to the Empire, and

Selected Bibliography

Unpublished Sources

Private Holdings. Many of the letters written by and to Paul Lafargue may be found in various published collections of Marx's and Engels' correspondence. The Lafargues had no surviving children and hence their correspondence (particularly the letters received from Engels), collected at the time of their death in 1911 by the family of Charles Longuet, found their way to Marx's great-grandson, Marcel-Charles Longuet. Subsequently they were given to Emile Bottigelli, who with Paul Meier published three volumes of the Engels-Lafargue correspondence (see "Published Works by or about Lafargue," below). The originals of letters included in these volumes were then sent to the Institute of Marxism-Leninism in Moscow. At the same time Bottigelli sent the remaining unpublished letters, all correspondence within the Marx family, to Paul Meier's widow, Olga Meier, who published most of them as *Les filles de Karl Marx* (see "Selected Published Works," below). Approximately two dozen letters and parts of letters, however, were not published in this latter compilation, and they were made available to me by Mme Meier. In the notes the source for these unpublished letters is abbreviated as Meier.

Archives Nationales (Paris). Lafargue communicated for many years with Gabriel Deville, one of the founders of *L'Egalité*. Seven cartons of Deville Papers are found under 51 AP 1-7, and cartons 2 and 3 contain fifty-two letters and cards from Lafargue. Other useful holdings include Ministry of Justice files: especially BB30 390, Rapports de l'année 1870; BB30 486, Rapports de l'année 1871; BB18 1848 (no. 849), Rapports sur Lafargue; BB30 727, BB30 731, Jugements de juin 1871. Material relating to the 1871 "disturbances" in Bordeaux and Lafargue's role in them, including the hostile testimony about him, is in Series C (Assemblée nationale), C 2882, C 2884, and C 2885, Dossiers préparatoire et rapport final de l'Enquête parlementaire sur l'insurrection du 18 mars 1871. They also contain assorted Bordeaux newspapers published in 1870–71 containing Lafargue's articles or references to him, particularly *La Fédération* and *La Tribune de la Gironde* (Bordeaux). The Sûreté Générale (national police responsible to the

Ministry of the Interior) files also useful are: F7 12490, Agissements socialistes, Congrès divers, 1876–1899; and F7 12552, Congrès divers, 1876–
1902.

Archives de la Préfecture de Police (Paris). The thick dossier on Lafargue
may be found under the classification B a/1135. Other especially useful files
include the following: B a/199, Le Socialisme en France, 1872 à 1881;
B a/200, Le Socialisme en France, 1882 à 1884; B a/430, Commune de Paris,
1871, Compte-rendu Londres, 1874–1879; B a/434, L'Internationale, 1865
. . . 1876; B a/439, L'Internationale en France, 1875–1878; B a/868, Auguste
Blanqui; B a/1287, Gustave Tridon; B a/1123, Victor Jaclard; B a/1482–84,
Parti guesdiste, 1882–1893.

Bibliothèque Marxiste de Paris. Formerly the Institut de Recherches Marxistes, which in turn resulted from the union in 1978 of the Institut Maurice
Thorez and the Centre d'Etudes et de Recherches Marxistes. The library
contains on microfilm some of the Lafargue correspondence found in the
Institute of Marxism-Leninism in Moscow, including Jules-Antoine Moilin's
letters to Paul Lafargue and Paul's letters to his sister-in-law Jenny.

Bibliothèque Nationale (Paris). The Manuscripts Division contains the Blanqui Papers, and Lafargue's letters to him are in Nouvelles acquisitions
françaises (N.A. fr.) 9592(2), ff. 512–515, and N.A. fr. 9588 (2), ff. 678–
679. There is also a letter to Edouard Lockroy, vice-president of the Chamber of Deputies, dated November 19, 1893, N.A. fr. 25162, f. 64. The
Periodical Room contains copies (but not always complete runs) of the newspapers in which Lafargue published: *Le Citoyen, L'Egalité, La Libre Pensée,
La Marseillaise, La Républicain de la Gironde, La Révolution française, La
Rive gauche,* and *La Tribune de la Gironde* (Bordeaux).

Bishopsgate Institute Library (London). The original "Minutes" of the first
International's General Council are found here because in 1872 the IWMA's
general secretary, John Hales, refused to hand over the Minutes for the
period October 1865–October 1869 to Marx. Although other IWMA material, after Engels' death, went to the German Social Democratic Party in
Berlin along with the bulk of the Marx-Engels papers, these remained in
England. This library also contains the International's original membership
list with the amount of dues paid and the notebook of Johann Eccarius,
general secretary of IWMA's General Council from 1867 to 1871.

Institut Français d'Histoire Sociale (Paris). Letters from Lafargue to Gabriel
Deville and from Deville to the twentieth-century historian Maurice Dommanget may be found in the Dommanget Papers, 14 AS 283. Lafargue's letter
to Benoît Malon is in the Eugène Fournière Papers, 14 AS 181 (2), no. 87.

Internationaal Instituut voor Sociale Geschiedenis (International Institute
for Social History) (Amsterdam). In the institute's Central European Depart-

ment there are ninety-two Lafargue letters (most of which fall outside the period covered by this book) in the Jules Guesde Papers. Also available is Guesde's 1881 letter to Lafargue and an undated letter from the English radical journalist C. Collet. In the Marx-Engels Papers there are fifteen letters from Marx to Lafargue (only six of which are the original drafts) from 1868 to 1880, C 395–409; twenty-three letters (twenty original) from Lafargue to Marx from 1868 to 1880, D 2860–85; ten letters from Lafargue to his sister-in-law Jenny Marx between 1868 and 1872, G 254–263. There are ninety-nine letters from Engels to Lafargue, dating from 1871 to 1895, only four of which are original drafts, however, K 829–927; and 242 letters (eleven original) from Lafargue to Engels dating from 1868 to 1895, L 3020–3262. There are sixteen letters from Marx to his daughter Laura (four original drafts) between 1866 and 1882, C 581–596; four letters from Laura to her father, three in 1870–71, D 3313, 3332–34; four letters from Mrs. Jenny Marx to Laura from 1854 to 1865, G 117–120; a letter from Laura to her sister Jenny in 1870, G 270; and 251 (five in the original) letters from Engels to Laura from 1867 to 1895, K 1144–1286 and L 4772–4879. Most of these letters have been published in the collected works of Marx and Engels and in the Engels-Lafargue correspondence.

Public Record Office, Census Room (London). Census material gives the Lafargues' address, occupation, etc., during their "exile" in the 1870s.

Dissertations. William Cohn, "Paul Lafargue: Marxist Disciple and French Revolutionary Socialist," University of Wisconsin, 1972; Joy Hall, "Gabriel Deville and the Development of French Socialism (1871–1905)," Auburn University, 1983.

Published Works by or about Lafargue

Lafargue's Writings. Most of Lafargue's writings consisted of newspaper articles, published singly or as part of a series. Often they were later presented in the form of pamphlets. The newspapers and reviews to which Lafargue contributed most extensively during 1865–1882 were *La Rive gauche* (1865–1868), *La Marseillaise* (1869–70), *La Libre Pensée* (1870), *La Défense nationale* (1870), *La Tribune de la Gironde* (1870), renamed *La Tribune de Bordeaux* (1871), *Le Républicain de la Gironde* (1870), *La Fédération* (1871), *La Emancipación* (1872), *L'Egalité* (1880–1883), *La Révolution française* (1879), *Le Citoyen* (1882), *La Revue socialiste* (1880).

Pamphlets published during the period covered by this book include: *A las Internacionales de la región Española* (Madrid,1872); *L'Alliance de la démocratie socialiste et l'Association internationale des travailleurs: rapports et documents publiés par ordre du Congrès de la Haye* (London, 1873), written and compiled with Engels and Marx; *Le Droit à la paresse, réfuta-*

tion du droit au travail, de 1848 (Paris and Brussels, 1883) and numerous
subsequent editions and translations. The Lafargues' correspondence with
Engels, collected and annotated by Emile Bottigelli and Paul Meier, was
published as *Friedrich Engels–Paul et Laura Lafargue: Correspondance*, 3
vols. (Paris, 1956–1959). Engels and Lafargue communicated in French,
Engels and Laura, in English. A complete English edition was published in
Moscow and London in 1959–60. Lafargue's memoirs of Marx, "Karl Marx:
Persönliche Erinnerungen," first appeared in *Die Neue Zeit*, 9th year, 1890–
91, 10–17, 32–42; they were published in an American edition as *Karl
Marx: The Man* (New York, 1947). Various collections of Lafargue's writings, usually introduced by the editor, include the following: Jacques Girault,
ed., *Paul Lafargue: textes choisis* (Paris, 1970); Jean Freville, ed., *Paul Lafargue: critiques littéraires* (Paris, 1936); Salvador Morales, ed., *Pablo Lafargue: textos escogidos* (Havana, 1976); Paul Lafargue, *The Right to Be
Lazy and Other Studies* (New York, 1973).

Writings on Lafargue. The introductions to the anthologies listed above
provide some biographical material. Little attention was paid to Lafargue's
life or works during the quarter century following his death in 1911. In the
1930s, however, the French Left, searching for a cultural identity in Marxism, resuscitated Lafargue in two (uncritical) book-length studies: J. Varlet,
Paul Lafargue, théoricien du marxisme (Paris, 1933) and Georges Stolz, *Paul
Lafargue, théoricien militant du socialisme* (Paris, 1937). The immediate
post–World War II success, and then Cold War setback, of the two large
French Marxist parties elicited another study, Jean Bruhat, "Paul Lafargue et
la tradition du socialisme révolutionnaire français," *Cahiers internationaux*
6 (July–August 1949), 65–76. Still, the writer showed more concern with
explaining the failings of French Communism than with providing a dispassionate account of Lafargue's life. Claude Willard's exhaustive study of the
French Workers Party, *Les Guesdistes: le mouvement socialiste en France,
1893–1905* (Paris, 1965), which despite the dates in the title discusses the
Party's origins, commends Lafargue's theoretical accomplishments, but does
this only within the larger context of the party structure that is emphasized.
Of greater relevance are Willard's articles, "Marx et la naissance du Parti
ouvrier français." *Cahiers de l'Institut Maurice Thorez* 10 (1968), 65–69;
"Paul Lafargue et la critique de la société bourgeoise," in Dominique Grisoni,
ed., *Histoire du marxisme contemporain*, 3 vols. (Paris, 1977), 3:183–204;
and "Paul Lafargue, critique littéraire," *Le Mouvement social* (April–June
1967), 102–110. Most useful is Willard's collection of letters written by the
founders of the Workers Party, *La Naissance du Parti ouvrier français* (Paris,
1981). Also important is Jacques Girault's article, "Mises au point sur certains aspects de la vie et du rôle du jeune Lafargue," *La Pensée* 153 (1970),
47–67. William Cohn's doctoral dissertation (see "Unpublished Sources"
above) surveys the life of and the analyses put forward by Lafargue.

Soviet historians have written on Lafargue, but aside from his correspondence, much of which is now available elsewhere, and his own writings, have tended to base their accounts on (largely French) secondary sources. A short biography by I. A. Boldyrev, *Lafargue,* was published in 1984. Articles include V. H. Balmashnov, "Freidk Engel's i Pol' Lafarg" (Friedrich Engels and Paul Lafargue), *Novaia i Noveisaia Istoria* 1976(1), 79–92, which is based on the Engels-Lafargues correspondence; E. M. Makarenkova, "Molodoi Lafarg" (The Young Lafargue), *Voprosy Istorii* 1981(6), 115–122, and "Lafarg i Sozdaniye Marksistskoy Rabochyey Parti Frantsyi" (Unpublished Writings: Paul Lafargue and the Creation of the Marxist Workers Party of France), *Voprosy Istorii* 1978(11), 116–127; I. A. Bakh, ed., "Neopublikovannye pis'ma Laury Lafarg i Zhenni Longe Karlu Marksu" (Unpublished Letters of Laura Lafargue and Jenny Longuet to Karl Marx), *Novaia i Noveisaia Istoriia* (1983(3), 3–10; and the original Russian version of the Novikova article mentioned below, "Bordoskaia Seksita i Internacionala vo Vremia Franko-Prusskoi Voiny i Parïzkoj Kommuny," *Novaia i Noveisaia Istoriia* 1961(2), 74–88.

Most recently, Cuban writers and journals have shown interest in their nation's most personal link with Marx, but have limited themselves to anthologies of Lafargue's writings or popularizations of his life. See Salvador Morales, "Pablo y Laura Lafargue," *Bohemia* 16 (April 1964), 68–71, and "Primeros años en la vida de Pablo Lafargue," *Santiago* 21 (1976), 73–100; Morales' collection of Lafargue's writings is referred to above. See also Ana Ortega, "Apuntes sobre Pablo Lafargue," *Santiago* 13-14 (December 1973– March 1974), 241–255; Raul Roa, "Evocación de Pablo Lafargue" *Cuba socialista* 6 (February 1962), 56–83; Michel Robert, "Lafargue: el yerno cubano de Marx," *Bohemia* 67 (January 31, 1975), 8-9; Stefan Morawski, "Pablo Lafargue y el desarrollo de una estetica marxista," *Casa de las Americas* 10 (1969), 25–37; Aida Mesa Martinez, "Paul Lafargue," *Bohemia* 65 (November 23, 1973), 107; and G. P. Novikova, "Pablo Lafargue y la Primera Internacional," *Academia de ciencias de Cuba, Instituto de historia, serie temas sociales* 2 (May 1969), 3–16.

Published Works

Unless stated otherwise, the place of publication is Paris.

Abramsky, C., and Collins, H. *Karl Marx and the British Labour Movement: Years of the First International.* London, 1965.

Alvarez del Vayo, Julio. *The Last Optimist.* London, 1950.

Andréas, Burt. "Briefe und Dokumente der Familie Marx aus den Jahren 1862–1873," *Archiv für sozialgeschichte.* 2 vols. Hanover, 1962.

Bacardi y Moreau, Emilio. *Crónicas de Santiago de Cuba.* 2 vols. Santiago, 1925.

Bartier, John. "Etudiants et mouvement révolutionnaire au temps de la Pre-
    mière Internationale: les Congrès de Liège, Bruxeles et Gand," in *Mé-
    langes offerts à G. Jacquemyrs. Brussels, 1968.*
Bernstein, Eduard. *Briefwechsel mit Friedrich Engels.* Assen, 1970.
—— *My Years of Exile.* New York, 1921.
—— "Paul Lafargue," *Sozialistische Monatshefte* 16 (1912), 20–24.
Bernstein, Samuel. *Auguste Blanqui and the Art of Insurrection.* London,
    1971.
—— *The Beginnings of Marxist Socialism in France.* New York, 1965.
—— "Jules Guesde, Pioneer of Marxism in France," *Science and Society* 4
    (1940), 29–56.
Berthaud, Pierre-Louis. *La Commune à Bordeaux.* Bordeaux, 1924.
Bookchin, Murray. *The Spanish Anarchists: The Heroic Years, 1868–1936.*
    New York, 1977.
Bottigelli, Emile, ed. "Documenti: lettres et documents de Karl Marx, 1856–
    1883," in *Annali dell' Istituto Giangiacomo Feltrinelli,* pp. 149–219.
    Milan, 1958.
Boxer, Marilyn, and Quataert, Jean H. *Socialist Women.* New York, 1978.
Braunthal, Julius. *History of the International, 1864–1914.* London, 1966.
Brenan, Gerald. *The Spanish Labyrinth.* Cambridge, 1943.
Brown, Bernard. *Socialism of a Different Kind.* Westport, Conn., 1982.
Bruhat, Jean et al. *La Commune de 1871.* 1960.
Buré, Emile. "Gabriel Deville, l'introducteur, en France, du marxisme,"
    L'Ordre, March 6, 1940.
Callejas, José Maria. *Historia de Santiago de Cuba.* Havana, 1911.
Carr, E. H. *Michael Bakunin.* New York, 1961.
Cavignac, Jean. "Paul Lafargue et ses parents à Bordeaux," *Bulletin de l'In-
    stitut aquitain d'études sociales* 21-22 (1975), 17–32.
Chapman, Guy. *The Third Republic of France: The First Phase, 1871–1894.*
    New York, 1962.
Cogniot, Georges. "La pénétration du marxisme en France," *Cahiers du
    Centre d'études et de recherches marxistes* (1965), 1–28.
Compère-Morel, Adéodat. *Jules Guesde: le socialisme fait l'homme, 1845–
    1922.* 1937.
"Correspondance de militants du mouvement ouvrier français, 1879–1882,"
    Annuaire d'études françaises, 1962. Moscow, 1963.
Da Costa, Charles. *Les Blanquistes.* 1912.
The Daughters of Karl Marx. See *Les Filles de Karl Marx.*
De Paepe, César. *Correspondance.* 1974.
Domenech, Francisco. *Tres vidas y una epoca, Pablo Lafargue.* Havana,
    1940.
Dommanget, Maurice. *Auguste Blanqui au début de la IIIe République,
    1871–1880.* 1971.

——— *Blanqui et l'opposition révolutionnaire à la fin du Second Empire.* 1960.

——— *Edouard Vaillant, un grand socialiste, 1840–1915.* 1956.

——— *Hommes et choses de la Commune.* Marseilles, 1937.

——— *L'Introduction du marxisme en France.* Lausanne, 1969.

———, ed. *Paul Lafargue: Le Droit à la paresse.* 1970.

——— Drachkovitch, Milorad. *Les Socialismes français et allemand et le problème de la guerre, 1870–1914.* Geneva, 1953.

———, ed. *The Revolutionary Internationals, 1864–1943.* Stanford, 1966.

Droz, Jacques, ed. *Histoire générale du socialisme.* 4 vols. 1972–1978.

Dunois, Amédée, ed. *Paul Lafargue: Le Droit à la paresse.* 1946.

Dupont, Léonce. *Tours et Bordeaux: souvenirs de la République à outrance.* 1877.

Edwards, Stewart. *The Paris Commune, 1871.* New York, 1971.

Engels, Friedrich. *The Housing Question.* New York, 1935.

Enquête parlementaire sur l'insurrection du 18 mars. 3 vols. Versailles, 1972.

Enzensberger, Hans, ed. *Gespräche mit Marx und Engels.* Frankfurt, 1973.

Fayolle, Roger. "Paul Lafargue, critique littéraire et propagandiste du matérialisme historique," *Philologica Pragensia* 3-4 (1976), 117–127, 161–171.

Fernbach, David, ed. *Karl Marx: The First International and After.* New York, 1974.

Ferrat, André. "Karl Marx et le mouvement ouvrier français après la Commune," *Cahiers du Bolchevisme*, March 14, 1933.

Les Filles de Karl Marx: lettres inédites. Comp. Olga Meier. 1979. Translated as *The Daughters of Karl Marx: Family Correspondence, 1866–1898.* New York and London, 1982.

Freville, Jean, ed. *Paul Lafargue: critiques littéraires.* 1936.

Freymond, Jacques, ed. *La Première Internationale: recueil de documents.* 4 vols. Geneva, 1962–1971.

García Venero, Maximiano. *Historia de las Internacionales en España, 1868–1914.* 3 vols. Madrid, 1956–57.

Gerth, Hans, ed. *The First International: Minutes of The Hague Congress of 1872.* Madison, 1958.

Girault, Jacques. *La Commune et Bordeaux, 1870–1871.* 1971.

——— "Les Guesdistes, la deuxième *Egalité*, et la Commune, 1880," *International Review of Social History* 17 (1972), 421–430.

——— "Mises au point sur certains aspects de la vie et du rôle du jeune Lafargue," *La Pensée* 153 (1970), 47–67.

Greenberg, Louis. *Sisters of Liberty: Marseille, Lyon, Paris and the Reaction to a Centralized State.* Cambridge, Mass., 1971.

Guillaume, James. *L'Internationale: documents et souvenirs, 1864–1878.* 2 vols. 1905–1909.

Halkin, Léon-Ernest. *Le Premier Congrès international des étudiants à Liège en 1865*. Liège, 1866.

Henderson, W. O. *The Life of Friedrich Engels*. 2 vols. London, 1976.

Higounet, Charles, ed. *Histoire de Bordeaux*. Toulouse, 1980.

—— *Histoire générale de la presse française*. 3 vols. Vol 1, *De 1871 à 1940*. 1972.

Howorth, Jolyon. *Edouard Vaillant: la création de l'unité socialiste en France*. 1982.

Hutton, Patrick. *The Cult of the Revolutionary Tradition: The Blanquists in French Politics, 1864–1893*. Berkeley, 1981.

Institute of Marxism-Leninism. *Documents of the First International*. 5 vols. Vol. 1, *The General Council of the First International, 1864–1866, Minutes*. Vol. 2, *The General Council of the First International, 1866–1868, Minutes*. Vol. 3, *The General Council of the First International, 1868–1870, Minutes*. Vol. 4, *The General Council of the First International, 1870–1871, Minutes*. Vol. 5, *The General Council of the First International, 1871–1872, Minutes*. London and Moscow, n.d.

—— *Documents of the First International: The Hague Congress*. Moscow, 1976.

Jellinek, Frank. *The Paris Commune of 1871*. London, 1937.

Jéloubovskaïa, E. A. *La Chute du Second Empire et la naissance de la Troisième République en France*. Moscow, 1959.

Judt, Tony. *Marxism and the French Left: Studies on Labour and Politics in France, 1830–1981*. Oxford, 1986.

Kapp, Yvonne. *Eleanor Marx*. 2 vols. Vol. 1, *The Family Years*. London, 1972.

Kelly, Aileen. *Mikhail Bakunin: A Study in the Psychology and Politics of Utopianism*. New Haven, 1987.

Kolakowski, Leszek. *Main Currents of Marxism*. 3 vols. Vol. 2, *The Golden Age*. New York, 1981.

Landauer, Carl. "The Origin of Socialist Reformism in France," *International Review of Social History* 12 (1967), 81–107.

Lefebvre, Jean-Pierre. "La Première Traduction française du *Capital*," *La Pensée* 233 (May-June 1983), 85–99.

Lefranc, Georges. *Le Mouvement socialiste sous la Troisième République, 1875–1940*. 1963.

Lettres de Communards et de militants de l'Internationale à Marx, Engels, et autres dans les journées de la Commune de Paris en 1871. 1934.

Lichtheim, George. *Marxism in Modern France*. 2d ed. New York, 1972.

Lida, Clara E. *Antecedentes y desarolla del movimiento obrero español, 1835–1888*. Madrid, 1973.

——, ed. *Anarquismo y revolución en la España del XIX*. Madrid, 1972.

Ligou, Daniel. *Histoire du socialisme en France, 1871–1961*. 1962.

Lindemann, Albert S. *A History of European Socialism.* New Haven, 1983.

Longuet, Charles, ed. *Karl Marx: La Commune de Paris.* Preface. 1901.

Longuet, Robert. *Karl Marx, mon arrière-grandpère.* 1977.

Lopez, Ernesto. *Historia de Santiago de Cuba.* Havana, 1947.

Lorenzo, Anselmo. *El Proletariado militante: memorias de un Internacional.* Madrid, 1974.

McInnes, Neil. "Les Débuts du marxisme théorique en France et en Italie, 1880–1897," *Cahiers de l'Institut de science économique appliquée* 102 (June 1960), 5–52.

———— "Les Partis socialistes français (1880–1895): lettres et extraits de lettres d'Engels à Bernstein," *Cahiers de l'Institut de science économique appliquée* 109 (January 1961), 41–78.

Maitron, Jean. *Histoire du mouvement anarchiste en France, 1880–1914.* 1951.

————, ed. *Dictionnaire biographique du mouvement ouvrier français, 1864–1871.* 9 vols. 1964–1971.

Malon, Benoît. "Le Collectivisme en France de 1875 à 1879," *La Revue socialiste* 4 (1886), 990–1016.

Marti, Casimir. "La Première Internationale à Barcelone (1868–1870)," *International Review of Social History* 4 (1959), 394–414.

Marx, Eleanor et al. *Reminiscences of Marx and Engels.* Moscow, n.d.

Marx, Jenny. "To the Editor," *Woodhull and Claflin's Weekly of New York* 23 (October 21, 1871), 477–485.

Marx, Karl, and Engels, Frederick. *Collected Works.* New York, 1975–.

———— *Le Mouvement ouvrier français.* 2 vols. Vol. 2, *Efforts pour créer le parti de classe.* 1974.

———— *Revolution in Spain.* New York, 1939.

———— *Werke.* 41 vols. Berlin, 1956–1968.

Marx, Karl, Marx, Jenny, and Engels, Friedrich. *Lettres à Kugelmann.* Ed. Gilbert Badia. 1971.

Masó, Calixto. *Historia de Cuba.* Miami, 1976.

Mauger, Charles. *Les Débuts du socialisme marxiste en France.* 1908.

Mayer, Gustav. *Friedrich Engels: A Biography.* New York, 1969.

Mermeix. *See* Terrail, Gabriel.

Molis, Robert. "Un Petit-fils de Karl Marx repose au coeur des Pyrénées," *Archistra* 76 (November 1986), 99–102.

Molnár, Miklos. *Le Déclin de la Première Internationale: la conférence de Londres de 1871.* Geneva, 1963.

Morato, Juan José. *Pablo Iglesias.* Madrid, 1931.

———— *El Partido socialista obrero.* Madrid, 1976.

Morawski, Stefan. "Pablo Lafargue y el desarrollo de una estetica marxista," *Casa de las Americas* 10 (1969), 25–37.

Moss, Bernard. *The Origins of the French Labor Movement, 1830–1914: The Socialism of Skilled Workers*. Berkeley, 1976.

Nettlau, Max. *Documentos inéditos sobre la Internacional y la Alianza en España*. Buenos Aires, 1930.

———— *Miguel Bakunin, la Internacional, y la Alianza en España, 1868–1873*. Buenos Aires, 1925.

———— *La Première Internationale en Espagne, 1868–1888*. Dordrecht, 1969.

Noland, Aaron. *The Founding of the French Socialist Party, 1893–1905*. Cambridge, Mass., 1956.

Padover, Saul. *Karl Marx: An Intimate Biography*. New York, 1978.

————, ed. *The Karl Marx Library*. 7 vols. New York, 1971–1977.

————, ed. *The Letters of Karl Marx*. Englewood Cliffs, 1979.

Patsouras, Louis, ed. *The Crucible of Socialism*. Atlantic Highlands, N.J., 1987.

Paz, Maurice, ed. *Lettres familières d'Auguste Blanqui et du docteur Louis Watteau*. Marseilles, 1976.

Peirats, José. *Los Anarquistas en la crisis política española*. Buenos Aires, 1964.

Perrot, Michelle. "Les Guesdistes: controverse sur l'introduction du marxisme en France," *Annales: économies, sociétés, civilisations* (May–June 1967), 701–710.

———— "L'Introduction du marxisme en France et les débuts du Parti ouvrier français, 1882–1889, à travers la correspondance Engels-Lafargue," in *Annali dell' Istituto Giangiacomo Feltrinelli*, pp. 740–751. Milan, 1960.

———— "Le Premier Journal marxiste français: *L'Egalité* de Jules Guesde, 1877–1883," *Le Mouvement social* 28 (July 1959), 1–26.

Pieper, Joseph. *Leisure: The Basis of Culture*. New York, 1952, 1963.

Puech, J.-L. *Le Proudhonisme dans l'Association internationale des travailleurs*. 1907.

Rébérioux, Madeleine. "Le Guesdisme," *Bulletin, Société d'études jaurèsiennes* 50 (July–September 1973), 2–10.

———— Preface to Louis Lévy, *L'Anthologie de Jean Jaurès*. 1983.

Roland, Lucien. "Dans l'intimité des Lafargue," *Le Populaire*, December 2, 1936.

Rougerie, Jacques, ed. *1871: jalons pour une histoire de la Commune de Paris*. 1973.

Seigel, Jerrold. *Bohemian Paris*. London and New York, 1986.

Seignobos, Charles. *Le Déclin de l'Empire et l'établissement de la IIIe République, 1859–1875*. 1921.

Shapiro, Ann-Louise. "Housing Reform in Paris: Social Space and Social Control," *French Historical Studies* 12 (Fall 1982), 486–507.

Stafford, David. *From Anarchism to Reformism: A Study of the Political Activities of Paul Brousse.* Toronto, 1971.

Stein, Robert. *Léger Félicité Sonthonax: The Lost Sentinel of the Republic.* Rutherford, N.J., 1985.

Stekloff, G. M. *History of the First International.* London, 1928.

Stolz, Ruth, ed. *Karl Marx: Wie ich meinen Schwiegersohn erzog.* Berlin, 1969.

Tchernoff, I. *Le Parti républicain au coup d'état et sous le Second Empire.* 1906.

Termes, José. *Anarquismo y sindicalismo en España: la Primera Internacional, 1864–1881.* Barcelona, 1972.

Terrail, Gabriel (Mermeix, pseud.) *La France socialiste.* 1886.

Thomas, Hugh. *Cuba: The Pursuit of Freedom.* New York, 1971.

Thomas, Paul. *Karl Marx and the Anarchists.* London, 1980.

Verdes, Jeanine. "B a/1175: Marx vu par la police française, 1871–1882," *Cahiers de l'Institut de science économique appliquée* 176 (August 1966), 83–120.

Vérecque, Charles. *Dictionnaire du socialisme.* 1911.

Vincent, Steven. *Pierre-Joseph Proudhon and the Rise of French Republican Socialism.* New York, 1984.

Vuilleumier, Marc. "Quelques documents inédits sur Paul Lafargue et la famille Marx en 1871," *Cahiers de l'Institut de science économique appliquée* 9 (August 1965), 231–253.

Weill, Georges. *Histoire du mouvement social en France, 1852–1910.* 1911, 1924.

Willard, Claude. "Chronique historique: une thèse sur les Guesdistes—quelques problèmes de méthode," *La Pensée* 123 (October 1965), 93–100.

——— "Engels et le mouvement socialiste en France (1891–1895) à travers la correspondance Engels-Lafargue," *Annali dell' Istituto Giangiacomo Feltrinelli,* pp. 752–767. Milan, 1959.

——— *Les Guesdistes: le mouvement socialiste en France, 1893–1905.* Paris, 1965.

——— "Marx et la naissance du Parti ouvrier français," *Cahiers de l'Institut Maurice Thorez* 10 (1968), 65–69.

——— "Paul Lafargue et la critique de la société bourgeoise," in Dominique Grisoni, ed., *Histoire du marxisme contemporain,* pp. 183–204. 3 vols. 1977.

——— "Paul Lafargue, critique littéraire," *Le Mouvement social* 59 (April–June 1967), 102–110.

Woodcock, George. *Pierre-Joseph Proudhon: His Life and Work.* New York, 1972.

Worobjowa, Olga, and Sinelnikowa, Irma. *Die Töchter von Marx.* Berlin, 1965.

Wright, Gordon. "The Distribution of French Parties in 1865: An Official Survey," *Journal of Modern History* 15 (1943), 295–302.

———— *France in Modern Times*. New York, 1987.

———— "Public Opinion and Conscription in France, 1866–1870," *Journal of Modern History* 14 (1942), 26–45.

Zévaès, Alexandre. *Aperçu historique sur le Parti ouvrier français*. Lille, 1899.

———— *De l'introduction du marxisme en France*. 1947.

———— *Jules Guesde (1845–1922)*. 1928.

Notes

In the notes, Jenny Marx refers to Laura Lafargue's sister (later Jenny Longuet); Mrs. Jenny Marx refers to Laura's mother. The following abbreviations have been used:

AN	Archives Nationales, Paris
Annali	Emile Bottigelli, "Documenti: lettres et documents de Karl Marx, 1856–1883," in *Annali dell' Istituto Giangiacomo Feltrinelli,* pp. 149–219 (Milan, 1958)
Annuaire	"Correspondance de militants du mouvement ouvrier français, 1879–1882," *Annuaire d'études françaises, 1962* (Moscow, 1963)
APP	Archives de la Préfecture de Police, Paris
BM	Bibliothèque Marxiste de Paris
BN	Bibliothèque Nationale, Paris
Cohn	William Cohn, "Paul Lafargue: Marxist Disciple and French Revolutionary Socialist" (Ph.D. diss., University of Wisconsin, 1972)
Daughters	*The Daughters of Karl Marx: Family Correspondence, 1866–1898,* comp. Olga Meier (New York and London, 1982)
Documents, GC Minutes	*Documents of the First International: General Council of the First International, Minutes,* 5 vols. (Moscow and London, n.d.)
ELC	*Friedrich Engels–Paul and Laura Lafargue: Correspondence,* comp. Emile Bottigelli and Paul Meier (Moscow and London, 1959–60)
IAES	Institut Aquitain d'Etudes Sociales
IFHS	Institut Français d'Histoire Social, Paris
IISH	Internationaal Instituut voor Sociale Geschiedenis, Amsterdam
IML	Institute of Marxism-Leninism, Moscow
ISEA	Institut de Science Economique Appliquée, Paris
MECW	Karl Marx and Frederick Engels, *Collected Works* (New York, 1975–)
MEW	Karl Marx and Friedrich Engels, *Werke,* 39 vols. (Berlin, 1956–1968)
Meier	Meier Papers; see Bibliography, Private Holdings

Naissance   *La Naissance du Parti ouvrier français,* comp. and ed. Claude
                 Willard (Paris, 1981)

Introduction

1. George Lichtheim, *Marxism in Modern France* (New York, 1966), 1.
2. Michael Kelly, *Modern French Marxism* (Baltimore, 1982), 1.
3. For writings on Lafargue, see the Bibliography.
4. See the excellent historiographical discussion in Cohn, 1–37, for the literature published before 1970.
5. Alexandre Zévaès, *De l'introduction du Marxisme en France* (Paris, 1947), 102, 108–109, 172.
6. Milorad Drachkovitch, *Les Socialismes français et allemand et le pro-blème de la guerre, 1870–1914* (Geneva, 1953), 9–11.
7. Georges Weill, *Histoire du mouvement socialiste en France, 1852–1924* (Paris, 1924), 308; Aaron Noland, *The Founding of the French Socialist Party, 1893–1905* (Cambridge, Mass., 1956), 53; Carl Landauer, "The Guesdists and the Small Farmer: Early Erosion of French Marxism," *International Review of Social History* 6 (1961), 214; Claude Willard, *Les Guesdistes: le mouvement socialiste en France, 1893–1905* (Paris, 1965), 28–31, 214; Leslie Derfler, "Reformism and Jules Guesde, 1891–1904," *International Review of Social History* 12 (1967), 72–73, 78–80.
8. Willard, *Les Guesdistes,* 134; see also Roger Fayolle, "Paul Lafargue, critique littéraire et propagandiste du matérialisme historique," *Philologica Pragensia* 3–4 (1976), 117–127, 161–171.
9. Neil McInnes, "Les Débuts du marxisme théorique en France et en Italie, 1880–1897," *Cahiers de l'ISEA* 3 (1960), 25; Lichtheim, *Marxism in Modern France,* 9; Leszek Kolakowski, *Main Currents of Marxism,* 3 vols. (New York, 1981), 2:141; Claude Willard, "Paul Lafargue et la critique de la société bourgeoise," in Dominique Grisoni, ed., *Histoire du marxisme contemporain,* 3 vols. (Paris, 1977), 3:183.
10. Willard, *Les Guesdistes,* 39–43, 164, 2–4; Cohn, 4; Michelle Perrot, "Les Guesdistes: controverse sur l'introduction du marxisme en France," *Annales* (May–June 1967), 701–710; Jacques Girault, "Le Guesdisme dans l'unité socialiste, 1905–1941," Mémoire principal du Diplôme d'Etudes Supérieures, 1964.
11. Daniel Lindenberg, *Le Marxisme introuvable* (Paris, 1975), 67–69; Maurice Dommanget, *L'Introduction du marxisme en France* (Lausanne, 1969), 184, 216–218.
12. Georges Lefranc, *Le Mouvement socialiste sous la Troisième République, 1875–1940* (Paris, 1963), 161, 266.
13. Georges Cogniot, "La Pénétration du marxisme en France," *Cahiers du Centre d'études et de recherches marxistes* (1965), 27.

14. Annie Kriegel and Michelle Perrot, *Le Socialisme français et le pouvoir* (Paris, 1966), 34–39; Robert Baker, "Socialism in the Nord, 1880–1914: A Regional View of the French Socialist Movement," *International Review of Social History* 12 (1967), 362–389; Donald Baker, "The Politics of Social Protest in France: The Left Wing of the Socialist Party, 1921–1939," *Journal of Modern History* 43 (March 1971), 2–41.
15. Bernard Moss, *The Origins of the French Labor Movement, 1830–1914* (Berkeley, 1976), xi, 1, 3, 6, 25, 82–84, 104–106.
16. Tony Judt, *Marxism and the French Left* (Oxford, 1986), 105–106, 29, 114.
17. *L'Humanité*, November 27, 1911.
18. Willard, "Paul Lafargue," 183.

1. Cuba

1. Salvador Morales, "Primeros años en la vida de Pablo Lafargue," *Santiago* 21 (1976), 73; Salvador Morales, ed., *Pablo Lafargue: textos escogidos* (Havana, 1976), 1.
2. Robert L. Stein, *Léger Félicité Sonthonax: The Lost Sentinel of the Republic* (Rutherford, N.J., 1985), 26.
3. Ibid., 26.
4. Ibid., 31, 35.
5. Hugh Thomas, *Cuba: The Pursuit of Freedom* (New York, 1971), 91–92; Ernesto Buch Lopez, *Historia de la Santiago de Cuba* (Havana, 1947), 47–48; Morales, "Primeros," 74. Perhaps twice that number emigrated to the United States.
6. José María Callejas, *Historia de Santiago de Cuba* (Havana, 1911), 66.
7. Lopez, *Historia*, 48–51.
8. Emilio Bacardi y Moreau, *Crónicas de Santiago de Cuba,* II, 44–45, cited in Morales, "Primeros," 74.
9. Act of baptism of François Lafargue reproduced in "Documents," *Bulletin de l'IAES* 23–24 (1975), 123–124, and in the collection of the Musée de l'Histoire Vivante, Montreuil.
10. The little information that exists on Lafargue's boyhood may be found in Charles Vérecque, ed., *Dictionnaire du socialisme* (Paris, 1911), 232–237. The data it contains was obtained by the editor from Lafargue himself prior to the latter's suicide in November 1911. See also Vérecque's introduction to the biographical account in *Le Travailleur*, a socialist newspaper of the Workers Party's Fédération du Nord, December 2, 1911, and Jacques Girault, "Mises au point sur certains aspects de la vie et du rôle du jeune Lafargue," *La Pensée* 153 (1970), 47–51.
11. Those who remained in Cuba became naturalized Spanish citizens. Lopez, *Historia*, 63–64.

12. Ibid., 66.

13. Vérecque, *Dictionnaire*, 232.

14. Certificate of marriage reproduced in *Bulletin de l'IAES* 23–24 (1975), 122–123.

15. Laura Lafargue to Engels, October 9, 1888, ELC, 2:156.

16. Ana Ortega, "Apuntes sobre Pablo Lafargue," *Santiago* 13–14 (December 1973–March 1974), 241. The name was also spelled Armagnac.

17. Jean Maitron, ed., *Dictionnaire biographique du mouvement ouvrier français, 1864–1871*, 9 vols. (Paris, 1964–1971) 6:449. On the one hand, the archivist at the Gironde departmental archives, Jean Cavignac, doubts that Lafargue's origins were so exotic, arguing that parish registers show the name Armaignac, which was probably Protestant, and that Tripier (*sic*) is not an Indian-sounding name. Cavignac, "Paul Lafargue et ses parents à Bordeaux," *Bulletin de l'IAES* 21–22 (1975), 26–27. On the other hand, based on family conversations, Lafargue had reason to believe his origins were as stated.

18. *Le Citoyen*, July 24, 1882.

19. *The Daily People*, November 28, 1911, cited in the introduction to Paul Lafargue, *Socialism and the Intellectuals* (New York, 1967).

20. A copy of the birth certificate attests that he was the legitimate son of Francisco Lafargue of Santiago de Cuba and Ana Virginia Armaignac of Kingston, Jamaica. Musée de l'Histoire Vivante, Montreuil. See also Ortega, "Apuntes," 241; *Bulletin de l'IAES* 23–24 (1975), 122–123. A copy of the baptismal certificate was sent to Maurice Dommanget at the latter's request. IFHS, Dommanget Papers.

21. *Bulletin de l'IAES* 23–24 (1975), 122–123.

22. Girault, "Mises," 48; *L'Eclair*, November 17, 1891. The family probably lived in Santiago's French community. A descendant on his mother's side recalled that the Lafargues owned a farm or ranch near the city called "La Maison de San Julian." Testimony of Dr. Bertha Armaignac, cited in Ortega, "Apuntes," 242.

23. Ortega, "Apuntes," 242.

24. Lopez, *Historia*, 164.

25. Morales, "Primeros," 78.

26. Paul Roa, "Evocación de Pablo Lafargue," *Cuba socialista* 6 (February 1962), 57.

27. Thomas, *Cuba*, 205; Lopez, *Historia*, 184; Calixto Masó, *Historia de Cuba* (Miami, 1976), 187.

28. Morales, "Primeros," 79–80.

29. Cavignac, "Paul Lafargue et ses parents," 26–27.

30. Ibid., 18; Marcelo Segall, "En Amérique Latine," in Jacques Rougerie, ed., *1871: jalons pour une histoire de la Commune de Paris* (Paris, 1973), 366.

31. Cavignac, "Paul Lafargue et ses parents," 20–21.

32. Ibid., 23; Jacques Girault, ed., *Paul Lafargue: textes choisis* (Paris, 1970), 9.

33. Paul Lafargue, "La Genèse du Gogo," *Le Citoyen,* May 30, 1892, cited in Cohn, 38.

34. Paul Lafargue to A. M. Simon, April 15, 1902. A. M. Simon Papers, Wisconsin State Historical Society, Madison, cited in Cohn, 38.

35. Testimony of Raoul Duval, reproduced in J. Girault, *La Commune et Bordeaux, 1870–1871* (Paris, 1971), 297. Lafargue took his degree in 1857 according to Maurice Dommanget; see Paul Lafargue, *Le Droit à la paresse,* ed. Maurice Dommanget (Paris, 1970), intro.; Flax, "Paul Lafargue," *Les Hommes du jour,* July 10, 1909.

36. A. Prost, *Histoire de l'enseignement* (Paris, 1968), 34, cited in Girault, *Textes,* 10; David Watson, *Georges Clemenceau, A Political Biography* (London, 1974), 21.

37. *Le Radical,* November 16, 1891, cited in Girault, "Mises," 51.

38. *Le Matin,* November 15, 1891; *L'Intransigeant,* November 16, 1891.

39. *Le Matin,* November 15, 1891; *Le XIXe Siècle,* November 18, 1891.

40. AN, C 2882, Documents préparatoires . . . sur l'insurrection du 18 mars 1871, no. 15; George Weisz, *The Emergence of Modern Universities in France, 1863–1914* (Princeton, 1983), 494.

41. Louis Liard, "L'Enseignement supérieur sous le Second Empire." *Revue internationale de l'enseignement* (1893), cited in Girault, *Textes,* 10.

42. *Statistique de l'enseignement supérieur* (Paris 1878), 1:282.

43. Edouard Charton, *Dictionnaire des professions* (Paris, 1880), 346–351.

44. Weisz, *Emergence,* 49, 51.

45. Charles Longuet, in *L'Eclair,* November 17, 1891.

2. The Student Radical

1. Gordon Wright, *France in Modern Times* (New York, 1987), 158; Georges Cogniot, "La pénétration du marxisme en France," *Cahiers du Centre d'études et de recherches marxistes* (1965), 2–3.

2. Wright, *France,* 147.

3. *La Rive gauche,* July 1, 1866.

4. Patrick H. Hutton, *The Cult of the Revolutionary Tradition: The Blanquists in French Politics, 1864–1893* (Berkeley, 1981), 21–22.

5. Ibid., 25–27.

6. Ernest Labrousse, "La Montée du socialisme en France depuis un siècle," *La Revue socialiste* (May, 1946), 21.

7. Paul Lafargue, *Le Droit à la paresse,* ed. Maurice Dommanget (Paris, 1970), intro.

8. K. Steven Vincent, "Pierre-Joseph Proudhon and the Rise of French Socialism" (Ph.D. dissertation, Univ. of California at Berkeley, 1981), 8–9.

9. Frank Jellinek, *The Paris Commune of 1871* (London, 1937), 35; E. H. Carr, *Michael Bakunin* (New York, 1961), 136. The literature on Proudhon is immense and the interpretations are conflicting. For example, Bernard Moss, *The Origins of French Labor, 1830–1914* (Berkeley, 1976), sees him as a nonrevolutionary socialist whose objective was the organization of skilled workers into producers' cooperatives to end the wage system; Steven Vincent, *Pierre-Joseph Proudhon and the Rise of French Republican Socialism* (New York, 1984), places emphasis on his moralism.

10. *La Révolution française,* April 20, 1879.

11. Lafargue, *Le Droit,* ed. Dommanget, intro.; Maurice Dommanget, *Blanqui et l'opposition révolutionnaire à la fin du Second Empire* (Paris, 1960), 142.

12. Jacques Girault, "Mises au point sur certains aspects de la vie et du rôle du jeune Lafargue," *La Pensée* 153 (1970), 51–52. Free thought preoccupied the Blanquists: perhaps because philosophical ideas could be debated while political ideas could not be, perhaps because atheism was the key to their political philosophy. I am grateful to Patrick Hutton for this comment.

13. George Woodcock, *Pierre-Joseph Proudhon: His Life and Work* (New York, 1972), 260; Moss, *Origins,* xi.

14. Dommanget, *Blanqui et l'opposition,* 110.

15. John Bartier, "Etudiants et mouvement révolutionnaire au temps de la Première Internationale: les Congrès de Liège, Bruxeles, et Gand," in *Mélanges offerts à G. Jacquemyns* (Brussels, 1968), 35–37.

16. The letter is in BN, Manuscript Div., Blanqui Papers, N.A. fr. 9589, f. 376.

17. Léon-Ernest Halkin, *Le Premier Congrès international des étudiants à Liège en 1865* (Liège, 1866), 20; Girault, "Mises," 49.

18. The Paris prefect of police, Symphorian Boittelle, estimated there were 2,000 students; *La Siècle,* a Paris newspaper, estimated 1,500. The official *compte-rendu* of the Congress gave 1,400, most from Liège, some from other Belgian cities, and perhaps 100 foreigners, chiefly French and Dutch. Halkin, *Le Premier,* 14–15.

19. APP, B a/1135, Paul Lafargue, undated report.

20. This was asserted by Benoît Malon and accepted in Dommanget, *Blanqui et l'opposition,* 110.

21. Bartier, "Etudiants," 38; Samuel Bernstein, *Auguste Blanqui and the Art of Insurrection* (London, 1971), 276.

22. Paul Lafargue, "Auguste Blanqui, souvenirs personnels," *La Révolution française,* April 20, 1879. See Dommanget, *Blanqui et l'opposition.*

23. I. Tchernoff, *Le Parti républicain au coup d'état et sous le Second Empire* (Paris, 1906), 334; Lafargue, *Le Droit,* ed. Dommanget, 15.

24. Cited by Boittelle in his report, "Le Congrès international des étudiants
...," cited in G. P. Novikova, "Pablo Lafargue y la Primera Internacional," *Instituto de historia, serie temas sociales* 2 (May 1969), 3.

25. Halkin, *Le Premier*, 25–26.

26. Bartier, "Etudiants," 38–39.

27. Halkin, *Le Premier*, 137; Bartier, "Etudiants," 39–40.

28. S. Bernstein, *Auguste Blanqui*, 276.

29. Blanqui's papers contain handwritten copies of articles from Paris newspapers covering the Congress. BN, Manuscript Div., N.A. fr. 9590(1):69–73.

30. *La Révolution française*, April 20, 1879.

31. J. P. Mayer, ed., *The Recollections of Alexis de Tocqueville* (New York, 1959), 130.

32. *La Rive gauche*, April 22, July 1, 1866; *La Révolution française*, April 20, 1879.

33. AN, BB30 374 (Ministry of Justice), cited in Jacques Girault, *La Commune et Bordeaux, 1870–71* (Paris, 1971), 26.

34. *Le Temps*, December 21, 1865.

35. Dommanget, *Blanqui et l'opposition*, 114.

36. Charles Longuet, reporting Lafargue's remarks to him in February 1866, in *L'Eclair*, November 17, 1891.

3. Arrival in London

1. Reporting of Charles Longuet, *L'Eclair*, November 17, 1891. The Kentish Town Road address was listed on Lafargue's marriage certificate. See Chapter 5, note 38.

2. Michael Harrison, *In the Footsteps of Sherlock Holmes* (Newton Abbot, 1971), 101.

3. Karl Marx to Engels, August 7, 1866, MEW, 31:247–248.

4. Harrison, *Footsteps*, 79.

5. According to *L'Humanité*, November 28, 1911, the letter was Jaclard's; according to Lafargue's own account, it was Henri-Louis Tolain's. Lafargue said this in his reminiscences of Marx, first published as "Karl Marx: Persönliche Erinnerungen," in *Die Neue Zeit*, 9th year, 1890–91, 10–17, 32–42. The translations are from an American edition, *Karl Marx: The Man* (New York, 1947), 7.

6. Lafargue, *Karl Marx*, 6–7.

7. Ibid., 7.

8. *L'Eclair*, November 17, 1891; Karl Marx to Laura Marx, March 20, 1866, MECW, 42:246; Marx to Engels, March 24, 1866, MEW, 31:194.

9. The IWMA's membership list is at the Bishopsgate Institute in London. G. P. Novikova, "Pablo Lafargue y la Primera Internacional," *Instituto de historia, serie temas sociales* 2 (May 1969), 4.

10. See the discussion in Cohn, 44–46, and Jacques Girault, "Mises au point sur certains aspects de la vie et du rôle du jeune Lafargue," *La Pensée* 153 (1970), 52.
11. Lafargue, *Karl Marx*, 7.
12. IML, *Documents, GC Minutes*, 1:168–169.
13. Milorad Drachkovitch, ed., *The Revolutionary Internationals, 1864–1943* (Stanford, 1966), 18–19; IML, *Documents, GC Minutes*, 1:174.
14. IML, *Documents, GC Minutes*, May 22, September 18, October 2, 1866, January 8, 1867, 1:183–184, 2:19, 59, 83; Yvonne Kapp, *Eleanor Marx*, 2 vols. (London, 1972, 1976), 1:73.
15. IML, *Documents, GC Minutes*, July 9, 1867, 2:136–138; Maximilien Rubel and Margaret Manale, *Marx without Myth* (Oxford, 1975), 227.
16. David Fernbach, ed., *Karl Marx: The First International and After* (New York, 1974), 16.
17. "A Victory of the Plebeians," June 3, 1866.
18. The council's meeting of June 26, 1866. IML, *Documents, GC Minutes*, 2:198, 201, 204, 417–418.
19. Cited in Novikova, "Pablo Lafargue," 6.
20. Karl Marx to Laura Marx, March 20, 1866, *Annali*, 161–162.
21. Karl Marx to Engels, June 7, 1866, MEW, 31:222; IML, *Documents, GC Minutes*, 2:417.
22. Karl Marx to Engels, June 20, 1866, MEW, 31:229.
23. IML, *Documents, GC Minutes*, 2:373–374; Rubel and Manale, *Marx without Myth*, 227; Girault, "Mises," 54. Marx took credit for having Lafargue admitted (through "a third party") to London hospitals to acquire "the necessary practical experience." Karl Marx to Engels, August 7, 1866, MECW, 42:304.
24. J. Freymond, ed., *La Première Internationale: recueil de documents*, 4 vols. (Geneva, 1962), 1:134.
25. IML, *Documents, GC Minutes*, vol. 4.
26. BN, Manuscript Div., Blanqui Papers, N.A. fr. 9594, ff. 310; Roger Garaudy, *Les Sources françaises du socialisme scientifique* (Paris, 1949), 218.
27. BN, Manuscript Div., Blanqui Papers, N.A. fr. 9592(2), ff. 512–515.
28. Maurice Paz, *Un Révolutionnaire professionnel, Auguste Blanqui* (Paris, 1984), 192, 194.
29. BN, N.A. fr. 9592, ff. 217–219, cited in Paz, *Révolutionnaire*, 191.

4. *Laura*

1. *Les Filles de Karl Marx: lettres inédites*, comp. Olga Meier (Paris, 1979). I have used the American edition, introduced by Sheila Rowbotham, *The*

Daughters of Karl Marx: Family Correspondence, 1866–1898 (New York and London, 1982). The daughters wrote to each other in English. See also MEW, esp. vol. 31.

2. Jerrold Seigel, *Marx's Fate: The Shape of a Life* (Princeton, 1978), 279.

3. Karl Marx to Engels, January 24, 1863, Saul Padover, ed., *The Letters of Karl Marx* (Englewood Cliffs, 1979), 165.

4. David Felix, *Marx as Politician* (Carbondale, 1983), 113.

5. Yvonne Kapp, *Eleanor Marx*, 2 vols. (London, 1972, 1976), 1:30, 56–57.

6. Eduard Bernstein, *My Years of Exile* (New York, 1921), 154–155.

7. Saul Padover, *Karl Marx: An Intimate Biography* (New York, 1978), 486.

8. Mrs. Jenny Marx to Luise Weydemeyer, March 11, 1861, cited in Olga Worobjowa and Irma Sinelnikowa, *Die Töchter von Marx* (Berlin, 1965), 51.

9. Ibid.

10. Robert Longuet, *Karl Marx, mon arrière-grandpère* (Paris, 1977), 206; Eleanor Marx et al., *Mohr und General: Erinnerungen an Marx und Engels* (Berlin, 1965), 183, 190.

11. R. Longuet, *Karl Marx, arrière-grandpère*, 204.

12. Karl Marx to Engels, May 1, 1865, MEW, 31:110.

13. Paul Lafargue, *Karl Marx: The Man* (New York, 1947), 22.

14. Mrs. Jenny Marx to Natalie Liebknecht, October 1866, cited in Padover, *Karl Marx*, 487.

15. R. Longuet, *Karl Marx, arrière-grandpère*, 212.

16. Karl Marx to Engels, August 7, 1866, MEW, 31:247.

17. Reproduced in Ruth Stolz, ed., *Karl Marx: Wie ich meinen Schwiegersohn erzog* (Berlin, 1969), 34–35, 48–49.

18. BM, microfilms 17077–81; 17094–97; 17098–17101; 17071–76.

19. *Annali*, 164.

20. Karl Marx to Engels, October 1, 1866, MEW, 31:255; Cohn, 47–48.

21. Jenny Marx to Karl Marx, n.d. (end of April 1867), Eleanor Marx to Karl Marx, April 26, 1867, *Daughters*, 17.

22. Karl Marx to Ludwig Kugelmann, August 23, 1866, MECW, 42:311–312.

23. Karl Marx to Engels, August 13, 1866, MEW, 31:252.

24. Original French version in IISH, C 395; German translation in MEW, 31:518–519. I have used the English translation in Kapp, *Eleanor Marx*, 1:298–299.

25. Cohn, 48–50.

26. Karl Marx to Engels, August 23, 1866, MEW, 31:253.

27. Ibid.

28. Ibid.

29. Mrs. Jenny Marx to Natalie Liebknecht, the first wife of family friend Wilhelm Liebknecht, Stolz, *Karl Marx,* 14; Kapp, *Eleanor Marx,* 1:74.
30. Karl Marx to Eleanor Marx, September 5, 1866, MEW, 31:527, MECW, 42:315–316. The German edition identifies the recipient as Laura; the English version (correctly), as Eleanor Marx.
31. *La Nouvelle Revue socialiste* 26 (November 1–December 15, 1928), 5.
32. Cited in Padover, *Karl Marx,* 487.
33. Karl Marx to Engels, November 8, 1866, October 4, 1867, MEW, 31:262, 354–356.
34. Karl Marx to Paul Lafargue, December 7, 1866, MEW, 31:538.
35. September 1, 1866, *Daughters,* 9–10.
36. BM, microfilms 17094–97.
37. Eleanor Marx to Karl Marx, April 26, 1867, *Daughters,* 18.
38. Kapp, *Eleanor Marx,* 1:81.
39. *Daughters,* 31; Mrs. Jenny Marx to Engels, December 24, 1866, MEW, 31:593; Mrs. Jenny Marx to Kugelmann, December 24, 1867, MEW, 31:596.
40. Karl Marx to Engels, September 11, 1867, MEW, 31:343.

5. Marriage and Politics

1. Robert Longuet, *Karl Marx, mon arrière-grandpère* (Paris, 1977), 217.
2. Ibid., 217–218; Jules Clère, *Les Hommes de la Commune* (Paris, 1971), cited in Jerrold Seigel, *Bohemian Paris* (London and New York, 1986), 183.
3. Eduard Bernstein, *My Years of Exile* (New York, 1921), 212.
4. Jean Maitron, ed., *Dictionnaire biographique du mouvement ouvrier français, 1864–1871,* 9 vols. (1964–1971), 7:181.
5. Seigel, *Bohemian,* 187–188.
6. *L'Eclair,* November 17, 1891.
7. Cohn, 55–56; Roger Fayolle, "Paul Lafargue, critique littéraire et propagandiste du matérialisme historique," *Philologica Pragensia* 3 (1976), 119–120; Paul Lafargue, "La Nouvelle Génération," *La Rive gauche,* July 1, 1966.
8. "La Méthode idéaliste et la méthode positif," *La Rive gauche,* April 22, 1866.
9. Karl Marx to Engels, June 7, 1866, MEW, 31:222.
10. Proposed three-part article in *La Rive gauche.* Only two appeared (July 15 and 22, 1866), because the newspaper ceased publication in late July 1866. It was later published as a twenty-four-page brochure, *La Lutte social,* n.d. Cohn, 56.
11. Georges Weill, *Histoire du mouvement social en France, 1852–1924* (Paris, 1924), 120.

12. IML, *Documents, GC Minutes,* 1:5; Maurice Dommanget, *L'Introduction du marxisme en France* (Lausanne, 1969), 6.

13. Guesde to Charles Fournière in 1913, cited in Dommanget, *L'Introduction,* 25.

14. *La Rive gauche,* April 22, 1866.

15. "Variétés, nature et sciences," *La Rive gauche,* May 13, 1866.

16. "L'Empire sauve par la guerre," *La Rive gauche,* July 1, 1866.

17. "Encyclique de l'église ...," *La Rive gauche,* June 5, 1866; Fayolle, "Paul Lafargue," 121.

18. "Une Victoire de la réaction," *La Tribune du peuple,* September 19, 1866, cited in Max Nettlau, *Miguel Bakunin, la Internacional, y la Alianza en España, 1868–1873* (Buenos Aires, 1925), 15, and Jacques Girault, ed., *Paul Lafargue: textes choisis* (Paris, 1970), 20.

19. According to Max Beer, it was Lafargue who in 1868 introduced Marx to Beesly. *Fifty Years of International Socialism* (London, 1935), 95. See also Karl Marx to Engels, January 8, 1868, MEW, 32:13.

20. Issue of May 13, 1866.

21. "La Grève et ses résultats," "Une Victoire plébéienne," *La Rive gauche,* May 13, 15, June 3, 1866, cited in Cohn, 65–67.

22. Paul Lafargue, "Souvenirs personnels sur Frédéric Engels," *Le Socialiste,* August 27–September 3, 1905.

23. Yvonne Kapp, *Eleanor Marx,* 2 vols. (London, 1972, 1976), 1:74.

24. September 11, according to Saul Padover, *Karl Marx: An Intimate Biography* (New York, 1978), 363.

25. Karl Marx to Engels, September 12, 1867, MEW, 31:347; *Le Courier français,* October 1, 1867; Dommanget, *L'Introduction,* 72.

26. César de Paepe, *Correspondance* (Paris, 1974), 191–192.

27. Dommanget, *L'Introduction,* 6, 72, 181.

28. Padover, *Karl Marx,* 94–95.

29. Lafargue, "Souvenirs personnels sur Frédéric Engels," *Le Socialiste,* September 10–17, 1905. The quotations in the next two paragraphs also come from Lafargue's article.

30. Karl Marx to Engels, December 16, 1867, MEW, 31:411.

31. Karl Marx to Engels, March 6, 1868, MEW, 32:38.

32. Karl Marx to Kugelmann, March 17, 1868, MEW, 32:540.

33. Engels to Karl Marx, March 19, 1868, MEW, 32:48.

34. Paul Lafargue to Engels, March 18, 1868, ELC, 1:2–3.

35. Paul Lafargue to Engels, March 25, 1868, ELC, 1:23.

36. Karl Marx to Kugelmann, April 6, 1868, MEW, 32:542.

37. Engels to Karl Marx, December 16, 1867, MEW, 31:411.

38. IISH, G 349. Original from Registry Book, no. 23, page 50, District of Pancras, Middlesex County. Copies in the Musée de l'Histoire Vivante, Montreuil, and BM, microfilm 16977.

39. Laura Lafargue to Engels, March 6, 1893, ELC, 3:246–247.
40. Laura Lafargue to Karl Marx, April 3, 1868, *Daughters,* 31–32.
41. Laura Lafargue to Jenny Marx, April 22, 1869, Meier.
42. Karl Marx to Engels, April 11, 1868, MEW, 32:58.
43. Karl Marx to Paul and Laura Lafargue, April 11, 1868, MEW, 32:32.
44. Karl Marx to Laura Lafargue, April 11, 1868, MEW, 32:544–545; Paul
    and Laura Lafargue to Jenny Marx, April 6, 1868, Meier.
45. Karl Marx to Engels, April 30, 1868, MEW, 32:75.
46. Karl Marx to Engels, July 23, 1868, MEW, 32:124. Possession of the
    MRCS, indicating membership in the Royal College of Surgeons, enabled
    the holder to practice surgery in England and Wales. The standard qual-
    ification in the 1860s was the MRCS and the LSA (Licentiate of the
    Society of Apothecaries), which permitted the practice of medicine, sur-
    gery, and midwifery, an ideal combination for a general practitioner of
    the day. It is not known whether Lafargue held the LSA. I. F. Lyle,
    Librarian of the Royal College of Surgeons, letter to the author, April 6,
    1990.
47. Kapp, *Eleanor Marx,* 1:91–92.
48. Karl Marx to Kugelmann, August 10, 1868, MEW, 32:556.
49. BM, microfilm 17109.
50. Karl Marx to Engels, March 18, 1868, MEW, 32:47.

6. Becoming a Revolutionary

1. Paul Lafargue, *Karl Marx: The Man* (New York, 1947), 11; Cohn,
   69–70; Jacques Girault, ed., *Paul Lafargue: textes choisis,* 20.
2. Engels to Karl Marx, April 19, 1869, MEW, 32:307.
3. Paul Lafargue to Jenny Marx, n.d., IISH, G 254.
4. APP, B a/1135, undated report (fall 1868).
5. Laura Lafargue to Jenny Marx, n.d., Meier.
6. Paul Lafargue to Jenny Marx, n.d., IISH, G 256–257; Laura Lafargue to
   Jenny Marx, April 30, 1869, Meier.
7. Laura Lafargue to Jenny Marx, February 28, 1869, *Daughters,* 38.
8. Karl Marx to Ludwig Kugelmann, February 11, 1869, MEW, 32:590.
9. Laura Lafargue to Jenny Marx, n.d. (mid-March 1869), Meier.
10. Laura Lafargue to Jenny Marx, February 9, 1870, *Daughters,* 62, xxiii.
11. Marilyn Boxer and Jean H. Quataert, eds., *Socialist Women* (New York,
    1978), 75.
12. Laura Lafargue to Jenny Marx, June 9, 1870, *Daughters,* 70, xxvi.
13. Mermeix (pseud. of Gabriel Terrail), *La France socialiste* (Paris, 1886),
    886.
14. Laura Lafargue to Jenny Marx, February 9, 1870, *Daughters,* 63–64,
    xxvi (Rowbotham, Introduction).

15. Karl Marx to Engels, November 7, 1868, MEW, 32:198; Karl Marx to Kugelmann, December 5, 1868, MEW, 32:581.
16. Laura Lafargue to Jenny Marx, n.d., Meier; Laura Lafargue to Karl Marx, October 26, 1868, *Daughters,* 34; Karl Marx to Engels, February 11, 1869, MEW, 32:590; Yvonne Kapp, *Eleanor Marx,* 2 vols. (London, 1972, 1976), 1:92.
17. Kapp, *Eleanor Marx,* 1:104.
18. Karl Marx to Paul Lafargue, June 2, 1869, IISH, C 398.
19. Karl Marx to Engels, March 1, 3, 1869, MEW, 32:264, 270.
20. Karl Marx to Jenny Marx, June 2, 1869, *Annali,* 50.
21. Karl Marx to Engels, March 14, 20, July 7, 1869, MEW, 32:278, 283, 618.
22. Karl Marx to Paul Lafargue, October 18, 1869, MEW, 32:635.
23. Paul Lafargue to Karl Marx, n.d., IISH C 2863.
24. Karl Marx to Kugelmann, March 3, 1869, MEW, 32:597.
25. Kapp, *Eleanor Marx,* 1:102; Karl Marx to François Lafargue, July 10, 1869, MEW, 32:622–623.
26. Karl Marx to Engels, July 14, 1869, MEW, 32:377; Karl Marx to Paul and Laura Lafargue, April 18, 1870, MEW 32:671–672.
27. Gordon Wright, *France in Modern Times* (New York, 1987), 147.
28. Edward Shorter and Charles Tilly, *Strikes in France, 1830–1968* (London and New York, 1974), 89, 93.
29. Paul Lafargue, "Souvenirs," *Le Socialiste,* January 1–8, 1911.
30. Patrick Hutton, *The Cult of the Revolutionary Tradition: The Blanquists in French Politics, 1864–1893* (Berkeley, 1981), 2, 10–11.
31. Maurice Dommanget, "Les Groupes Blanquistes de la fin du 2e Empire," *La Revue socialiste* 44 (1951), 225, 228.
32. Lafargue, "Souvenirs," *Le Socialiste,* January 1–8, 1911.
33. Paul Lafargue to Auguste Blanqui, BN, Manuscript Div., Blanqui Papers, N.A., fr. 9594, f. 310.
34. Samuel Bernstein, *Auguste Blanqui and the Art of Insurrection* (London, 1971), 323.
35. Karl Marx to Engels, March 1, 1869, cited in E. A. Jéloubovskaïa, *La Chute du Second Empire et la naissance de la Troisième République en France* (Moscow, 1959), 129.
36. Laura Lafargue to Karl Marx, April 6, 1870, IISH, D 2681.
37. Maurice Dommanget, *Blanqui et l'opposition révolutionnaire à la fin du Second Empire* (Paris, 1960), 181–182.
38. BN, Manuscript Div., Blanqui Papers, N.A. fr. 9588(2), ff. 734–737.
39. Paul Lafargue, "Auguste Blanqui, souvenirs personnels," *La Révolution française,* April 20, 1879; Lafargue, "Souvenirs," *Le Socialiste,* January 1–8, 1911.
40. Lafargue, "Auguste Blanqui"; Dommanget, *Blanqui et l'opposition,* 182.

41. Laura Lafargue to Jenny Marx, February 28, May 9, 12, 1869, *Daughters,* 37, 48; Paul Lafargue to Karl Marx, n.d., IISH, C 2684.
42. Karl Marx to Jenny Marx, June 2, 1869, MEW, 32:611.
43. S. Bernstein, *Auguste Blanqui,* 257, 260; Lafargue, "Souvenirs," *Le Socialiste,* January 1–8, 1911.
44. Jéloubovskaïa, *La Chute,* 557, 245–246.

7. *The International*

1. Julius Braunthal, *History of the International, 1864–1914* (London, 1966), 125–126, 130, 134, 136.
2. Friedrich Engels, *La Question du logement* (Paris, 1936), 40.
3. Maurice Dommanget, *L'Introduction du marxisme en France* (Lausanne, 1969), 26–27.
4. Ernest Labrousse, "La Montée du socialisme en France depuis un siècle," *La Revue socialiste* 1 (May 1946), 21.
5. Maurice Dommanget, *Hommes et choses de la Commune* (Marseilles, 1937), 217.
6. Paul Lafargue to Karl Marx, n.d. (end of May 1869), IISH, D 2865; E. A. Jéloubovskaïa, *La Chute du Second Empire et la naissance de la Troisième République en France* (Moscow, 1959), 201. It is possible that Lafargue, like other revolutionary admirers of Proudhon, was disappointed that the latter upheld the status quo concerning women. See Claire Moses, *French Feminism in the Nineteenth Century* (Albany, 1984), 154–157.
7. October 23, 1869, Jéloubovskaïa, *La Chute,* 223.
8. Paul Lafargue to Karl Marx, October 13, 1869, IISH, D 2866; Cohn, 92.
9. *La Marseillaise* was not controlled by the IWMA. Paul Lafargue to Karl Marx, April 20, 1870, IISH, D 2868; Karl Marx to Engels, October 18, 1868, October 23, 1869, Jenny Marx to Engels, August 10, 18, 1870, cited in Jéloubovskaïa, *La Chute,* 243.
10. Laura Lafargue to Karl Marx, April 18, 1870, IISH, D 2860; Jean-Pierre Lefebvre, "La Première Traduction française du *Capital,*" *La Pensée* 233 (May–June, 1983), 87.
11. Karl Marx to Engels, April 15, 19, 1869, MEW, 32:302, 307.
12. Karl Marx to Paul and Laura Lafargue, April 18, 1870, MEW, 32:671, cited in Jacques Girault, ed., *Paul Lafargue: textes choisis* (Paris, 1970), 22.
13. Engels to Laura Lafargue, April 18, 1884, ELC, 1:194–195.
14. Engels reporting his conversation with Louise Kautsky to Laura Lafargue, June 20, 1893, MEW, 39:85, cited in Helmut Hirsch, "Une lettre inconnue de Laura Lafargue," *Economies et sociétés* 2:12 (1968), 2536.
15. Ibid.

16. David Fernbach, ed., *Karl Marx: The First International and After* (New York, 1974), 19.

17. Louis Lévy, *Vieilles histoires socialistes* (Paris, 1933), 61–62; Rappoport cited in Labrousse, "La Montée," 21; APP, B a/439, L'Internationale à Paris, 1869–1889.

18. APP, B a/439, L'Internationale dans les Départements, no. 5037.

19. G. P. Novikova, "Pablo Lafargue y la Primera Internacional," *Instituto de historia, serie temas sociales* 2 (May 1969), 7.

20. Frank Jellinek, *The Paris Commune of 1871* (London, 1937), 38; Charles Seignobos, *Le Déclin de l'Empire et l'établissement de la IIIe République, 1859–1875* (Paris, 1921), 80.

21. Edouard Dolléans, *Eugène Varlin* (Paris, n.d.), 5–7, 15.

22. Braunthal, *History,* 109.

23. Louis Patsouras, "Jean Grave and the French Anarchist Tradition," in L. Patsouras, ed., *The Crucible of Socialism* (Atlantic Highlands, N.J., 1987), 23–25.

24. Seignobos, *Le Déclin,* 80.

25. Laura Lafargue to Karl Marx, April 18, 1870, IISH, D 2860.

26. Paul Lafargue to Karl Marx, n.d., IISH, D 2866; Karl Marx to Engels, July 14, 1869, MEW, 32:33; Karl Marx to Engels, July 22, 1869, MEW, 32:344; Laura Lafargue to Jenny Marx, August 16, 1869, Meier.

27. Karl Marx to Engels, August 2, 10, 18, September 25, 27, 30, 1869, MEW, 32:355, 359, 367, 373, 375; Cohn, 83; Paul Lafargue to Karl Marx, n.d. (1869), IISH, D 2865; Laura Lafargue to Karl Marx, n.d. (1868), Meier.

28. Laura Lafargue to Jenny Marx, August 16, 1869, Meier; Karl Marx to Laura Lafargue, September 25, 1869, Saul Padover, ed., *The Letters of Karl Marx* (Englewood Cliffs, 1979), 263.

29. Novikova, "Pablo Lafargue," 8; Jéloubovskaïa, *La Chute* 223; Laura Lafargue to Karl Marx, April 18, 1870, IISH, D 2860.

30. Laura Lafargue to Engels, January 17, 1870, MEW, 32:706.

31. Paul Lafargue to Jenny Marx, January 9, 1870, *Daughters,* 60; George D. Sussman, *Selling Mothers Milk: The Wet-Nursing Business in France, 1715–1914* (Urbana, 1982), 8, 11, 102–103, 122, 126–129, 165; Valerie Fildes, *Breasts, Bottles and Babies* (Edinburgh, 1986), 302; Valerie Fildes, *Wet-Nursing: A History from Antiquity to the Present* (Oxford, 1988), 90, 236, 203–204. The death attests to the high fertility rates and infant mortality rates of the period. Laura, though doubtless aware of birth control, was to have three children in four years; her sister Jenny, six in eight years. Yet of Marx's nine grandchildren, only three, the sons of Jenny, survived their sixteenth birthday.

32. Karl Marx to Paul and Laura Lafargue, March 5, 1870, Padover, *Letters,* 269–270. Copy of original in MEW, 32:657.

33. Ibid.
34. Paul Lafargue to Karl Marx, about January 15, 1871, *Daughters*, 87; Laura Lafargue to Jenny Marx, June 9, 1870, *Daughters*, 70.
35. "La Viande," July 21, 1870.
36. Laura Lafargue to Jenny Marx, March 20, 1870, *Daughters*, 66; Maurice Dommanget, *Blanqui et l'opposition révolutionnaire à la fin du Second Empire* (Paris, 1960), 179–183; Cohn, 84.
37. Karl Marx to Paul Lafargue, April 19, 1870, *Annali*, 171–172; IML, *Documents, GC Minutes*, 4:224, 316; Maximilien Rubel and Margaret Manale, *Marx without Myth* (Oxford, 1975), 255; Jean Maitron, ed., *Dictionnaire biographique du mouvement ouvrier français, 1864–1871*, 9 vols. (Paris, 1964–1971), 8:200.
38. See also IML, *Documents, GC Minutes*, 4:224, 316.
39. Karl Marx to Paul Lafargue, April 19, 1870, *Annali*, 173; Rubel and Manale, *Marx without Myth*, 255.
40. Laura Lafargue to Karl Marx, April 6, 1870, IISH, D 2681; Paul Lafargue to Karl Marx, n.d., IISH, D 2869; Jéloubovskaïa, *La Chute*, 240.
41. Dommanget, *Blanqui et l'opposition*, 220; Laura Lafargue to Jenny Marx, June 9, 1870, *Daughters*, 70.
42. Roger Fayolle, "Paul Lafargue, critique littéraire et propagandiste du matérialisme historique," *Philologica Pragensia* 3–4 (1976), 122; Paul Lafargue, "Les Contradictions de la Bible," March 5, April 2, May 14, 1870, and "Querelles de ménage," March 20, 1870, *La Libre Pensée*.
43. "La Pangenese darwinienne," *La Libre Pensée*, February 12, 1870.
44. *L'Eclair*, November 17, 1891.
45. Eleanor Marx to Laura Lafargue, June 24, 1888, IISH, G 304; Cohn, 88.
46. March 12, 1870; Cohn, 88.
47. Fayolle, "Paul Lafargue," 122.
48. Girault, *Textes*, 85, Cohn, 90.
49. Two such articles appeared on May 28 and June 4, 1870. Cohn, 92.
50. IML, *Documents, GC Minutes*, 4:228.
51. Novikova, "Pablo Lafargue," 8; Jéloubovskaïa, *La Chute*, 268. Apparently Lafargue, at least at this time, saw no inconsistency between the internationalism of Marxism and the Jacobinism of the Blanquists and the Libres Penseurs.
52. Jéloubovskaïa, *La Chute*, 244.
53. IML, *Documents, GC Minutes*, 4:228.
54. Jéloubovskaïa, *La Chute*, 268–270; Girault, *Textes*, 23–24.
55. Jéloubovskaïa, *La Chute*, 272; K. Steven Vincent, *Pierre-Joseph Proudhon and the Rise of French Republican Socialism* (New York, 1984), 232.
56. Jéloubovskaïa, *La Chute*, 276–277; Dommanget, *Blanqui et l'opposition*, 221.

57. Jéloubovskaïa, *La Chute,* 293.

'58. Letters of April 18, 20, 1870, to Marx, cited by Jéloubovskaïa, *La Chute,* 272–273, and Girault, *Textes,* 24.

59. H. Collins and C. Abramsky, *Karl Marx and the British Labour Movement* (London, 1965), 288; Braunthal, *History,* 106–119.

60. IML, *Documents, GC Minutes,* 4:472, 240; Karl Marx to Paul Lafargue, April 19, 1870, *Annali,* 172; Rubel and Manale, *Marx without Myth,* 255.

61. Novikova, "Pablo Lafargue," 9; Jéloubovskaïa, *La Chute,* 283–284, 295, 297–298.

62. Jéloubovskaïa, *La Chute,* 312–313; Paul Lafargue to Karl Marx, n.d. (end of July 1870), IISH, D 2781; Cohn, 94–95.

63. Paul Lafargue to Karl Marx, n.d. (end of July 1870), IISH, D 2781.

64. Paul Lafargue, Laura Lafargue to Jenny Marx, January 9, 1870, *Daughters,* 61, 64.

65. Renamed three times, and now Place du Général Leclerc. Yvonne Kapp, *Eleanor Marx,* 2 vols. (London, 1972, 1976), 1:124.

66. Laura Lafargue to Jenny Marx, June 9, 1870, *Daughters,* 68–69.

67. Paul Lafargue to Karl Marx, in July 1870, *Daughters,* 72–73.

68. Kapp, *Eleanor Marx,* 1:124.

69. G. Dupliex, *Histoire de Bordeaux,* 6:328, cited in Jean Cavignac, "Paul Lafargue et ses parents à Bordeaux," *Bulletin de l'IAES* 21–22 (1975), 32; Léonce Dupont, *Tours et Bordeaux: souvenirs de la République à outrance* (Paris, 1877), 257.

70. Paul Lafargue to Karl Marx, n.d. (July or August 1870), IISH, Marx Papers, D 2860–65.

71. Laura Lafargue to Karl Marx, between August 23 and 27, 1870, *Daughters,* 74–77.

72. Karl Marx to Engels, September 6, 1870, MEW, 33:55.

8. Bordeaux

1. Charles Higounet, ed., *Histoire de Bordeaux* (Toulouse, 1980), 282–287, 309, 312, 314.

2. Ibid., 7, 71, 309.

3. Louis Greenberg, *Sisters of Liberty: Marseille, Lyon, Paris and the Reaction to a Centralized State* (Cambridge, Mass., 1971), 9; Higounet, *Histoire,* 282, 314.

4. Gordon Wright, "Public Opinion and Conscription in France, 1866–1870," *Journal of Modern History* 14 (1942), 29, 39–40; Jacques Girault, *La Commune et Bordeaux, 1870–1871* (Paris, 1971), 49.

5. Léonce Dupont, *Tours et Bordeaux: souvenirs de la République à outrance* (Paris, 1877), 353; *L'Egalité,* September 24, 1882.

6. Paul Lafargue to Karl Marx, September 12, 1870, IISH, D 2873; Cohn, 96.

7. Dupont, *Tours et Bordeaux*, 253–255.

8. Paul Lafargue to Jenny Marx, n.d., IISH, G 258–263; Burt Andréas, "Briefe und Dokumente der Familie Marx aus den Jahren 1862–1873," *Archiv für Sozialgeschichte*, 2 vols. (Hanover, 1962), 2:229–230.

9. Paul Lafargue to Jenny Marx, n.d., IISH, G 257, 259.

10. Laura Lafargue to Jenny Marx, October 6, 1870, *Daughters*, 78; Paul Lafargue to Karl Marx, October 28, 1870, IISH, D 2874.

11. Laura Lafargue to Jenny Marx, December 12, 1870, *Daughters*, 81.

12. Laura Lafargue to Jenny Marx, December 12, 1870, *Daughters*, 80–82.

13. Archives Municipales de Bordeaux, 1E 290, cited in Robert Molis, "Un Petit-fils de Karl Marx repose au coeur des Pyrenées," *Archistra* 76 (November 1986), 99.

14. Karl Marx to Paul Lafargue, February 4, 1871, MEW, 33:176.

15. Jean Cavignac, "Paul Lafargue et ses parents à Bordeaux," *Bulletin de l'IAES* 21–22 (1975), 28.

16. Cavignac, "Paul Lafargue et ses parents," 21, 23, 30, 32. A notarial act shows that Mme Lafargue gave her son the management of her New Orleans property. Ibid. 25.

17. Paul Lafargue to Marx, n.d., (about January 15, 1871), *Daughters*, 87.

18. *L'Egalité*, . . . September 24, 1882.

19. *Le Matin*, November 15, 1891.

20. *La Libre Pensée*, April 16, 1870; Maurice Dommanget, *Hommes et choses de la Commune* (Marseilles, 1937), 218.

21. *Le Paris*, November 17, 1891, cited in Jacques Girault, "Mises au point sur certains aspects de la vie et du rôle du jeune Lafargue," *La Pensée* 153 (1970), 59.

22. BM, microfilms U 17176 and 65909; G. P. Novikova, "Pablo Lafargue y la Primera Internacional," *Instituto de historia, serie temas sociales* 2 (May 1969), 9; Girault, *La Commune*, 75–76; Paul Lafargue to Jenny Marx, n.d. (September 1870), BM, microfilms 17164–65.

23. Pierre-Louis Berthaud, *La Commune à Bordeaux* (Bordeaux, 1924), 6. Copies of *La Tribune* are missing from the Bordeaux Municipal Library. Girault, "Mises," 62; Jacques Girault, ed., *Paul Lafargue: textes choisis* (Paris, 1970), 25–27.

24. Girault, *La Commune*, 303.

25. Also reproduced in Girault, "Mises," 59–61.

26. Paul Lafargue to Jenny Marx, date illegible (April 1871), IISH, G 260.

27. According to Berthaud, *La Commune à Bordeaux*, 6, and Maurice Dommanget, *Auguste Blanqui au début de la IIIe République, 1871–1880* (Paris, 1971), 39, the Bordeaux section was reconstituted by Lafargue.

28. Jacques Rougerie, ed., *1871: jalons pour une histoire de la Commune de Paris* (Paris, 1973), 121.

29. Paul Lafargue to Marx, n.d. (near September 25, 1870), cited in E. A. Jéloubovskaïa, *La Chute du Second Empire et la naissance de la Troisième République en France* (Moscow, 1959), 517–518.

30. Girault, "Mises," 63.

31. Ibid., 62.

32. The thesis of Robert Molis, who says the Spanish Legion arrived in Bordeaux September 2. Molis, "Petit-fils," 100. In the short-lived Bordeaux biweekly newspaper, *La Fédération* (April 16–May 21, 1871), Dargance regularly advertised his pamphlet describing the history of the legion.

33. *Le Paris,* November 17, 1891, cited in Girault, "Mises," 62.

34. Paul Lafargue to Karl Marx, October 28, 1870, IISH, D 2874; IML, *Documents, GC Minutes,* 4:83.

35. IML, *Documents, GC Minutes,* 4:79.

36. Berthaud, *La Commune à Bordeaux,* 7.

37. BM, microfilm 65905; Girault, "Mises," 61.

38. *Enquête parlementaire sur l'insurrection du 18 mars 1871,* 3 vols. (Versailles, 1872); APP, B a/1175, November 1891.

39. Paul Lafargue to Karl Marx, about January 15, 1871, *Daughters,* 86–87.

40. Paul Lafargue to Karl Marx, February 4, 1871, *Daughters,* 91; APP B a/439, L'Internationale, report no. 5037.

41. Paul Lafargue to Karl Marx, February 9, 1871, cited by Cohn, 97.

42. Paul Lafargue to Jenny Marx, February 28, 1871, *Daughters,* 93–94.

43. Girault, *La Commune,* 221.

44. Paul Lafargue to Jenny Marx, n.d., IISH, G 261.

45. Reproduced in *La Tribune,* March 1, 1871.

46. Dommanget, *Hommes,* 221–222.

47. Cited in Dommanget, *Hommes,* 222.

48. Paul Lafargue to Jenny Marx, March 23, 1871, BM, microfilms 17157–58; Girault, *La Commune,* 221.

49. Berthaud, *La Commune à Bordeaux,* 8–10.

9. *The Commune*

1. Paul Lafargue to Jenny Marx, March 19, 1871, wrongly dated 1870, IISH, G 261; Cohn, 99; Jacques Girault, ed., *Paul Lafargue: textes choisis,* 30.

2. Jenny Marx to Ludwig Kugelmann, April 3, 1871, Burt Andréas, "Briefe und Dokumente der Familie Marx aus den Jahren 1862–1873," *Archiv für sozialgeschichte,* 2 vols. (Hanover, 1962), 2:240–241.

3. Jaclard was later to escape to Switzerland. APP, B a/1135, dossier Jaclard.

4. Karl Marx to Wilhelm Liebknecht, April 10, 1871, Saul Padover, ed., *On the First International* (New York, 1973), 525.

5. J. Varlet, *Paul Lafargue, théoricien du Marxisme* (Paris, 1933), 9; Jean Bruhat, "Paul Lafargue et la tradition du socialisme révolutionnaire français," *Cahiers internationaux* 6 (July–August 1949), 68; Maurice Dommanget, *Hommes et choses de la Commune* (Marseilles, 1937), 223; Claude Willard, *Les Guesdistes: le mouvement socialiste en France, 1893–1905* (Paris, 1965), 27.

6. Jenny Marx to Kugelmann, April 18, 1871, Karl Marx, Jenny Marx, and Friedrich Engels, *Lettres à Kugelmann,* ed. Gilbert Badia (Paris, 1971), 192.

7. Laura Lafargue to Jenny Marx, n.d. (between April 7 and 18, 1871), Jenny Marx to Laura Lafargue, April 18, 1871, *Daughters,* 98–100.

8. Lafargue published a series of letters, "Une Visite à Paris," in *La Tribune de Bordeaux,* April 24, 25, 28, and May 3, giving his impressions.

9. Dommanget, *Hommes,* 222–223; Paul Lafargue to Karl Marx, April 8, 1871, *Lettres du Communards . . . à Marx . . .* (Paris, 1934), 25.

10. Karl Marx to Kugelman, April 12, 1871, MEW, 33:205; IML, *Documents, GC Minutes,* 4:181.

11. *La Tribune,* May 3, cited in Jacques Girault, *La Commune et Bordeaux, 1870–1871* (Paris, 1971), 243–246.

12. Cited in Dommanget, *Hommes,* 219–220.

13. *Le Socialiste,* April 9, 1892; "Socialism in France from 1876 to 1896," *Fortnightly Review,* September 1897, 452.

14. *Le Socialiste,* July 9, 1887.

15. *Le Patriotisme de la bourgeoisie* (Paris, 1906); Dommanget, *Hommes,* 219–220.

16. *La Fédération,* April 16–May 4, 1871; Louis Greenberg, *Sisters of Liberty: Marseille, Lyon, Paris and the Reaction to a Centralized State* (Cambridge, Mass.; 1971), 296; for *La Tribune,* see Girault, *La Commune,* p. 142.

17. AN, C 2882, Dossiers préparatoires et rapport final de l'Enquête parlementaire sur l'insurrection du 18 mars 1871; Girault, *La Commune,* 144, 271, 278.

18. AN, C 2882; *Enquête parlementaire sur l'insurrection du 18 mars,* 3 vols. (Versailles, 1872), 2:615–616; Greenberg, *Sisters,* 297–299; Girault, *La Commune,* 164–169.

19. Girault, *Textes,* 31–32.

20. Paul Lafargue to Karl Marx, May 12, 1871, IISH, D 2878; *La Fédération,* May 7, 1871; AN, C 2882; Girault, *La Commune,* 164.

21. *La Tribune,* May 9, 10, 12, 13–16; Girault, *Textes,* 31–32.

22. Paul Lafargue to Karl Marx, February 9, 1871, Dommanget, *Hommes,* 222.

23. *Le Socialisme et la conquête des pouvoirs publics* (Paris, 1899), cited in Dommanget, *Hommes,* 223.

24. Robert Molis, "Un Petit-fils de Karl Marx repose au coeur des Pyrenées," *Archistra* 76 (November 1986), 100–101.

25. APP, B a/1135, dossier Paul Lafargue; Dommanget, *Hommes,* 225.

26. *Enquête parlementaire,* 1:462–463, 544. Original in AN, C 2882, no. 15; reproduced in Marc Vuilleumier, "Quelques documents inédits sur Paul Lafargue et la famille Marx en 1871," *Cahiers de l'ISEA* 9 (August 1965).

27. *Enquête parlementaire,* cited in Girault, *La Commune,* 269.

28. AN, C 2882; Girault, *Textes,* 34; Girault, *La Commune,* 196.

29. Jenny Marx to Karl Marx, May 24, 1871, *Daughters,* 102.

30. Cohn, 101; Jenny Marx's account published in *Woodhull and Claflin's Weekly of New York,* no. 23 (October 21, 1871), reproduced in MEW, 37:477–485.

31. Laura Lafargue to Karl Marx, June 3, 1871, cited in Salvador Morales, ed., *Pablo Lafargue: textos escogidos* (Havana, 1976), 38.

32. *Enquête parlementaire,* 1:544; Vuilleumier, "Quelques documents," 232.

33. The official's penciled comment in APP, B a/1135; Cohn, 101.

34. De Kératry's report to Paris, July 4, 1871, AN, C 2882, no. 15; the report of the Toulouse public prosecutor, Baron Desazaras, dated August 17, 1871, AN, C 2884, no. 52.

35. AN, C 2882, no. 15; C 2884, no. 52. Both the Haute-Garonne prefect and the Toulouse public prosecutor agreed a Paris "radical," identified by Desazaras as a man named Spont, found the cottage and otherwise aided Lafargue.

36. Dommanget, *Hommes,* 226.

37. AN, C 2882, cited in Vuilleumier, "Quelques documents," 243; Karl Marx to Edward Beesly, June 12, 1871, *Marx-Engels, Selected Correspondence* (Moscow, 1955), 250.

38. Karl Marx to Jenny, Laura, and Eleanor Marx, June 13, 1871, cited in Yvonne Kapp, *Eleanor Marx,* 2 vols. (London, 1972, 1976), 1:128.

39. Jenny Marx to Kugelmann, October 3, 1871, MEW, 33:684; APP, B a/1135.

40. Paul Lafargue to Karl Marx, August 1, 1871, *Lettres de Communards,* 46–48.

41. APP, B a/1135; Jacques Girault, "Mises au point sur certains aspects de la vie et du rôle du jeune Lafargue," *La Pensée* 153 (1970), 64.

42. Dommanget, *Hommes,* 225; Vuilleumier, "Quelques documents," 243.

10. Escape

1. AN, BB18 1848, "Rapports sur Lafargue," cited in Jean Bruhat et al., *La Commune de 1871* (Paris, 1960), 407.

2. *L'Egalité,* January 18, 1883; Yvonne Kapp, *Eleanor Marx,* 2 vols. (London, 1972, 1976), 1:128–131; Cohn, 102–104; Eleanor's account to Liebknecht, December 29, 1871, Wilhelm Liebknecht, *Briefwechsel mit Karl Marx und Friedrich Engels* (The Hague, 1973), 413–414. Jenny's lengthier account was published in *Woodhull and Claflin's Weekly of New York,* no. 23 (October 21, 1871), reproduced in MEW, 37:477–485. Marx sent Jenny's story to Woodhull's in late September 1871 to show the character of the French republican government. Although he was not happy with the ardent feminism shown by "Woodhull & Co." and prepared to dismiss them as "humbugs that compromise us," the European press was closed to him. Karl Marx to Laura Lafargue, February 28, 1872, MEW, 33:412. Marx also sent a letter complaining of his daughters' treatment to Charles Dana, which was published in the *New York Sun* on September 9, 1871, cited in Saul Padover, *Karl Marx: An Intimate Biography* (New York, 1978), 453.

3. Jenny's account is corroborated by the dossier of the parliamentary committee investigating the insurrection of March 18, AN, C 2882, C 2884. That Lafargue was warned by a "brave republican" was confirmed by Charles Longuet, *L'Eclair,* November 17, 1891. This is Engels' version as well. See Max Nettlau, *La Première Internationale en Espagne, 1868–1888* (Dordrecht, 1969), 96; Jacques Girault, "Mises au point sur certains aspects de la vie et du rôle du jeune Lafargue," *La Pensée* 153 (1970), 64; Marc Vuilleumier, "Quelques documents inédits sur Paul Lafargue et la famille Marx en 1871," *Cahiers de l'ISEA* 9 (August 1965), 244.

4. Vuilleumier, "Quelques documents," 242.

5. Cohn, 106–107.

6. Maurice Dommanget, *Hommes et choses de la Commune* (Marseilles, 1937), 225.

7. Paul Lafargue to Karl Marx, August 16, 1871, IISH, D 2880; *L'Egalité,* December 19, 1882, cited in Girault, "Mises," 65.

8. *L'Egalité,* December 19, 1882; *La Verité,* August 22, 1871; Salvador Morales, "Pablo y Laura Lafargue," *Bohemia* 16 (April 1964), 70; ELC, 3:498.

9. Paul Lafargue to Engels, October 2, 1871, ELC, 1:26–27; José Termes, *Anarquismo y sindicalismo en España: la Primera Internacional, 1864–1881* (Barcelona, 1972), 138.

10. Dommanget, *Hommes,* 225.

11. Laura Lafargue to Karl Marx, December 9, 1871, IISH, D 2862; Karl Marx to Laura Lafargue, December 18, 1871, *Annali,* 193.

12. Laura Lafargue to Karl Marx, December 12, 1871, reproduced in I. A. Bakh, ed., "Neopublikovannye pis'ma Laury Lafarg i Zhenni Longe Karlu Marksu" (Unpublished Letters of Laura Lafargue and Jenny

Longuet to Karl Marx), *Novaia i Noveisaia istoriia* 1983(3), 6. On Lachâtre see Jean-Pierre Lefebvre, "La Première Traduction française du *Capital*," *La Pensée* 233 (May–June 1983), 87.

13. According to Anna Corvin's letter to Karl Marx of November 12, 1872, cited in ibid., 88.

14. Charles Longuet to Karl Marx, January 13, 1872; Jenny Marx to Ludwig Kugelmann, January 22, 1872, cited in ibid., 88.

15. Lefebvre, "La Première Traduction," 89–90, 92. Marx eventually expressed satisfaction with Roy's translation, and even said in 1875 that the French translation "had a scientific value the original did not and must be consulted by German language readers." Engels remained critical. See Jacques d'Hondt, "*Le Capital* et la France," in Georges Labica, ed., *1883–1893: l'oeuvre de Marx, un siècle après* (Paris, 1985), 131–137.

16. Paul Lafargue to Engels, December 21, 1871, ELC, 3:404.

17. Karl Marx to Laura Lafargue, December 18, 1871, MEW, 33:363.

18. In 1875. Karl Marx and Friedrich Engels, *Revolution in Spain* (New York, 1939), 7–8, 12–13.

19. Lafargue then signed his letters "Toole," or "Toole I," taking the name of an Irish comedian then popular in London. Karl Marx to Paul Lafargue, November 24, 1871, Saul Padover, *On the First International* (New York, 1973), 550–555; *Annali*, 192–193. Engels' postscript in ELC, 3:402–403.

20. Paul Lafargue to Engels, December 12, 1871, ELC, 3:403–405.

21. *Naissance*, 30; Dommanget, *L'Introduction du marxisme en France* (Lausanne, 1969), 138–139.

22. Paul Lafargue to Engels, October 2, 1871, ELC, 1:24–29.

23. ELC, 1:24–29; Engels to Paul Lafargue, December 3, 1871, ELC, 1:32.

24. December 9, 1871, ELC, 1:29–30; Miklos Molnár, *Le Déclin de la Première Internationale: la conférence de Londres de 1871* (Geneva, 1963), 174–175.

25. December 26; Max Nettlau, *Miguel Bakunin, la Internacional, y la Alianza en España, 1868–1873* (Buenos Aires, 1925), 103.

26. December 26, 1871, ELC, 3:409–410; January 7, 1872, ELC, 3:412.

27. Paul Lafargue to Engels, December 23, 26, 1871, ELC, 3:407, 408–411.

28. Paul Lafargue, *A las Internacionales de la región española* (Madrid, June 27, 1872), a thirty-two-page pamphlet cited in Max Nettlau, *Documentos inéditos sobre la Internacional y la Alianza en España* (Buenos Aires, 1930), 64.

29. Jenny Marx to Kugelmann, January 22, 1872, in Burt Andréas, "Briefe und Dokumente der Familie Marx aus den Jahren 1862–1873," *Archiv für sozialgeschichte*, 2 vols. (Hanover, 1962), 2:273–274.

30. Paul Lafargue to Engels, January 25/26, 1871, ELC, 3:415–421; Karl Marx to Paul Lafargue, February 28, 1871, *Annali*, 194–195.

31. Cited in G. P. Novikova, "Pablo Lafargue y la Primera Internacional," *Instituto de historia, serie temas sociales* 2 (May 1969), 12.
32. Karl Marx to Paul Lafargue, March 21, 1872, MEW, 33:436.
33. Paul Lafargue to Engels, December 26, 1871, ELC, 3:410.
34. Nettlau, *Bakunin,* 104.

11. *The Anarchist Alternative*

1. Gerald Brenan, *The Spanish Labyrinth* (Cambridge, 1943), 132; E. H. Carr, *Michael Bakunin* (New York, 1961), 150.
2. Julius Braunthal, *History of the International, 1864–1914* (London, 1966), 139.
3. Cited in Murray Bookchin, *The Spanish Anarchists: The Heroic Years, 1868–1936* (New York, 1977), 17; Carr, *Michael Bakunin,* 356.
4. Carr, *Michael Bakunin,* 351–352, 359; Braunthal, *History,* 177–178.
5. Bakunin to Tomás Morago, reproduced in Max Nettlau, *Documentos in-editos sobre la Internacional y la Alianza en España* (Buenos Aires, 1930), cited in Brenan, *Labyrinth,* 137.
6. Carr, *Michael Bakunin,* 444; Braunthal, *History,* 179–184.
7. Carl Landauer, *European Socialism* (Berkeley, 1959), 1:80–83.
8. Braunthal, *History,* 179; Carr, *Michael Bakunin,* 362–363.
9. Brenan, *Labyrinth,* 131.
10. Karl Marx to Paul Lafargue, April 19, 1870, MEW, 32:673–678; Cohn, 113–114.
11. David Felix, *Marx as Politician* (Carbondale, 1983), 176; Carr, *Michael Bakunin,* 443.
12. Braunthal, *History,* 183.
13. Brenan, *Labyrinth,* 38–39.
14. Braunthal, *History,* 222.
15. Bookchin, *Spanish Anarchists,* 21, 34, 41.
16. Juan Antonio Lacomba, *Introducción a la historia económica de la España contemporain* (Madrid, 1969), 185; Salvador Morales, ed., *Pablo Lafargue: textos escogidos* (Havana, 1976), 41.
17. Casimir Marti, "La Première Internationale à Barcelone (1868–1870)," *International Review of Social History* 4 (1959), 413; Josep Fontana, *Cambio económico y actitudes politicas en la España del siglo XIX* (Barcelona, 1973), 94, cited in Morales, *Textos,* 40.
18. Braunthal, *History,* 222–223.
19. Bookchin, *Spanish Anarchists,* 15.
20. Anselmo Lorenzo, *El Proletariado militante: memorias de un internacional* (Madrid, 1974), 40–41; Bookchin, *Spanish Anarchists,* 14.
21. Cited in Max Nettlau, "Bakunin und die Internationale in Spanien, 1868–1873," *Archiv für die Geschichte des Sozialismus und der Arbeiter Be-*

wegung 4, 2 Heft (1913), 250; Miklos Molnár, *Le Déclin de la Première Internationale: la conférence de Londres de 1871* (Geneva, 1963), 177.

22. Brenan, *Labyrinth*, 142–143.
23. Clara E. Lida, ed., *Antecedentes y desarolla del movimiento obrero español 1835–1888* (Madrid, 1973), 25.
24. Lorenzo, *El Proletariado*, 255; Bookchin, *Spanish Anarchists*, 14–15.
25. Brenan, *Labyrinth*, 140.
26. Ibid., 143. According to a report given at the Cordoba Congress in December 1872, the Spanish Federation had 101 local federations with 322 trade union branches, 66 other affiliated local groups, and 10 sections of individual members. Braunthal, *History*, 184.
27. Bookchin, *Spanish Anarchists*, 51–52.
28. G. P. Novikova, "Pablo Lafargue y la Primera Internacional," *Instituto de historia, serie temas sociales* 2 (May 1969), 12.
29. Bookchin, *Spanish Anarchists*, 72–73.

12. *Our Man in Madrid*

1. Maximiano García Venero, *Historia de las Internacionales en España, 1868–1914*, 3 vols. (Madrid, 1956–57), 1:193; Juan José Morato, *El Partido socialista obrero* (Madrid, 1976), 61.
2. Paul Lafargue, "Souvenirs de 1872," *Le Socialisme*, December 16, 1908. Not to be confused with *Le Socialiste*. Jacques Girault, ed., *Paul Lafargue: textes choisis* (Paris, 1970), 38.
3. José Termes, *Anarquismo y sindicalismo en España: la Primera Internacional, 1864–1881* (Barcelona, 1972), 138.
4. G. D. H. Cole, *A History of Socialist Thought*, vol. 3, *The Second International* (New York, 1956), part 2, 750.
5. Morato, *El Partido*, 62.
6. Max Nettlau, *La Première Internationale en Espagne, 1868–1888* (Dordrecht, 1969), 66; Girault, *Textes*, 38.
7. On November 14, 1871. Jean Cavignac, "Paul Lafargue et ses parents à Bordeaux," *Bulletin de l'IAES* 21–22 (1975), 25, 32.
8. IISH, Marx Papers, D 2881, D 2882, D 2883; Max Nettlau, ed., *Documentos inéditos sobre la Internacional y la Alianza en España* (Buenos Aires, 1930), 65.
9. Paul Lafargue to Engels, April 27, 1872, ELC, 3:438.
10. Engels to Paul Lafargue, March 11, 1872, ELC, 1:43.
11. Paul Lafargue to Engels, March 6, 1872, ELC, 3:425.
12. Nettlau, *Documentos inéditos*, 65.
13. José Peirats, *Los Anarquistas en la crisis política española* (Buenos Aires, 1964), 190; Max Nettlau, *Miguel Bakunin, la Internacional, y la Alianza en España, 1868–1873* (Buenos Aires, 1925), 105.

14. *Le Socialisme,* October 8, 1911.

15. Salvador Morales, ed., *Paul Lafargue: textos escogidos* (Havana, 1976), 45–46.

16. Murray Bookchin, *The Spanish Anarchists: The Heroic Years, 1868–1936* (New York, 1977), 74.

17. Clara E. Lida, ed., *Anarquismo y revolución en la España del XIX* (Madrid, 1972), 164; Termes, *Anarquismo,* 132.

18. Bookchin, *Spanish Anarchists,* 74; Miklos Molnár, *Le Déclin de la Première Internationale: la conférence de Londres de 1871* (Geneva, 1963), 176.

19. G. P. Novikova, "Pablo Lafargue y la Primera Internacional," *Instituto de historia, serie temas sociales* 2 (May 1969), 13.

20. Paul Lafargue to Engels, March 20–25, 1872, ELC, 3:426–427.

21. Mora to the General Council, ELC, 3:427–428; Venero, *Historia,* 1:196; Morales, *Textos,* 45. Mora gives the number of delegates as 45; Guillaume as 40. James Guillaume, *L'Internationale: documents et souvenirs, 1864–1878,* 2 vols. (Paris, 1905–1909), 2:276.

22. Paul Lafargue to Engels, April 12, 1872, ELC, 3:428–431.

23. Ibid.; Jacques Droz, ed., *Histoire générale du socialisme,* vol. 2, *1875–1918* (Paris, 1974), 308; Morato, *El Partido,* 63; Termes, *Anarquismo,* 428.

24. G. M. Stekloff, *History of the First International* (London, 1928), 215; Girault, *Textes,* 38.

25. IML, *Documents, GC Minutes,* 5:548; García Venero, *Historia,* 1:197.

26. Termes, *Anarquismo,* 142.

27. Molnár, *Le Déclin,* 177.

28. Paul Lafargue to Engels, May 17, 1872, ELC, 3:440.

29. Paul Lafargue to Engels, April 12, 1872, ELC, 3:428–429.

30. IML, *Documents, GC Minutes,* 5:293; Engels to Theodore Cuno, April 27, May 7–8, 1872, Karl Marx and Friedrich Engels, *Letters to Americans* (New York, 1953), 103–104. See also W. O. Henderson, *The Life of Friedrich Engels,* 2 vols. (London, 1976), 2:539.

31. Engels to Wilhelm Liebknecht, May 15, 1872, Wilhelm Liebknecht, *Briefwechsel mit Karl Marx und Friedrich Engels* (The Hague, 1963), 69.

32. Engels to Laura Lafargue, March 11, 1872, ELC, 1:42; Nettlau, *Documentos inéditos,* 90.

33. Girault, *Textes,* 38–39; Paul Lafargue to Engels, May 17, 1872, ELC, 3:441–442.

34. Engels to Wilhelm Liebknecht, May 7, 1872, MEW, 33:455; Engels to Cuno, May 7–8, August 4, 1872, MEW, 33:459, 510; Engels to Laura Lafargue, March 11, 1872, ELC, 1:42.

35. Termes, *Anarquismo,* 145; Morales, *Textos,* 47.

36. Clara E. Lida, ed., *Antecedentes y desarrolla del movimiento obrero español, 1835–1888* (Madrid, 1973), 27.
37. Novikova, "Pablo Lafargue," 14.
38. Nettlau, *Miguel Bakunin,* 107.
39. García Vereno, *Historia,* 1:198; Novikova, "Pablo Lafargue," 14. Text reproduced in Lida, *Antecedentes,* 245–265.
40. Nettlau, *Documentos inéditos,* 108; Paul Lafargue to Engels, June 5, 1872, ELC, 3:457.
41. Paul Lafargue to Engels, May 29, 1872, ELC, 3:444–450.
42. Paul Lafargue to the editors of the *Bulletin de la Fédération jurassienne,* July 12, 1872, ELC, 3:466–468.
43. *L'Alliance de la démocracie socialiste et l'association internationale* (London, 1873).
44. Paul Lafargue to Engels, July 12, 1872, ELC, 3:465; Cohn, 120–121.
45. Cole, *Socialist Thought,* 3:751.
46. Nettlau, *Miguel Bakunin,* 111.
47. Bookchin, *Spanish Anarchists,* 75.
48. Julio Alvarez del Vayo, *The Last Optimist* (London, 1950), 180.
49. Paul Lafargue to Engels, May 29, 1872, ELC, 3:445.
50. Paul Lafargue to Engels, mid-July 1872, ELC, 3:469–470; Nettlau, *Documentos inéditos,* 132.
51. Engels to Theodore Cuno, July 5, 1872, Engels to Adolphe Hefner, August 4, 1872, Marx and Engels, *Letters to Americans,* 110–111.
52. Some historians, following the example of Guillaume, have accepted this interpretation. Fritz Brupbacher, ed., *Socialisme et liberté* (Paris, 1955), 139, cited in Girault, *Textes,* 40.
53. Paul Lafargue to Engels, mid-July 1872, ELC, 3:469–470.
54. Paul Lafargue, "Souvenirs de 1872," *Le Socialisme,* February 23, 1908. The issue of March 22 published letters from Iglesias and Mora certifying the accuracy of Lafargue's account.
55. Girault, *Textes,* 41.
56. Paul Lafargue to Engels, April 12, 1872, ELC, 3:434.
57. Yvonne Kapp, *Eleanor Marx,* 2 vols. (London, 1972, 1976), 1:144.
58. Paul Lafargue to Engels, July 1, 1872, ELC, 3:463.
59. Jenny Marx to Karl Marx, May 3, 1872, Burt Andréas, "Briefe und Dokumente der Familie Marx aus den Jahren 1862–1873," *Archiv für Sozialgeschichte,* 2 vols. (Hanover, 1962), 2:278–279.
60. Juan José Morato, *Pablo Iglesias* (Madrid, 1931).
61. Stanley Payne, *The Spanish Revolution* (New York, 1970), 63–64.
62. Paul Lafargue to Engels, May 29, 1872, ELC, 3:445.
63. Morato, *Pablo Iglesias,* 32.
64. Morato, *El Partido,* 21, 60; Morato, *Pablo Iglesias,* 32.
65. Engels to Laura Lafargue, March 11, 1872, ELC, 1:45.

66. Nettlau, *Miguel Bakunin,* 119–120; Nettlau, *Documentos inéditos,* 138.
67. Nettlau, *Miguel Bakunin,* 104.
68. Ibid., 114.

13. The Hague

 1. Paul Lafargue to Engels, August 8, 1872, ELC, 3:471. The date appears to be in error. Lafargue said he had been in Portugal for eight days, and a later letter from Holland was dated August 4.
 2. Paul Lafargue to Engels, August 4, 1872, ELC, 3:473–474.
 3. IML, *Documents of the First International: The Hague Congress* (Moscow, 1976), 640 (hereafter *The Hague Congress*).
 4. Paul Lafargue to Engels, May 17, 1872, ELC, 3:443; Max Nettlau, *Documentos inéditos sobre la Internacional y la Alianza en España* (Buenos Aires, 1930), 96–97.
 5. David Felix, *Marx as Politician* (Carbondale, 1983), 178.
 6. David Stafford, *From Anarchism to Reformism: A Study of the Political Activities of Paul Brousse* (Toronto, 1971), 14–15.
 7. Maximilien Rubel and Margaret Manale, *Marx without Myth* (Oxford, 1975), 275; Georges Haupt, *Aspects of International Socialism* (Cambridge, 1986), 2–3. Apparently Marx's opponents, at the time the Communist League was dissolved, spoke of a "party of Marx," and in 1853–54 Wilhelm Weitling's supporters used the adjective "Marxian" to draw a distinction with Lassalle. See the discussion in Haupt's *L'Historien et le mouvement social* (Paris, 1980), 78–79.
 8. From the Amsterdam newspaper *Algemien Handelsblad,* cited in IML, *The Hague Congress,* 635.
 9. Theodore Cuno, "An Agitator's Notebook," draft ms. (1883), cited in IML, *The Hague Congress,* 626–633.
10. IML, *The Hague Congress,* 638–639; Franzisca Kugelmann, in *Reminiscences of Marx and Engels* (Moscow, n.d.), 284.
11. Cited in Haupt, *Aspects,* 38.
12. Paul Lafargue to Engels, ELC, 3:465.
13. On September 3. Maltman Berry's reports were originally published in the British newspaper *The Standard,* September 6–10, 12–13, 1872, and reproduced in IML, *The Hague Congress,* 261–262.
14. IML, *The Hague Congress,* 391.
15. Ibid., 66, 72, 148–149, 269.
16. There were 13 abstentions. Ibid., 222, 83; G. P. Novikova, "Pablo Lafargue y la Primera Internacional," *Instituto de historia, serie temas sociales* 2 (1969), 14–15.
17. IML, *The Hague Congress,* 361.
18. Novikova, "Pablo Lafargue," 15–16.

19. IML, *The Hague Congress,* 228–229.
20. Ibid., 200, 272, 316.
21. H. Gemkow, *Karl Marx: Eine Biographie* (Berlin, 1967), 361.
22. Cuno's draft memoirs, cited in Padover, *Karl Marx,* 361.
23. Alexandre Zévaès, *De l'introduction du marxisme en France* (Paris, 1947), 71–73.
24. Gerald Brenan, *The Spanish Labyrinth* (Cambridge, 1943), 145.
25. Cited in Jacques Rougerie, ed., *1871: jalons pour une histoire de la Commune de Paris* (Paris, 1973), 237.
26. Brenan, *Labyrinth,* 145.
27. Ibid., 146–149.
28. José Mesa to Engels, September 19, 1872; according to Engels, the Lafargues returned to London on October 27, Engels to Theodore Cuno, October 29, 1872, MEW, 33:534; Eleanor Marx to Jenny Longuet, November 7, 1872, 113–114.
29. APP, B a/1135, report dated January 21, 1873; Eleanor Marx to Jenny Marx, November 7, 1872, *Daughters,* 113–114; Jacques Girault, ed., *Paul Lafargue: textes choisis* (Paris, 1970), 42. A letter from Engels reveals that Lafargue was in London in late October. Engels to Theodore Cuno, October 29, 1872, MEW, 33:354.
30. Yvonne Kapp, *Eleanor Marx,* 2 vols. (London, 1972, 1976), 1:144, 161.
31. *Daughters,* 113–114.
32. Robert Longuet, *Karl Marx, mon arrière-grandpère* (Paris, 1977), 208, 216; Kapp, *Eleanor Marx,* 1:153, 161.
33. APP, B a/1135, undated report, cited in Girault, *Textes,* 42.

14. *The London Exile*

1. *The Labour Annual of 1897* (Brighton, 1971); Benedikt Kautsky, ed., *Friedrich Engels, Briefwechsel mit Kaul Kautsky* (Vienna, 1955), 56; Eduard Bernstein, "Paul Lafargue," *Sozialistische Monatshefte* 16 (1912), 22.
2. Jenny Marx Longuet to Ludwig Kugelmann, Mrs. Jenny Marx to Ludwig Kugelmann, December 23, 1872, Karl Marx, Jenny Marx, and Friedrich Engels, *Lettres à Kugelmann,* ed. Gilbert Badia (Paris, 1971), 71, 222.
3. Yvonne Kapp, *Eleanor Marx,* 2 vols. (London, 1972, 1976), 1:170.
4. Paul Lafargue to Jenny Marx, BM, microfilm U17 176.
5. *L'Egalité,* January 29, 1882.
6. Paul Lafargue to Mrs. Jenny Marx, February 10, 1871, Meier; Paul Lafargue to Karl Marx, February 4, 1871, *Daughters,* 91–92.
7. Jenny Marx to Laura Lafargue, April 18, 1871, *Daughters,* 100.
8. Laura Lafargue to Engels, October 4, 1883, ELC, 1:155–156.
9. *L'Egalité,* January 29, 1882.

10. Engels to Kugelmann, July 1, 1873, MEW, 33:594; Cohn, 129; Engels to Friedrich Sorge, July 23, 1873, MEW, 33:599.

11. Karl Marx to Engels, August 30, 1873, MEW, 33:89; Paul Lafargue to Le Moussu, Paul Lafargue to Sam Moore, Lafargue's attorney and Engels' friend, September 1, 1873, IISH, uncatalogued, cited in Cohn, 129.

12. E.g., February 11, 25, March 10, 1880. See page 8 of each issue. Cohn, 128.

13. Paul Lafargue to Engels, June 5, 1875, ELC, 1:51–52.

14. Mrs. Jenny Marx to Friedrich Sorge, January 20 or 21, 1877, cited in Saul Padover, *Karl Marx: An Intimate Biography* (New York, 1978), 500.

15. Paul Lafargue to Engels, January 4, 1877, ELC, 1:62.

16. Paul Lafargue to Karl Marx, January 15, 1871, cited in *Daughters*, 87; Engels to Paul Lafargue, September 9, 1880, ELC, 1:72–75; Paul Lafargue to (first name illegible) Grant, IISH, Marx-Engels Papers, R 59.

17. Engels to Paul Lafargue, September 12, 1880, ELC, 1:76–79.

18. Paul Lafargue to Engels, December 28, 1874, ELC, 1:50.

19. Paul Lafargue to Engels, August 11, 1875, ELC, 1:54–55.

20. Paul Lafargue to Engels, n.d., ELC, 1:57.

21. Paul Lafargue to Engels, May 9, 1878, ELC, 1:68.

22. Public Record Office (London), Census Room, Doc. Ref. Group RG, Class 11, Piece No. 246, page 39.

23. Paul Lafargue to Engels, December 28, 1874, ELC, 1:50.

24. Paul Lafargue to Engels, December 13, 1874, July 19, 1875, ELC, 1:48–49, 53.

25. Laura Lafargue to Karl Marx, September 8, 1876, n.d. (end of September 1876), Meier.

26. Paul Lafargue to Engels, June 9, 1874, ELC, 3:477–478.

27. Paul Lafargue to Karl Marx, July 26, 1874, IISH, Marx Papers, D 2883; Cohn, 131.

28. Jean Cavignac, "Paul Lafargue et ses parents à Bordeaux," *Bulletin de l'IAES* 21–22 (1975), 22, 31.

29. Engels to Paul Lafargue, September 3, 1880, ELC, 1:70–71.

30. Laura Lafargue to Engels, August 13, 1881, ELC, 1:81.

31. IML, *Documents of the First International: The Hague Congress* (Moscow, 1976), 407–447 (hereafter *The Hague Congress*); Marx to Sorge, April 4, 1874, cited by Jeanine Verdes, "B a/1175: Marx vu par la police française, 1871–1883," *Cahiers de l'ISEA* 176 (August 1966), 111.

32. Engels to Sorge, July 26, 1873, IML, *The Hague Congress*, 605; J. Freymond, ed., *La Première Internationale, imprimés, 1864–1876*, 3 vols. (Paris, 1961–1963), 2:537–538.

33. Cohn, 132.

34. Paul Lafargue to Paul Brousse, undated draft (end of April 1881), *Naissance*, 115.

35. Cited in *Naissance*, 52.

36. Paul Martinez, "Amis, épreuves et sûrs: les réfugiés Blanquistes en Angleterre, 1871–1880," in M. Agulhon et al., *Blanqui et les Blanquistes, colloque internationale* (Paris, 1981), 154; APP, B a/430, Commune de Paris, 1871, Comptes-rendus, Londres, 1874–1879, December 31, 1878; Verdes, "B a/1175" 108–110.

37. Jules Vallès cited by Stewart Edwards, *The Paris Commune, 1871* (New York, 1971), 349.

38. Patrick Hutton, *The Cult of the Revolutionary Tradition: The Blanquists in French Politics, 1864–1893* (Berkeley, 1981), 103, 106; Charles Da Costa, *Les Blanquistes* (Paris, 1912), 42–43; Maurice Dommanget, *Edouard Vaillant, un grand socialiste, 1840–1915* (Paris, 1956), 56; Jolyon Howorth, however, questions the extent to which Vaillant, a Proudhonian in the 1860s and ultimately to draw close to Marxism, was a Blanquist. *Edouard Vaillant: la création de l'unité socialiste en France* (Paris, 1982), 57–59.

39. Robert Longuet, *Karl Marx, mon arrière-grandpère* (Paris, 1977), 221–222.

40. Ibid., 224; Jenny Marx Longuet to Kugelmann, December 23, 1872, Marx, Marx, and Engels, *Lettres à Kugelmann*, ed. Badia, 222; Yvonne Kapp, *Eleanor Marx*, 2 vols. (1972, 1976), 1:143; *Daughters*, 113.

41. Kapp, *Eleanor Marx*, 1:170, 177.

42. R. Longuet, *Karl Marx, arrière-grandpère*, 224.

43. Eduard Bernstein, *My Years of Exile* (New York, 1921), 211–212; APP, B a/1135, report dated January 20, 1874.

44. Kapp, *Eleanor Marx*, 1:176.

45. Georges Cogniot, "La Pénétration du marxisme en France," *Cahiers du Centre d'études et de recherches marxistes* (Paris, 1965), 11.

46. *Naissance*, 13.

47. Ibid., 13–15; Alexandre Zévaès, *Aperçu historique sur le Parti ouvrier français* (Lille, 1899), 8–12.

48. Letter dated September 26, 1880, in *Le Citoyen*, in October; clipping in APP, B a/1135, Paul Lafargue.

49. Paul Lafargue to Auguste Blanqui, June 12, 1879, BN, Manuscripts Div., Blanqui Papers, N.A. fr., 9588(2), ff. 678–679.

50. Marx to Sorge, December 14, 1872, cited in Verdes, "B a/1175," 108–109; Samuel Bernstein, *Auguste Blanqui and the Art of Insurrection* (London, 1971), 348.

51. Jules Guesde to Karl Marx, n.d. (March or April 1879), *Annuaire*, 447–448.

52. Paul Lafargue to Guesde, June 1879, *Annuaire*, 450–451.

53. Paul Lafargue to Guesde, June 1879, *Annuaire,* 451.
54. Paul Lafargue to Guesde, June 1879, *Annuaire,* 450–451; José Mesa to Paul Lafargue, June 9, 1879, *Naissance,* 52.

15. The Guesdists

 1. Initial French publication dates for a number of Marx's and Engels' works are as follows: Volumes 2 and 3 of *Capital* were not published in France until 1900–1902; *The Communist Manifesto,* almost ignored in its 1848 edition, was not reprinted (in *Le Socialiste*) until 1885; *The Civil War in France* (as *The Paris Commune*) was not published until 1887 (in the same newspaper, serialized, but not completed, because *Le Socialiste* ceased publication); *The Eighteenth Brumaire of Louis Napoleon* was published only in 1891; *The Poverty of Philosophy,* first published in French in 1847, was reproduced in *L'Egalité* in 1880 and republished as a book in 1896; the *Introduction to the Critique of Hegel's Philosophy of Right* appeared in 1895; *The Class Struggles in France* was published in 1900; and the *Theses on Feuerbach* (in *L'Ere nouvelle*) in 1894. Engels' *Socialism: Scientific and Utopian* appeared in *L'Egalité* in 1880; his *Origins of the Family* was not published in France until 1893; and *Revolution and Counter-revolution in Germany* was published there only in 1900.
 2. Samuel Bernstein, "Jules Guesde, Pioneer of Marxism in France," *Science and Society* 4 (1940), 31.
 3. Joy Hall, "Gabriel Deville and the Development of French Socialism (1871–1905)" (Ph.D. dissertation, Auburn University, 1983), 92.
 4. IFHS, 14 AS 283, Dommanget Papers, Deville dossier.
 5. Charles Mauger, *Les Débuts du socialisme marxiste en France* (Paris, 1908), 19–20.
 6. Patrick Hutton, *The Cult of the Revolutionary Tradition: The Blanquists in French Politics, 1864–1893* (Berkeley, 1981), 111.
 7. Mauger, *Les Débuts,* 14–15.
 8. Paul Lafargue to Engels, January 10, 1886, ELC, 1:329–330.
 9. Hall, "Gabriel Deville," 438.
10. Madeleine Rébérioux, "Le Guesdisme," *Bulletin, Société d'études jaurèsiennes* 50 (July–September 1973), 2.
11. Hall, "Gabriel Deville," 94–95; Yvonne Kapp, *Eleanor Marx,* 2 vols. (London, 1972, 1976), 1:157.
12. Deville to Maurice Dommanget, May 21, 1935, IFSH, 14 AS 283(7), Dommanget Papers; Hall, "Gabriel Deville," 93–94.
13. Deville to Dommanget, June 2, 1936, cited in Maurice Dommanget, *L'Introduction du marxisme en France* (Lausanne, 1969), 134.
14. Benoît Malon, "Le Collectivisme en France de 1875 à 1879," *La Revue socialiste* 4 (1886), 998; *Daughters,* 130.

15. *Naissance,* 28.

16. Mermeix (pseud. of Gabriel Terrail), *La France socialiste* (Paris, 1886), 77–78.

17. Michelle Perrot, "Le Premier Journal marxiste français: *L'Egalité* de Jules Guesde, 1877–1883," *Le Mouvement social* 28 (July 1959), 1.

18. Gabriel Deville, *Le Capital,* 7–8, cited in Hall, "Gabriel Deville," 111.

19. Hutton, *Cult,* 119.

20. *La Révolution française,* April 29, 1979.

21. Hutton, *Cult,* 115–116.

22. Louis Mattia, cited in Léon de Seilhac, *Le Monde socialiste* (Paris, 1904), 42.

23. Cited in Georges Weill, *Histoire du mouvement social en France, 1852–1910* (Paris, 1911), 219.

24. *Naissance,* 29.

25. Willard, *Les Guesdistes: le mouvement socialiste en France, 1893–1905* (Paris, 1965), 14, 172; Rébérioux, "Le Guesdisme," 3.

26. Jules Guesde, *Ça et la* (Paris, 1914), 155–183, cited in Samuel Bernstein, *Auguste Blanqui and the Art of Insurrection* (London, 1971), 348.

27. Guy Chapman, *The Third Republic of France: The First Phase, 1871–1894* (New York, 1962), 188.

28. Robert Hunter, *Socialists at Work* (New York, 1908), 62.

29. Rébérioux, "Le Guesdisme," 3–4.

30. Cited in *Naissance,* 35. I am grateful to Steven Vincent for allowing me to see the relevant chapter in his draft manuscript of a Malon biography.

31. *Le Socialisme progressif* 4 (1878), cited in S. Bernstein, "Jules Guesde," 38.

32. José Mesa to Paul Lafargue, November 16, 1879, *Naissance,* 54; Paul Lafargue to Jules Guesde, undated draft, January 1880, *Naissance,* 61–62.

33. These letters are reproduced in both *Annuaire* and *Naissance.*

34. Paul Lafargue to Guesde, June 1879, BM, N4017, 060; *Annuaire,* 450.

35. November 29, 1882, APP, B a/1482.

36. Paul Lafargue to Guesde, June 1879, *Annuaire,* 450–451.

37. J. M. Brohm, introduction to Paul Lafargue, *Le Droit à la paresse* (Paris, 1965), 15.

38. Mermeix, *La France socialiste,* 98, 108.

39. Paul Lafargue to Pasquale Martignetti, November 4, 1891, cited in Willard, *Les Guesdistes,* 17. He later criticized the word as a bad Belgian synonym for Communist, but admitted it made little difference if the theory was applied. Ibid.

40. Hutton, *Cult,* 117.

41. Paul Lafargue to Guesde, November 29, 1879, *Annuaire,* 455–456.

42. Ibid.

43. The second series of *L'Egalité* ran from January 20 to August 25, 1880; the third, from December 11, 1881, to November 5, 1882. These first three series were weeklies; only the fourth, October 29 to December 28, 1882, was a daily.

44. Albert Lindemann, *A History of European Socialism* (New Haven, 1983), 134–135.

45. Frederick Engels, *Socialism: Scientific and Utopian* (New York, 1985), 73.

46. Paul Lafargue to Engels, July 12, 1885, ELC, 1:297. The original introduction to the pamphlet, though signed by Lafargue, was written by Marx. MEW, 19:181–182, 564, cited in Terrell Carver, *Engels* (New York, 1981), 47.

47. Paul Lafargue to Guesde, November 29, 1879, *Annuaire*, 456.

48. Paul Lafargue to Guesde, January 1880, *Annuaire*, 459.

49. Paul Lafargue to Guesde, November 29, 1879, *Annuaire*, 455; *L'Egalité*, August 11, 1880.

50. Paul Lafargue to Guesde, January 1880, *Annuaire*, 458–459.

51. *La Revue socialiste*, April 1880, 218; Cohn, 147.

52. "Le Rachat des chemins de fer et l'économie française," *La Revue socialiste*, May 1880, 269–274; *L'Egalité*, January 28, February 11, 18, 25, March 10, 1880.

53. "Les Accapareurs et leur impôts sur le blé," *La Revue socialiste*, January 1880.

54. Paul Lafargue to Guesde, January 1880, *Naissance*, 62.

55. "Le Parti ouvrier et l'alimentation publique," *La Revue socialiste*, February 20, 1880, 5–6.

56. Paul Lafargue to Guesde, November 29, 1879, *Annuaire*, 455; also Lafargue's article, "La Lutte de classes," *L'Egalité*, June 2, 1880, and a series of three articles in *La Revue socialiste*, February, April, and May 1880.

57. *La Revue socialiste*, April 20, 1880, 296–297.

58. Paul Lafargue to Guesde, January 1880, *Naissance*, 64.

59. Cited in *Naissance*, 18.

60. Paul Lafargue to Gabriel Deville, n.d., AN, 51 AP 2, Deville Papers.

61. Jacques Girault, "Les Guesdistes, la deuxième *Egalité*, et la Commune," *International Review of Social History* 17 (1972), 421–427, 429–430.

62. *L'Egalité*, February 18, 25, March 3, 18, April 14, 21, 1880.

63. *L'Egalité*, February 11, 1880.

64. Guesde to Paul Lafargue, December 31, 1880, IISH, Guesde Archives, G 7735, cited by Cohn, 138.

65. Paul Lafargue to Guesde, June 9, 1881, *Annuaire*, 473.

66. Paul Lafargue to Guesde, January 1880, *Annuaire*, 459.

67. José Mesa to Paul Lafargue, February 10, 1880, *Naissance*, 68–69.

16. A Pamphlet and a Program

1. *L'Egalité*, June 23, 30, July 7, 14, 21, 28, August 4, 1880. Many subsequent editions. Citations here are from the 1893 English edition, trans. James Blackwell, reprinted in pamphlet form from *Justice* by the Labour Literature Society with minor changes.

2. Cited in Joseph Pieper, *Leisure: The Basis of Culture* (New York, 1963), 54.

3. Paul Lafargue, *Le Droit à la paresse*, ed. Maurice Dommanget (Paris, 1970), 23.

4. Leszek Kolakowski, *Main Currents of Marxism*, 3 vols. (New York, 1981), 2:141–149.

5. Cohn, 161.

6. Cited in George Woodcock and Ivan Avakumović, *The Anarchist Prince: Peter Kropotkin* (New York, 1971), 320.

7. Stefan Morawski, "Pablo Lafargue y el desarrollo de una estetica marxista," *Casa de las Americas* 10 (1969), 37.

8. Paul Lafargue, *Pamphlets socialistes* (Paris, 1900).

9. Cited by Dommanget in his introduction to *Le Droit*, 8–9.

10. Karl Kautsky, *The Class Struggle* (New York, 1971), 157–158.

11. Bernard Brown, *Socialism of a Different Kind* (Westport, Conn., 1982), 34–35; Daniel Lindenberg, *Le Marxisme introuvable* (Paris, 1979), 68, n. 3.

12. For example, the discussion in *Le Nouvel Observateur*, December 1969, and *Le Monde*, May 16, 1970. *Le Monde* saw Lafargue's work as a "radical critique . . . not different from that elaborated by Herbert Marcuse in *Eros and Civilization*." Present-day strikes were seen as aiming not only for higher wages but for leisure time. Eric Larrabee and Rolf Myersohn, eds., *Mass Leisure* (Glencoe, Ill., 1958), 105–118; Cohn, 161–162.

13. In *Paris-Match*, August 1967.

14. Maurice Cristal (pseud. of Maurice German), *Les Délassements du travail*, cited in Lafargue, *Le Droit*, ed. Dommanget, 41.

15. Lafargue, *Le Droit*, ed. Dommanget, 44–45. Brissac cited by Dommanget. The need for leisure appears in several of Brissac's pre-1880 writings. In 1886, after Lafargue published his *Right to Be Lazy*, Brissac's *Travail et prolétariat* appeared.

16. Pierre Jaclard, *Histoire sociale du travail de l'antiquité à nos jours* (Paris, 1960), cited by Dommanget in his edition of Lafargue, *Le Droit*, 42.

17. Lafargue, *Le Droit*, ed. Dommanget, 46.

18. Ibid., 35.

19. Claude Willard, ed., *Jules Guesde: textes choisis, 1867–1882* (Paris, 1959), 25.

20. Victor Jaclard to Paul Lafargue, December 7, 1881, *Naissance*, 168.

21. Samuel Bernstein, "Jules Guesde, Pioneer of Marxism in France," *Science and Society* 4 (1940), 42.

22. Georges Lefranc, *Le Mouvement socialiste sous la Troisième République, 1875–1940* (Paris, 1963), 42–44; *Naissance*, 67.

23. First published in *La Revue socialiste*, 1881, English trans. in *The New International* (December 1938), 374–381.

24. Benoît Malon to Jules Guesde, April 3, 8, 27, 1880, cited in David Stafford, *From Anarchism to Reformism: A Study of the Political Activities of Paul Brousse* (Toronto, 1971), 160–162.

25. Adéodat Compère-Morel, *Jules Guesde: le socialisme fait l'homme, 1845–1922* (Paris, 1937), 153–154, 164.

26. Guesde's recollections, as told to Amédée Dunois in July 1911; Paul Lafargue, *Le Droit à la paresse,* ed. Amédée Dunois (Paris, 1946), intro.; Engels to Eduard Bernstein, October 25, 1881, cited in Karl Marx, *Selected Works,* 2 vols. (New York, 1936), 2:635–636. According to Engels, the program was dictated to Guesde. *Marx-Engels, Selected Correspondence* (Moscow, 1955), 324. The Bibliothèque Marxiste de Paris has a microfilm of part of the program, written by Lafargue with additional notes in Marx's handwriting. P[aul] L[afargue] and J[ules] G[uesde], *Le Programme du Parti ouvrier: ses considérants et ses articles,* 6th ed. (Paris, 1902). Complete text also in Willard, *Guesde: textes choisis,* 47.

27. J. Varlet, *Paul Lafargue, théoricien du marxisme* (Paris, 1933), 15; *Marx-Engels, Selected Correspondence,* 324.

28. Paul Brousse to César de Paepe, December 24, 1883, cited in César de Paepe, *Correspondance* (Paris, 1974), 266; Engels to Eduard Bernstein, October 25, 1881, cited in Stafford, *From Anarchism,* 163.

29. Engels to Eduard Bernstein, October 25, 1881, reproduced in "Les Partis socialistes français (1880–1895): lettres et extraits de lettres d'Engels à Bernstein," *Cahiers de l'ISEA* 109 (January 1961), 51.

30. Brousse to Paul Lafargue, July 14, 1880, *Naissance*, 83.

31. Stafford, *From Anarchism,* 382.

32. *Naissance,* 31–33; Stafford, *From Anarchism,* 383–384. Brousse, like the Bakuninists, used the term "Marxist" in a pejorative sense, not so much to describe a partisan of Marx's ideas as to describe one who seeks to impose those ideas in their entirety, e.g., German socialists and their French "appendages." Georges Haupt, *L'Historien et le mouvement social* (Paris, 1980), 95.

33. Undated letter from Paul Lafargue to Malon, cited in Stafford, *From Anarchism,* 162.

34. Malon received a copy of the program from Lafargue. Malon to Paul Lafargue, May 18, 1880, *Annuaire,* 468–471.

35. Paul Lafargue to Malon, May 5, 1880, IFHS, Fournière Papers, 14 AS 181 (2), no. 807.

36. Brousse to Hermann Jung, undated (1882), IISG, Jung Papers, 512/1; Stafford, *From Anarchism,* 164.

37. *La Revolté,* July 24, 1880; Daniel Ligou, *Histoire du socialisme en France, 1871–1961* (Paris, 1962), 40–41; Jean Maitron, *Histoire du mouvement anarchiste en France, 1880–1914* (Paris, 1951), 100–101.

38. Lafargue's article entitled "Le Parti ouvrier et l'état capitaliste." It was unsigned, but Lafargue did not hide his identity. Stafford, *From Anarchism,* 166–167.

39. De Paepe to Malon, January 2, 1882. Both he and Bernstein are cited in Stafford, *From Anarchism,* 319, n. 64.

40. Paul Lafargue to Brousse, undated (end of 1880), *Naissance,* 95–97.

41. IISH, Guesde Papers, 550/3; Joy Hall, "Gabriel Deville and the Development of French Socialism (1871–1905)" (Ph.D. dissertation, Auburn University, 1983), 162; Stafford, *From Anarchism,* 319–320.

42. Yvonne Kapp, *Eleanor Marx,* 2 vols. (London, 1972, 1976), 1:215.

43. Paul Lafargue to Brousse, undated (end of 1880), *Naissance,* 97–98.

44. Lefranc, *Le Mouvement socialiste,* 44; *Naissance,* 19.

45. Karl Marx to Friedrich Sorge, November 5, 1880, MEW, 34:476.

46. Paul Lafargue to Karl Marx, April 18, 1881, cited in Georges Weill, *Histoire du mouvement social en France, 1852–1910* (Paris, 1911), 239.

47. From October 31 to November 24, Hall, "Gabriel Deville," 166.

48. Mermeix, (pseud. of Gabriel Terrail), *La France socialiste* (Paris, 1886), 226. That Guesde and Lafargue needed the money was acknowledged by Mesa, who regretted their participation. Mesa to Paul Lafargue, December 14, 1880, *Naissance,* 94.

49. Paul Lafargue to Brousse, undated (April 1881), Brousse to Paul Lafargue, April 24, 1881, *Naissance,* 108–109, 111.

50. Michelle Perrot, "Le Premier Journal marxiste français: *L'Egalité* de Jules Guesde, 1877–1883," *Le Mouvement social* 28 (July 1959), 4.

51. Paul Lafargue to Guesde, June 9, 1881, Compère-Morel, *Jules Guesde,* 202.

52. Karl Marx to Sorge, November 5, 1880, MEW, 34:477.

53. A theme of Claude Willard and Jacques Girault.

54. Boris Nicolaievsky, *Karl Marx: Man and Fighter* (Harmondsworth, 1973), 402; Engels to Eduard Bernstein, October 25, 1881, MEW, 35:232.

17. *The Road to Schism*

1. The exchange, the references for which I have combined here in the interests of space and readability, consists of the following letters by

Brousse and drafts of letters by Lafargue. Paul Lafargue to Paul Brousse, dated only April 1881, *Naissance,* 108–110; Paul Brousse to Lafargue, April 24, 1881, *Naissance,* 111–113; Lafargue to Brousse, dated "end of April 1881," *Naissance,* 114–119; Brousse to Lafargue, May 27, 1881, *Naissance,* 120–122; Lafargue to Brousse, dated only June 1881, *Naissance,* 123–126.

2. Paul Lafargue to Jules Guesde, June 9, 1881, *Naissance,* 128.

3. Georges Lefranc, *Le Mouvement socialiste sous la Troisième République* (Paris, 1963), 45; Carl Landauer, "The Origins of Socialist Reformism in France," *International Review of Social History* 12 (1967), 84–85.

4. Paul Lafargue to the staffs of *L'Egalité* and *Le Prolétaire,* draft, October 21, 1881, *Naissance,* 142–144.

5. Paul Lafargue to Benoît Malon, draft, n.d. but November 1881, *Naissance,* 164; Paul Lafargue to *L'Egalité,* November 30, 1881, *Naissance,* 166.

6. Lefranc, *Le Mouvement socialiste,* 45.

7. Paul Lafargue to José Mesa, October 26, 1881, draft, *Naissance,* 157.

8. *Naissance,* 48.

9. Engels to Eduard Bernstein, October 25, 1881, MEW, 34:228–231.

10. Ibid.

11. Karl Marx to Laura Lafargue, December 14, 1882, MEW, 35:407–408; Engels to Bernstein, November 2–3, 1881, MEW, 34:388.

12. Engels to Karl Marx, January 13, 1882, cited in André Ferrat, "Karl Marx et le mouvement ouvrier français après la Commune," *Cahiers du bolchevisme,* March 14, 1933, 431; Karl Marx to Engels, January 13, 1882, MEW, 35:37–38; Karl Marx to Engels, February 17, 1882, MEW, 35:41; Cohn, 168.

13. Paul Lafargue to the Danish Social Democratic Party, June 4, 1889, ELC, 2:271–272.

14. Mesa to Paul Lafargue, November 6, 1881, *Naissance,* 160–161.

15. Eduard Bernstein, "Paul Lafargue," *Sozialistische Monatshefte* 16 (1912), 24.

16. Cited in Neil McInnes, "Les Partis socialistes français (1880–1895): lettres et extraits de lettres d'Engels à Bernstein," *Cahiers de l'ISEA* 109 (January 1961), 45.

17. McInnes, "Les Partis socialistes," 45–46.

18. Paul Lafargue to Guesde, July 17, 1881, cited in Jacques Girault, ed., *Paul Lafargue: textes choisis* (Paris, 1970), 49; Guesde to Paul Lafargue, n.d. (December 1881), *Naissance,* 170.

19. Roger Fayolle, "Paul Lafargue, critique littéraire et propagandiste du matérialisme historique," *Philologica Pragensia* 3–4 (1976), 123.

20. For example, *L'Egalité,* March 26, 1882.

21. Adéodat Compère-Morel, *Jules Guesde: le socialisme fait l'homme, 1845–1922* (Paris, 1937), 231.

22. Karl Marx to Laura Lafargue, December 14, 1882, *Annali,* 215.

23. "Le Possibilisme," *L'Egalité,* February 5, 1882.

24. Maurice Dommanget, *L'Introduction du marxisme en France* (Lausanne, 1969), 66–68. The *Manifesto* was serialized in *Le Socialiste* between August 24 and November 7, 1885, reprinted in the provincial socialist press, then in the monthly Marxist review, *L'Ere nouvelle,* in 1895.

25. For example, Alexandre Zévaès, *Une Génération* (1922). See David Stafford, *From Anarchism to Reformism: A Study of the Political Activities of Paul Brousse* (Toronto, 1971), 182, 325, n. 106.

26. Leslie Derfler, "Reformism and Jules Guesde, 1891–1904," *International Review of Social History* 12 (1967), 66–80.

27. Stafford, *From Anarchism,* 183.

28. Ibid., 184–187.

29. Mesa to Paul Lafargue, April 14, 1881, *Naissance,* 102.

30. Brousse to Paul Lafargue, April 18, 1881, *Naissance,* 107.

31. Mesa to Paul Lafargue, November 6, 1881, *Naissance,* 160.

32. Mesa to Paul Lafargue, March 20, 1882, *Naissance,* 196; APP, B a/1135, dossier 1882.

33. The amount proved to be 3,600 francs. Gabriel Deville to Paul Lafargue, March 23, 1882, Léon Camescasse to Paul Lafargue, March 25, 1882, *Naissance,* 199–200.

34. Deville to Paul Lafargue, March 27, 1882, *Naissance,* 201.

35. Jenny Marx Longuet to Laura Lafargue, April 22, 1881, *Daughters,* 131.

36. Eleanor Marx to Jenny Marx Longuet, October 18, 1881; Laura Lafargue to Jenny Marx Longuet, n.d., *Daughters,* 137–139.

37. Eleanor Marx to Jenny Marx Longuet, January 8, 1882, *Daughters,* 144–146.

18. *The Marxists Found a Party*

1. He changed his residence the following month to 49 rue du Cherche Midi. Jenny Marx Longuet to Laura Lafargue, April 12, 1882, IISH, Marx-Engels Papers, G 236; Cohn, 173.

2. APP, B a/1135, April 7, 8, 15, May 4, 12, 17, 1882; Cohn, 173.

3. APP, B a/1135, April 27, June 15, 21, 26, 30, 1882.

4. Edith Thomas, *Louise Michel* (Paris, 1971), 219.

5. APP, B a/1135, January 27, April 6, 8, 15, letter dated May 19, 1882.

6. APP, B a/1135, April 7, May 12, 1882.

7. APP, B a/1135, April 26, 1882.

8. APP, B a/1135, August 7, September 2, 1882.

9. Testimony to the Septième Bureau of the Chamber of Deputies, holding hearings on seating Lafargue as a deputy in 1891; summarized in *Le Matin*, November 15, 1891. Cohn, 172.

10. Laura Lafargue to Engels, August 9, 1882, ELC, 1:92–93.

11. Paul Lafargue, *Socialism and the Intellectuals*, cited in Paul Lafargue, *The Right to Be Lazy* (New York, 1973), 93–94.

12. Laura Lafargue to Engels, July 23, 1884, ELC, 1:220–221.

13. APP, B a/439, L'Internationale.

14. Karl Marx to Engels, August 3, 1882, MEW, 35:77; Laura Lafargue to Engels, August 2, 1882, ELC, 1:73.

15. Karl Marx to Engels, July 4, 1882, MEW, 35:75.

16. Editorial note, ELC, 3:501; *Naissance,* 26.

17. Gabriel Deville to Paul Lafargue, October 12, 1883, BM, microfilm 17067. Here Deville thanked Lafargue for correcting a manuscript and promised to follow his instructions.

18. Karl Marx to Engels, November 11, 1882, MEW, 35:109–110.

19. Karl Marx to Engels, September 30, 1882, MEW, 35:100; Engels to Eduard Bernstein, November 2–3, 1882, MEW, 35:388.

20. Karl Marx to Laura Lafargue, December 14, 1882, MEW, 35:407–408; Cohn, 169.

21. Engels to Bernstein, December 16, 1882, cited in Neil McInnes, "Les Partis socialistes français (1880–1895): lettres et extraits de lettres d'Engels à Bernstein," *Cahiers de l'ISEA* 109 (January 1961), 74; Karl Marx to Laura Lafargue, October 9, 1882, cited in Saul Padover, ed., *The Letters of Karl Marx* (Englewood Cliffs, 1979), 393.

22. Paul Lafargue to Engels, August 30, 1882, ELC, 1:96.

23. Karl Marx to Laura Lafargue, June 17, 1882, Padover, *Letters,* 387–388; Paul Lafargue to Laura Lafargue, August 29, 1882, *Annuaire,* 479.

24. APP, B a/1135, September 5, 1882.

25. Paul Lafargue to Deville, October 8, 1882, IFHS, Dommanget Papers, Deville dossier.

26. E. M. Makrenkova, "Lafarg i Sozdaniye Markistskoy Rabochyey Parti Frantsyi" (Unpublished Writings: Paul Lafargue and the Creation of the Marxist Workers Party of France), *Voprosy Istorii,* 1978(11), 126; APP, B a/1135, April 18, 1882; Jacques Girault, ed., *Paul Lafargue: textes choisis* (Paris, 1970), 59; Paul Lafargue to Engels, October 10, 1882, ELC, 1:104–105.

27. David Stafford, *From Anarchist to Socialist: A Study of the Political Activities of Paul Brousse* (Toronto, 1971), 191–193.

28. Lafargue's editorial, October 19; Mermeix (pseud. of Gabriel Terrail), *La France socialiste* (Paris, 1886), 236–237.

29. Paul Lafargue to Engels, November 24, 1882, ELC, 1:111; Girault, *Textes,* 60.

30. Cohn, 177–182. I am indebted to William Cohn for this interpretation.

31. *L'Egalité,* January 1, 8, 22, February 18, 1882.

32. *Le Citoyen,* May 11, 1882; Cohn, 185–186.

33. *L'Egalité,* March 19, 1882.

34. The argument of Samuel Bernstein, *The Beginnings of Marxist Socialism in France* (New York, 1965), 174.

35. *L'Egalité,* May 28, 1882; Cohn, 186.

36. *L'Egalité,* June 18, 1882.

37. *L'Egalité,* February 18, 1882; Cohn, 182.

38. *L'Egalité,* June 25, August 3, 1882; Cohn, 189.

39. *L'Egalité,* March 12, 1882.

40. *Le Citoyen,* March 23, May 19, 30, June 10, August 19, September 11, 1882; *L'Egalité,* November 27, 28, December 4, 7, 8, 1882; Cohn, 191–192.

41. Paul Lafargue to Engels, June 16, 1882, ELC, 1:84.

42. APP, B a/486, Enquête sur les loyers à Paris, 1871–1891, cited in Ann-Louise Shapiro, "Housing Reform in Paris: Social Space and Social Control," *French Historical Studies* 12 (Fall 1982), 493–494.

43. APP, B a/486, reports dated March 18, June 4, July 11, 1881, cited in Shapiro, "Housing," 494.

44. Friedrich Engels, *The Housing Question* (New York, 1935), 7, 29, 77.

45. APP, B a/1135, reports of June 24, July 5, 6, 1882.

46. *Le Citoyen,* June 12, 18, 23, November 14, 1882; Cohn, 194.

47. *Le Citoyen,* August 21, 1882; *L'Egalité,* July 23, 1882; Cohn, 194.

48. *L'Egalité,* July 9, 1882; Cohn, 194.

49. *Le Citoyen,* June 20, 1882.

50. APP, B a/486, report of July 4, 1882.

51. Shapiro, "Housing," 495.

52. Ibid., 496, 507.

53. *L'Egalité,* July 9, 1882.

54. *Le Marxisme dans l'Internationale et dans le Parti ouvrier;* Stafford, *From Anarchist,* 192–193.

55. Paul Lafargue to Engels, October 10, 1882, ELC, 1:102.

56. Engels to August Bebel, October 28, 1882, MEW, 35:382–383.

57. Engels to Bebel, October 28, 1882, MEW, 35:382–383; Engels to Eduard Bernstein, October 20, 1882, MEW, 35:373–374.

58. Paul Lafargue to Engels, October 10, 1882, ELC, 1:103.

59. Parti ouvrier socialiste révolutionnaire français, *Compte-rendu du 6me congrès national tenu à Saint-Etienne, septembre 24–30, 1882* (Paris, 1882), 70–94; Engels to Bebel, October 28, 1882, MEW, 35:382–383; Cohn, 164–165.

60. Stafford, *From Anarchist,* 199. The Possibilists retained a separate identity until 1899, when in the attempt to achieve socialist unity in a general

congress, they became part of the new French Socialist Party (Parti Socialiste Français).

61. Paul Lafargue to Engels, November 13, 1882, ELC, 1:108.
62. Stafford, *From Anarchist,* 196.
63. Claude Willard, *Les Guesdistes: le mouvement socialiste en France, 1893–1905* (Paris, 1965), 25–26.
64. Ibid., 79.
65. Claude Willard, "Chronique historique: une thèse sur les Guesdistes— quelques problèmes de méthode," *La Pensée* 123 (October 1965), 93.
66. Maurice Duverger, *Political Parties* (New York, 1962), 54.
67. Paul Lafargue to Engels, October 10, November 13, 1882, ELC, 1:101– 104, 108–109.
68. *L'Egalité,* June 25, 1882.
69. Paul Lafargue to Engels, November 13, 1882, ELC, 1:108–109.

Conclusion

1. George Lichtheim, *Marxism in Modern France* (New York, 1972), 20.
2. Thierry Paquot, *Les Faiseurs de nuages: Essai sur la genèse des marxismes français (1880–1914)* (Paris, 1980), 69–70.
3. Jean Bruhat, "Paul Lafargue et la tradition du socialisme révolutionnaire français," *Cahiers internationaux* 6 (July–August 1949), 71.
4. Maurice Dommanget, *L'Introduction du marxisme en France* (Lausanne, 1969), 20–21; Georges Weill, *Histoire du mouvement social en France, 1852–1910* (Paris, 1911), 120.
5. Claude Willard, "Chronique historique: une thèse sur les Guesdistes— quelques problèmes de méthode," *La Pensée* 123 (October 1965), 99.
6. Cited in Michelle Perrot, "Les Guesdistes: controverse sur l'introduction du marxisme en France," *Annales: économies, sociétés, civilisations* (May–June 1967), 707.

Index